RIMBAUD IN ABYSSINIA

RIMBAUD IN ABYSSINIA

ALAIN BORER

TRANSLATED FROM THE FRENCH
BY ROSMARIE WALDROP

WILLIAM MORROW AND COMPANY, INC. NEW YORK

Alain Borer published simultaneously with Editions Iachenal et Ritter a work entitled *Un Sieur Rimbaud Se Distant Negociant* in collaboration with Philippe Soupault and Arthur Aeschbacher. This work also contains an important iconographic dossier: maps, old photographs (by Arthur Rimbaud, Jules Borelli and the Vigneras mission), and modern photographs by Francois Margolin.

Copyright © 1984 by Alain Borer

First published in France, 1984, by Editions du Seuil as *Rimbaud en Abyssinie*

It is the policy of William Morrow and Company, Inc., and its imprints and affiliates, recognizing the importance of preserving what has been written, to print the books we publish on acid-free paper, and we exert our best efforts to that end.

Library of Congress Cataloging-in-Publication Data

Borer, Alain.
   [Rimbaud en Abyssinie. English]
   Rimbaud in Abyssinia / Alain Borer : translated from the French by Rosmarie Waldrop.
      p.   cm.
   Translation of: Rimbaud en Abyssinie.
   ISBN 0-688-07594-0
   1. Rimbaud, Arthur, 1854–1891—Journeys—Ethiopia. 2. Poets, French—19th century—Biography. 3. Ethiopia—Description and travel. I. Title.
PQ2387.R5Z558813   1991
848'.803—dc20   91-8807
                                                                        CIP

Printed in the United States of America

First Edition

1 2 3 4 5 6 7 8 9 10

BOOK DESIGN BY JAYE ZIMET

To Pierre Prentki
To Marc, Marisa, and Jacques Prentki

Acknowledgments

I would owe this book to many friends even if they had not dedicated themselves to it. Let me express my deep gratitude here. They will recognize themselves, in particular: Zéno Bianu, Jean-Paul Corsetti, Émilie Daniel, Katia Krivanek, Lydie Lachenal, Ken Ritter, Philippe Soupault, Agnès et Pierre Rosenstiehl, Jean-Luc Steinmetz, Suzanne Strube, Jean Voellmy.

CONTENTS

1
DEPARTURE

Forward!
The march, the backpack,
the desert, boredom and anger.
—Arthur Rimbaud

Taking big strides, Charles sinks up to his knees in the snow. The snow crunchy like a meringue. The camera follows his tracks, calling up Rimbaud's early escapades: In a corner of the Ardennes, he and his friend Delahaye illegally crossed the border into Belgium to buy tobacco. The sun is setting behind the pines; the snow takes on a purple cast: "When the dark drools over the woods . . . "* At the end of the road, the customs official tries to get warm stomping his feet on the frozen ground. The red and white roadblock has been taken down for the occasion: The place is deserted. "This must be the end of the world, ahead."† The TV trucks are parked in a ditch. You might think we were filming Erskine Caldwell's *Tobacco Road.* We have just gone through Boulzicourt, the dismal village Delahaye mentions in their itinerary. Boulzicourt! Nothing to write home about. A few ghostly farmhouses in the winter night. René Daumal was born here, in 1908. It was hot in Harar, last month. My

*"Les Douaniers" ("The Customs Officials").
†"Enfance" ("Childhood") IV, *Illuminations.*

notebook ends here, with these footprints in the snow.

Holzwege, wrong tracks wide of the mark, Rimbaud's early running away gets him nowhere. As in the Christmas story where a child follows at night, in the snow, the tracks of the stranger who just brought him a present; the tracks stop abruptly in the middle of a field. But we remain fascinated with the impossible gap between the footprints and the body they do not lead to: The trace enchants us because it is worth an unreachable body. "Oh wandering feet, can I find your imprint in sand or stone?" writes his sister Isabelle in *Mon Frère Arthur (My Brother Arthur).* "Luminous feet of statues of Mary!" The trace of a dream is no less real than a footprint.

Rimbaud escapes us: After his adolescent adventures (endless tramping through the town and country[1]), real flight. His running away from Charleville, to Paris and Douai, then to Belgium and England, his traveling all over Europe, to Java, all seem so many rehearsals for his great departure for Africa: for Harar, his last and most successful running away.

Why did we feel so strange following the red trails of his caravans around Harar? Our Land Rover stuck in a river ford; we asked the way of a group of blacks going to the market in Harar with guns slung over their shoulders: Burka? Wachu? Baroma? They answered with a slow and precise gesture, as if they had met him on the way. We imagined him disappearing around the bend, still on the move. "Those I met *perhaps did not see me,*" he wrote in *A Season in Hell.* Disillusioned question that the lost ship in *Moby Dick,* the *Pequod,* addresses to all passing vessels.

"Rimbaud as he was," wrote Jean-Paul Vaillant.[2] Who could know? It's Rimbaud as he escapes. Rimbaud always beats it, gets the hell out! No doubt this impression of mine comes from the fiction inherent in following someone's traces: But is it not like what the people close to him felt? No sooner had you spotted him than he was reported missing. He had announced his departure and threatened the "Mad Virgin" with it: "One day perhaps he will miraculously disappear," he made her say in "Delirium," Part I. "He is the kind of person," writes Mauriac, "who does not even turn to look at the footprints he left on earth as a child."[3] When he starts his great voyages, his friends exchange information or fantasies: Verlaine sees him robbed by a coachman in Vienna ("Dargnières nouvelles," 1875); Delahaye, among the Kaffirs or as a Negro king (1876). "Still no news from our Hottentot," Delahaye frets, and later: "The best informed geographers suppose he is near the 76th parallel."[4] During his ten years in Harar, they will not know where he has gone: "Hérat," Verlaine throws out, "Hérat in Afghanistan, or maybe Harat"[5]—while the town registrars put down "J.N.A. Rimbaud, professor in Hazar." As time goes by, they think of more distant countries, of the Orient as a passageway to unreality. His mother, without mail for eight months, worries: "Are you no longer in Aden? Could you have gone on to the Chinese Empire?"[6] Verlaine lays it on in his biographical note: "He is now around thirty-two and traveling in Asia, occupied with works of art."[7] Or else, and it comes to the same thing, they assume the worst: three issues of *La Vogue,* which in 1886 had printed the *Illuminations,* speak of "the late Arthur Rimbaud." The living-dead was at that point languishing by the Red Sea, in Tadjoura. A few months later, the *Illuminations* appeared as a volume prefaced by this appeal of Verlaine's, a kind of message in a bottle: "There have been several reports of his death. We do not know anything certain, but it would make us very sad. We would like him to know this, in case there is nothing to the rumor."[8]

On November 28, 1887, Verlaine asks Delahaye for "Rimbesque informations." The latter sends him a short and truculent biography. The ending (not by him) is magnificent: "He was lost track of around 1879, but somebody ran across him in Aden. He had lost a leg, but other information allows us to affirm that Arthur Rimbaud will be back shortly, completely restored, to revise the edition of his works."[9] One might say, an impresario climbing on stage before the closed curtain to reassure the fans the concert will take place. This was the period when Maxime Gaucher denigrated the "decadents" in his *Causeries littéraires, 1872–1888,* published in 1890, and had barely a word for "Rimbaud, at present king of a wild tribe." In 1891, as a student, Paul Valéry tried to find out what had become of Rimbaud: "He is said to be a colonel in Algeria, after having sold cattle in India." In December of the same year, one month after the poet's death, his very brother, "Rimbaud Frédéric, bus driver at Attigny (Ardennes)," replies to Rodolphe Darzens that "he is supposed to be at Harar, or Horor, and as far as I know in business."[10] To all the false news his forgotten friends made up, I prefer the letter Germain Nouveau wrote Rimbaud from Algiers, saying he would like to join him in Aden: "I would be happy to hear from you, very happy." That was in 1893; Rimbaud had been dead and buried for two years. This moving appeal beyond death, this message that was perhaps *received* after a fashion, is the only important one for those who are still questioning the work and life of Rimbaud. In December 1891, the *Echo de Paris* had announced Arthur Rimbaud's death, a month late, with an obituary of ten lines.[11] The poet's death, like Icarus' falling out of the sky in Brueghel's painting, made no splash. Only an image. During those years and long before, Rimbaud was wandering in terra incognita, in the region the Arabs called Barr Adjam,[12] or "unknown land": in Ethiopia, which the ancient Egyptians considered the kingdom of black and evil spirits, where they would not venture, not beyond the Second Cataract of the Nile. In the century when explorers began to search for the sources of the Nile in this "beyond," Rimbaud disappeared there, in Abyssinia, like Nectanebo, last pharaoh of the thirtieth dynasty, who, chased out of Memphis, fled to the kingdom of spirits and never came back.

★ ★ ★

The chimes of the airport at Roissy—crystal dissolving into the sound of a sitar, followed by the roar of a plane taking off—the hostess's voice, languorous like a warm breeze in the Postojna grotto, and the metallic click of the "Departures" board combine constantly to engender all possible dream destinations. "Leaving for affection and new noise."* It is there, in Rimbaud, the poetry of departures, the ever live urge to pull away—from places, ties, the duties and worries that hold us back. From it I draw the strength to say today, in the face of our rehashed problems of unemployment, inflation, wars: "Enough seen . . . Enough known."† Let's leave! Change maps. "Onward! Hat, coat, hands in pockets, off we go!"†† To go to the end of the world,[13] anywhere out of the world, we need only make one first step, the step onto the escalator: In the womb of any airport, travelers standing still are sucked into crossroads of transparent cylinders and—propelled by rolling sidewalks through long, undulating guts with raw-silk walls and soft lights toward the satellite—delivered into yet another belly: the plane. But I feel the energy of departure as the plane races down the runway with a roar of jets, feel the rush of morning and, at takeoff, birth, hope, pure beginning, geographic future, and conquest found in the *orders* Rimbaud gives himself: "*Forward march!* Ah! . . . my temples roar!" in *A Season in Hell;* "Onward, road!" in *Illuminations;* and again, in his letter on crossing the St. Gotthard, "Let's be off."[14] It is the "indefinite desire to be gone" Victor Segalen talked about, the world opening in the rift between clouds.

Magic of space-time: leaving Paris at 7:00 P.M. to land in London at 7:00 P.M. astonishes even those people who can sort out time zones and local clocks.

---

* "Départ," *Illuminations.*
† Ibid.
†† Letter to Georges Izambard, November 2, 1870.

Africa begins in London—or, rather, at Heathrow, an airport really nowhere, with transit halls channeling passengers from all over the world. The planes, head to tail, wait for their turn at the runway. A first image of Ethiopia awaits me at the end of the corridor to the Boeing of the Ethiopian Airlines: The plane snoring in the dark, all windows aglitter, a group of travelers in turbans, djellabas, sandals, with kids and caboodles, both mournful and voluble, gathered at the gate for Addis Ababa and Nairobi, the gate with a strong odor of cotton—you could find your plane "by smell."

The lights of the city and the dark areas tilt. For a moment, I took the little blinker at the end of our wing for a star. In a plane, as in a movie theater, you disturb your neighbors when you get up. But it is easy to get talking on long flights. Our bird has done two thousand hours of flight time. The "Afronauts," as the brochure of the Ethiopian company—Africa's oldest—calls them, are gentle and beautiful.

A wing-beat in the night: Already we are at Rome's Fiumicino Airport. I had tried to make out the shimmering coastline of northern France through the window. France went by so fast! The country where we have lived for so many years—where one needs so many years to live—does not exist. Or only too much. Rimbaud must have understood very quickly. And on foot.

Then, with another beat, with the feeling of extreme power we get from the seemingly immobile plane, the sun rises over a different continent: pink snow, the Egyptian desert in the morning!

Like an astronomer asking, "At which longitude am I?" the aviator gets no answer: The desert is a nonplace, its reliefs unnoticeable, its colors improbable. From the plane, Africa shows again the barely known outline of the early mariners' charts, with the interior remaining mysterious and the desert labeled in big letters: "Ubi Rugiunt Leones."

In a plane that crosses the immensity of the pole, even the most experienced travelers will lose their true north and no longer know time or place: Those earthly notions no longer make sense when one sees night out of the left window, and day out of the right one. As if the plane followed a precise demarcation line or itself divided night from day. Neither time nor space, but a planet between near past and immediate future. Beside the living and the dead, Socrates distinguished a third category of men: sailors. Among his thirty-six proofs of the existence of God, there is one especially for sailors at sea—and the empire will legislate special recourse for them, in the department of the "lower Ems."
. . . On the sailors' model, today a portion of mankind is permanently up in the air.

My neighbor seems a *khouan* (bigotted) Muslim, telling his beads without touching his tray or offering it to me, and not inclined to conversation. So I concentrate on my notebook.

Outward bound, waiting for Ethiopia. Traveling in books and beyond. The world as book: "The universe is a kind of book of which you only read the first page if you know only your own country" (Paul Morand). The book of travel: *The Complete Works of Rimbaud*. Travel as a book—a spring binder filling up, in Heine's manner, with *Reisebilder*. These notes were written while traveling. Without the rigorous plan of a book, which would only try to keep the truth hidden. The contradictions of library and travel resolved in my person. A book, perhaps, but one to crumple and stick in your pocket.[15] A book that begins with the sun at the moment when Rimbaud feels its irresistible pull. In Ethiopia for an "ethi-epic," a "painting of the customs of a country or portrait of a personage," as Littré defines. My head full of singing idea-phrases. A notebook rather than a project, illegible passages marking the moments when, according to the Japanese word, we notice the *ah!* of things. It quickly became as indispensable as my passport—which did not keep me from forgetting both in turn. Full of scribblings, sketches of meeting places, a few words of Amharic, it could resemble the houses painted with the story of their owner's pilgrimage to Mecca.

Rimbaud not only transcends poetry, he arms the desire to write. He even forced people around him to take up the pen: All the Rimbauds are writers. Vitalie's journal joins her brother's *Works;* his mother's letters are collected in a volume;[16] Isabelle declares herself the keeper of the flame, corresponds abundantly, writes *My Brother Arthur.* Then the vestal virgin feels a tremor in her pen and rides her own Pegasus—not with very strong wings, more like a farm horse—to write a chronicle of the First World War in the *Mercure.* Even brother Frédéric will write to the editor of the *Petit Ardennais,* the *Pétard* as it is called locally. Izambard, attacked by Rimbaud's brother-in-law Berrichon, goes through his drawers, where his former student's letters have lain dormant for forty years, and writes *Rimbaud as I Knew Him.*[17] Not only the family honor is at stake: Isabelle, who did everything she could to keep Vanier from publishing a complete edition of the *Poems*—she wanted to remove some and modify others—ends up, in 1895, *wanting* just that. And the desire kept growing from this slimmest body of work into a gigantic Rimbaudrary: Writings on Rimbaud constitute a literary genre of their own, said Jean Paulhan.

Hence my notebook is content to limit its desire to the "wide open" subject of the "Ethiopian Rimbaud." The dream of joining the-man-who-gets-away can only be sustained by a tenacious examination of his poetry, not by any encounter, albeit without illusion: another of his childhood friends, Ernest Millot, imagines meeting him after several years of separation in the middle of the Sahara. "We are alone, moving in opposite directions. He stops for a moment: 'Hello, how's it going?'—'Fine, so long.' Not a trace of effusiveness. Not a word more."[18] Yet there were many who felt "the temptation of Rimbaud's itinerary."[19] Looking for

Rimbaud's footprints means finding and joining the caravan of their tales: "Sulle Trace di Rimbaud" by Adele Luzzatto; "Sur les Traces africaines de Rimbaud" by André Provost; "En Abyssinie sur les traces de Rimbaud" by Henri d'Acremont; *Sur les Traces d'Arthur Rimbaud* by Robert Goffin; "Sur les Traces de Rimbaud" by Pierre Arnoult; "Sur les Traces de Rimbaud" by Enid Starkie; "Sur les Traces de Rimbaud" by Philippe Soupault; and "Sulle Trace di Rimbaud" by Augusto Orsi.[20] This obligatory title recurs again and again like a badge, like the scallop shell of the pilgrims to Santiago de Compostela.

We can distinguish two categories of Rimbaldians: no-. madic and sedentary. The former repeat; the latter contradict each other. Rimbaud was a nomad *and* contradictory. The idea of pilgrimage suggests accomplishment, revelation. But Rimbaud took his secret with him. Let us admit that he is not where we look for him: He remains Loxias, the mysterious. In his portrait of Arthur Rimbaud, Mallarmé wrote, in 1896: "To arrange somebody else's life into intelligible and likely fragments in order to translate it, is simply impertinent: all I can do is push this kind of mischief to its limit. Only, I try to get information."[21] The traveler knows there is nothing to discover, no document, few testimonies, not even "the key to this wild parade"* if he chanced to lose it on the way—that the essential remains to be understood. If you spend ten years of your life in a distant country, you leave a bit of yourself there. But then, it is not the *bit of him* we must look for in Ethiopia, but the bit of ourselves through which alone we could understand him better.[22] Rimbaud cannot be duplicated. He does not suffer any disciples: Do not go to see if he is there, but to feel your own self. If he was able to lead an "inimitable life," as Verlaine claims, his permanent freedom, his desire for solitude, his dreams of distant lands, his thirst for knowledge, can be felt and shared like so many aspirations

*"Parade," *Illuminations*.

in which the young recognize themselves in this century, which Rimbaud anticipated in revolt and adventure. One does not imitate the gods: One adores them. But Rimbaud, "angel or demon," is no icon. "He was neither the devil nor the Lord God," writes Verlaine; "he was Arthur Rimbaud, that is to say, a very great poet, absolutely original, with a unique savor."[23]

In Perrot d'Ablancourt's *Voyages imaginaires, Histoire véritable de Lucien* (*Imaginary Voyages, the True Story of Lucien*) (1787), there is a delightful vision we may take seriously: "I saw two marvels in the king's palace: a well, not very deep, but if you went down into it, you could hear all that was said in the world; and at the bottom, a mirror where you could see all that was happening." These two "marvels" are now joined into a single piece of furniture: TV. Charles Brabant has the merit of having filmed the first feature-length TV program about Rimbaud,[24] a phenomenon the poet-turned-merchant in quest of oblivion at the Abyssinian borders could not have imagined. Rimbaud once, toward the end of his life, evokes the Eiffel Tower he was not to see—he saw only the makeshift, scaled-down replica Armand Savouré built in 1890, in Djibouti, with the help of fifty masons—it is a tangible symbol of the world to come after him, of a century of stupefying technological developments (cars, aviation, electricity, and even a seventh art form, film, were invented within a single lifetime), in spite of which he remains, such is his strength, totally contemporary.

A search for identity? La Pérouse was not to see France again; so another navigator published a *Voyage à la Recherche de La Pérouse*—taking himself for La Pérouse. According to the scenario of our film, *Le Voleur de feu* (*The Fire Stealer*), I research (simply search, rather) a book. In realizing this desire, the *I* speaking does not take himself for anybody else. . . . An exception made for scholars; we tend to have one of two distinct relations to Rimbaud: identification or revelation. The former is represented by Henry Miller,[25] who basically says: Rimbaud is me. In the crowd of sub-Rimbauds—not every writer is Rimbaud—he alone holds up next to his model. Paul Claudel heads the second group: By reading Rimbaud he became Claudel. This is more important than what he says about the "mystic in the raw."[26] Rimbaud, purest image of a poet, of immediate perfection, acts—for most, at an age when "one is not serious"—as a *revealer* of desperate desire. His giving up poetry, symbolized by Harar, seems the more vertiginous the closer one comes to it.

The traveler senses a secret murmuring among the passengers that approach their country, as a ship's crew catches whiffs of an island long before it can be seen. Then, as the plane loses altitude, I am overcome with finally seeing Ethiopia, as green and broken up as the Auvergne under an unknown sun.[27] The din of jets sets us down on the ground of Addis Ababa, the "new flower."[28] Here I am, ready to soak up all the juices of Africa through the soles of my Clarks.

My nap in the plane, the time differences among Paris, London and Addis Ababa, the length of the flight itself, lack of sleep and quickened desire have abolished all sense of continuity: Sleep means the heaviness of my European body, which this other world offers to transform. The sun occupies an unusual, formidable place. Ethiopia is on the same latitude as the Sierra Leone, Guinea, Liberia, the Ivory Coast, Togo, Benin, Nigeria, Cameroon, the Central African Republic, the Sudan, all names to conjure with. It alone does not have an equatorial climate, because of its altitude.

I am arriving here at the same age as Rimbaud: twenty-seven. A century after him, we covered the six thousand kilometers as the crow flies, in a few hours—reaching the end too quickly, robbed of the excessive distance.

International smell of kerosene. We have taken the vertical shortcut of meteorites and dead birds. But I step off a rolling carpet, whereas Rimbaud, after drifting along the Red Sea all the way to Hodeida, arrived in Ethiopia in summer

1880: "sick and completely helpless," writes his first employer, Alfred Bardey. "He was picked up by M. Trébuchet, of the firm of Morand-Fabre of Marseille, who sent him on to Aden with a recommendation to M. Dubar. The latter hired him temporarily as a foreman, a job consisting in receiving shipments of bales of coffee." But it is no longer possible to drift like Rimbaud, to find work or drag on in misery. States have arisen everywhere, and going to Harar takes visas, vaccination, and urine samples.

November 23? Impressions of Africa. Beauty. Misery. The traveler landing in Africa for the first time is struck by the misery as one is struck by the number of fat people in the United States. The misery hits the traveler right at the airport. A child with feverish eyes remains part of my first picture of this country: his legs inert, he drags himself with the help of two flat irons. "*Baksheesh, baksheesh,*" cry the little girls holding out their hands. I don't have any Ethiopian *birrs* yet, and charity seems suddenly an odious Western idea.[29] Hardened Europeans know it is the beginning of trouble on a daily basis—"Eat your hand and keep the other for tomorrow." "I abhor misery" (*A Season in Hell*).

The customs official who opens my suitcase for a conscientious search indifferently moves the couple of books that fall out, then shows surprise and finally concern at finding still more books: Works on Rimbaud outnumber and certainly outweigh the underwear. A way of travel for a few friends. The books come to face the test of reality. A trunkload of books on Rimbaud arrives, a century later, in the country where he thought he could "disappear . . . without any news ever getting out."* His life too comes back in form of this part of the larger library devoted to him, of which he could not have had any inkling. Return of knowledge from elsewhere, which he had fled. A trunk full of books, a suitcase full of words. Crates of television supplies, symbol of unbridled communication, in the country of his

*Letter to his family, Harar, May 6, 1883.

silence and solitude. He traveled without baggage—the tin knife and fork he carried with him preserved in the Charleville Museum! Possessions make sedentary. "Who could wrong me when I own nothing but my person?"* An anti-Rimbaud, Byron arrived in Italy with his silver and furniture piled high on five carts. And Burton, the famous translator of the *Arabian Nights* and first European to enter Harar, came in 1854 (the year of Rimbaud's birth) disguised as an Arab trader, accompanied by a camel caravan carrying his library. The soldier lets me pass with an expression of disgust.

More misery. In order to think about Rimbaud, I must push aside the kids. (The apocalyptic Burroughs arriving in Pasto, Colombia, which is rife with leprosy, encounters a boy of fourteen "with a body puffed up like a rotten melon": same here.) Literature suddenly appears as a luxury of countries where one eats one's fill. "Why a modern world if it invents such poisons!!" †

*To his mother, Aden, April 15, 1882.
†"L'Impossible," *Une Saison en enfer* (*A Season in Hell*).

2
LIVING

Oh! To be over there! to scalp
my European brain!
—Jules Laforgue

The journey begins after the arrival. It takes two stages to reach Harar: First we go to Diredawa, the city at the foot of the plateau on which Harar is situated. The Addis railroad station is at the end of the great avenue that leads up to the town hall. I expected a station like that of Bobo-Dioulasso, an enormous neo-Moorish pastry from the 1930s, but it turned out more like that of Bar-le-Duc. The quais crowded in the morning. Kids shout, *"Farengi!"* ("Foreigners!"). Beggars hold out enamel bowls.

At the head of the long gray and white train, a parlor car with the green upholstery of Paris locals, then several dark third-class cars that give off a strong smell of musk. Hundreds of Ethiopians are crammed into them, with dignity and a few animals. We seem to go from Boeing to Wells Fargo without transition. After a flight at nine hundred kilometers per hour at an altitude of ten thousand meters, it is a puddle jumper taking off with the speed of the mule of the Strasbourg explorer René Binger. If you like the trains in old westerns, this one is a feast. It is like the Mossi emperor's pretty little train that runs between Abidjan and "Bobo" and "Ouaga." But these tin ashtrays with "SNCF" stamped on them? I am in fact in the CFE, the Franco-Ethiopian Railroad, which has been covering the eight hundred kilometers between Addis Ababa and Djibouti since 1917. "From Harar to Entotto, Menelik's present residence, it's a twenty days' trek across the Itous Gallas Plateau," Rimbaud wrote in the *Bosphore égyptien*. Nowadays, leaving in the morning, the CFE arrives in Diredawa in the evening—this is as precise as it gets. It is the very railroad Rimbaud prophesied—"It will happen . . . in the more or less near future"—that takes us to Harar, the train wanted by Menelik and connected with the names of the engineers Ilg, Chefneux, and Soleillet.[1] At eighty kilometers per hour, images are quickly superimposed. After the suburbs of the capital with crowds swarming through stony streets under gray eucalyptus leaves, we are leaving the high plateaus. The train plunges into grass higher than the cars. The locomotive pants along the slopes. The abundant, virgin vegetation rapidly thins out.

Here it is finally, the great thrill. In a long traveling shot we discover Africa, untouched. Today, everybody has an idea of Venice or New York without feeling any need to have been there. This makes early travel reports, like Hippolyte Taine's *Voyage aux Pyrénées,* obsolete, but so delectable. Now, the exhilarating surprise of the CFE is that it shows us an Africa exactly like the picture we have of it, and does not disappoint us. We are crossing the Dankali Desert, territory of the Danakil, terror of caravans. Quick like lizards gliding across lava blocks the color of elephant skin, they held Rimbaud's caravan for a whole year at Tadjoura: "They treated all travelers the same, letting them pass only after stripping them of everything they had."[2] A dozen camels break into a run to follow our convoy for a moment. Bands of monkeys take off screaming, the *guerezas* peculiar to Ethiopia, fur striped black and white like the "All Blacks"

T-shirt. Tiny dik-dik antelopes jump and run away at the approach of the train. Waders, zebras, ostriches, bob up and disappear. We can watch the most curious and motionless for a long time because of the meandering tracks. All species of the African bestiary seem assembled to see the train pass by. The question of the day: Will we see His Magnificence the lion, symbol of Ethiopia—"the Lion of Judah"—whose most splendid breed occurs here. But an Ethiopian lion does not stoop to watching a puddle jumper. There are some endangered species of gazelles and rare birds that still exist in this region and the neighboring Kenya. I am told Ethiopians do not eat game—but they hunt monkeys (it takes forty-five to make a rug).

The stretches of semidesert that are now going by the train windows allow me to dig out the letter to the editor of the *Bosphore égyptien* and reread it, use it on location, where every word suddenly takes on the relief and color of the unfamiliar reality it talks about. Rimbaud as Baedeker! At the Haouach, that "tortuous ditch obstructed at every step by trees and rocks," the train stops for an hour. Time for refreshments and relief of the handful of reckless soldiers who secure the area against rebels, *chiftas* (bush bandits) and the "desert blacksmiths."[3] Rimbaud was the first to tell geographers that the Haouach is not navigable. Menelik had had "tree trunks thrown across for simple foot bridges . . . I crossed it on foot at several points, over several hundred kilometers." Today, the train crosses the river on a bold viaduct[4] lined with banana and orange trees. Has my "guide" (I am thinking of Rimbaud's bust in Charleville, which celebrates the "poet and explorer") not been recognized as the "most daring type of explorer?"[5] The letter to the *Bosphore* is undeniably an event for geography, but, as Rimbaud says himself, it presents "only a few notes . . . on the actual state of this region." In his *Rapport sur l'Ogadine* (*Report on Ogaden*) (1881), which brought him honor with the Geographical Society, Rimbaud speaks of "the tribes visited by

M. Sotiro," his Greek colleague at the Harar depot, who, we now know, must be credited with the exploration. Then, at Bubassa, where he had gone by himself in 1881, it was to "open markets in the bush." He did for some time want to become an explorer, but remained an adventurer. "I am giving up the idea of Rimbaud as an explorer of genius," Segalen will write, "except as a prototype of heat resistance." When the Geographical Society asks for his photo, Rimbaud does not send it.

In its daily run across the desert, the train stops at every little village: Debre Zeit, Dukem, Mozo, Nazareth, Kora, Asabot. The arrival of the big diesel is the event of the day. Out of cylindrical, straw-covered huts they come, men in loincloths, a large knife stuck in their belt; old men with frizzy white hair; bands of children who storm the cars at the head with ready cries of "*Baksheesh,*" but laughing; cripples exhibiting their stumps.

Women wrapped in a single piece of multicolored cloth, with clanking rings around their ankles, walk along the train, baskets full of papayas, fritters, lentils, guavas balanced on their heads, at window height. Others pass, shaking the souls imprisoned in calabashes to the rhythm of the cassava pestles. Farther off, still others with huge sugarcanes on their shoulders. They swing their hips, scratch their armpits, and spit herb juice in great arcs from between filed teeth. We admire the keen curve of the hips, the nude amber breasts. Images without eroticism, but waking a sentiment of infinite motherhood. It was in the Ethiopian Rift that a French expedition discovered the oldest human skeleton we know to date, a woman's, five million years old. They named her Lucy, after the Beatles song, "Lucy in the Sky with Diamonds" (understood as LSD). Lucy's fifty-two bones in the sun, under the perfect blue sky! In the beginning there was Lucy! No need to go further.

Land of origins, fertile and nourishing. Land without ruins, where time seems in immemorial harmony with space.

In Ethiopia, time is absent, only extension is given: I am in eternal Abyssinia, beyond Shoa, in the land of once-upon. You enter it like a book that allows you to dream of the past. Ethiopia is a political abstraction: These women and men are the Abyssins[6] in the engravings of Jules Borelli's *Southern Ethiopia*. Going back in time, this train puts us in immediate touch with adventure, with imaginary hopes and sufferings, with the stuff of dreams. What I see, Rimbaud saw. Immense fields of lava cut through the savanna. The train stops at a village smaller than the row of cars. The heat is crushing: black, burned trees, their leaves like red paper. On these "horrible roads that recall the supposed horror of lunar landscapes" (writes Rimbaud, laying it on a bit, all the same), I see him passing in the distance with his caravan, his *gaflah* of ninety years ago, October 1886. He walks in front, at the slow pace of the camels, carrying only his small stash of grilled millet in his white linen jacket, followed by a straggling crowd of thirty-four camel drivers and an interpreter, armed with heavy St.-Étienne rifles or carrying shepherd's spears and round shields of hippopotamus hide, some goats and thirty camels loaded with two thousand scrap rifles from Liège and seventy-five thousand cartridges. The year before, he had quarreled with the Bardey brothers, then thought he could make a quick fortune by selling arms to Menelik, king of Shoa, at war with Emperor John IV.[7] His partner, Labatut, and his second partner, Soleillet, die one after the other during the preparations. Later, he had to mope for an entire year in the sinister village Tadjoura, held by the Danakil—but also by French government recantations and British pressure to keep French nationals from selling arms to Menelik. Then he moves on, alone with his caravan—"My journey will take . . . a year," he had written his family on September 15, 1886—an exhausting trek through unexplored and hostile regions. It ought to be possible to tell him that Menelik is not in Ankober where he is headed, that he should look in Entotto, that Menelik has no intention of paying him, that he ought to return straight to Harar, which is devastated by war, that this expedition is disastrous. But he would not hear.

We are going through Shalenko, one of the villages to be razed, like the preceding ones, by the Somali Air Force during the Ogaden war, three months after our trip. Shalenko where, Rimbaud remembers in passing, the three thousand warriors of the emir of Harar "were sabered and killed in the blink of an eye" by the angry Menelik's thirty thousand Abyssins. Night falls on the Harargué, an area half covered by stiff parasol mimosas and candelabrum purslane, all curves. The CFE climbs to a thousand meters onto a plateau covered with shrubs, sisal, and termite colonies.

The train's arrival in Diredawa, at night, is a carnival. A colorful crowd of Wa-Gallas (people of Gallaland) mob the station under the French flag and mill around the lampion-lit square in high excitement. In a bottleneck of horse-drawn carts, small carriages and cabs waiting for travelers, familiar Peugeots blowing their horns—"Pijos" crammed full with barely visible blacks—I am glad to spot my friend Sancerni,[8] his black Somali hair, his pointed face of a Coptic Christ—and we are off in his jeep.

Before the millet fields on the plateaus, shaded by a few large sycamores at the edge of the precipice, we give the first turn of the crank to our film. A pan across wild, rocky mountains dotted with spiny mimosa, with dazzling red and yellow aloes, beautiful like anything untouched by man. In the back of the Land Rover, in the cool of early morning, the director asks me what I want in Harar. . . . The Land Rover takes off, followed by the supply truck, I have fifty kilometers to answer—or find a few seconds for the answer. We cross a sandy wadi which the torrents must play havoc with in the rainy season. Then the road twists up the steep slopes of the Engago Pass to the Harar Plateau: Diredawa is one thousand meters above sea level; Harar, seventeen hundred (these are zebu mountains); whereas Addis, perched at twenty-five hundred, makes your ears pop. "Would you repeat your question, Charles?" But one finds it in all the books. Question of library-"sitters," which we could dismiss with Gide's famous reply on starting for the Congo: "I'll know when I get there." Moreover, I am already there, or almost, and the question of "knowing" is literally *out of place*.

"No Harar for me!" André Breton threw out proudly. We should rather question this resistance of the homebodies. "Real life"* is elsewhere. It is Rimbaud who holds the "Key to the Fields," even if it is Breton's title. So Breton smears him with cowardice. The explicit insult ("very ordinary cowardice") that the author of the pale *Constellations* throws at the author of the *Illuminations* in the *Second Manifesto of Surrealism* only shows Breton's intolerance and misunderstanding of the problem. As if it were inadmissible to flee from the bistro revelations of the "Surrealist Revolution"! No Breton for me! (At any rate not the one of the *Second Manifesto*.) All admiration is due the man who can free himself from what constrains others. Even if he fails. With a grandiose failure, if one could put it in aesthetic terms. To the people who would prevent any departures for Harar, we could show the beautiful testimonial penned by René Char: "You were right to leave, Arthur Rimbaud!" But I do not like this chumminess, calling Rimbaud *tu* and by his first name, which suggests such a fake, back-slapping brotherhood. I like even less the "gratuitous substitution of one's own consciousness," as Mallarmé put it. And after all, Rimbaud was wrong to leave—for so many misfortunes.[9]

A kind of Prometheus retired into plumbing? And in Africa? Not on Place Ducale? That story would interest me!— in another genre. But it is not our case. Rimbaud led a life of high risk. You arrive in Africa at age twenty-seven—in

*"Délires," ("Delirium") I, *A Season in Hell*.

the nineteenth century—and you spend ten long years alone, absolutely alone, having nothing, absolutely nothing, in vast countries with barely forty Europeans, among hostile tribes speaking unfamiliar languages, countries where you must never say "never," where you encounter wild beasts, real ones, and corpses, also real. Ten years of "unimaginable fatigue," of "the most abominable privations,"* of "sleeping out in the open for a year,"† without care in your first illness,[10] and where the smallest error may be fatal. "Imagine how one feels after exploits of this kind: crossing the sea in a fishing boat, travel on horseback, without clothes, food supplies, water, etc., etc."†† We have to take Rimbaud literally when he claims to "feed on afflictions as vehement as they are absurd."§ As for me, going "up to" Harar in a Land Rover with an enormous cyclops of a camera in back— all that is lacking is a motorcycle escort—I do not kid myself, I would not have survived one month. The silence of these infinite spaces (and these mountains so beautiful you want to sing) frightens me. But to many, this young man "working for a remote firm,"‖ was but a "tradesman" (as they said in the past century). Some even spread around that Rimbaud became "bourgeois," that his life faulted his work, that it "flouts and dishonors his youth."[11] Now there's judgment!

The cars climb slowly. We encounter Peugeots doing duty as village buses, brave trucks and indefatigable hikers with their goats, sheep, resigned donkeys with backbreaking loads. From the turns in the road we discover round huts with conical roofs, the *guimbi-gallas*. Lake Aramaya shimmers in the early morning light, peopled with multitudes of ducks, wild geese, ibis, and pink flamingos. As we

---

* Letter from Rimbaud to his family, Cairo, August 23, 1887; "troubles" and "privations" (Harar, August 26, 1883).
† To his family, Aden, January 15, 1883.
†† To his family, Cairo, August 23, 1887.
§ To his family, Harar, May 25, 1881.
‖ To his family, Harar, May 6, 1883.

come closer, flocks of metallic blue blackbirds take off. The "nomadic" Rimbaldians have given us only spotty stories, but among some twenty works dealing with Rimbaud's African years, not a single author went to Harar[12] to check, compare, learn, walk, experience—not even Miss Starkie, who worked thirty years on her *Rimbaud* and published two versions of her *Rimbaud in Abyssinia*. They did not go, but they had heard about it. . . . Inflation often corresponds to a void, a hole. Nobody would think of analyzing a text without having read it, but the same people speak of an experience without having lived it—or tried to, in their own fashion. As if life were not at least as singular as a text, as if experience were general, immediate, given to all. Yet no two people have the same body: Clearly no two have the same life. When you get down to it, there is nothing "unthought," but there is much "unlived."

Never banal—especially not in Abyssinia—Rimbaud's life is so short that we must not neglect any detail that might help us understand his fate. Moreover, Rimbaud did not separate poetry from life, language from experience and the world, or, rather, "experience" was not a category for him, but an integral part of poetry, the part that "advanced"* poetry would transform. For the Rimbaud of the two letters called *du voyant,* "of the Seer," May 1871, poetry could not be an aim in itself, but a means of cognition *and,* in the same movement, of transformation. (The group around *Le Grand Jeu* understood the metaphysical and esoteric dimension of this statement, whereas the Surrealists retained only the oniric and revolutionary aspect.) We may find it difficult today to understand the *voyant*'s enterprise because we no longer share his conception of the symbolic. A symbol, the Greek *symbolon,* is a coin broken in two, of which two parting friends or lovers each take one half, with the idea of restoring the coin, the whole, when they meet again. The coin represents *the* value; it is not "symbolic," but the Symbolic:

*Letter to Paul Demeny, May 15, 1871.

the circle of Totality, the sphere of absolute identity of cosmos and logos, Heraclitus' One, the union of words and things (of man and man, man and nature, of being-in-the-world). It is the paradise of Genesis before the fall, that is, nonseparation from God. Harmony. "The time of universal language,"* said Rimbaud. In this vision of the world, idealistic and religious in the most literal sense, the poet, who creates (his master Baudelaire's famous *poieien*), gets through the Word the power to act on things, to create by naming. It is in this sense that Rimbaud, following a long tradition (*the* Tradition[13]), could think of himself as "God's equal" and Promethean rival: "The poet is truly a fire stealer."† It is in this sense, again, that Rimbaud opposes to his teacher's "subjective and insipid" poetry a "language of the soul for the soul, containing all, perfumes, sounds, colors, thoughts seizing thoughts and pulling,"†† a language that he declares "objective" and "materialist" because it can change the world. . . . We must oppose *catalogue* thinking (Aristotle classifying everything, even the winds) with thinking by *analogue* (Plato and myths). We must supplant Descartes's diurnal, rational, prospective *therefore* with the poet's *like:* nocturnal, imaginary, primitive.[14] Rimbaud climbs his own Mount Analogue. He is possessed by the demon of analogy.

So Rimbaud's project was nothing less than the end of *A Season in Hell:* "to possess the truth in soul and body." This is no doubt why, unlike Mallarmé, Rimbaud is of little interest to formalists (who periodically surface as a school in French literature), but returns to favor in times when ideas and dogmas are in crisis. We cannot separate life and work. Even one of the *Tel Quel* poets, Marcelin Pleynet, admitted that with Rimbaud "life and work are intimately, one cannot put it better, bound," which is what Verlaine had claimed

* Ibid.
† Ibid.
†† Ibid.

back in 1895: "Both life and work are superb as they are, in their unutterably proud *pendet interrupta.*"[15]

Rimbaud wanted to "change life:"* Life changed him. But we have too long neglected and even despised the Abyssinian Rimbaud, a Rimbaud of the dark, traitor to the ideas of his youth, the opposite, in all points, of the Commune revolutionary, the "nigger" crying his innocence and horror of Western values. When Rimbaud stops writing, he stops being of interest. The *poète maudit* is celebrated, the "tradesman" disqualified! We even avoid trying to find out more, as if the question were settled in advance or as if, knowing already, one had to hide some shameful part. An apostate of the religion of Poetry, Rimbaud died of abandoned writing—in the eyes of those who continue. Hence this strange sentence of Verlaine's: "Afterwards he did nothing but travel horribly and die very young."[16]

It seems to me, on the contrary, that Rimbaud's silence, his wanderings in the unfamiliar reality of a mysterious country, pose the fundamental questions of writing in a very *pure* manner. Harar could even be the *episteme,* the "fundamental search for knowledge" in literature. With these pure questions, Rimbaud's anonymous and singular existence attains even the "universal" Yves Bonnefoy talks about, and radically. As my notes begin where Bonnefoy's *Rimbaud par lui-même (Rimbaud by Himself)* ends, I dedicate my quest to the poet and Rimbaldian who wrote that "Harar is not the negation of Rimbaud's past life, but rather its continuation"[17]—concrete and symbolic. In his reply to Roger Munier, Yves Bonnefoy also observed rightly of Rimbaud's silence: "We must consider the opposition of such intermittent, then final, silence to the profound muteness of rhetoric."[18]

In choosing to be silent with Rimbaud, Yves Bonnefoy's book prepares for these questions. But it risks to aban-

*"Délires," I, *A Season in Hell.*

don Rimbaud to the "cursed part" that marked him since his flight from Europe. *Rimbaud par lui-même* closes with the words "Let us not read Rimbaud's African letters," even though it began with "In order to understand Rimbaud, let us read Rimbaud." The best possible advice: "Let us read Rimbaud." All of him.

Nevertheless, I place Bonnefoy's book in the heaven of the "Rimbaudrary" where we must distinguish, without discrimination, four hierarchical levels, all of which no book has ever covered. Ground level: the basics (establishing correct texts, historical documents). Second level: the dimension of analytical criticism (exegesis, gloss, commentary). Third level: the dimension of synthesizing interpretation (Rimbaud within the sweep of the great ideas—of Dhotel, Fondane, Gengoux, Rivière, Starkie, Thisse—for which criticism has shown no taste in half a century now). Fourth level: heaven, or access to literature itself through Rimbaud's work; the dimension of rarefied air. Beside Bonnefoy's book and Henry Miller's, there are a few essays (by Blanchot, Bounoure, Char, Claudel, Gilbert-Lecomte, Macé, and Segalen), which belong not only to the "literary" kind of Rimbaud studies, but to literature itself.

Today the humanities—so inhuman, really!—accentuate this break, this first death: Categorical thought (catalogical, we might say), whether psychoanalysis or linguistics, divides language from the world. Montaigne already defined this conception—to announce a loss of the divine: "A name is not part of the thing or substance, it is an extraneous piece joined to the thing, but outside it" (*Essais,* II, 16). Here the symbol is precisely one half only of the Greek coin or torn bill: One part designates the thing (the referent), the other constitutes merely the symbol that stands for the thing. It is this latter part of the bill, again divided into signifier and signified, that Saussure declares the strict equivalent of the recto and verso of a sheet of paper. Now, by separating words from things, life from work (subject from text), the poet from the African (the latter *persona non grata*), formalist analyses (or those with "scientific" pretensions) devitalize Rimbaud's poetry and miss its essential dimension, given in *A Season in Hell:* the poet's failure to transform the world, the mission he had felt chosen for. A confusion of Mallarmé's "disappearance into elocution" and Rimbaud's "I is another."[19]

So I would hold with Kenneth White that "in Rimbaud's work, literary criticism in the narrow sense misses the point." To understand Rimbaud you must love him. And I prefer to listen to his commonsense sigh of January 6, 1886, in Tadjoura, his invitation to "come and spend some time here in order to learn philosophy!" I used to think that with a paragram, a pinch of oxymoron, and some repetition compulsion one could deal with any text. But it is the *nature* of poetry that it cannot be reduced to discursive thought.[20]

At the wheel of the Land Rover, my friend Sancerni, with a scarf on his head against the wind (which threatens to scatter the Amharic alphabet printed on the cloth), speeds across the high plateau he knows so well. We continue our conversation, shouting to be heard. We wonder about alternatives to Albert Thibaudet's way of relating life (unknowable, irreparable, undecidable) and writing. I don't know, I shout. But once, during a radio program, I asked Laurent Terzieff to read Rimbaud's letter from Harar of May 6, 1883, and was overcome by the feeling of hearing something like *Rimbaud's voice.* What brought on this simple hallucination? No doubt Terzieff's interpretation—he had played Rimbaud in a television film[21]—or perhaps the huge baffles of the studio, whose vibrations one feels physically, as in a concert of the Who. When I consulted Barthes about this, he was perplexed—and yet anybody who has heard the unforgettable "grain" of his voice will hear it in his writings. But then, I tell myself, we *cannot fail* to hear Rimbaud's voice in a text as powerful as *A Season in Hell* not as the causal breath of a

Golem, but because *the more written it is, the more one hears the voice.* Artaud: "Life gives off sound."

No doubt, the voice gives different structures to the literary texts and the African correspondence, which is not "written" in this sense. But I still hear it, its different relation to the symbolic, remote in its renunciation, silence, and reality. Listening to it forces us to admit the integrity of person and destiny, to give up distinguishing "the two Rimbauds" (of J.-M. Carré) in order to celebrate one and condemn the other. This has been a litany: "The Double Rimbaud" (of Segalen); "The Two Aspects of Arthur Rimbaud" (by Lucien Lagriffe); "The Double Personality of A.R." (by Jules de Gaultier); the poet and rebel (according to Hugo Ball); or even lunar period versus solar period (according to Henry Miller). We must stop opposing the Ardennais to the Ethiopian, Renéville's *voyant* to Fondane's *voyou* or "hooligan," Seer to non-Seer, and so on. I draw two gravestones in my notebook, side by side: "Arthur Rimbaud, poet, 1854–1875" and "Arthur Rimbaud, explorer, 1875–1891."[22]

In the rapidly rising sun, I am struck by the red soil of the Harar Plateau, cultivated in the traditional way and extremely fertile: All you need to do is plant, and everything grows.[23] Maize all over, *cat,* lemons, coffee, of which I grab a few green beans as the car passes. Rimbaud had only negatives, only concessions for this country he settled in: "The land [is not] infertile. The climate . . . not unhealthy. . . . The countryside is not unpleasing, . . . not entirely wild."* From September 1881 on, he begins to grumble: "I'm still very unhappy with this area . . . The climate's grouchy."† The climate? Or his mood? Later, in 1886, Rimbaud will write from Tadjoura that Abyssinia is "the African Switzerland." He may have read the phrase in Achille Raffray's book

*Letters to his family, December 13, 1880; January 15, 1881; February 15, 1881.
†September 2, 1881.

on Abyssinia (1876)—"Abyssinia is Africa's Switzerland"—but then it is a traveler's cliché about this country.[24] Let us not confuse Ogaden and Engadine! Why did Rimbaud make contradictory statements about the climate? why did he have to be out of Harar to join the chorus of travelers as summed up by Raffray: "The poetical image of a perpetual spring is reality here"?

We are finally catching sight of Harar, the millennial city. We turn off the engine. When Rimbaud heard Bardey and Dubar talk of this mysterious city in Aden,[25] he "instantly" begged to be sent there. From a distance, Harar seems to spread heaps of brown, terraced houses and white buildings within wild ramparts. It stands out against the surrounding green of rows of fields, called gardens* here, that stretch to the distant mountain range, the Condoudo Rimbaud talks about, with its flat top where wild horses are said to roam. Point of view, heart of the tale. Burton: "From afar, the city looks like a freshly ploughed field with big lumps of earth." Bardey: "We come to a hill from which we suddenly see the reddish mass formed by the city of Adare or Harar, built on an elongated hill."

It seems as if roads here did not lead to cities, but this city had been placed here as a mythical rest for those forever on the road. We are approaching the Bab-el-Fouth (Gate of Conquest), an Arc de Triomphe in crumbly clay with a look of scraped bone, decorated with Arabic motifs. For me, it marks less the end of the journey than the blazing beginning of a cosmogony, the entrance into the unknown, the irreversible passage into another dimension. And, as the Buddha did Benares, we enter Harar through the western gate.

*"I might be able to buy some gardens" (letter to his family, May 5, 1884).

3
THE PLACE

Talk has no bearing on the
reality of things except in a
commercial sense.
—Stéphane Mallarmé

Some cities, like İstanbul or Babylon, are built on a sea
coast, on the banks of a river. Harar is a city without water,
without fountains, a city of earth, a city without memory,
where the same is forever regenerated at a slow pace—a city
for Rimbaud, who wanted to forget. Some cities have no
reason to exist, either good or bad: They suit perpetual travelers like Rimbaud for whom nobody and no place are necessary anymore, for whom everything has become
contingent. Some cities have grown under the wings of a
miracle, like Jerusalem or Mecca. But Harar possesses neither marvels nor miracles of any kind: It is a sacred city
without a sacred history. It suits the wanderings of the man
who has given up finding "the place and the formula."* It
is his "flagrant and empty" place. For a city to be alive, it
needs a totem: the Kaaba, the Coliseum, the Eiffel Tower.
So that people will come and mill about. So that they will
put on their feathers and dance. Harar is a taboo city, a city
that suits a traveler like Rimbaud, whose feathers have been

*"Vagabonds," *Illuminations.*

plucked, who does not look for the center, but drifts toward the periphery, a dusty city growing into the desert.

Some cities are open to the wind from the sea, like Dakar; some cities perfume their island and the sea around, like Zanzibar. The main sensation one associates with Harar's brown is olfactory: Harar's sunbaked clay without gutters or waterways gives off a powerful fetid stench, which neither the unleavened bread baking on hot stones in the alleys, nor the scent of cloves and pepper trees is strong enough to mask. The city takes us by the throat with the heavy breath of lives squeezed between slabs of dry clay and, at nightfall, exhales a false, putrid vitality from orifices in hot stones, which seems to rise all the way up to the cold stars. Harar is an excremental city—not really in the sense of being repulsive, to tell the truth, but of a kind of infantile well-being; it is a comfort station. One could very nearly be tempted to walk around with an herb cup over one's nose, the kind used during the great plagues. But these over-powering smells please the man who curses salons and sniffs with pleasure at this surest sign of being far from the "crude modern metropolis."* Rimbaud reserves the supreme obscenity of the French language for literary men; one letter to Verlaine (of April 1872) contains nothing else: In the African correspondence the word does not appear. It would not be surprising, though, especially if we think of Harar after the battle of Shalenko, when the area was ravaged by Menelik's warriors, famine, sickness—a scene of defilement on which Rimbaud arrives unprepared, exhausted, pursued by bad luck and Labatut's creditors. You had to have your heart set on it to come back into the rubble and stench of the city† crowded with Menelik's soldiers who, according to Borelli, "left excrement and waste of slaughtered cows all over the place, while packs of dogs, under the indifferent eyes of the Amharan guards, devoured

---

* "Ville" ("City"), *Illuminations*.
† "The city has become a cesspool" (letter to Alfred Bardey, August 26, 1887).

bodies of Gallas who had died of hunger."[1]

In Rimbaud's letters, sarcasm remains, obscenity disappears. No doubt he no longer needs to provoke. Harar with its one-eyed walls would be a kingdom for the blind: nothing but ochre to dream of, clay to finger, odors to touch, nothing but a sky to guess above braille city.

The Land Rover with the camera on its stand in back looks like a mounted machine gun. Its way is soon blocked by a growing crowd of children dressed in flour sacks, crying, "*Baksheesh!*" "*Farengi!*" "Rimbo house!" An Abyssinian church[2] overlooks Makonnen Square, named after the Ras who, in the Egyptian metaphor, "had to eat" the land of Harar that he governed as faithful follower of King Menelik.[3] On the left, in front of *Dedjazmatche,* Makonnen's old *guêbi,* was the Bardey trading depot—"Viannay, Bardey et Cie."—the only house with more than one floor, which Alfred Bardey rented on arrival from the Egyptian governor Raouf Pasha. "Arthur Rimbaud and Constantin Righas lived on the second floor with the two windows," he specifies in *Barr Adjam.* The ground floor was taken up by the store. When the Egyptian troops evacuated the city, the English delegate chose the house for his temporary residence and raised the British flag on it—all while Rimbaud ran around the desert with his caravan.[4]

I can see it, this house no longer there, with mud walls like the others, flat plaster roof, cool inside because of the thick walls. "Among the beams that support the ceiling of reeds reinforced with beaten clay, many red birds are fluttering about without minding the people." The dark corners, crawling with flat-backed ants and earwigs dropped from the ceiling, must have been stacked with cowhides and panther skins; elephant tusks from Ogaden or Guraghe; fragrant Harar coffee beans; musk *okiètes* (which the Abyssins obtain by scraping the belly of civet cats); gold in the form of bracelets or dust; *wars,* the precious, saffronlike powder used for dyeing cloth, and which the Sidamo and Ouaglala chiefs fake with iron. "They come from the most distant tribes, out of curiosity," notes Bardey. "Everybody seems happy. It's a honeymoon between the depot and the area." The honeymoon did not last. But when the firm wound up its affairs in Africa, at the end of 1883, the Aden, Harar, and Zeila branches had important assets. Today, young men are selling Lenin's *Little Red Book* and detective stories in front of the old store. I have seen a few talers in circulation, those beautiful big silver pieces that ring and tip the scales through ten years of Rimbaud letters, coins bearing the effigy of Maria Theresa of Austria, which were currency in the last century and gave their name to the dollar. There are still a few around in the country, where the peasants call them *martresas*. Sancerni takes me to a bar, a dark *bounabète* where people drink Harar coffee at all hours. Coffee, as its name indicates, comes from the kingdom of Kaffa, not far south of here. The Arabs load and transport it across to Mocha, where the Ethiopian coffee is blended into Arabian coffee. I immediately contract a habit of taking a cup of this very black liquid—the beans being grilled rather than roasted according to local custom: divine coffee. "Cursed coffee,"* cries Rimbaud because the firm paid him in coffee against the forced loan of his talers! "Cursed coffee," because the kind he bought for resale was laced with earth: "dirt scratched up from the floor of Harar houses!"† So Rimbaud wishes the governor "caravans rich in rotten coffee."†† Divine coffee whose taste lingers on the tongue all day.

In an unfamiliar city, you go slow. Camera on shoulder, microphone under Charles's arm, our crew ventures into the labyrinth of alleyways intersected here and there by ridges of real rock, through clusters of square, terraced houses of

---

* "Maudits cafés" (letter to Ilg, February 24 and March 1, 1890).
† Letters to Messrs. Mazeran, Viannay, and Bardey, August 25, 1883.
†† December 20, and again, October 3, 1889: "this muck called coffee"; December 20, 1889: "this coffee, always very dirty, very impure"; February 24, 1890: "miserable coffee"; April 1890: "your vile coffee"; June 15, 1890: "horrible coffee!"

dried marl, brimming over with inhabitants. In Harar (forty thousand inhabitants? seventy-five thousand? it is difficult to estimate the growing population confined within the city walls), the crowds are dense, but almost immobile. Only the children run. In every shady corner, an invalid is napping. Christian beggars lean against the church wall. As in Rimbaud's days, the sick lie in the street—in Rimbaud's days the system was to leave them there until they either got well or died. They became the natural prey of wild beasts that managed to get into the city at night, in spite of the ramparts, as Philippe Paulitschke reports in *Harar* (1888). In town and all over the region, the men are chewing *cat* leaves. Rimbaud "tried it out on himself,"[5] this green, stimulant plant with the licorice taste, whose shoots are nibbled. Everywhere, blacks with green teeth. Cheeks puffed out by balls of *cat,* they are chewing time.

All of a sudden, Ato Chami, an old Oriental storyteller, emerges from the shadows to ask us into his cool and smoky house where his wife, like an ancient slave, brings in the *tief* (a cereal) mill and the jar of fermenting *talla,* the Ethiopian beer . . . *Salaam aleikum.* Ato Chami offers us the ritual coffee, first round for the men, second for the women, third for the servants. Then the storyteller, dressed in his *gourbi,* lights up together with the projectors. Ato Chami's act is very much to the point. On an old map of Harar, he points out the various houses where Rimbaud is supposed to have lived. He tells of a traditional song, which he modifies for our benefit into a celebration of the poet's presence in Harar. Then he fans the interest I have shown in his anecdote about Rimbaud—my incredulity quickly gave way before his pleasure in being believed. He promises to do further research on it, provided, this time, that we pay: Two old friends of his now in their nineties remember how they were fiercely chased off by a European whom they used to bother in his courtyard at the edge of town, when they were kids. They called him *hiraregna* in Amharic, literally "the irascible man."

Which reminds me that the coffee sorters in Aden called Rimbaud *Karani,* "the Meanie." The anecdote is probably made up, but it fits Rimbaud: solitary, uncompromising with everybody and himself, the man who once wanted to "become a very mean madman," whose "vicious plans" scandalized Verlaine, and who wrote "mean" letters from Harar and Arabia, which I prefer to his others: "I have cast off this woman without appeal!"[6]

I believed the old con man's story, believed in discovering an unknown trace, the glimmer of an image—another mirage. Back in the half-light, I thought of Rimbaud's eternal difficulties, his infinite patience, the constant trickery he had to deal with, the insane harassments that made up his daily life. His worst moment of distress, the climax of his 1886 arms deal, was certainly his encounter with Menelik.

Meeting Ato Chami's malicious eyes, I can see Menelik before me: Triumphant, athletic, in a huge embroidered black cape over a confusing mass of white linen, and a black, broad-brimmed Quaker hat under which protrudes the silk scarf knotted around his head, Menelik faces Rimbaud, who can only counter with a mask of pain and toughness. Menelik, who personally supervised all the traders in his kingdom and was a kind of stock market all by himself, makes the point that he no longer needs arms after his victory, temporizes, and finally brings out an IOU of Labatut's. Other creditors turn up. Rimbaud has wandered into a veritable den of thieves. He has to leave his stock without getting paid. "I'm convinced the Negus robbed me."* In Menelik he found his match. Rimbaud breaks, but does not bend. The Negus was the more cunning. A rake at the business. *A rake of rakes.*

Too honest to be a merchant, Rimbaud. Intransigent where he ought to be supple, not duped, but indignant, unable to learn from his experiences, to turn his failures to advantage, he even sympathizes with the others, enters into

*To M. de Gaspary, Aden, November 9, 1887.

their reasons. And bad luck! "As for business," Segalen will say, "he has a capital fault: he failed." A good salesman would have imagined Menelik naked, whereas Rimbaud was the one who felt naked before Menelik. He was a matchless caravaneer, but as a diplomat, a zero to the second power. He had ideas and could count, but that is not enough to make a businessman: Rimbaud *did not like to sell*. Though he had had the idea. As always in his life. Only the idea.

We are going down Arthur Rimbaud Street—the street signs have been ripped off, street of the forgotten poet, nameless street—which leads to the center of the city, the marketplace, *faras magalah* (horse market), or *souk magalah*. It used to be enclosed by a high wall, pierced on one side by a gate crowned with two lions and locked with elephant tails. Soldiers would unlock the gate at dawn, and the traders (*nagadiés*) spread over the city. Along with the main mosque, "Rimbaud House"—an Indian-style house with a wooden facade—dominates the square. The joists inside the handsome oval space bear the construction date: 1900! It is no doubt because it is the most beautiful house in town that it is offered to the "naive tourist"* as a sublime false clue, homage to an unknown name that returned to them vaguely famous, glorifying the city in turn. We could do the market by camera: You would see brief images of women arriving single-file from neighboring villages, with produce on their heads. You would recognize them by their clothes: The Galla women wear mostly brightly colored material and long kerchiefs on their heads; the Argobas (among whom Rimbaud was said to have taken his wife) seem more ferocious in their khaki tunics. You would see merchants in heavily mended clothes sit cross-legged before small heaps of red coffee beans or boxes of *cat*. We would do a close-up on this blind old black with the wooden rod on his shoulders that passes behind his neck, his arms dangling from it by the elbows, or on this woman sauntering by with impecca-

*"Soir historique" ("Historic Evening"), *Illuminations*.

bly braided hair, simpering under her wicker parasol. We could stock up on images. . . . Enough seen! But if you have *lived* a morning in the hubbub of the Harar market, you will never forget the mix of odors—as if Europe made us lose our sense of smell—and being carried by the crowd that churns slowly among the wares, dense like an ear of corn and armed with big sugarcanes.

This plumber's stall could be Rimbaud and his Greek bazaar! Arabian incense mingles with casseroles, *matads,*[7] gewgaws, lengths of cotton, *aboudjedide,* still worn by the peasants. You open a door, climb some rickety steps: to find a feline storekeeper napping among gimcrack mirrors, earthenware pots, armchairs with two indentations in the upholstery. In a basin or a *counna* of braided straw, piles of "magic scrolls" or *dabtaras,* books handwritten in red and black ink on parchment or gazelle skin, bound in wood or vellum: Korans or books written in Ge'ez, the liturgical language of the orthodox. Out the window, the market, bright and silent. In 1880, the Bardey store on Makonnen Square in the upper city meant hope, but in 1890, the market was the end of an adventure, ridiculous and tragic. After his lowly employment in Bardey's office, Rimbaud was dreaming: "From these savings I'll have some small, steady income."* And he was still dreaming before his arms deal: "I certainly hope this deal will work. . . . If the King pays me promptly I'll come right back to the coast with about twenty-five thousand francs profit."† It was counting chickens before they were hatched. He tried everything. Then, in the last months of his life, resigned himself to not getting rich quick. Working for himself and with César Tian, an Aden businessman, he buys and sells anything, runs after deals and bargains, all to no purpose. Rimbaud as retailer! "Enclosed duplicate invoice pots." He says himself: "My bric-a-brac," "my junk!"†† Alfred Ilg makes fun of his "bazaaritis," sneers

*To his family, Aden, May 5, 1884.
†Aden, November 18, 1885.
††To Ilg, Harar, October 7, 1889 and November 20, 1890.

at the unsaleable goods Rimbaud stores with him: rosaries and crucifixes—at a time when Menelik is trying to oust the missionaries—notebooks for an illiterate population, pearls from Decran et Compagnie. Why not bootjacks, mocks Ilg, who also makes fun of Brémond, another trader, and his "three-penny bazaar." But Alfred Ilg himself had, only a year and a half earlier, imported color reproductions of Raphael's "Sistine Madonna."[8] Wild-eyed, on the wrong track, all of them. Then collapse of the myth, tragic version: Rimbaud amputated in Marseille, a few months later, writing from his hospital bed: "Farewell marriage, farewell family, farewell future."[*]

Struck by "the fatal thirst for gold," of which he wrote in his Latin poem "Jugurtha" when he was fourteen, Rimbaud turned in Harar into a "very tight and very hard dealer," according to the Righas brothers interviewed by Segalen. "One gets stingier and stingier here, it's terrible."[†]

"I shall have gold!" This symbolic exclamation from *A Season in Hell* is sized up in the reality of the eight kilos of gold that Rimbaud carries in his belt to Cairo in 1887 and which, he says, gave him dysentery. Even when he went from Harar to Aden in 1884, he carried 12,000 to 13,000 francs on him: "You have to drag your nest-egg around with you and keep an eye on it at all times."[††] Lack of security and real dangers make these precautions of Rimbaud's necessary. Still, we cannot help being reminded of his mother, the lady in black, who during the last two years of her life carried her money and IOUs in a kangaroo pouch on her body.[9] Rimbaud has *somebody he takes after* in scraping for "redeeming coins."[§] He too becomes bent on gain like his grasping mother, Vitalie Cuif, "widow Rimbaud," and the whole Cuif family, Ardennais peasants rooted in their land in Roche, in the canton of Attigny. "Mama ad-

---

[*] To Isabelle, July 10, 1891.
[†] To Ilg, Harar, November 18, 1890.
[††] Aden, May 5, 1884; and from Cairo, on August 24, 1887: "I can't go on carrying this money on my back, it's too stupid, too tiring and too dangerous."
[§] To Ilg, Harar, November 16, 1889.

vises to take good care of your money," writes Isabelle in 1891, "and watch out you don't lose it or get robbed on the trip back."[10]

In Abyssinia, a sober and somber Rimbaud went back to *being a Cuif*. No doubt he had never stopped being one. Even the schoolboy good in French (and all other subjects) tried to make his efforts pay off in prizes. But in the African correspondence, money takes the place it occupies in his mother's life. Now they speak the same language. "You can be pleased with me. I know the value of money, and if I take a risk I know what I'm doing."[11] Except for "business" connections, the letters from Africa and Arabia are addressed to his mother and sister exclusively. Rather than with a formula of affection, many end "with prosperous greetings."* Rimbaud writes in his mother tongue. This is no doubt where we got such an exaggerated image of him as a businessman of painfully boring conversation, laboriously amassing rupees and talers. The letters are as if "aspirated" by their recipient, as if dictated by his mother: The son talks of what interests her, what she expects to hear about—marriage, money, employment—tends to conform to his mother's ideal of him. But this fact is new and certainly not accidental. Rimbaud shows yet more Cuif traits in Ethiopia: a pride that cannot stand to be beholden to anybody, strong will and stubbornness in errors, inflexible tenacity, worry about being respectable, scrupulous honesty, a taboo against tenderness. Under the tropical sun, we find a very gloomy Rimbaud.

"To smoke, above all, to drink liquor strong as boiling metal!"† The excesses of *A Season in Hell* are followed by inflexible harshness against himself: "I drink absolutely nothing but water, *fifteen francs'* worth a month! I never smoke" (Rimbaud's italics).†† Righas corroborates: "He was

---

* Or with "health and prosperity" (December 3, 1885).
† "Mauvais Sang" ("Bad Blood"), *A Season in Hell*.
†† Aden, April 14, 1885.

very sober, never drank any alcohol, only coffee Turkish style, as one does here." "I dress in calico; my clothes don't cost me fifty francs a year."* Ottorino Rosa remembers that he made himself "suits of white American cotton" ("simple denim pants and a cotton shirt"; "I am always badly dressed,"†) and "lived like a native: When Lieutenant Harrington, the English Resident in Zeila, saw him in his bizarre outfit he took him for a simple mason." And Augustin Bernard said he looked more like "some poor Armenian or Greek bugger than a Frenchman."

He showed the same harshness toward others. Ilg reproaches him with "never taking enough provisions. Every single caravan of yours has arrived starved, with all hands in deplorable condition. Everybody complains bitterly about you."[12] "I marched with all possible economy,"†† taking for food only a handful of *dabokolo,* a mixture of grains, in his jacket and cooked rice in his saddle pocket: "I carefully avoid any unnecessary expense!"§

During his long travels in Europe and Java, he had practically not written to his mother at all. For one thing, he was getting away from her . . . but we might say that going to the end of the then known world allowed his likeness with his mother to surface. Distance is the very condition of their dialogue: Disobedient and rebellious when with her, he can get close to her when away. "I think of you, I even think only of you";‖ "The only thing that interests me is news from home. . . . I am pleased to think that your little business is doing alright. If you need it, take what is mine: it's yours."¶ These letters, born from lack of communication, are a camouflaged asking for love, which, never answered, contributes to their distance. We do not have the

* Ibid.
† To Isabelle, July 15, 1891, and to his family, Aden, January 15, 1885.
†† Letter to the *Bosphore égyptien,* August 20, 1887.
§ Aden, January 15, 1885.
‖ Harar, July 22, 1881.
¶ To his family, Harar, May 6, 1883 and November 7, 1881.

replies of this renewed dialogue with "mother," though we can guess some of them.[13] But their absence, their loss, their distant, inaudible voice as it were, is the proper symbol for this correspondence of two voices that never meet.

In spite of his diffuse presence in Harar, I feel Rimbaud is absent from any particular place: from the houses he lived in, long washed away by the rain, from the stores and markets our fancy rides, as from this fake "Rimbo house" where he might have liked to live, which might represent his daydreams, his castle in Spain.[14]

Can I even imagine the absent, the fugitive? "If it is so difficult to imagine Rimbaud (physically, even), is it not because in reading him we feel his own vain obsession: to steal, one day, along with the fire, his own image?"[15] Rimbaud is certainly nothing like the troubadour in oriental costume his sister Isabelle drew in 1893—clean-shaven but for a mustache, strumming an Abyssinian harp, and heaving a sigh to make the whole Bosporus groan—which inspired Verlaine to write a three-penny sonnet: "I admire you in this drawing's naive lines."[16]

"A poet's life belongs to everyone," declared Nerval.[17] But Rimbaud is alone: As an adolescent poet, he did not want to be first, but "other." In Abyssinia, he always feels a "barbarian," as Ovid did in exile among the Getae. Another singularity: He is mysterious. When the Massawa police arrest him on August 5, 1887, and take him to Consul Alexandre Merciniez, the latter immediately writes to his colleague in Aden for information about "Sieur Rimbaud, a supposed tradesman" who "looks like a rather shady customer."[18]

In reaction against the legendary portrait drawn by his brother-in-law Berrichon, Rimbaud has often been belittled, made normal, a tradesman among others, judged on appearances. But there is always a troubling difference that sets him apart, a strangeness in the old sense of the stranger who comes from the other side, across the sea. "We would like to help you," a correspondent writes, "but you are so bizarre." Rimbaud—"that extraordinary original," said Savouré[19]—is indeed *different* from the handful of Europeans who lived at that time in East Africa. As in Balzac's novels, there is an abundance of secondary characters. In the group of tradesmen, everybody has his personality. Rimbaud is caught in their net, one of them. But knowing them better would show up his extravagant individuality. I can see them, as if in one of those old Félix Potin albums where we used to paste the "celebrities of our time": Brémond, the oldest; Eloy Pino, former commander of the brig *Oronoco,* a sea captain like Labatut, who became quite by chance the "first link between Menelik and Europe"; the Bienenfeld brothers, Vittorio and Giuseppe, from Trieste, and their Italian colleagues Ottorino Rosa and Pietro Felter; Armand Savouré,[20] the shadiest and most rooted; Ernest Laffineur, a grocer from Fécamp. The photographer Bidault, an original, "always deep in contemplation," banters Rimbaud.* But once we have named them, what do we do with them? A TV show? They share a flair for situations, an absence of moodiness; aquatic or landlubbers, they are all more or less confidence men. The two Swiss, however, are distinguished by unfailing honesty and an equal lack of subtlety: the mechanic Ernest Zimmermann, called Zimpi, and especially Alfred Ilg, veritable sidekick of the story, square head, crew cut, shell glasses and handlebar mustache, the engineer who became Menelik's "prime minister," *bihoadded.*[21]

We may regret that Rimbaud wrote only one letter to young Léon Chefneux, the future consul general of Abyssinia, "intelligent, subtle, likeable" according to Scarfoglio. His boss at that time, Paul Soleillet, could be the subject of an English-style monograph. "Soleillet is only concerned with his name," a classified note in the Foreign Office (from Savouré?) insinuates. He would have had good reason—his name already makes him attractive—but he was actually

*To Jules Borelli, February 25, 1889.

concerned with many other things: Author of *Voyages en Éthiopie* and *Obock, Choa, Kaffa,* the "famous traveler in the Algerian Sahara,"[22] the first to conceive of a trans-Sahara railroad, was also the singlehanded founder of the French protectorate of Somaliland. For months he flew the French flag in the furnace heat of the Red Sea coast, to the annoyance of the British on their ships, whose field glasses kept spotting, always in a different place, the flag they had shot down the night before. "The purpose of all my eighteen years of traveling is to open roads," Soleillet wrote, in vain, to the Ministry of Education on January 30, 1883. Rimbaud too had defined himself in this way well before going into business. Like him, Soleillet had the worst troubles. "The thousand Remington rifles" he had imported, Rimbaud notes, "are still stacked in the only palm grove of the village nineteen months later."* They had planned the arms caravan for Menelik together. On September 9, 1886, Soleillet died in Aden, felled by sunstroke as his name might seem to foreshadow. "The late Soleillet," Rimbaud says bitterly. But the difference between them and Rimbaud? It is that we have no desire to write a book on these pitiful or picturesque characters. Rimbaud does not continue to interest us because he stopped being a poet, but because he was not altogether the "supposed tradesman."

The explorers? Rimbaud leaves them behind, like Borelli on the route to Harar while he gallops ahead to get paid by Makonnen. If he encountered Captain Cecchi or the Marquis Antinori at the beginning of his stay, they did no more than greet each other according to custom. Rimbaud did not seek their company, though a few stayed with him in Harar: the engineer Luigi Robecchi-Bricchetti and the Hungarian Count Téléki on his return from an expedition to Kenya. They remembered him cordially and with curiosity. Likewise Ugo Ferrandi, author of *Itinerari Africani* (1897), and Augusto Franzoj,[23] whom he knew for more

*Letter to the *Bosphore égyptien,* Cairo, August 20, 1887.

than six months in Tadjoura. He did not speak about them. The "Ambition, O Mad Ambition!" that he admitted to the "Dear Master,"* Theodore de Banville, is long gone, but the loss of ambition, hence of models, does not abolish his difference. Rimbaud continues to feel distinct, that is to say, alone: "As I am the only somewhat intelligent employee in all of Aden . . ."† Bardey notices and trusts him with his depot in Harar. Even Borelli, always condescending to him, declared in 1936: "What cannot be denied is his more than average intelligence." He obviously has a range different from that of his peers of the moment, employees like Sotiro, the bighearted Greek whose taste for adventure he shared; or Pinchard, with whom he made his first trek from Aden to Harar in December 1880; not to mention the Righas brothers, nice people of the kind it takes four to have an idea. "As for Europeans, there are only a few idiotic business employees,"†† he one day throws out in disgust. But he saw neither more nor less or them than of the explorers, engineers, journalists, businessmen, diplomats, or priests. He did not join any group of the small European society in Abyssinia at that time. As always, he did not feel superior, but singular. Untouchable. All the testimonies of the different groups agree on his austerity and bizarre character. Ironical, but not arrogant, the former rebel is even liked by a wide range of people: Proud and modest, he always had the gift of knowing how to talk to the powerful— the imperial prince or the Negus—as well as to the humble, the workers he hung out with as a young man[24] or the natives in his caravans. His "damn upbringing"§ (so remote from the Anglo-Saxon, Protestant empiricism favorable to commerce) and the latent Cuif Catholicism continue to show in charity, this noncontradictory *key* of avarice: Rimbaud,

---

* To Théodore de Banville, March 24, 1870.
† To his family, September 22, 1880.
††Aden, April 14, 1885.
§ "L'Éclair" ("Lightning"), *A Season in Hell*.

the robbed merchant, pays his partner's debts, though the creditors proliferate, come out of the bushes with "flatteries to make you pale": "As these poor people were nevertheless in good faith, I was touched and paid." To a certain Dubois's request for twenty talers, he adds interest and a pair of shoes—"the poor devil complained of being barefoot."* This "heartless A. Rimbaud,"† as he used to sign himself, severe and unexpansive, hips hugged by his gold belt, can at the end of his road, in 1890, write to his family, as if asking for absolution: "In the country and on the road I enjoy a certain consideration because of my humane conduct. I have never wronged anybody. On the contrary, I do a little good when I find occasion to, and that is my only pleasure."†† At the end of his *Souvenirs,* Alfred Bardey holds up a placard bearing his personal motto, as if revealing the secret of his success: *C.O.S.—Confidence. Optimism. Solidarity.* Of these virtues, Rimbaud practices only the third.§ His letters are all defiance, pessimism, and distress signals: SOS. But Charitable he was, says Bardey: "His charity was very discreet and large . . . probably one of the few things he did without scoffing or pleading disgust."[25] On his bed of pains in Marseille, the strange tradesman will receive echoes from this capital of affection: "Do not fear," Sotiro writes to him, "you have no family, but you have good friends." Savouré confirms from Harar that Ras Makonnen "does not think of anything else: He was very disturbed by the operation you had to have, he talked to all of us about it *twenty times* a day, saying you were the most honest of men and had often proved a *true friend* to him" (Savouré's italics).[26] Bienenfeld too tries to console him: "A leg more or less

* To M. de Gaspary, Aden, November 9, 1887.
† To Georges Izambard, November 2, 1870.
††Harar, February 25, 1890.
§ Ilg's reproach must be put in the context of their complicated relations. Rimbaud replied: "As for your reproach that I starve men and beasts on the road, you must be joking. I am on the contrary known for my generosity in these matters. . . . But it goes to show the gratitude of natives!" (To Ilg, Harar, December 11, 1889).

won't keep you from making your way in life." And there is this note from Dimitri Righas, a *natural* Rimbaldian:

> Harar, July 15, 1891
>
> My dear Monsieur Rimbaud,
>   Got you letter jus tooday, where you menshon you had the opperation, I mean you lost your leg, and I'm very sorry and so are all your frens in Harar. I rather loose my own leg than yourn. Well I hope you get well soon. Since you gon I think I lost the hole world. I never go out exept to the Zaptié.

We are just passing the *Zaptié,* the prison, still as overcrowded . . . and, at the city limits, there is again the countryside and its islands of mud-wall *toukouls* with their straw roofs. Red trails run through the gardens toward the distant sea and legendary names: Aden, Ogaden, Sidamo. We feel the call of the road, or its silence, and the promised names at the end. "Sensitive to the quality of his gimcracks? Maybe not," said Mallarmé with relish, "but to the landscapes drunk in with a thirst for vastness and independence." At the south gate of Harar, the Buddha Gate (of the "evil eye") where the caravans used to start, I have a kind of fleeting vision, which I keep like a postcard without anybody to send it to. It is suggested by this passage in Bardey's souvenirs: In May 1881, Rimbaud asks to be sent south, to Bubassa. So as not to arouse the hostility of the natives nearly naked in their scraped and reddened goatskins, Rimbaud wants to pass for a rich Muslim merchant. On leaving at the head of a convoy of camels loaded with cotton, he winds a white napkin around his head as a turban and drapes a red blanket over himself. He laughs himself at his get up and, spurring his horse, sets out to "traffic in the unknown."*

*Harar, May 4, 1881.

4
TIME

The daily mechanics of being
on the road make for a flagrant
opposition between two
worlds: the one in your head
and the one you collide with.
—Segalen

In the land of the beginning of time, Ethiopians of today
count 6:00 A.M. the first hour of the day. We generally rise
with the sun, without keeping track of the clock, in order
fully to use the light. If you want to get to know a country,
you must join the movement of its inhabitants, follow the
local rhythm, take part in social constraints: Every morning, Sancerni takes me in his jeep from Diredawa to Harar,
each of us wrapped in a blanket against the nippy cold of
dawn. Down in the narrow valleys, camel caravans are already on the road. The basalt mountains seem higher and
more compact, more abrupt and blacker in the light of the
rising sun. This could be a morning in the first century.

The sun keeps the appointment—the only one you can
count on. At six o'clock (1:00 P.M. in France), we leave on
a "scouting expedition" for a distant wadi that a traveler in
the last century had described in the epic terms of South Sea
tales: "We headed East from the town, through wild and
bare ravines where we encountered large dog-faced ba-
boons."[1] In the sand of the dry, meandering riverbed, our

jeeps and Land Rover skid and slide like camels on firn, raising clouds of white dust. All along the rutted and washed-out trails that Rimbaud used to take, we are bumped on our iron seats as on a trotting horse. But the trails give out, paths divide, and in the mountains, the cars, almost vertical, get stuck in the middle of nowhere. Without the Rover we would be lost. It took this impass and the fatigue of an after all very brief expedition to make me understand Rimbaud physically, take his word for it when he traces the beginning of his pains to forced marching, as he writes his mother, asking for an orthopedic stocking for varicose veins: "I've got this infirmity from too much effort on horseback and also fatiguing marches. For we have in this country a laby-rinth of steep mountains where one cannot even stay on horseback. All this without roads or even trails."* Ever since he had shown his enormously enlarged knee to the British doctor in Aden, he repeated doubtfully and as if to himself: "This certainly comes from the fatiguing treks to Harar on foot and horseback."† "The man with soles of wind" suf-fered from the malady of long marches under a leaden sun. But the cancerous tumor in his knee was complicated by—did he hide it?—the syphilis he had contracted early in his stay, which Dr. Traversi confirms he treated. Alfred Bardey will say that "he had unmistakable signs of it in his mouth."[2]

Contemplating the rocky landscape as far as the eyes can reach, my attention is suddenly caught by a rough spot on the hill opposite. Looking carefully, I think I see a crouched man whose stillness and brown clothes make him blend al-most completely with the "steppe of high grass and stony clearings." With the zoom lens, we make out several men and a child among the bushes and rocks, impassive in the heat. These are Ogadens, of whom Rimbaud said: "Their daily job is to go hunker in groups . . . they are completely

*Letter to Ilg, Harar, February 20, 1891.
†Aden, April 30, 1891.

inactive."* I automatically look at my watch: eleven-thirty. What did I do last week at this hour? Run madly through stifling subway tunnels. It is hard to believe that these Ogadens are our contemporaries. I see them just as Rimbaud saw them, just as they have no doubt always lived. They do not give an impression of big-city misery: They are not third world, but of a different world. "True life" has perhaps been here from the start, essentially, tied to the earth they blend into, untouched by any superfluous worry or new need created by our time-conscious society, which looks at them right now through our big optical instrument. Was Rimbaud tempted to learn from them, as we can from African societies, how to live completely "here and now," without the anxiety or greed our notion of "the future" brings with it? We might smile and ask which era, rather than which hour. For the Ogadens, days follow and resemble one another, succession is abolished and, with it, the running out of time that sends us chasing after "progress." They live in suspended time. The past is not dead: It is not even past.

The Ogadens are outside time. Rimbaud saw them through his obsession with space: He scoured endless expanses for his place. No longer the magic place and formula, but the *y*, the "there" of the unfindable place, the "there" we can circle in red in his poems: "black . . . water, no invalid fell down *there* even in his dreams."† "Among strangers without age . . . *there* I might have died."†† He searches for "a heart, to rest *there*."§ (Italics added.) It is the "there" we find again in the correspondence: The Rimbaldian place is both somewhere and nowhere. If we listen for the *ici*, the "here" in all his letters, the little adverb of place is repeated as if it had no reference, like the "here" of the

---

* *Rapport sur l'Ogadine*, December 1883.
† *Proses évangéliques*.
††"Adieu," *A Season in Hell*.
§ "Délires" I, *A Season in Hell*.

Illuminations: "Nothing happens here . . . one gets stifled here": Charleville. "What delights me here": Paris. "Who could invent atrocities here": Roche. "If you don't want to come back here": London. "Verlaine has arrived here": Stuttgart. Then three "heres" ring out in a letter from Alexandria, three in a letter from Larnaca, three "up to heres" from Mount Troodos, two "heres" from Limassol on Cyprus.* The first mention of Abyssinia appears in a letter of 1880, mailed in Aden on August 17: "I've come here." Rimbaud arrives in Harar: "I am here."† He thinks of leaving the next year: "I don't think I'll stay here long."†† "Here" will mean Egypt in 1887, or Marseille, in his last days: "I'll lose no time taking the boat from here."§ The boat in question goes to Aphinar, and he asks for its departure time right before dying, mysterious boat of his delirium, that will carry him to the nonplace beyond. Always dreaming of elsewhere, all places seem the same to an unsettled, indifferent Rimbaud. Does his correspondence not reiterate in its own fashion: "We are not in the world?"‖ Rimbaud moves constantly, but he does not really travel. "Good-bye, be seeing you here, wherever."¶ His journeys are abstractions.

I lie low faced with the Ogadens. Laboring and pressed for time, we are the idlers of their inaction. But Rimbaud, incapable of *being there,* what could excite him, spur him

---

* August 25, 1870; September 12, 1871; "Junphe," 1872; May 1873; July 4, 1873; March 5, 1875; December 1878; February 1879; May 23, 1880.
† December 13, 1880.
†† February 15, 1881.
§ August 23, 1887; June 29, 1891. "There is nobody here and there is somebody" ("Nuit de l'enfer" ("Night of Hell"), *A Season in Hell*). But what does it mean to affirm being there when it accelerates, hammering six times in a few lines of a letter from Aden: "M. Bardey has left . . . to continue his business *here*. . . . He told me to wait for him *here*, but if there is no satisfactory news by the end of this month I'll look for employment elsewhere. There is no work *here* at this point, the big firms that supply the branches *here* having all gone under in Marseille. . . . Life is unaffordable *here* . . . and you know it is the hottest place in the world *here*!" (to his family, May 5, 1884).
‖ "Délires," I, *A Season in Hell*.
¶ "Démocratie," *Illuminations*.

on?[3] Nothing. Or boredom, most likely. Boredom worthy of the Ardennes winters, his favorite diversion. A prayer. He must have been afraid of being deprived of it. Aden was "the most boring place in the world, that is, after the one where you live."* On arriving in Harar: "May we finally enjoy a few years of real rest in this life . . . since we cannot imagine another life more boring than this one!"† In Harar, seven years later: "I am often, always, bored; I have never known anybody more bored than I am." ". . . *qui s'ennuyât autant que moi.*"†† *Qui s'ennuyât!* This subjunctive goes beyond grammar. It suggests a yawn and, even more, an absolute kind of *ennui* that gives the word its seventeenth-century, nonpassive sense of torment and impatience.[4] Boredom, said Baudelaire, "dreams of gallows while smoking a houkah." But there is a particular Rimbaldian boredom that is another constant in his life. It did not begin in Abyssinia, but in Charleville, where Rimbaud was "ineffably bored."§ He was bored at the Café Duterme, according to his classmate Louis Pierquin. His sister Vitalie wrote in her private diary in London: "Sunday, July 1. Arthur is bored." Action is not the sister of dreams, Rimbaud's *ennui* is not the "O for action" that Mallarmé smiles at while blowing a few cigar rings. Gide was very poorly informed to evoke a Rimbaud in Harar "who spent his days smoking, crouched in the Oriental manner"! When Rimbaud is bored it is in action, spending energy, in constant dynamism. He suffers from the act of being bored. In this indolent empire, he displays a stupendous activity, gives of himself to the point of exhaustion, without really finding anything to devote himself to. Absolute boredom means perhaps precisely that action never finds its true object any more than Rimbaud finds his exact "here." What makes Ar-

* To his family, September 22, 1880.
† To his family, Harar, May 25, 1881.
††To his family, Harar, August 4, 1886.
§ To Georges Izambard, July 12, 1871.

thur Rimbaud run? What goal has he set himself that precipitates him onto the trails? People believe[5] that Rimbaud's
aim was to get rich in Abyssinia. Not at all. His only aim
was *rest*. Only, he made *work come first*. What an error!

To accumulate money is indeed not itself his aim: It is
the means for attaining rest. His program is clear, he repeats
it all through the ten years: "to scrape up, at the price of
fatigue, enough to settle down and rest." In other words,
to work hard in hope of not working later: "to get to live
on my revenues," "to rest a little after long years of suffering," "to see a time of rest arrive before my death." As he
wrote to Isabelle before dying: "I marched and worked hard,
more than ever."[6]

This reiterated goal, "to live on my revenues," is not
one of those bouts of fever Rimbaud suffered in Africa, but
his oldest childhood project: "Sapristi, I'll be a stockholder,"
he scribbles in his "Notebook at Seven."* Of course, Rimbaud hates and detests work! "I have a horror of all trades."
But this horror, expressed in *A Season in Hell* and permeat-
ing his letters from Africa and Arabia, is linked to the bib-
lical idea of the punishment for man who, wanting to know,
tasted the forbidden fruit of the tree of knowledge of good
and evil. Like Adam chased from the Garden of Eden, Rimbaud is condemned to "eat his bread in the sweat of his
brow." In *A Season in Hell,* work, the fatal punishment is
associated with the white man, the Christian Occident: "The
White men are landing. . . . We must submit to baptism,
wear clothes, toil."† By contrast, idleness, one of the reasoned vices of the *voyant,* the Seer, is low, dirty, black in
the unacceptable mythical sense the white man has given it:
"Yes, I close my eyes against your light. I am a beast, a
nigger."[7] Without recourse to oriental wisdom, the black
man in "Bad Blood" makes fun of human toil: "Life flour-
ishes through toil, an old saw: . . . my life takes wings and

*1862.
†"Mauvais Sang" ("Bad Blood"), *A Season in Hell.*

floats above the action, the point dear to the world." "I shall never work," the "Infernal Husband" screams at the "Mad Virgin."* "Let's sham and shirk our work for pity's sake."†

Even the "idle time of youth, enslaved to all," this "lost life," was not inactive: the reclaimed "Negro" past ("idler than a toad I've lived everywhere") and the "Negro" future he aspired to ("I'll be idle and brutal") were the object of work during the *voyant* period and the crisis of 1873. If Rimbaud claims to be "idle," prey to heavy fever, it is because he found "sacred the disorder of [his] mind": Idleness flaunts its rejection of Western values, but it even more exalts his project of poetic transformation: "I work at making myself *Voyant*, a Seer."†† Poetry has become insipid through subjectivity, he believes, because "man did not work on himself."§ So the experiment of the "reasoned *disordering of all the senses*," which "was first of all study," required "superhuman strength." Putting in his effort, Rimbaud writes to Delahaye, in the letter dated "Parmerde, Junphe 72": "I am working." After him will come other *voyants*, other "horrible workers" like him.

"If he were less wild we would be saved!"‖ Taking stock of the failure of his poetic experiment—"I am . . . a nigger. But I can be saved"¶—Rimbaud believed in redemption through a "new" kind of toil: "When shall we go across shores and mountains to salute the birth of a new kind of toil."** But his entire correspondence, always and increasingly dramatic, though written in a different symbolic mode—in haste and for a recipient—documents his backsliding in the test of Reality. His letters, which we might never have known, repeat in solitude this bitter statement

---

* "Délires" I, *A Season in Hell*.
† "Éclair" ("Lightning"), *A Season in Hell*.
†† May 13, 1871.
§ May 15, 1871.
‖ "Délires" I, *A Season in Hell*.
¶ "Mauvais Sang" ("Bad Blood"), *A Season in Hell*.
** "Matin" ("Morning"), *A Season in Hell*.

of *A Season in Hell:* "Sleep among riches is impossible." I understand why Rimbaud gallops past the Ogadens, why happiness is never "here": He has the tendency to "defer existence until later" of which Bataille speaks in *L'Expéri-ence intérieure.* Rimbaud works at deferring rest until later. . . . He procrastinates against his life! Work becomes his punishment for failing to reach the inaccessible state of rest, punishment that condemns him to wander "like a soul in purgatory": "So I must spend the rest of my days wander-ing."* Fatal punishment, "since every man is the slave of this miserable fate."† His perpetual projection of rest drives Rimbaud on the road, but Sisyphus will not get the impos-sible reward for so much fatigue and suffering. "After all, man counts on spending three quarters of his life suffering in order to rest the last quarter; and most often he dies of misery without knowing how far he has gotten in his plan."†† Rimbaud will find his rest indeed—in the fourth quarter he will never live, the eternal rest of death.

On the scale of values from black to white, what be-comes in Abyssinia of the man who in Europe had called himself a "nigger"? What kind of Melano-European or Af-ricandidus does he become in Harar?[8] A far cry from Ernest Delahaye's little white man's game of drawing an African Rimbaud ("still no news from our Senegalese") in his "Ne-gro Series" (1876, reply to a drawing of Verlaine's that shows Rimbaud as "native chief"): "Rimbaud with the Kaffirs" (an arrow through his nose), "Negro Farandole" (Rimbaud, an arrow through his hat, waves a bottle of "firewater," flanked by the Hottentot dictionary), and finally "The Ne-gro King" (Rimbaud on his throne, a crowned butcher being supplicated by his native subjects).[9]

---

* Cairo, August 23, 1887.
† Aden, September 10, 1884. On the meaning of this "punishment," see Chapter 10.
††Tadjoura, January 6, 1886.

*　　*　　*

"In Harar . . . you live with Negroes exclusively."* The
ambiguity of his symbolic and actual situation grows into
an additional contradiction. Rimbaud reproaches the natives
for their ingratitude, screams with "constant rage at living
among stupid Negro riffraff,"† claims to be "lost among
Negroes whose conditions I would like to improve, but who
in return try to exploit me and make it impossible to con-
clude deals without delay. Obliged to speak their gibberish,
eat their filthy food, suffer a thousand aggravations because
of their laziness, treachery, stupidity."†† Elsewhere he writes:
"These stupid Negroes expose themselves to consumption
and pleurisy by staying naked in the rain. Nothing can get
sense into them."

But we must read on to the next sentence: "I sometimes
come home naked under my burnous, having clothed some
of them on the way." Rimbaud comes home naked in the
rain, and the blacks leave with his white cotton underwear.
When his anger has boiled down, Rimbaud explains to his
mother and sister: "The people in Harar are neither more
stupid nor lower than the white Negroes of the countries
we call civilized; it's simply not on the same order, that's
all. They are rather less mean and can occasionally show
gratitude and fidelity. It's a matter of being decent to them."§

Exchange of colors, crossovers. . . . In the land of Lucy,
which we too quickly confuse with black Africa, the inhabitants do not have that bluish shimmer at the temples that
Rubens dared in his "sketches of Negroes," nor Mick Jag-
ger's thick painted lips. . . . The Manichean distinctions are
residues of medieval disputes, when, as we know, scholars
were divided on the question if "Negro" flesh was black or
like ours.[10] I remember the old black man we filmed in the

---

* To his family, Harar, November 10, 1890.
† To his family, Harar, February 20, 1891.
††To his family, Harar, August 4, 1888.
§ To his family, February 25, 1890.

CFE, in a third-class car, dark and sad like the one drawn by Daumier. His face seemed red in the half-light, and I was reminded of Emperor John of Abyssinia, whom his subjects called Yoannès the Red for the color of his skin.[11] In Abyssinia, you could reconstitute the pharaonic infantry one admires in the Cairo museum: small terra-cotta soldiers with a regiment of black Nubians and red pike-bearers from Abyssinia. The Ethiopians see their likes in colors, not in black and white, and distinguish a whole range of skin shades from bright red to brown to black. All nineteenth-century travelers noted this distinctive trait of the Abyssins.[12] Rimbaud himself calls the Ogadens "tall, more often red than black."* So that in reality there are few "Negroes" (as the last century called them) between the Red Sea and the Blue Nile. (In Icelandic, Ethiopia is called *Blaland,* "Blue Land.")

But if the term "Negro" is pejorative for Rimbaud (himself "Negro" in Europe, white in Africa, always in opposition), he applies it symbolically to both Europeans and Africans without any difference. The term tends to change in value as he abandons literature, as he voices his persistent disgust with the "white niggers" and is in sympathy with the blacks he encounters. But if the "nigger" home in the Roche attic, writing his *Livre Païen ou Livre Nègre*† (his *Pagan Book or Negro Book,* first title of *A Season in Hell*) was searching for some impossible negritude in Africa, it was in vain that he later burned himself out with activity, with the white passion for work as salvation, while becoming more and more of a stranger to Europe. The exchange of colors takes place inside him: I see Rimbaud "red as an Amhara."

In spite of khaki hats, *bobs,* and Canadian caps with long visors, our staff are red too from the violent desert sun, on this morning early in our stay. . . . We rest up on the shady terrace of a *bounabète* in Diredawa with a haciendalike green

* *Rapport sur l'Ogadine.*
†To Enrest Delahaye, Roche, May 1873.

wood fence, while kids mob to shine our shoes. Sancerni tells me of his hunting exploits and promises to take me hunting warthog in his jeep. We agree that Rimbaud was surely not "inactive" in Abyssinia, but that we cannot simply oppose the man of action to the poet, the rebel to the businessman: heads or tails! "Had not his master Michelet said that the modern hero was to be the man of action?" writes Starkie.[13] No doubt, but he had to be at it constantly, the horrible toiler!

Poetry was inseparable from action for him, Yves Bonnefoy reminds us and quotes: "In Greece, I said, verse and lyric *give rhythm to Action*. . . . Poetry *will be the vanguard*."* In Abyssinia, Rimbaud constantly tells himself, "Go in this direction." He gives himself *notice*. One thinks of the famous beginning of Sartre's *Baudelaire:* "Baudelaire is a leaning man." So is Rimbaud, differently, leaning forward in a projective movement, head always in search! His whole life long he was a man of projects. So many abrupt departures. His first change of direction was actually the most brutal and most decisive: After the prize-giving in July 1870, in the full glory of his academic success, Rimbaud refused to come back to school for his graduation year. As classes, at the restoration of the empire, were held in the building of the municipal theater, Rimbaud declared he had "no taste for the stage." This was the beginning of his flights (*Schübe*, the Germans would say: actions, pushes, drives) and also the period when he began to show his will to strangeness in his clothes and behavior. His poetics very quickly evolved from parody to mastery in a brief philogenesis of the history of modern poetry.

The period of *voyance* that culminates in the crisis of *A Season in Hell* constitutes only one—the most intense—phase of it, preceding partly his "diamond prose," as Verlaine called the *Illuminations*. Nevertheless, Rimbaud tried hard to become a journalist—and to make sure nobody would hire him.

*May 15, 1871.

After giving up on poetry, one project followed on the heels of another: He wanted to learn languages by traveling in England and Germany, more shortly in Italy, possibly in Spain.[14] Henri Pauffin ran across him in the Havetière woods around Charleville "learning Russian from an old Greek-Russian dictionary." Louis Pierquin tells how he used to lock himself in a closet to be undisturbed—and no doubt to keep out of the rain. He sometimes stayed there "twenty-four hours without food or drink," absorbed in studying Russian, Arabic, Amharic, and perhaps Hindustani.[15]

In 1874, he wanted to study music and practiced scales on a keyboard he had carved on the edge of a piece of furniture until his mother agreed to rent him a piano. With his music teacher, Louis Létrange, he searched for "*new sonorities.*"[16] "In general, an unstable, lazy, undisciplined and demanding child becomes an adult in need of adventures, a deserter or vagabond," says classical psychology. But "mental instability," as described by ludicrous and outmoded psychiatrists, *programs* its conclusion: "superior dilettante," "degenerate talent."[17] All his life, Rimbaud searches. For what? We do not know. Maybe he did not either. A quest is not a pathological symptom. He does not search for *something,* but exists in the act of searching. Rimbaud is ever ahead of himself, carried away in his own advance. He is in exodus, but from himself: dispossessed always. Rimbaud's life does not look like a construction. But his multiple projects have the logic of relays. He moves like a knight on a chessboard.

Abandoning literature, then the neighboring disciplines—languages, music—he takes more pragmatic initiatives. Rimbaud is foreman of sixty or so workers in a Cyprus quarry in 1878, when he, probably, learns of his father's death.[18] A psychoanalyst[19] has dated his "dyptic asymmetry," his "radical change from this event": "On one side, running away fourteen times . . . on the other, two journeys that fuse into one continuous project." It seems to me, on the contrary, that the rhythm of the projects does not change, no matter how we finally identify Rimbaud, that all his enterprises proceed essentially by interruptions and successive choices, part of a logical evolution that is not even deflected by the news of his father's death. It is true that Rimbaud never explained himself in this regard, and the opinions of people "who would hinder departures for Harar," radically inept at sorting out Rimbaud's "spiritual chase," are no help in understanding his actions; but everything indicates that it is *the same* Rimbaud who follows the destiny he chose at the end of *A Season in Hell*, who, after a moment's belief in his own supernatural powers, declares himself "returned to the earth with . . . rough reality to embrace."* After leaving the Cyprus quarry, he signs a contract in Aden with the firm of Mazeran, Viannay, Bardey et Compagnie, asks immediately to be sent to Harar, and tries to go in search of ivory from there: "He was always impatiently waiting for the next occasion to set out on adventures," writes Bardey. "I could sooner have held on to a shooting star."[20] He glimpses a chance to become an explorer, then a correspondent for *Le Temps*. He even thinks of writing a book: "I'm going to write a work on Harar and Gallaland for the Geographical Society, with maps and engravings."† Photography becomes a project by itself: Rimbaud has "a complete photographic apparatus" sent "with the idea of taking it to Shoa, where such a thing is unknown and will bring a fortune in no time."†† His contract terminated on April 23, 1884, he takes employment with Alfred Bardey in June, then with Pierre Bardey in January 1885. He organizes his arms caravan for Menelik, first with Soleillet, then with Labatut and finally by himself, then gives up arms deals and founds his own trading post in Harar. As a businessman, Rimbaud has a new idea every day: Breed

* "Adieu," *A Season in Hell.*
† Aden, January 18, 1882.
††Aden, September 28, 1882.

a better strain of mules, import sheets from Sedan, and so on.

The first words of the first extant letter of his are a request to Izambard: "If you have and can lend me . . ."* All his life, Rimbaud remains *demanding*. "I beseech you . . . don't make me do without what I'm asking for."† In spite of being implored in this manner repeatedly, it seems his mother never noticed: "My poor Arthur who has never asked for anything . . ."†† How can we fail to see in this fear of lacking—not everything, Rimbaud lives in poverty and does lack everything, but *always something in particular*—the major operation of a mind that moves from being to essence? And the list of books he asks to have sent to Africa, which so disconcerts critics and biographers, must be understood as so many ideas and projects pursued for a moment, an infinite quest of the provisional:

Album of Agricultural and Forestry Power-Saws; The Carpenter's Handbook; Treatise on Metallurgy; Urban and Agricultural Hydraulics; Steamship Commander; Naval Architecture; Powders and Saltpeter; Mineralogy; Masonry; Artesian Wells; Manual for the Construction of Saw-Mills; Textile Matters; Illustrated Catalogue of Agricultural Machines; The Wheelwright's Manual; The Tanner's Manual; The Perfect Locksmith; Mine Management; Glazier's Manual; The Brickmaker; Earthenware and Pottery; The Potter; All-Metal Smelting; Candlemaking; Guide to Weapon Manufacturing; Complete Catalogue of the Bookshop of l'École Centrale; Manual of Telegraphy; The Little Cabinet-Maker; The Housepainter; Traveler's Guide or Theoretical and Practical Manual for the Use of Explorers; Complete Manual for the Fabrication of Precision Instruments; Metal Construction; Dictionary of Military and Civil Engineering; Shipbuilding; Trigonometry; Hydrography; Meteorology; Industrial Chemistry; Traveler's Handbook; Instructions for the Preparation of Voyages;

---

* 1870.
† Aden, January 22, 1882.
††Mme. Rimbaud, June 1, 1900.

The Sky by Guillemin; Directory of the Bureau of Longitudes for 1882; Complete Railroad Treatise on Mechanics of the Châlons School; Treatise on Topography and Geodesics; Mineralogy and Geology; Contract Fulfillment; Abridged Embankment Computations; Geodesics; Hydraulics; Treatise on Curves; Elementary Mechanics; Applied Astronomy; Practical Manual of Railroad Construction; Earthworks Marketing; Tunnels and Underpasses; "the best French translation of the Koran"; Dictionary of Commerce and Navigation; Dictionary of the Amharic Language.

The above is a list of books that indicates distress, boredom with action, mockery of practical knowledge, an arid absence of literature, the paradox of the "overgifted" student and "genius" of a poet thinking naively that he can instruct himself as if by correspondence. An encyclopedic enterprise like that of Bouvard and Pécuchet or the queer Chinese nomenclature reported in Foucault's *Les Mots et les Choses* (*The Order of Things*). But it also shows continuity in the swarming of ideas and their surprising sequence, his unimpaired curiosity, his bulimia for action, his intensity in spending energy, the dispersion or consumption of a self.

Utterly confident, as if it were a matter of course, Rimbaud communicates to a librarian his desire to "know about all the best French (or foreign) mathematical, optical, astronomical, electrical, meteorological, pneumatic, mechanical and mineralogical instruments." And he adds with a touch of (involuntary?) humor: "I am not concerned with chirurgical instruments."[21]

There was obviously only one possible location in the world for this weighty and soulless library of books arrived too late, disappointing, tossed on the road, into the fire or sea, scattered and turned from their purpose. It was between Aden and Harar, strange in an empire without printing or technology. Rimbaud assembled more books—manuals and treatises, that is—than you could find in all of Abyssinia.

But the wind is sometimes very strong in Harar and was certainly all that turned the pages.

This inventory is telling enough: In Abyssinia, Rimbaud was always *inquiet* (in the sense of the Latin *inquietus,* without rest, or the English "unquiet" or, even better, "restless": The person who cannot find rest, cannot stay in one place). He lost himself in "enormous useless labors," said Segalen. The real question connected with Rimbaud's poetical enterprise is not the phantom problem of a break in his life, but the permanence of renunciation, of repeated abandonment, of a passion for failure.

Beyond the cacti and acacias, out in the desert where we continue "scouting," in the vastenss of these steppes and regions without water, it suddenly occurs to me that Rimbaud was not likely to encounter his image and therefore forgot himself. "Finally, by dint of groans and grimaces,"* he would become entirely his grimace, would lose his face. But lack of mirrors is a deprivation that may be compensated for by photography.

The camera, ordered from Lyon in 1881 and long awaited as a possible means to a quick fortune, insistently punctuates Rimbaud's correspondence.† Rimbaud is curious about the image of himself he might get from this object arriving slowly with a detour via Mauritius, arriving not slowly enough, as if Rimbaud were afraid of knowing, of seeing himself—of disappointment.

Then, one day, in "the dirty liquid of the developer," Rimbaud sees his face appear.†† "Enclosed two photo-

---

* To Ilg, Harar, October 7, 1889.

† January 15, 1881; January 18, 1882; September 28, 1882; November 16, 1882; November 18, 1882; December 8, 1882; January 6, 1883; January 15, 1883; March 14, 1883.

†† May 6, 1883: "These photographs show me standing in front of the house, standing in the garden of a café, another one with crossed arms in a banana grove." We note that Rimbaud sends three photographs and announces only two, that one portrait is "forgotten."

graphs of myself by myself." But he does not recognize himself in his portrait, graying and aged. He does not feel his identity confirmed by his image as he had in London, when Verlaine and he had gone to the National Gallery to look at their portraits in Fantin-Latour's "The Table Corner"—unless in a Dorian Gray exchange. Even his famous "forget-me-not-blue eyes" have lost their sparkle. "The gray eyes and nearly blond mustache" the consul in Massawa noted, these features drawn by fatigue and syphilis are not "myself," are not the "boy with pink cheeks and a little bowler hat" Delahaye remembered, nor "the perfect oval face of an angel in exile" that Verlaine evoked five years later in *Les Hommes d'aujourd'hui* (*Men of Today*). This head of his does not *strike home*. He is nearly ashamed of it: "This is only to recall my face." Not to admire, "only to recall." In other words, his disclaimer begs, don't look at how ugly, how strange I am, but don't forget me—the latent, ever renewed reproach of the unloved. "To recall": to avoid the oblivion he seeks and into which he feels he is sinking. "This is . . . my face." But nobody has ever seen this face, this person. Fantin-Latour liked to paint people returning from trips, but he would not have recognized Rimbaud.

The desert has only one dimension: space. Rimbaud is bored, kills time. The more he works, the more he kills time with activity, the more he accelerates its rotation for himself alone. "A year here ages you as much as four years elsewhere," he says in 1884.* By the next year, the speed has increased: "A year here counts as five elsewhere."† And it is as if everything else is as it were carried along in the movement: The newspapers he sends are already old "and will get older yet in transit," and money seems to follow the rate of time (one to five, in the same letter of April 1885): "One franc elsewhere is worth five here." Rimbaud

*Aden, May 5, 1884.
†Aden, April 14, 1885.

says in his own way that *time is money,* an absurd slogan in a country where nobody would think of digging a tunnel to "save time." "Time passes, and nothing's amassed." Time presses. Rimbaud sets it in motion, we might say, runs toward its end. "I fear I am shortening my life."*

The long Harar evenings with doors closed? Evenings of a hurried man moping, sending off occasional, minimal letters, "telephonings," notes thrown at a caravan.† The *Illuminations* must no doubt be considered instances of an absolute impatience requiring brevity, juxtaposition, drive, as opposed to Mallarméan honing: simultaneity of saying and the moment of writing, texts where, for the first time, what is about to be said is exactly what is in process of being written. . . . But in Abyssinia, where all action is put off till the day after, this impatient man who once claimed to "be in a hurry to find" (the place and the formula), submits to the horrors of endless waiting, of patience in the etymological sense of suffering and enduring. He will die impatient to leave (perhaps his impatience led to his death), nagging Isabelle to pack his suitcase, twelve days before his death: "Quick, quick . . . let's close the suitcase and leave!"[22]

"I feel I am getting very old very fast."†† This is Rimbaud at thirty. And in the year of his death, at thirty-seven: "One ages very fast here."§ Yet Alfred Bardey and Alfred Ilg, both born in 1854 as he was, look fixed in their forties. Rimbaud lived more in thirty-seven years than others in sixty. This fast-forward of time can be observed, in a nutshell, in the story of his hair: the carefully combed black hair, "smoothed down with sugar water," of his first communion (1866), his ample Parnassian mane to which he owed

* Harar, May 25, 1881.
† Harar, December 21, 1883: "I'm still well and hope you are too. On this occasion I wish you a happy new year 1884. No news here. All yours, RIMBAUD"; Harar, July 22, 1881: "I've always been in a hurry"; Cairo, August 26, 1887: "There is much to do, and those who hurry and go economically will do it."
†† September 10, 1884.
§ February 20, 1891.

the village boys' hostility (1872), his shaved Buddhist skull
at the death of his sister Vitalie in December 1875[23]—and
finally "hair quite gray."*

"I'm not sending my photograph,"† he will write his
mother, clearly in reply to her request. This refusal, under
pretext of economy, can be understood as reservations against
his image, against the threat of being reduced to *exposure
time:* "My hair grows white by the minute."†† Rimbaud's
face would seem like those elementary particles too short-
lived to leave a trace on the photo plate.

This is what became of the "meteor" Mallarmé saw
shooting across the sky of letters in 1872. He continues his
course (a "shooting star," says Bardey) far from the little
sphere of Paris poets, continues to turn ever faster in his
course around some enormous, slow planet.

Rimbaud lives in a parallel universe. His life cannot sta-
bilize in either space or time. "It is consumed like a line that
disappears the very moment it is drawn."[24] A life without
place or present. Like the "here" he uses everywhere, the
phrase "at present" recurs constantly. As early as 1875,
Rimbaud wrote to Delahaye from Charleville: "I have no
intentions in that direction at present," as he will write a
hundred times from Abyssinia, for example, on May 6, 1883:
"But you have spring at present, and your weather corresponds to mine here in Harar, at present." This achronol-
ogical present does not, however, give a sense of permanence,
but is tinged with melancholy. "Once!" Rimbaud had been
nostalgic for the "once" that opens *A Season in Hell,* for the
very ancient times "when all hearts opened and the wine
flowed."§ In these "at presents," there is the bitterness (or
secret relief, or resignation) of the formula of *A Season in*

---

* Cairo, August 23, 1887.
† Aden, January 15, 1885.
††Harar, April 21, 1890.
§ *A Season in Hell.*

Hell: "This happened." His "at present" seems to *have always said* "from now on."

Rimbaud will never have met a single contemporary. He gets to the point of writing from Abyssinia as if he had *drifted* out of time: "Finally, at present, I no longer keep track of dates."*

The most overwhelming surprise of our trip is the sun. We seem to get more heat from it in one day than in an entire winter in France. It makes for a heavy head, for bloodshot eyes, if one is sensitive. You end up fearing as much as wanting it. Rimbaud sought out this excessive sun. He had a pagan passion for it. In *A Season in Hell,* but also in his correspondence from Africa and Arabia, the sun is always sovereign: Both "beneficial, liberating" and "murderous, devouring,"[25] the sun is the most powerful of the Rimbaldian constants. The attraction gets more pronounced in Ethiopia and Yemen, land "where it never rains."† His passion for sun is even one of the explicit reasons why Rimbaud leaves Europe for good: Charleville "stinks of snow."†† Having walked "without a rest eight or ten miles in the snow" of the Ardennes Forest with his friend Delahaye, a winter Sunday in 1879, he declared: "I shall not stay in France. I get fevers. I need the warm climate of the Levant." Delahaye had been astonished to see the "athletic walker" shiver at the first autumn wind: "I need warm countries, the Mediterranean coast at the very least," Rimbaud replied. "On the road from Attigny to Chesne, he suddenly left me: 'The fever! The fever is after me!' I was not to see him again." His horror of the cold keeps Rimbaud from coming back ("Pity that it's so cold in your place in winter"§), holds him at the point of no return. It makes him lose the rhythm of

---

* Harar, May 6, 1883.
† Aden, January 15, 1883.
††October 14, 1875.
§ Harar, March 6, 1883. "It's forty degrees [centigrade] here . . . I only wish it were sixty" (to his family, Aden, September 22, 1880).

seasons, modifies his sense of time. If the sun once had a mythic value of eternity, "at present" it stands for Rimbaud's obsession with enduring the climate, the longest possible time in the sun before death. Of the grand eschatological dream worked out in the night of *voyance,* there remains only the hope for a long, tangible period of rest in the sun, for salvation by riches, a hope for an Indian summer. This long summer that he often wishes his family, this wish for "fifty years of summer without end"* is the ideal time Rimbaud longs for, his conception of paradise. Not the Christian paradise of his childhood catechism, eternal and accessible only in the next world, or the immense paradise Mohammed compared to the cool shadow of a banana tree, so vast a galloping horse would take eighty years to cross it, but a paradise in this world—and rather, in this other promising image of the prophet's, an uninterrupted orgasm. Fifty years at least during which he would do nothing but endlessly "enjoy his earnings"† under the real sun. Such is the paradise toward which Rimbaud strains with all his might and which he holds at bay with all his might, the horizon he feels within range and always out of reach. Such is the paradise for which he climbs the steps of an interminable summer.

Rimbaud is surprised by the passage of time: "Already fall . . ."†† "Rimbaud is nothing but a filthy skunk who will turn into a vulgar bourgeois at thirty," Verlaine announced in 1875.[26] This is, by the way, what the poet of *Sagesse,* of *Wisdom,* thinks of age thirty in general: "What an old brute one becomes at thirty," he confides that same year to Delahaye. But Rimbaud is twenty-one in 1875, whereas Verlaine turns thirty that same year. When Rim-

---

* Ibid. "May your winter be short" (January 15, 1885). "Spring is perpetual green" (February 28, 1886).
† Aden, May 5, 1884.
†† "Adieu," *A Season in Hell.*

baud in turn reaches thirty, in 1884, he writes: "In July '86 or '87. I'll be thirty-two or thirty-three then. I shall start growing old."* And a few days before: "I see that I will reach the age of thirty (half of life!) and have made much effort to diddle the world."† Hearing him speak of "half of life," when he will actually die in another seven years, one might say he missed a whole phase of life. Old age? He already feels old, has *done his time,* this personal time that consumes him. He dies young, however, in terms of life expectancy.[27] Rimbaud belongs to the generation of Freud, Buffalo Bill, Pétain: He could have died after 1914. He should not have died when he did! But it is the *silenced* poet in him that died young, killed within him. Verlaine is right to say: "Rimbaud is a poet who died young."[28] Yves Bonnefoy remarks that he "was both an adolescent too soon and a little child too long." It is perhaps a result of living that one becomes a child: "Basically," said Malraux, "there are no adults." The adult in Rimbaud never survived his adolescence? But if Rimbaud stands for adolescent revolt, he nevertheless stands out by the maturity of his best poetic work. If he realized a childhood dream in Africa, only an adult could last a decade under such painful conditions, in the Africa of that time. So it is his own time that spins more rapidly, that he makes spin with action, from the time he pretended to be a year older in order to approach Banville,†† when he wrote, at sixteen; "You can't be serious when you're seventeen," to the time of maturity when he inquired about life annuities at thirty-three§ and felt prematurely aged in the heat of the sun: In Europe, "I would be regarded as an old man."‖ So which phase did he miss? Not the winter of life, the fourth and noxious season which he knew physi-

* Aden, May 29, 1884.
† May 5, 1884.
†† To Théodore de Banville, May 24, 1870.
§ To his family, Aden, November 22, 1887: "Where does one place money for a life annuity? . . . Can I get one at my age?"
‖ To his family, May 29, 1884.

cally, but the infinite he vainly pursued, accelerating his end in proportion to thinking he was getting closer: the supplementary season, the inaccessible "fourth quarter"—after hell, a season in paradise.

If he never saw himself, he felt himself—age, suffer, become another, not in the eternally misconstrued sense of "I is another," but in that of his other, repressed identity, which he projects and turns into, which pursues or accompanies him, the poet in him that he wants to flee.

The Other appears in the photographs: He finds him pretty strange, *altered:* "I regret I cannot make a trip to the World's Fair this year. . . . It'll have to be the next one, and at the next one I'll be able . . . to exhibit myself because I think one gets to look extremely baroque after a long stay in countries like these."*

The Other, who has no name and cannot be named, takes on different masks. It is the officer father, about whom the whole family is silent. It is his brother Frédéric, the "perfect idiot" who bears the father's name, the black sheep of the family who, thrown out by mother Rimbaud, would sell the newspaper *Le Petit Ardennais* in the streets of Attigny. Frédéric, his double, who will attend in a top hat the inauguration of his brother's bust on the "shabby lawn"† of the Square de la Gare in Charleville, whereas Mme. Rimbaud was hiding that day.[29] "It would bother me," wrote Rimbaud, "if people knew I had that kind of a bird for a brother. . . . You don't need to tell me not to write to him."††

"What he thinks," Rimbaud wrote already in 1880, "doesn't concern me, doesn't touch me in any way, and I wish him all happiness possible on earth and particularly in the county of Attigny (Ardennes)."§

* Harar, May 18, 1889.
† "À la musique" ("To Music").
†† Aden, October 7, 1884.
§ Aden, September 22, 1880.

The Other is perhaps Verlaine, the most repressed name, the one he most wishes to forget, the *unnamable*.

He is the other *Rimbaud*,[30] his mysterious and very real homonym who turned up around the Red Sea at that same time, who has left no trace and might be the "*Remban*" mentioned in Cecchi's report.* "Be careful in writing my address because there is another Rimbaud who works for the Messageries Maritimes."†

The Other is also the desire for rebirth in a child, not a daughter, but a son who would succeed where he has failed, "the genealogical dream in which he engenders himself":[31] "At least to have a son whom I could spend the rest of my life bringing up in my way."††

But Rimbaud did not encounter himself. And the Other is finally "himself" in the past without memory, the strange "Estrus," as Verlaine called him, not daring to name him. This is the *Other he has always been*.

And we, the fine crew of modern times, are driving over hill, over dale, with our full schedule nailed to the calendar, held to a drastic "shooting plan," haunted by the question, Are we on time? Yes, we are on time, in search of a man who fled his past, pursued an impossible future, and, by dint of saying "here" and "at present," left no trace.[32] In search of a nineteenth-century poet here, outside time, in the years 7476 of the "era of the world," 3261 of the "era of martyrs," and 1969 of the three Ethiopian calendars, here in Harar, in the year 1345 of the Hegira.

* See Chapter 10.
† Aden, September 22, 1880.
††Harar, May 6, 1883.

5
WANDERING

How does it feel
To be on your own
With no direction home
A complete unknown
Like a rolling stone.
—Bob Dylan

This clap has been heard everywhere: On the little black-board that is hit against a black-and-white bat at the beginning of each take of the film to synchronize the sound and number the takes, we have chalked all the places Rimbaud has been. On his tracks we too have much "wagoned and steamered"[1]—and airplaned. During the—indispensable—siesta on this mild afternoon, my neck on a traditional wooden pillow in shape of a flared anvil, I think of my friends working in the cold and hum Bob Dylan's song, "Like a Rolling Stone," which seems as if written by Rimbaud—with whom Dylan has often identified. Sometimes a piece of music sticks in your head like an itch. When you are obsessed by a tune, you just have to sing along. It happened to Ernest Delahaye, whose humming irritated Germain Nouveau—until he joined in.[2] Dylan's tune, brought back from forays into the steppe, pursued me all through the "briefing" to take stock of the images already shot. Now, along with the song, the miles of film condensing the miles covered by Rimbaud come to me in a personal flashback during my siesta, like a trip within the trip.

Charleville. The Place Ducale, a beautiful replica of the Place des Vosges seen from the top of a belltower and (with traffic barred for a few hours and all cars removed) returned to the nineteenth century. It seemed to be an early morning in 1870. Snow, slush, the deadly boredom of "pale Sundays in December."* Hypnotic. It is easy to imagine the paramilitary procession of the Rimbaud family: Vitalie and Isabelle hand in hand in front, the two boys forming the second rank, also hand in hand, and Mme. Rimbaud bringing up the rear at a fixed distance, like a mother duck following her ducklings.[3]

"My hometown is the most idiotic of all provincial towns."† There is the old mill by the green water of the Meuse: The family lived nearby when Arthur wrote "Le Bateau ivre," "The Drunken Boat." The Square de la Gare, "where everything is correct," where he made fun of the "wheezing bourgeois," where Vitalie had met Captain Rimbaud at a Sunday parade. On this Station Square, the same "military band" he had mocked in the poem "À la musique," would "perform an adaptation of Émile Ratez's symphony on the theme of 'The Drunken Boat' " for the inauguration of Rimbaud's bust in 1905![4] For ten years, his hometown remained the epicenter of his departures and returns, point of departure for a waltz of excursions when the child "felt the strong call of sails,"†† but also his winter refuge at the bosom of maternal law. I love Charleville like a second hometown. Rimbaud loved it also, I am sure, if contrarily. It was the hated, fled, and missed mother-town ("I miss this atrocious Charlestown"§ as one "misses plump

---

* "Les Poètes de sept ans" ("The Seven-year-old Poets").
† To Georges Izambard, August 25, 1870.
†† "The Seven-year-old Poets."
§ Letter to Ernest Delahaye, May 1873.

arms"*), place of anchorage and unmooring.

Everybody has his favorite posture for thinking. Rimbaud thinks while he *walks*. And since he never stopped walking, we must assume he never stopped thinking either. Rimbaud was called "the man with soles of wind" by Verlaine and ended up, by an irony of fate, with his leg amputated almost entirely. "He tramped through mountains, woods, plains—what a walker!"[5] "The high road in any weather, supernaturally sober . . ."† I promise myself to come back in the fall, when the Ardennes woods are so beautiful, and retrace on foot his legendary walk from Charleville to Charleroi, to find in the colors and smells the words of his poems, to understand them, as he recommends, through *dromomania:* "I am sending you some verses: Read them in the morning sun as I wrote them."†† To read his poems to the point where we can do without commentaries, we must *incorporate* them, follow his advice to Delahaye to "read and walk."§

"His long legs would calmly take formidable steps," Delahaye remembers. "His long, dangling arms moved in very strict rhythm, torso and head erect, eyes vacant, his whole figure expressed a *resigned defiance,* a sense of being ready for anything, without anger or fear" (italics added). Walking satisfied his impatient character. Whether it is "an expansion of the infinite I and its loss in the world" or, on the contrary, "a solitary experience, cut off from the world, directed toward a quest for the new,"[6] traveling is the motion to conquer space in which Rimbaud finds his autonomy and *identity in freedom.* In a laconic phrase he summed it all up. I thought of it yesterday on the Harar trails, as I had in the Ardennes countryside: "I am a pedestrian, nothing more."‖

* "Mémoire."
† "L'Impossible," *A Season in Hell.*
†† To Georges Izambard, Charleville, August 25, 1870.
§ "Junphe," 1872.
‖ To Paul Demeney, August 28, 1871.

*   *   *

If Rimbaud sometimes represents himself lying down ("Happily I stretched my legs under the green table";* Delahaye found him on a couch in Paris, smoking hashish), it is a posture of defiance. Rimbaud detested the symbolic position of "Les Assis," "The Sitters," in libraries. He wrote while walking or, rather, walked *murmuring* his poems, says Delahaye, especially the *Illuminations,* which seem written on the slopes or recopied, *finished,* in one swoop on coming home.[7] A kind of writing worked out, without written or oral trace, in the unpredictable motion it fuses with, formulating the secret, which he will leave behind, but where we can hear the *walk-murmur:* "I am the pedestrian of the high road through dwarfed woods. Sluices drown out my footsteps with their noise. I take a long look at the melancholy golden wash of the setting sun."†

Roche. "Laïtou, my village." A small group of tile roofs. "*The mother* put me in a sad hole here."†† Among humid, dark green bushes, a dilapidated wall of the attic Rimbaud retired to in 1873 seems still to hold some of the vociferations of *A Season in Hell.*

My brown *deux-chevaux,* with crew and supplies piled in back, went through the woods tilting like an outboard motor boat. In the freezing early morning countryside ("What a horror, the French countryside"§), I thought—without wanting or managing to say it into the microphone on the dashboard—that here one could indeed feel how a poet is tied to his soil, could physically sense his "Bohème" between Voncq and Attigny without evidence other than the rhymes rattled off by his "dreamy Tom Thumb."

---

*   "Au Cabaret-Vert" ("At the Green Inn").
†   "Enfance" ("Childhood") IV, *Illuminations.*
†† To Ernest Delahaye, Roche, May 1873.
§   Ibid.

". . . 1879–1880, seen unloading cartfuls of harvest on his mother's farm and walking those meager paths with his matchless legs"[8]—for once we must take the expression "matchless legs" as referring to stamina rather than in the sense Maurras reproached Verlaine with. We were driving toward Vouziers, "Subprefecture of ten thousand souls,"* where I met Émilie Teissier,[9] Frédéric Rimbaud's daughter. She was only five or six years old when Arthur came back to Roche in 1891—and both she and her father were *banned* by mother Rimbaud. It was fascinating to get a direct sense, across the years, of hatred of *the mother,* "mother Rimbe," the "Gate of Night," or, as Verlaine said, *"daromphe"*—who has already joined Mme. Lepic and Folcoche in literary history. Indulgent for Isabelle who "secretly" saw her in Paris, Émilie Teissier, on the threshold of death, defends her father Frédéric like a child. Her unquenched bitterness leaves me pensive as to the violence once exercised by the grandmother. "Was she strict with Arthur? I should say so. That's why he wasn't very successful."

Mme. Rimbaud was one of many family tryants the middle class produced during the last century and a half. Victor Segalen for example, born in 1878, likewise had to suffer an authoritarian, dominating, narrowly Catholic mother. But we must try to understand Vitalie Cuif, a peasant woman of thirty-five, during the Second Empire in Charleville. She married a captain. She has four children, two boys and two girls. How does she see the future? Perhaps not without misgivings, but she must have pictured herself growing old in the company of a colonel, her boys well educated and in respectable or even eminent social positions, her two girls brought up religiously and well married. She is far from imagining her fate as we know it: The captain leaves her shortly after Isabelle's birth—Delahaye dates it around 1860. Then war. Her first daughter, Vitalie, dies young, at seventeen (1875). One son goes to the dogs. The

*Ibid.

other, her pride, with a learning capacity that would be the envy of today's elite students, Arthur (whose headmaster said, "Nothing banal will germinate in this head") runs away and torments her, dies young in 1891—and continues to harass her even posthumously. Of Vitalie Cuif's ruined dream, only Isabelle is left, her double, vestige of her vision of life, the only one to survive as late as 1917.

"Mme. Rimbaud, who is always described as bigoted and narrow, dried up with lack of love, worried what the neighbors will say, nevertheless was to accept some stupefying compromises": [10] There was indeed the astonishing moment when she rang the doorbell of Verlaine's in-laws, on the rue Nicolet, to demand her son's manuscripts. She had made a special trip, her first to Paris, and was well aware of her son's liaison with Verlaine (a supreme scandal to her) and the welcome she was likely to get! She took in her son when he returned from the capital hairy and filthy. She rushed to London—that far!—when he needed her. She tolerated that her "favorite" (as she will say much later) did not do his share of farm work, but sat in the attic writing this book of which she understood nothing. Nevertheless, she may have paid for the first printing. "This excellent woman," said Delahaye. She had kicked Frédéric out for much less, at the birth of Émilie Teissier-Rimbaud. "True, she doled out her help in the coin of sighs and tiresome advice, but she always kept the door open for her prodigal son" [11]

She took him in, but also said: "A job by such and such a date . . . or out,"* kicking him out in the same gesture. The Commune, which for Rimbaud occurs in the middle of the family drama, precipitates their misunderstanding. "She has gotten to the point of constantly wishing I would be rash and leave, run away!"† Later there was gossip in Roche. Eugène Mery, a farmhand questioned by Robert Goffin, declared that "Rimbaud said the foulest things about his mother,

*To Paul Demeny, August 28, 1871.
†Ibid.

and that's surely why he went to the colonies."[12] Segalen gets an echo of this comment from Righas in Djibouti: "There was something or other with his family."[13] Yet it is Arthur who *provokes* (he says so) the "atrocious resolution of a mother as inflexible as seventy-three administrations in steel helmets."* But had his mother not provoked these provocations? As in a children's quarrel, who can tell who started it all? It is an error to label the mother (abused by some, rehabilitated by others) as *cause*. Mother and son could not live with each other. Their painful relation recovered when they were separated, but turned virulent on reunion in Charleville or Roche, even during Rimbaud's last stay, as witnessed by Dr. Beaudier: "I remember one single big impression of my visits to Roche: Arthur Rimbaud's indifference (not to say aversion) toward his mother. You could feel how her mere presence made him physically uneasy. There were several occasions when she stuck her head in the door while I talked with him. Immediately, Rimbaud's features became tense, and once, I remember he rudely jumped down her throat and asked her to get the hell out."[14]

I went to Charleville another winter, with Allen Ginsberg. The great poet of the Beat Generation, who had just recorded an improvised chant on Rimbaud with Bob Dylan, discovered Charleville, which he had wanted to visit for twenty years. He stood plunged in thought at Rimbaud's grave, recited poems preceded by the "OM" of meditation next to the old mill, and asked a hundred questions about the life of the most famous European poet—yet so little known in the United States—while we crossed a chilly Place Ducale open to the four winds, resplendent with orange lights under the arcades and a large Christmas pine lit up in the middle of the market. We had gone to Roche, "the wolf hole,"† stopped in silence before the dilapidated wall of *A*

*Ibid.
†To Maurice Riès, 1891.

Season in Hell, walked through the countryside, which seemed cold and hostile, but bathed in an undefinable, magic light where we saw the carriage, pulled by the pony "Comtesse," taking a feverish, amputated Rimbaud for rides on the Sundays of his last summer.

Ginsberg was astonished that Rimbaud continued to despise his brother Frédéric in Abyssinia, that he could nurse his rancor so long and so far, without ever reaching inner peace. He remembered Jack Kerouac's guilt about his homosexuality and attributed it to his mother's excessive moral domination. Like Rimbaud, he said, Kerouac never came free of Puritan values or maternal authority. No matter how far the poet (either one) traveled, he "dragged his ego along with him," when it was so easy to break with the I, give up the Christian concept of the full, suffering, guilty subject and make an empty space inside oneself, in harmony with others and with nature, taste all experience with detachment and understand that life has *one taste* only, whether in hate or happiness.

In this sense, Rimbaud's misfortune was his own self that he could not escape. And the man for whom love was to be reinvented had simply never known love. But then, Rimbaud's case is not an experience of wisdom, but suffering. It is precisely because this exceptional *I* defied God through language that he left the world. Because he pursued his life in terms of a fatal guilt, he represents our entire culture. And if he was unable to say with Leconte de Lisle, our only Buddhist poet: "Deliver us from Time, from Number and from Space/And give us our rest that life has troubled," if the blood of *A Season in Hell* was still steaming on his face in Harar, it was because Thirst and Will—the cause of suffering according to the Buddha (and Schopenhauer)— carried him to the *religious* limits of poetic creation, where escape from the damned *I* is impossible, carried him even to a thirst for annihilation.

"Paris is but a belly!" Rimbaud declared to Delahaye.

But the belly attracts him. "There's the holy City, sitting in the West."* Ambition or anger pushed him toward "Paris, the whore." "At seventeen, in 1872, he made his fourth trip there, on foot like the earlier ones," notes Mallarmé. After the "rotating hospitality" organized by Cros, Banville, and Verlaine, the latter found him "wandering aimlessly" in the capital. Then, the belly cast him out. The radical nature of his poetic project—but also his shyness—pushed Rimbaud toward deliberate provocation in order to be rejected. He immediately despised the "all too artistic milieu"† and reproached Baudelaire for frequenting it. Pierre Petitfils has given us an eyewitness account of the dinner of the "Vilains Bonhommes" at the end of which Rimbaud wounded Carjat with Verlaine's sword stick.[15] Pierre Gascar has explained Rimbaud's "Communal spirit" to us, his adhesion to the ideals of the Commune.[16] But we know that Rimbaud was not one of its glorious combatants. He was at the same time communal and solitary. He was thrilled with the insurrection and was deeply disappointed by its defeat—if not by the Commune itself. The Commune and his *voyance* intersected only for one moment. "The Commune is the history of one springtime," says Gascar. The time of cherries. Nevertheless, Pierre Gascar, faithful humanist of the left, sees the Commune everywhere. It's Rimbaud rewritten by Guy Mollet!

Paris. Jean-Louis Baudry speaks of transference of the paternal image: Georges Izambard, the young composition professor, was no doubt for a few months the father Rimbaud lacked. He heard the first confessions of literary ambition. He responded to his wanting books—against mother Rimbaud, who reproached him for making her son read "Victor Hugot [sic]." "*My hope lies in you* as in my mother" (Rimbaud's emphasis), Rimbaud writes to him when arrested in Mazas. "I love you as a brother and will love you

---

*"L'Orgie parisienne ou Paris se repeuple" ("Parisian Orgy or Paris Repopulated").

†May 13, 1871.

as my father."* Izambard in turn confides: "My affection for him grew with his moral distress." But, himself henpecked (by his aunts Gindre from Douai), he also took the fugitive back to his mother—"his mother never knew how much of an ally she had in me."[17] But the teacher quickly reached his degree of incompetence before the soaring of Rimbaud's poetry: "You will not understand at all,"† Rimbaud wrote him after carving a good-bye poem on his dark green door.

Verlaine, prestigious poet to the Charleville boy, next filled the vacant position of father figure. But Rimbaud very quickly was the one to seduce Verlaine, a cruel Rimbaud to bewitch the weak Verlaine, who shuttled forever between bar and confessional and surrendered with feminine abandon. But no analysis can account for the quality of a text or the intensity of a destiny. It is not the homosexuality of the two poets that matters, but that Verlaine was to such a degree *spellbound* by Rimbaud, who wanted to "convert him back to his original state as son of the Sun."††

"Once the prestige of Paris wore off," says Mallarmé, Rimbaud suddenly quit his noxious hotel and kidnapped Verlaine on Montmartre,§ where he was buying medication for his wife. Verlaine followed him *on the spot:* "The regretted Arthur Rimbaud and I, smitten with a masculine rage for travel, one fine day took off" for Belgium, "daughter of belfries," where Rimbaud certainly lived the only moment of happiness in his life. "It's too beautiful!" cries Verlaine,[18] and Rimbaud echoes: "It's too beautiful! Too much! Let's keep mum." ‖

We walked—do you remember where?
That day has gone, O traveler—

* September 5, 1870.
† May 13, 1871.
†† "Vagabonds" *Illuminations.*
§ July 7, 1872.
‖ "Bruxelles" ("Brussels").

One might have said two jolly ghosts
Slipping through the subtle air.[19]

I seemed to see them one winter night when I was driving through a deserted Bruges, "the never banal Bruges."[20] And again in Ostende where, giving in to the call of the sea which both of them saw for the first time, they took the mailboat to Dover the very same night, "with very little underwear."*

On a Belgian ship, listening to the "foghorns," those signals of boats crossing in the fog—heartrending like the song of whales—voice of Neptune, of "boats lost in the hair of coves,"† I too had a "somewhat rough crossing" from Ostende to Dover and the "*sea sickness* of which most of our fellow travelers set an example."[21] At the head of this Belgian ship, whose planks groaned in the raging sea, I did an experiential, *total* reading of the poem "Marine"—"Chariots of silver and copper/Prows of silver and steel/Beat the foam"—Rimbaud's first poem in free verse, which this crossing inspired in the author of "The Drunken Boat" on a later ("unbelievably beautiful") voyage from Anvers to Dover, in May 1873. Finally, the famous white cliffs rose out of the fog.

London. "The misery . . . The brick so monotonous . . . everything sticky with smoke . . . oozing fog and coal tar . . . the smell between here and the docks insidious, a smell of wet sulfur and moist tobacco, it clings to your skin, stays with you."[22]

The misery in the working-class neighborhoods of London in the nineteenth century—as Gustave Doré has shown it in his engravings, as one feels it in "Ville" ("I see new ghosts float through the eternal thick coal smoke")—this misery was a shock to the two cronies, as much as the mo-

---

*September 7, 1872.
†"Le Bateau ivre" ("The Drunken Boat").

dernity. If we believe Delahaye, Rimbaud "came back enthusiastic about London: everything there was stronger . . . it was the big city, *the City!*"[23] The poems called "Villes," "Cities," probably came out of memories of London (though they cannot be reduced to that): "With a peculiar taste for the enormous they have copied all the marvels of classical architecture."*

"Chalets of crystal and wood move on invisible rails and pulleys"†—a vision of the London Underground? Arthur took the two Vitalies on it, when they joined him in July 1874. On the upper deck of a red bus, I am now floating among Piccadilly's flashing signs, above the City and Westminster Bridge (where you still see business men with bowler hats and umbrellas), above Soho (where the exiles of the Commune gathered). Through the fogged window of a black taxi, I see the Thames docks loom in the mist, or the small frozen fountain on Sloane Square ("Arthur drinks from the London fountains"), as in Félix Régamey's drawing of Rimbaud and Verlaine appearing out of the *fog,* in front of a pointillist *bobby.* . . .

We drink tea in huts whose Tudor style dates from after the war, ale in pubs, but especially the pure, fresh air—the air of freedom—in the large parks of the city: "By arranging the buildings into squares, closed mews and courtyards, they have cheated the cabdrivers. The parks represent primitive nature shaped with proud art."†† Walking in Hyde Park, I imagine Rimbaud in the top hat he was so proud of (he still laughs about it in Harar[24]), passing Vincent van Gogh without knowing him, in the same kind of stiff hat, also twenty years old, also in London in May 1873.

The candor of Vitalie's diary gives us a glimpse of her brother as if in a rediscovered old home movie: "Arthur reads . . . Arthur goes out in the evening . . . Arthur takes

---

* "Villes" ("Cities") II, *Illuminations.*
† "Cities" I, *Illuminations.*
†† "Cities" II, *Illuminations.*

us to the docks . . . Arthur smiles at me . . . Arthur leaves
. . . Arthur back from the British Museum."[25]

In Camden Town, at 8 Great College Street where the
"herring scene"[26] took place, a red telephone booth (the same
one that appeared in *Blow Up,* but more necessary in the
film). I called V. P. Underwood, who had talked of the two
poets' life in "Leundeun" (as Verlaine pronounced it), of
"this life all violence and uncalled-for *drama* you fancied
fucking me up with!"[27] Underwood interviewed Camille
Barrère who indeed remembered their "eternal fights."[28] "I
would like to add," writes Verlaine with tongue in cheek,
long afterward, in 1894, "that my stay in London was on
the frivolous side, to put it mildly, and that it hung by a
hair that I didn't lose all sense of seriousness, from which I
have hardly strayed since."[29] On the frivolous side? The life
of the "pitiful brother" who "would get up with a sour
mouth, eyes starting out of his head,"* the "Mad Virgin's"
"slavery," as told in "Délires"? Freedom, misery, orgies, all
understood and condensed by Mallarmé: In London, "the
couple lived in orgiastic misery, inhaling the floating coal
smoke, drunk with reciprocity."

If I could pick a place to meet the-man-who-escapes—
cherished fantasy[30]—I would not hesitate to choose Stuttgart in March 1875. Rimbaud is no longer the *encrapulé,* the
profligate wretch of Paris, not yet *anxiety-ridden* as in Harar.
He is back from it all and going everywhere. He is in the
bloom of youth—twenty-one years old—everything is possible. But above all, Rimbaud is at the height of his poetic
mystery: *A Season in Hell* lies behind him, lived through,
published, and burned. He "frenetically flogs the language,"
he says in what has become a catch phrase. The German
language? Or that of the *Illuminations,* which he had no doubt
with him since he thought at the time of publishing a book
"written between trips to Belgium and England, and all over

*"Vagabonds," *Illuminations.*

Germany."[31] Verlaine, out of jail, runs to join him in "Stuttgarce," the whore of a city his pun creates. He expected him to be "unchanged," as he will later say, and came "dressed on the romantic side." He found a "very correct Rimbaud in a family pension,"[32] but if anything even more sarcastic (in the literal sense of *sarkasmos*, biting the vanquished adversary's flesh), violent and cynical: "Verlaine arrived the other day, a rosary in his paws. . . . Three hours later we had denied his God and torn open the ninety-eight wounds of Our Lord."* Rimbaud will not see Verlaine again, whom he abandoned black and blue on the bank of the Neckar.

Back from a trip, one shows photos. This one for example, taken in Harderwijk, Holland, on the morning of May 19, 1876. It is a photo in the form of a story, but authentic,[33] forgotten between the pages of a book. A crowd mills about the harbor to watch the parade of a detachment of the army of the Dutch Indies. In front, the standard-bearer with the Dutch Tricolor, then the band with brass and drums, playing "Auprès de ma blonde." The two hundred odd soldiers marching in step, Beaumont rifles on their shoulders, are mercenaries enlisted for three years, due to leave for Batavia on June 10. You can distinguish their blue serge uniforms, gray capes, and kepis with orange braid. Rimbaud is the tall, gaunt one right in the middle.

"I voyage to the point of vertigo," Verlaine had written to Lepelletier in August 1872. But "voillaging" (except for the pun on sail) was not Verlaine's way. He was *dragged off* to the point of vertigo. Then two years in jail. Rimbaud passed once more through the "departure gate"—Charleville—on the way to Harderwijk and Java, then deserted in Salatiga, on August 15, 1876. Let us reconstitute a small reel of film: Rimbaud discreetly leaves the caserne in white co-

*To Ernest Delahaye, Stuttgart, March 5, 1875.

lonial uniform and disappears among exuberant vegetation, craters, and cascades. (There are no paths; but serpents and some tigers.) He feeds himself from the abundant fruit trees or in the *warongs,* tiny native restaurants (the region is among the most densely populated in the world). He sleeps in shelters built of dry banana leaves for the field workers. Then, after three or four days (surely not a whole month, as Isabelle claimed[34]) of walking and taking coaches or palanquins incognito, he reaches Semarang, fifty kilometers from Salatiga. In the Semarang port, a Scottish windjammer, *The Wandering Chief,* seems to expect him in particular, with a name like that! "He's come back!" Delahaye exclaims to Ernest Millot.[35] From a little journey, hardly worth mentioning. Here are the stages: Brussels, Rotterdam, Le Helder, Southampton, Gibraltar, Naples, Suez, Aden, Sumatra, Java (two months), the Cape, St. Helena, Ascension, the Azores, Queenstown, Cork (Ireland), Liverpool, Le Havre, Paris, and, always, ending up in "Charlestown." As Delahaye also says, in a footnote to his account of his friend's travels: "I ask the reader's pardon, but the frequent repetition of the words *gone, returned, come back* cannot be avoided in Rimbaud's story."[36] Rimbaud leaves again for Vienna, Bremen, Hamburg, Sweden and "a stroll in Norway," visits Rome this same year of 1877, returns to Charleville, and leaves again via the St. Gotthard Pass for Egypt. "He ran through continents and oceans in proud poverty (though rich, if he had wanted, by family and position)."[37] After having explored all the spiritual spheres of an unfamiliar project, it seems he wanted to touch physically all the places on the globe.

We usually learn from our first travels how little it matters to be here or there. After many false starts, the "infatuated traveler"[38] had unawares crossed to the other side, the irreversible. Philippe Soupault has told us how people who have lived some years by the Red Sea have this feeling of a river crossed, of having toppled over, to the other side of the coin, "the other side of Africa."* The page is turned. Rimbaud was not to return to Paris except to pass through twice without stopping: in December 1876, in a British sailor's outfit, which suggested to Germain Nouveau the nickname "Rimbaud the Mariner"; and on a rainy night in 1891, from Roche, shouting at the coachman to take him straight to the Gare de Lyon—to go to Marseille to die.[39]

Aden. On an earlier trip, the dream began on wings. "A cloud of sand vanishes into the sea: latitude 12° 45' north, longitude 4° 4' eastern: Aden. I have made it. Nothing to be proud of."[40]

The Red Sea, green from a distance, brown on the coast. One of the hells mentioned in sailing dictionaries. In front of the famous and depressing purple rock, during some hours of steam bath stopover, I dreamed of melons. A goat was eating the *Daily Mail*. Already an enormous red disk, the sun, was still growing larger, like an Elf gas station sign. Hard to imagine an Ardennes man in these dog days. A pine tree in Yemen!

"Aden. May 5, 1909. Aden made a painful specter of ambiguous omen rise before me: Arthur Rimbaud" (writes Segalen in an appendix to his book *Equipée*). "It was here that he suffered anxieties unsuspected by anyone." Segalen enters into a dialogue with an echo of Rimbaud's complaints, which he catches in the dry caverns: "See my complaints, my infinitely disappointed hopes, my surprisingly vain efforts." I have to move on, says Segalen: I'm going. And I tell you: "You fought for the Real: You struggled with it body against body. But you were vain! You first stripped off your most splendid armor. You knew yourself a poet! But you flattered yourself for having muscles and bones. The poet you despised was still leading you, and you

*May 5 1884.

ignored him out of spite—to your own loss." Dialogue that goes to the heart of the matter. "This is the Rimbaud Myth," concludes Segalen. Indeed, the only one worthy of a quest.

Djibouti. Flat country. Black soldiers in camouflage tops and beige shorts. In the shade of hovels, tables are put close together; very black hands play with all-white dominoes— sugar cubes handled with surprising speed. And a noise of metal balls. Abandoned airplane skeletons give full meaning to their name: Mirages. A tugboat by the quai: the *Arthur Rimbaud*. Instead of a municipal bust, this little boat with its black prow, which *for no good reason* carries the name Arthur Rimbaud out to the sea he had dreamed of and crossed. It continues his wanderings in his name and seems to me the only conceivable monument for him. In the distance, AMX tanks raise once more the dust of Paul Soleillet's empire, which for a moment forms in the torrid air remote images of the lost harbors I am searching for—Obock, Zeila—then gently settles back on the sand. You meet everybody at the Zinc Palm, the Deux Magots of the African Horn, buzzing successor of the two facing bistros the Righas brothers were running when Segalen came to interview them. I am sitting by the sea, thinking of nothing.

But the main feeling one gets from the Rimbaldian itinerary—even with shortcuts, in company, on a "mission," and in comfort—is freedom. The general tendency is to trade it in for a more peaceful inner life. The Buddha said freedom is won at the price of losing home. Rimbaud paid it more dearly yet—with his life. He was not bound to any person for any length of time, except himself, always. Freedom is the most beautiful Rimbaldian constant in the work of his life.

> *The winds coming down the great mountains of Norway*
> *Had whispered to you of bitter freedom.**

*"Ophélie."

But "free" freedom. "I'm terribly stubborn in loving free freedom," he threw at Izambard in November 1870. Then he knew "The pride of being freer/Than the most free," which Verlaine envied him in "Laeti et Errabundi." "With me alone can you be free,"* Rimbaud had written him while trying to track him down in the docks of London, while Verlaine tried to escape, a few days before the "Brussels drama." And Verlaine, who never got over having tasted this kind of freedom, admits still with a touch of bitterness in 1884: "The man in M. Rimbaud is free, that is only too clear."

He does not know where he is going or why, but everywhere he goes, Rimbaud feels free: in Tadjoura in 1886, where he leads a "free and gratuitous life;"† in 1887 in Cairo, where he declares: "I am used to a free life."†† "Have you lost your freedom of action?" his mother worries, but he preserves it, on the contrary, in Harar: "Harar . . . you can leave whenever you want."§ And a year to the day before dying, in 1890: "in Harar . . . But after all one is free here."‖

"Rimbaud's greatness remains that he refused the meager freedom which, in his place and century, he could have made his," writes Yves Bonnefoy rightly,[41] distinguishing between freedom defined as choice of several possibles and an *absolute* desire of freedom. It is this absolute that carried Rimbaud, which his sister Isabelle understood at his deathbed ("he had too strong a taste for the rare and unique"[42]). It marked him: Freedom is a question of high metaphysics, and the various interpretations (flight from the mother, search of the father, etc.) cannot grasp it for their ontological thrust. Throughout his wandering and free life, *as unsociable as possible,* Rimbaud restores for himself, in his own fashion, Nietzsche's "ancient sovereignty of the I." He understands,

* London, July 5, 1873.
† February 28, 1886.
†† August 26, 1887.
§ February 1, 1888.
‖ November 10, 1890.

at the same time, this fatal "Impossibility": He will not or cannot help choosing endlessly; hence he does not really choose at all, and everything leads to his end. But Rimbaud remains on a human scale in limitless Ethiopia; he is natural size. He felt his freedom in the vast spaces. But the prison was inside him. He remained a prisoner of his *rib cage,* of the absolute within him, which could come free and expand only in movement, in the positive fullness of the finite world, which at the same time breaks through its limits and returns to the infinite of matter[43]—and in abandoning his body, in death, which makes the body invisible, dissolves its unity. Then Arthur Rimbaud's soul was finally delivered of his convict body, free to wander forever through the airy, sunny deserts of Abyssinia.

(And while the Dylan song fades away, I imagine Rimbaud on his horse now and then singing some simple song that, at night, fades into a hymn.)

After siesta and coffee, we drive again through the steppe to a dinner of Nile turkey. After my reminiscing on recent travel, the desert, which still overwhelms me with its endlessness, brings home to me the obvious continuity of Rimbaud's wanderings. Yet most books on him claim that Rimbaud, after "staggering"[44] travel, settled down in Harar, that he found his "niche" in Abyssinia. His journeys formed as it were an encephalogram at first frantic, then straight. But Rimbaud is only "based" in Harar, his new point of departure. As Verlaine saw him "tramping" through the Ardennes, Righas sees him in Abyssinia: "He was a great walker, Oh! an astonishing walker, with coat open* and just a little fez on his head in spite of the sun."[45] As Baudelaire said of Poe: "He went through life as through a desert and changed locations like an Arab."

*"Ma Bohème," 1870: "I went on, fists in my torn pockets;/My coat was also becoming ideal."

*　　*　　*

No matter how far back we trace Rimbaud's genealogical tree,[46] its roots go into the soil: beginning with the ancestor who is a "farmer and vintner" in the eighteenth century, and continuing to Jean-Nicolas Cuif, his maternal grandfather, "farmer and stockholder." Rimbaud had declared himself a "peasant!"* Mallarmé had not failed to notice his "big washerwoman hands . . . red with frostbite." "The hand that wields the pen is worth the hand that guides the plow."† In Abyssinia, Rimbaud is nostalgic for the farm in Roche, in the manner of Millet's inevitable "Angelus": "I am always happy to dwell on the picture of your working the farm."†† But while in Roche, he refused stubbornly to take any part in the work.§ "As you said, my vocation will never be farming."‖ His relation to the soil is not in question. What Rimbaud fears above all is becoming sedentary. He loves nature, but detests the countryside. His soil is the "magic soil" that Wiechert talks about. Rimbaud does not have the *vézou,* as people of the region say (which André Dhotel translated for me as the inability to walk ten paces without sitting down). "Living always in the same place I would always find very miserable."¶ We need only listen to his ever repeated fear of being held in some place, to consider his ten years of refusing to come home and settle in the country, as his mother advises, to admit that movement (which far from giving out, gains momentum in Abyssinia**) defines his entire life and was

---

* "Adieu," *A Season in Hell*
† "Mauvais Sang" ("Bad Blood"), *A Season in Hell*.
†† Harar, May 6, 1883. And the following year: "I love to picture your peaceful life and occupations" (Aden, May 5, 1884).
§ Except once, in the summer of 1879.
‖ Aden, December 30, 1884.
¶ Aden, January 15, 1885.
** "I prefer leaving to being exploited" (Aden, September 22, 1880). "It is certain that I can no longer live a settled life" (Aden, October 8, 1887). "I am too used to a wandering and gratuitous life" (Cairo, August 23, 1887). And again in Harar, a year before his death, on November 10, 1890: "Moreover one thing is impossible for me: a sedentary life."

already clearly expressed by the poet in 1871: "I want to work in freedom."*

Unawares, we all have an anniversary of our death every year. The letters of the various November 10 seem marked by a tone of truth or fatality, like the contract with Bardey of 1880, the refusal of a settled life in 1890, and especially the letter of November 10, 1888, three years before his death, in which Rimbaud writes two dry sentences that might serve as epigraphs for his entire life: "I work. I travel." Mme. Létrange remembers that "Rimbaud could not sit still" in 1875.[47] In 1885, he writes his family: "In any case, don't count on me becoming less of a vagabond; on the contrary, if I had the means to travel, without having to stay places to work and make a living, you would never see me two months in the same place."

This perpetual desire to leave, the call of adventure, the attraction of the Orient, the conflicts with Vitalie Cuif, and some biographical details all push us toward remembering Frédéric Rimbaud, captain in the French Colonial Army, the all the more unknown father because the abandoned family tacitly agreed to act as if he had never existed. "The poverty of information we have about Rimbaud's father must in itself be considered significant": A psychoanalyst has put this absent father . . . back in his place.[48] Without refuting the psychoanalyst's hypothesis of Rimbaud's "fantasized identification" with his father, let us try to eliminate it by considering how it dovetails with the classical, binocular, and sedentary vision of the "two Rimbauds": "The departure of November 1878 . . . marks *the end of his former nomadism.*" And to make his "rather bold hypothesis" still more pointed, the analyst says: "It would not be the Arthur Rimbaud of the poetical period who wandered through continents to settle down in Africa, but a psychically different personality with a strong unconscious relation to his father."[49] In a previous

*To Paul Demeny, Charleville, August 28, 1871.

essay, a first sketch of the one we are speaking of, the psychoanalyst compared Rimbaud to "the Rat Man, who was likewise the prey of an unconscious identification." In some way, "the Arthur Rimbaud" of "Cities," then "the Arthur Rimbaud" of fields. Rimbaud was in the desert ("the Rimbaud of the desert"), and the desert was in him! I have already stated my reasons for not seeing any "dyptic asymmetry" in the departure of November 1878, or any dissolved continuity in Rimbaud's destiny. First, Ethiopia is no desert. The high plateaus of Harar where Rimbaud lived are as like a desert as the Rhone delta around Aix-en-Provence. . . . But above all, Rimbaud did not stop moving through this territory two and a half times the size of France—he is even most on the move here. At least seven thousand kilometers on horseback and foot. Charleville—Zanzibar. They seem to be next door for him. "Add marches of fifteen to forty kilometers a day on foot, insane cavalcades through the steep mountains of the country."*

John Arthur Rimbaud, born 1854, still going strong![50] Strong tail wind. He remains a footloose pebble-pusher, a nomad or, as he insists, a "vagabond," a "wanderer," and, as the English word says so well, a *"drifter."* The difference of his wanderings in Europe or Java lies in the greater attraction of solar energy and in the *real, not symbolic* fact that Rimbaud, who is no longer supported by anybody and refuses to be so (he had allowed himself to be "cynically supported" by old school friends, Verlaine, his mother), finds himself more and more caught in a net of relationships and interests, in the web of long itineraries he has spun. This speaks rather for an identification with mother Cuif. The meshes of the net are tighter toward the end of his life: "I would leave . . . but I'm owed much money and cannot leave because I would lose it."†

*To Isabelle, Marseille, July 15, 1891.
†Harar, February 20, 1891.

Hence, *in self-defense,* the shuttle movement, the "back and forth"* he complains of by 1883, back and forth between Harar and Entotto, between the coast near Aden or Zeila and Harar, where he organized a dozen caravans ("runs on the cursed coffee and raising those talari of Satan"†). But it was a shuttling he was familiar with, which could not have felt much different around Harar or around Charleville, which must even have taken his mind back from Harar to Charleville, and which did not hinder his trying out all directions.††

So we cannot cut Rimbaud in two in order to "godchotize" him.[51] However, the probable fact of Rimbaud's having become a Cuif does not contradict identification with his father, but rather furnishes a counterpoint to that theory: Rimbaud did not begin unconsciously imitating his father the moment he learned of his death, but there is an eventual, complex, and constant *alternating* of identifications. I am reminded of another farmer, M. Girard who, leaning on his pitchfork, told Robert Goffin: "Be sure to tell that his mother and sister Isabelle were two hypocritical bigots, and that the whole village said the captain and Arthur weren't all wrong to clear out."[52] No matter how dubious village gossip, even when unanimous, Rimbaud, who had seen his father come home on leaves, return, after domestic quarrels (and not without having fulfilled his conjugal duty) to his garrison, and finally leave for good, identified with his father at least in the manner in which he left his mother,§ in his *desire to worry her.* Which succeeded: from his first escapade in August 1870, when his mother desperately searched for her son in all the cafés of Charleville, which was then occupied by

---

* Harar, June 10, 1881: "I'm just back from an outside campaign and am leaving again for ivory." Harar, July 2, 1881: "Just got back from the interior. . . . I'm leaving . . . for a country completely unexplored by Europeans." To Ilg, Aden, March 29, 1888: "Back from Harar. . . . I have indeed made the trip to Harar, 6 days going, 5 coming back. . . . I'm leaving very soon again for Harar . . ."
† To Ilg, February 24, 1890.
†† See below: "the elsewhere." On "what keeps" Rimbaud, see Chapter 11.
§ Also by his enlisting in various armies, from 1876 on: see Chapter 7.

the Prussians. Provided we do not reduce it to this interpretation, we may hear the mother's anxiety at the flight of the "man" in one of Rimbaud's most beautiful poems, "Mémoire":

> *Madame stands too upright in the fields* . . .
> *He* . . .
> *is leaving across the mountain! She, all*
> *cold and black, runs! after the man taking off!*

There is the same unconscious wish to worry mother in 1884, from Aden: "I cannot give you an address to reply to because I myself do not know where I'll be off to next, by which route, whereto, why, and how!"★

Thus the "worrier" of Harar transfers his worrying to his mother by a latent exchange of anxiety and reproaches, causes her maternal pain, which, by understatement or syllogism, leads to the no doubt desired declaration of love. The mother breaks down:

> Arthur, my son,
>
> Your silence has been long, and why this silence? Happy those who have no children, and very happy those who do not love them: They are indifferent to what may happen to them. Perhaps I should not worry. Last year around this time you already did not write or reply for six months, no matter how urgent my letters. But this time it is over eight long months since we have heard from you. There is no use talking about us since we interest you so little. Yet it is impossible that you should forget us like this: What has happened to you? . . . Are you no longer in Aden? . . . To tell the truth, we are going mad trying to search for you. And I come back to

★To "my dear friends," Aden, May 5, 1884.

saying: Happy, O very happy those who have no children
or do not love them!*

Rimbaud did not keep his mother's letters—except for
this one, of October 10, which he had with him even on his
stretcher. The replies to his other letters are in the wind, the
fresh breeze I breathe tonight coming back with Sancerni.
Rimbaud once said of these letters, that he "lost them somewhere in the country."†

But perhaps it is mostly our own contemporary preoccupations that enter into these concepts. Perhaps the "fantasized identifications" will some day end up on the shelf of
outdated tools, next to the "bovarism" with which Segalen
thought he could explain Rimbaud. The reality of Harar attracts me differently, no doubt because I have plunged into
it and because it is directly tied to a dream. What could
Rimbaud have done, for example, on May 22, 1889? It was
Kremt, the rainy season in Abyssinia. Torrential rains kept
him from working, but he still claimed to be "very busy."††
On that same day, at a great distance, Jules Renard wrote in
his *Journal:* "At sunset it seems that just beyond our horizon
there begin the fantastic countries, the scorched ones, Tierra
del Fuego, countries that plunge us into dreams . . . Egypt
and its great sphinx, Asia and its mysteries, anything but
our own poor little meager and sad world."

Without knowing it and at a distance, Jules Renard was
formulating Rimbaud's dream, Rimbaud's heliotropic
reality.

"At seven he wrote novels about life/In the great desert
. . ./Forests, suns, coasts, savannahs."§ Following Baudelaire "to the bottom of the unknown to find something new,"
searching for the pearl, the truth, like the diver in Victor

* Mme. Rimbaud to her son, Roche, October 10, 1885.
† February 15, 1881.
††Harar, May 18, 1889.
§ "The Seven-year-old Poets."

Hugo's *L'Homme qui rit (The Man Who Laughs)*, Rimbaud had tried to build up a universe "delivered from its origins and longings."[53] "From indigo straits to Ossian's sea, over rose and orange sand washed by wine-colored sky, there rise and intersect boulevards of glass."* In *A Season in Hell*, he plumed himself on "possessing all possible landscapes."† Disillusioned, he abandoned "simple hallucination," a moment taken up in an existential manner in *Illuminations*. Rimbaud then pursues in reality his insatiable search for an elsewhere, leaving from any coast swept by the compass rose, haunted by the place never to be found. Even in Arabia, he still dreams of elsewhere: "The world is very large and full of magnificent lands that could not be visited in a thousand lifetimes."††

His letters from Africa and Arabia are dominated by inchoative verbs marking the beginnings of action—"leave," "clear out," "go away"—which came into my head as I left in the plane. "I'll buy a horse and leave."§ In 1879, Rimbaud was indignant that Izambard did not leave for Russia since he had the opportunity. In the different "here," Rimbaud constantly thinks of "elsewhere." In Ethiopia, he is in his utopia (*utopia*, the "not place"), but still dreams of the Eldorado, Eden, Cythera, Fortunate Isles, and Cloud-cuckooland of his first reading. He has already gone far (from where?[54]) and is still unsatisfied: "I count on finding something better a bit farther on . . . push on. . . find something better farther on."‖

Zanzibar! Who knows what great unquenched depar-

---

* "Métropolitain," *Illuminations*.
† "L'Alchimie du verbe" ("Alchemy of the Word"), *A Season in Hell*.
†† To his family, Aden, January 15, 1885.
§ May 4, 1881. And again: "I'll know . . . if I should stay here or clear out" (March 12, 1881); "I am nearly decided to change air" (September 2, 1881); "I'll soon go on a great expedition" (September 22, 1881); "I'll leave very soon, and it's not too likely I'll come back here" (Harar, December 9, 1881); "I'm definitely leaving Aden" (February 8, 1883).
‖ "I'm in Gallaland. I think I'll have to push on soon" (Harar, December 13, 1880); "I'm not counting on staying long . . . I count on finding better farther on" (Harar, February 15, 1881); "I won't stay here long," etc.

tures this name alone evoked for Rimbaud. For seven years of his life in Arabia and Abyssinia, Zanzibar* represents the accessible elsewhere, the earthly paradise just a journey away, the alphabetical end of all wandering. . . . All Rimbaud's writings show a kind of spatial optimism, the elsewhere being the implicit superlative of the "here" for him—elsewhere it will be better than here.

Today, it is mostly Europeans who dream of America. The young Africans we meet dream of Europe—America is too far, a different planet, one or two civilizations ahead. Not so travelers of the last century, like Gérard de Nerval: "In Africa one dreams of India as, in Europe, one dreams of Africa; the radiant ideal is always beyond our actual horizon."[55] "India is more agreeable than Arabia. I could also go to Tonkin,"† Rimbaud writes. In Cairo (a turning point in his African life), Rimbaud thinks of "returning to the Sudan," feels "called to Madagascar," dreams of "long trips through Africa and perhaps China, Japan, who knows where?"†† Ever since his arrival in Arabia, he had thought of pushing on as far as the Panama Canal.§

So we can imagine a possible destiny taking Arthur Rimbaud to the United States of America. It was actually the period of the highest immigration rate in its history (thirteen and a half million immigrants between 1860 and 1890). "Florida, it seems, is the most beautiful country in the world," say the characters of Knut Hamsun's novel *Vagabonds*. Chateaubriand inserted in his *Voyage en Amérique* (which he undertook in 1791) a fragment of an "undated

* He writes from Aden: "I'm leaving for Zanzibar" (August 17, 1880); then from Harar: "I'll probably stop at Zanzibar" (March 12, 1881); back in Aden the next year: "If I leave, and I count on leaving soon, it'll be for . . . Zanzibar" (February 12, 1882). In Cairo for three days, seeing boats leave for Zanzibar, he feels its call like a bout of fever: Zanzibar is mentioned on August 23, 1887, then five times on August 24 to the tune of "here: whereas in Zanzibar." And on August 25: "I am called to Zanzibar."
† Aden, September 28, 1885.
†† August 23 and 25, 1887.
§ Aden, September 28, 1885.

journal" of which young Rimbaud might have savored every word: "Original freedom, finally I have found you! . . . Here I am as the Almighty has created me, lord over nature. . . . Run and lock yourselves up in your cities, go and obey your little laws. . . . I shall go wandering in my solitude, not a single heartbeat of mine shall be compressed, not a single thought fettered. I shall be free like nature."

While Rimbaud drifted through "these countries of Satan,"* everything he ever longed for was happening over there: the conquest of large spaces; adventure; the lure of the new; the gold rush; arms; Colorado sun; the Arizona desert; unashamed piling up of riches in free, even a little too free, freedom: It was the period of the Wild West, of cowboys and Indians. . . . Rimbaud, who corresponded with the Negus of Abyssinia and Armand Savouré, would have exchanged letters with Buffalo Bill or John Wesley Harding. . . .

> Dear Bill Cody,
>
> I have received with pleasure your letter of January 16. I am back from a trip to Nevada: six hundred kilometers, which I covered in eleven days on horseback. The two thousand Winchesters have still not arrived in this damn hole of Tucson. I am convinced that Geronimo has robbed me. I should have known, since those Redskins are all thieves and knaves. Since the English landed on the Coast, trade is ruined in the whole area.
>
> Nothing doing here, at the moment; moreover, I've found something in New Mexico. Gold is way down because of the rise of the dollar. The owners here refuse to sell at $18 and go to Miami.
>
> I suffer from black *vomito* and cannot digest anything in this excessive heat. My health is broken; a year here counts like fifteen elsewhere.
>
> Well, I hope for your sake that this circus is soon going

*Harar, March 18, 1889.

to be over and you can go back to hunting your buffalos in peace. I wish you a summer sixty years long, health, and prosperity,

Yours faithfully,
Rimbaud

Enclosed duplicate of invoice of shoehorns.[56]

Rimbaud had in fact intended to go to the United States. . . . What might his life there have been? Can we imagine his posterity if the man who tried to sign up for the American Navy under the name of John Arthur Rimbaud, in Bremen, in 1877, had taken part in the modern mythology of the conquest of the West, the Iliad of the New World? What influence might one of the greatest European poets have had on American literature, which, barely out of the almanac period, would have discovered his work while not yet daring to acknowledge the preeminence of its own first classics?[57] We would see only him on American TV or in John Ford's peplums. He would have had his "oval face of an exiled angel" carved on Mount Rushmore. Allusions to his work would be as obligatory in presidential addresses as those to Lafayette. But let's not get carried away by this cartoon. America is not the mythic destiny of Rimbaud. "I talked to him of his old project to go to the United States to complete his tour of the world," Delahaye remembers. "He had given up."[58] The salvation he looked for lay in one direction only: the East. "Philosophers, you belong to your Occident."* Rimbaud thinks only of the Orient, his "original fatherland.† Where could he go, the unlucky fellow? He went wherever one could be unlucky. The United States in gestation would have suited him too well, he might have been successful there! Perhaps Rimbaud was wrong about America. But though we can replace a few words in his letters,

*"L'Impossible," *A Season in Hell.*
†Ibid.

they cannot change his destiny. Rimbaud had to follow his star.

No essential truth, no matter how elevated, can stop a man made for action, a *rajasique,* from acting. Rimbaud tends toward the Orient as if he were moved by the idea (more troubling than Nietzsche's "eternal return") that everything is fated, and that we are "acted" within ourselves. A large part of his suffering comes from his inability to reach the ever close and ever distant elsewhere. All the roads he takes are dead ends, but he has a gift for pushing off their known limits and marking for our benefit the impossible satisfaction that turns his life into a destiny under the sign of mystery.

We could say that Rimbaud steps into the *same spot* of divers rivers. "Here" and "elsewhere" will coincide hopelessly: "As well in Aden as elsewhere," he writes in 1884. Even his dream of Zanzibar vanishes in the end: "And perhaps I won't leave for Zanzibar or anywhere else."* "Here is elsewhere."[59]

Yet in Marseille, suffering tortures before his death—"I who am barely able to put my shoe on my one leg"—Rimbaud is still obsessed with wandering: "I spend day and night thinking of means to get moving . . . I would like to do this and that, go here and there, see, live, leave."†

If Rimbaud became a Cuif in Abyssinia, it was not a Cuif from Roche, like his uncle in the Ardennes who was called "the African," but the man of vast space that he had always been: *le Cuif errant*—a wandering Jew of a Cuif!

*November 5, 1887.
†To Isabelle, Marseille, July 15, 1891. When he is given his crutches after the amputation, he desperately tries to run.

6
SOLITUDE

The door to the invisible must
be visible.
—René Daumal

You cannot get lost in a Muslim country: Five times a day
part of the population crouches down facing north. . . .
Yet when seizing Harar, Menelik had written to the English
minister: "Everybody knows this is not a Muslim country."[1] In fact, Tekle Haymanot, the only Ethiopian saint
recognized by Rome, is the patron saint protecting the empire of the "conquering lion of the tribe of Judah." The liturgical splendors of the holy city of Aksum, the procession
of the Tables of the Law in Addis Ababa, bear witness to
an ancient Christianity that never broke with the rites of the
Old Testament and mixed Mosaic custom with Christian
rites, as if in memory of King Solomon.

The *aboun,* patriarch of the Monophysite Ethiopian
Church, kisses the wall of the church. Draped in his *kaba*
(the subterranean church is chilly), he joins a group of priests
chanting by the light of two petroleum lamps. In the shadow,
clergymen called *debceras* lean on their prayer sticks—the
ceremony lasts seven hours—and respond with incessant invocations, chants, and readings from the Bible.

In the twelfth century, churches were carved into the red tuff everywhere in Ethiopia, from Gondar to Asmara. They remain mysterious for the traveler, like the monastery of Debra-Domo which can only be entered by a sixteen-meter rope and where every monk lives walled into his cell, dead to the world.

Rimbaud has fallen asleep on the altars of Solomon.* Pursuing a different mystery, we might say, he indifferently passes by these octagonal sanctuaries you can see from the road; unless he considers himself unworthy to enter, as the faithful sometimes do. Or unless he *already* carries within him the essential disappointment of the apocryphal Abyssinian gospel, *Fecra Yasous* ("Love of Jesus"[2]), which announced that a certain Theodor would appear in Greece and convert the world to Christianity. Then, in 1830, a follower of this gospel came to see a Christian missionary and said sadly: "The time fixed for this prophecy has passed, and Theodor has not appeared."

Early in the morning, Father Émile Foucher with his white beard and black robe welcomes us to the Catholic Mission of Harar, at the end of a small street, next to a mosque whose bright minaret pierces the sky. A Capuchin, Father Émile[3] is the worthy successor of the two "apostolic vicars of Gallaland," Monsignor Taurin-Cahagne, bishop of Adramyth, who arrived in Harar in March 1881 together with Alfred Bardey, and Monsignor Jarosseau,[4] who settled in Harar in 1884 and became the teacher of Haile Selassie.

"A troop of French missionaries has arrived,"† Rimbaud tells his family, as if it were a distraction in the course of a Sunday sunny with boredom, carrying the unexpected pleasure of meeting compatriots. One day, he went to see Monsignor Jarosseau and asked for something to read. "I had only my New Testament," the latter replied. "I gave it to

---

*"How I sleep! how I'm boiled/On the altars of Solomon," *A Season in Hell*.
†Letter to his family, Harar, Sunday, April 16, 1881.

him." The author of the forgotten "Proses johanniques" found nothing to read in Harar except Monsignor Jarosseau's New Testament. . . . The latter added: "He was happy about it, the poor fellow!" And a guest of the bishop wrote in 1948: "I wrote these words down as soon as we left the table. They are exact."[5] But they mean nothing. Unless Monsignor Jarosseau thought "Rimbaud had missed his vocation: He should have been a Trappist or Carthusian monk."[6] Alfred Bardey, who sometimes, for the pleasure of dressing and "thinking of the fatherland," went to mass in Harar, in a mission room doing duty as chapel, said that Rimbaud never went to the services. "He was quietly indifferent to religious matters. But he had most cordial relations with the missionaries. He liked their company, whereas he generally avoided all Europeans."[7] Rimbaud had once thought of becoming a missionary or simple lay brother: "There are lay brothers in the East," he is supposed to have said to Delahaye, "it's a way like any other." This detail, comments Delahaye, "will give you an idea of his erratic frenzy. He envied the missionaries that are sent to the end of the world."[8] And when missionaries join him at the end of the world, Rimbaud is happy because he hopes to leave with them "for countries hitherto unaccessible to white men."*

   Did the "Fire Stealer" see himself as "God's equal"? For all the admitted failure of *voyance, A Season in Hell* does not return to the Christianity the poet had rejected without outgrowing it philosophically. His contempt for Catholic institutions goes back to the time when Rimbaud chalked "death to God" (or "shit on God," depending on the witnesses' intensity) on park benches. And this break in "Les Premières Communions" ("First Communion") was definitive, whatever the precise date of the poem (1870?):

> *Then the Virgin is nothing but the virgin of the book.*
> *The mystical fervor loses its thrust . . .*

*Harar, April 16, 1881.

Add the bad taste of the pictures, old cuts
With atrocious colors glazed by a bored look.

The eternity Rimbaud pursues "at present" is not the one Monsignor Jarosseau preaches in the desert of Gallaland. "Luckily this life is the only one, that is clear."* His "charity" in everyday life? Perhaps; but as a matter of ethics; it is an aspect of his personality, not of transcendence. Besides, it is too hot here to be Catholic.

"Your brother has faith, my child . . . never, in fact, have I seen faith of this quality," the chaplain of the Conception Hospital told Isabelle "with a strange expression."[9] The clergy, it is true, excells in administering sacraments, baptism, or extreme unction, by surprise. Here is a heartrending detail: The dying Rimbaud was unable to receive holy communion. "He spits constantly . . . we were afraid of profanation." And just a few days before his conversion, he accused "the nurses and even the nuns of abominable things."[10]

"I'm only asking for one thing: that he have a good death," declared Isabelle on October 5, 1891. Rimbaud's conversion rests exclusively on her testimony: the letter to her mother of October 28, 1891. On the following December 15, Isabelle wrote to the *Petit Ardennais* that her brother "died like a saint." But it is only in 1892 that an article by Anatole France makes her discover Rimbaud's literary past. When she finally agrees to the publication of her brother's work, it is on condition that they be expurgated and accompanied by her commentary.[11] "As for biography I only admit one version: mine. . . . Not only do I have the right . . . to mutilate, but it is my strict duty."[12] And about the correspondence of Rimbaud and Verlaine (sublime, if we may judge by Verlaine's extant letters), the thirty-some so-called "martyr" letters of 1872, Isabelle writes to Mathilde, Verlaine's ex-wife: "Above all, yes, above all, I am glad that

*Harar, May 25, 1881.

you burned those papers, whatever they contained, rather than put them in the hands of strangers."[13] The details of the poet's edifying death appear first in a letter Isabelle writes to her future husband, Paterne Berrichon, on December 30, 1896. This allows us to suspect[14] that the famous letter of October 28, 1891, telling of Abbé Chaulier's visit and Rimbaud's return into the bosom of the Church ("he is one of the just, a saint, a martyr, an elect!") was modified, if not all written later, at the time when pious Isabelle fought to save the family honor. This letter (which Paul Claudel quoted in 1912, in his preface to Berrichon's edition, and which was published in its entirety only in 1921, in Isabelle's book, *Reliques*) blends "marvelous visions" into the story of the conversion, as if the memory of Rimbaud's delirium were retroactively influenced by reading her brother's poems, which Isabelle had discovered in the meantime.

But I can believe that the power of approaching death, the dilation of the person before extinction (which is for man what suns exploding into red giants are to the stars), I can believe that these moments reawakened Rimbaud's exhausted faculty of hallucination, quickened by atrocious pain. A delirium ("amethyst columns, angels of marble and wood") that his astounded sister did not invent, only—prettified in her recall.

"On my hospital bed, the odor of incense came back to me so potently."* Reminiscence of his stay in the St.-Jean Hospital in 1873, after the "Brussels drama": pure fiction or prophecy? Impossible to decide. The beauty of poetry. Nobody can say or could have said then what lucidity this "almost immaterial" being had.[15] At that point he was, as Vera Daumal said of Roger Gilbert-Lecomte, "in Reality." Isabelle's notes of October 4 refer to unlikely things the dying man tells: "I have to use my wits all day long to keep from saying foolish things." The preceding July, in Roche, "he saw his end near," said Dr. Beaudier, "which did not keep him from swearing and using certain exclamations which

*"L'Éclair" ("Lightning"), *A Season in Hell*.

tell their own story about his supposed religious convictions."[16] So if we consider the blasphemies of his last summer, the sick man's behavior (and state) in the Marseille hospital, the Islamic habits of his last African years, and especially the quest that drove Rimbaud in Abyssinia, we are perplexed by Isabelle's testimony: His deathbed conversion seems . . . smuggled in. The term "conversion," though presented as a solution, is after all only a threshold of further questions. But at the end of his road, in the fall of 1891, Rimbaud had more reason to die than to live. He was tempted by suicide: What use falling back on the self? Abandoning the self assuages pain, prepares for Nothingness or God. Rimbaud had eliminated the last toxins of time; he was ready for eternity. We have seen false witnesses appropriate the death of someone close before. But a man about to die may also change his direction. What thoughts does the mind hold once the body gives up? "I am greedily waiting for God,"* Rimbaud cried in 1873: Perhaps God kept the appointment. Nobody will ever know. It is better this way. Rimbaud's death belongs to him alone. We must only refuse to make it significant.

Menelik told Sadi Carnot, in a letter of April 1891, that his kingdom was "a Christian island in a sea of pagans." But in 1887, Lucien Labosse, the French consul at Suez, observed: "There has not been a single example of conversion since the missionaries came to the Muslim countries."[17] The holy city of Harar, Madinet al-Auliya, is surrounded by about a hundred graves of sheiks venerated by faithful Muslims and also boasts one of the densest concentration of mosques in the world: eighty-two within the city walls.[18] "The man who builds a mosque will own a palace in paradise." Every morning at sunrise, Father Émile is awakened by the muezzin (here called *lazim*), who chants from the top of the neighboring mosque that it is better to pray than to sleep. Rimbaud, who for some time was the only Catholic in the

*"Mauvais Sang" ("Bad Blood"), *A Season in Hell.*

area, lived mostly among Muslims—Somalis, Afars, Danakil, or the Oromos whom the Amharas, their conquerors under Menelik, call Gallas.

If we think of the Koran annotated by his father, of the copy Rimbaud ordered from Hachette in 1883, of the business seal he used on occasion: *Abdoh Rinbo* (for Abdallah Rimbaud, "servant of God," "purveyor of incense"), it is easy to paint him green, the color of Islam. Rimbaud "became Mohammedan in manners and spirit," claims Pierre Petitfils. And Sheik Si Hamza Borbakeur, with all his authority, annexes Rimbaud quite cavalierly in his work on the Koran, claiming as historical fact that he "converted to Islam."[19] A postmark need not be proof! As Islam recommends, Rimbaud observed personal cleanliness, abstained from smoking and drinking. But these dispositions are part of a personal morality, of his Cuif heritage, his repeatedly mentioned care to live as economically as possible. In fact, he adapted perfectly to Gentile custom: His Muslim style shows an elementary social conformity—and security required the costume of the Arab merchant he sometimes wore. Sotiro, the Greek, was no more Muslim than our Ardennais, but he also traveled Arab-style and called himself Adj (or Ali) Abdallah. And the posture Rimbaud adopted for urinating (not "kneeling" but crouching!)[20] seems to me no more decisive as proof than the costume. "He advised me to do likewise," wrote Ugo Ferrandi.[21] We tried it out, Sancerni and I, while the jeep, the brake not properly on, raced down the Harar hills all by itself. . . . We readily believe the same Ferrandi when he says that "everybody around him claimed Rimbaud had become a Muslim."[22] When you are white, and Catholic on top of it, and want to make a living from business, this is wisdom itself. "The inhabitants of Harar are such fanatic followers of the strictest Islam," wrote Rochet d'Héricourt, one of the first travelers, in 1841, "that they do not let Christians enter their country. The European who dared venture among them would pay his daring with his life."[23] Savouré said that "he left [around 1886–1887]

preaching the Koran as a means of penetrating into then unknown regions of Africa." He certainly read the Koran, *in
his fashion:* "He would talk with his camel drivers in the
camp, could show them up on their religion, and read fluently
the Koran, which he knew to interpret to his interest." His
personal interpretations even aroused anger. Once Rimbaud
was attacked near Harar by a group of Integrists who beat
him up with cudgels. "The only reason they did not kill
him is that Muslims do not kill madmen," Henri d'Acremont
explains.[24] On the other hand, Léonce Lagarde, who had
not known Rimbaud, wrote Paul Claudel what he wanted
to hear: that Rimbaud had "surrounded himself with faithful Christians who considered him of divine inspiration."
Ambassador talk, and transmitted by Isabelle![25] Already
d'Hervilly, one of the extras in Fantin-Latour's painting "Coin
de table," labeled him "Jesus among the doctors," when he
was introduced to the literary dinners of the Vilains
Bonshommes in 1871.[26] According to Ferrandi, "Rimbaud
gave veritable lectures on the Koran in his house."[27] Rimbaud himself said that he was "educating the pickanin-
nies."* Certainly with suras rather than the Gospel. Was the
Koran a new technique of salvation? Its place on his book
order is between *Underpasses and Tunnels* and *Dictionary of
Commerce and Navigation.* If he asked in 1881 for his father's
Arabic Dictionary and various "Arabic papers," it is because
these documents are "useful in learning the language."†
Rimbaud "reconverts," but in a professional sense. His intellectual curiosity, strong capacity for adaptation, and indispensable opportunism do not make him a *hafiz.* Basically
he shows the same indifference for Mecca.

"I was not aiming for the bastard wisdom of the Koran,"†† we hear in *A Season in Hell.* In Africa and Arabia,
in spite of his personal "interpretations," which I would like
to know, Rimbaud still does not have the "wisdom . . . of

* Harar, August 4, 1888.
† Harar, February 15, 1881.
†† "L'Impossible," *A Season in Hell.*

the Koran." But you cannot live "on the other side" for ten years without undergoing some assimilation. At thirty-seven, "the old man had metamorphosed," to Isabelle's surprise.[28] The Rimbaud "back from the hot countries"* was marked like a miner coming up from the tunnels. Exhaustion and disappointment at not being able to reach his goal led to deep tiredness: "I do not know how all this will end. Well, I am resigned to anything."† The only true encounter of Islam and Rimbaud was: acceptance. Harar, 1883: "Like the Muslims I know whatever will be will be, that's all."†† Aden, 1884: "I shall neither live nor die in peace. Well, as the Muslims say: It is written!—There's life for you: It's not funny."§ And the dying man on his bed in Marseille who cries in his delirium "*Allah kerim,*" ‖ ("It is God's will") is all that remains of the "Muslim" Rimbaud: a solitary, resigned man in pain, who says *Mektoub.*

Islam does certainly not play a role in the daily utterances of this bitter man. The concept of fate that emerges from them is rather Graeco-Latin, a peasant "fatalism" that cannot oppose the physical order: "In wind or frost, it's idle talk to contradict facts with words," Bounoure commented in *Le Silence de Rimbaud*.[29] But above all, crossing desert or sea, he never submits to obstacles or pain as divine law. He keeps protesting, never renounces action or projects, or the freedom of roving. In the end, his "it is written" equals "such is life."¶ Rimbaud has simply hardened: "I'm used to it all now; I don't fear anything."** It is striking to observe how Rimbaud, unlike any Muslim, is marked by "the curse of never being tired," as Verlaine put it,[30] cursed to risk his life—his physical and moral integrity—in constant enter-

* "Bad Blood," *A Season in Hell.*
† Marseille, June 17, 1891.
††Harar, May 6, 1883.
§ Aden, September 10, 1884.
‖ Isabelle to Paterne Berrichon, Roche, October 12, 1896.
¶ Aden, September 10, 1884.
**Harar, July 22, 1881. Or again to Isabelle, from Marseille, June 17, 1891: "In any case, we must be resigned and not despair."

prises without ever finding either success or peace, cursed to wander without ever reaching recognition or salvation.

The poet, who had transgressed all taboos without managing to "change life," vainly searches for salvation in redeeming action. In this sense, the Wandering Cuif with his desperate efforts remains under the same sign as the *poète maudit*.

The connotations of restless wandering, destitution, anxiety, and the curse that we associate with the legendary figure of the Wandering Jew, the *Juif errant,* can be taken in my formula of the *Cuif errant,* the Wandering Cuif, as a strictly interior affair of Rimbaud's. But Rimbaud himself uses the legend to support his dreams of travel:

> *Norway's Wandering Jew,*
> > *Tell me all about snow.*
> *Old exiles dear to me,*
> > *Tell of the sea.* ★

At the time of his first running away, his mother wondered under her breath: "Don Juan or Wandering Jew?" A jolly drawing by Delahaye, titled "The New Wandering Jew," shows Rimbaud crossing the Black Forest with giant steps (1876). And in 1905, Delahaye writes of his friend: "An honest, unselfish vagabond, without even the Wandering Jew's five pennies, he has traveled over almost all of Europe."[31] Verlaine likewise refers to the "good Wandering Jews" that Rimbaud and he were in their escapades:

> *Joys of the open road,*
> *Trains ready to cruise . . .*
> *What windfalls for*
> *Good Wandering Jews!*[32]

★"L'Esprit," 1872.

This frequent and apparently trivial stereotype of the period, reduced by the poets to the idea of mere perpetual vagabonding, is also sung by Germain Nouveau:

> *If your reason proves the stronger at last*
> *And breathes easy after dealing its death-blow to doubt,*
> *Go on your way, man, like the Wandering Jew.*
> *Be content without soul, happy without a heart.*[33]

In its own language, the word "Hebrew" means passerby, nomad, ferryman, the man in touch with the beyond. Rimbaud's lonely wandering is, as we have seen, without beyond, without revelation. His *inquietude,* his restless anxiety, may be on the order of ontology (in the sense of Heidegger's *Angst*) or simply existential. It is by no means the anxiety of Judaism before what Lévinas calls transcendence, an anxiety mainly ethical and oriented toward concrete forms of brotherhood and justice, as the ritual is to make God appear in our neighbor's face: "anxiety of man before God's Infinite, which he could not contain, but which inspires him."[34]

As a pure existential category, experience is irreducibly opposed to writing, which it feeds. Writing is not living. A writer is a person who cannot live without writing. Rimbaud wrote little during his life, in actual time, but his poetic experience was *vital* (integral to both his life and his will to "change life"). However, we cannot speak of the experience of writing without considering Judaism, which links this very experience to survival and salvation. With the invisible God present in the book, what is written must always be deciphered as a secondary utterance, an incessant questioning of the letter, text of an infinite that turns life into the condition of writing.[35] Then experience (in the sense of *Erlebnis,* of what is *lived*) would not be opposed to writing as potentiality of the book.

In Rimbaud's concept of the Seer, the *voyant,* writing was linked with the divine, not through subjectivity (the sovereign and creative *I* of the Romantics), but as it were in the *idealist objectivity* of the "Fire Stealer" (who has stolen the Word from God in order to create by naming). Once Rimbaud renounces the *formula,* only the place is left. Or, rather, the nonplace. In giving up literature, Rimbaud does not find the "true life" that was the stake. He cuts off communication, abandons all hope of sharing, of being with others, whoever they might be. He enters into life to the exclusion of writing, into their unraveling, and remains the purest figure of this contradiction. What falls away with writing is objectivity (not only the relation to the collective, but the mediation through the universal). What is left is an absolutely solitary man. Hence it is precisely in and through Rimbaud's silence that a philosophy of the absolute, of a singular consciousness (him or me, whoever comes "here" to live rather than to know) can be felt "in the act of being-there where it is a mystery, in life."[36]

> He lived, he died,
> he sang in solitude.
> —Shelley

What moves me most in the *Memories of My Nervous Illness,* are the opening lines, in which President Schreber pleads for his release so that he may "live with people of a certain culture"—we do not live in social classes, but in separate Indian tribes that recruit their members through "passionate attraction" or "elective affinities."[37] Now, if Rimbaud got along with everybody, he never found anybody *to talk to.* The poet Banville did not respond to his overtures; his teacher Izambard stopped understanding him at the crucial moment; Verlaine was much too weak to become the "son of the Sun."* Rimbaud is not only isolated in regard to religion: He also lived in cultural misery. In 1870, after he had

---

*"Vagabonds," *Illuminations.*

absorbed the public library of Charleville as well as Izambard's, to which he had the key, his bulimia for reading remained unsated: "Not a single new book! This is deadly! . . . your library, my last hope, was exhausted!"* Likewise in Roche (this green and purple desert), in 1873, during *A Season:* "I am absolutely stumped. Not a book . . ."† In Aden in 1885, he still complains that "there is no library."†† In 1888, he deplores being "without intellectual occupation." "Without these books," he says, thinking of the treatises he expects and which would be the true light, "I would be like a blind man" in the desert sun.§

The man who declared "I am an inventor . . . even a musician!" did certainly not know the pleasures of music.[38] What could he have heard during his life? Some hypothetical concert in London, church chants, military bands, cabaret songs: "popular tunes, snatches of anthems,"‖ which drove the mocking Seer to "old-fashioned operas, inane refrains, artless rhythms."¶ But the "masterly music"** he desired was ever lacking. Music remained entirely within him, in his head and body. Alone at night in Roche, he could only dream his concerts, dream or dance "a hellish concert," "a suave sacred concert."††† Basically, the given is "ancient discord."§§ The poet, he thought, was the one who could number and organize this chaos, carry it to "new harmony:"‖‖ "One stroke of the bow, and the symphony stirs in the depths or leaps onto the stage."¶¶ His prose poems

* To Georges Izambard, Charleville, August 25, 1870.
† To Ernest Delahaye, "Laïtou," May 1873.
†† Aden, April 14, 1885.
§ Aden, August 4, 1885.
‖ "Les Ponts" ("The Bridges"), *Illuminations.*
¶ "Alchimie du verbe" ("Alchemy of the Word"), *A Season in Hell.*
** "La musique savante manque à notre désir" ("Our desire lacks masterly music"), "Conte" ("Tale"), *Illuminations.*
††† "Nuit de l'enfer" ("Night in Hell"), *A Season in Hell.*
§§ "Matinée d'ivresse" ("Morning of Drunkenness"), *Illuminations.*
‖‖ "À une raison" ("To a Reason"), *Illuminations.*
¶¶ Letter called *du voyant* ("of the Seer"), May 15, 1871. Application: "One tap on the drum releases all sounds and begins the new harmony." "À une raison" ("To a Reason"), *Illuminations.*

contain the rhythms and sounds of a mental score that he felt in his body, his movements, his sleep, a score with ties to nature, architecture, to a universe where the orphic poet brought to life "rings of muted music,"* captured the "unfamiliar music . . . coming from castles built of bone,"† heard with delight the "music of the ancients,"†† or the "bands of rare musicians"§ wandering through the country. . . . If we have ears to hear, the *Illuminations* hold this "fabulous opera,"‖ symphonic in the Greek sense, cosmic and silent like Harmony.

One thing that will stay with me is no doubt the strangeness of African voices in the warm air and a few songs, the best conducting wires of memory—the sonorous identity of a country still spared international noise. Did Rimbaud listen to the chants and strange instruments of Harar? The opera lights had gone out for him. He had rejected the Seer's creative listening, he was no longer in harmony with the universe. In the steppes, he became master of silence. And I suspect that for ten years he heard little other music than the blocks of salt that are sawed all day long in Harar, to make pieces of exchange money.

Leaving the Harar Plateau, you can walk for hours without meeting anybody. "When the grass is high," writes Bardey, "it is easy to get lost in the immense plain of Mandao." This was always the direction Rimbaud took: "from the crowd to the beach."¶ Solitude tempered his bad character, tanned his soul and body. On the highways of Europe, he walked alone, "proud to have neither country nor friend."** Now he had arrived at great inner solitude. Every day he took the risk of getting lost.

* "Being Beauteous," *Illuminations.*
† "Villes" ("Cities") I, *Illuminations.*
††"Métropolitain," *Illuminations.*
§ "Vagabonds, *Illuminations.*
‖ "I became a fabulous opera," "Délires" II, *A Season in Hell.*
¶ "Génie" ("Genius"), *Illuminations.*
**"L'Impossible," *A Season in Hell.*

Nevertheless, he writes, "solitude is a bad thing here."*
It is the deepest, maybe also most cherished, emotional solitude that he suffers most from. The wail of the man who,
in "Bad Blood," proclaimed himself "always alone, without
family," can still be heard throbbing in Harar: "And isn't it
miserable, this life without family . . . ?"†

The solitude he sought out leads him to paroxysms of
despair, to a self-induced delirium of abandonment, which
forms the third movement of the implacable disposition he
shares with his mother: impossible life together alternates
with the reproach of "having been abandoned":†† "What
makes me sad is that you end your letter declaring that you
will have nothing more to do with my business. This is not
the way to help a man thousands of miles from home, traveling among wild tribes and having not a single correspondent in his country!"§

Rimbaud was almost totally devoid of good manners.
This goes for breaking the objects Mathilde Verlaine cared
for (*on purpose!* she fumed[39]), for his youthful provocations
as well as for his daily life in Africa and Arabia. Demanding, he did not know how to say thank you;[40] authoritarian,
perhaps like his officer-father and like *the mother,* he was
incapable of politeness owing to pride, independence, a horror of hypocrisy. He expressed himself always in the imperative. "*Take this train,*" he wrote to his professor when he
was sixteen, at the time of their best understanding, "come
here. . . . Do all you can . . . I command you."‖ Every
letter to his family contains a request, abrupt and dry as a
stock market bid: "pay"; "send"; "write." Friendship played
no part in his "tiger" love for Verlaine, only passionate
domination. Their shared taste for books and strong drink,

---

* Harar, May 6, 1883.
† Harar, August 4, 1888.
†† "It is not agreeable to be so abandoned" (Aden, November 5, 1887).
§ Aden, December 8, 1882.
‖ To George Izambard, September 5, 1870.

for scandal and *"carousses"* ("red-haired caresses") as Laurent Tailhade punningly put it was peppered with sadistic meanness. Rimbaud threatened to destroy Verlaine: "Think again what you were before you met me."* In school, Ernest Delahaye had sought his friendship: Rimbaud has even forgotten his first name when he writes after seven years of silence, without asking how he is, to demand that he send a list of books and scientific instruments: "Wrap carefully. Meanwhile, make haste."[41] Rimbaud felt himself to be too different to confide in anybody. But a friend need not be a confidant, but somebody who is always close, constant. All relationships change with time; only friends remain: One sees them rarely, one often thinks of them with pleasure, it is a relation of identity. Rimbaud had no alter ego. He never wrote a letter of friendship. In Harar he wanted to think only of himself—and succeeded.

His only tie was his family—what was left of it: his mother and one sister ("I have only you"). Neither receiving nor giving any signs of tenderness, he addressed them with the bizarre formula, "my dear friends," as if these two remote women compensated for his lack of friendship with their absence of affection.

Rimbaud never spoke of his young servant Djami, who was approximately twenty and remained devoted to him for several years. But it is Djami he calls in his agony. Djami, in whose name reverberates as if by magic the word *ami,* "friend," was no doubt the only human being from whom Rimbaud received signs of loyalty and affection. Rather than a suppressed passion, this young man is considered to have been a pal, as in a Kipling story. After Rimbaud's departure, Djami vanished among his family. It is for him that Rimbaud made his only testamentary disposition, charging Isabelle to leave him a portion of his fortune, as if this unknown servant represented all he had in this world. Isabelle tried through César Tian and later through Monsignor Taurin to

*To Verlaine, July 5, 1873.

send him the substantial sum Rimbaud had left him. When Djami's family was finally found (he had married and had a child), Djami Wadaï was dead.[42]

A lonely wanderer, Rimbaud again shows his distress in the wish to "find a family."* Would marriage make up for what he lacked? "As for me, I regret not being married and having a family."† "Marriage" rather than woman—though he does certainly not exclude loving, and being loved by, a woman—this is the sense of the project entrusted to the two women of his family. Rimbaud had long ago renounced being understood. He was now to come thoroughly to know the absurdity of asking to be loved.

The idea of conjugal happiness, like his regret at not having passed his baccalaureate or succeeded in his project of getting rich—this return to so-called bourgeois values (which is only logical once the Seer gives up reinventing love) contradicts the ambitions of the poet in revolt. No doubt he also repudiated homosexuality,[43] of which he had once conceived as a procedure of initiation, as part of the "reasoned disordering of all the senses."†† But the various forms of moral contradiction that discredit the Abyssinian Rimbaud—most often in the eyes of the best representatives of the Order he fled—are superficial. Rimbaud does not return to traditional values. He would like to! Here is the core of the African Rimbaud's problem: He would *so much have liked to* "marry and have a family";§ he would *so much have liked to* "become an engineer respected for his knowledge";‖ reach salvation through wealth, and so forth! "I! I who called myself a magus or angel above all morality, I am back down to earth with a duty to seek."¶ Rimbaud always asks for

---

* Harar, May 6, 1883.
† Ibid. (This letter is the living counterpart to "The Impossible" of *A Season in Hell*.)
†† May 13, 1871.
§ Ibid.
‖ Ibid.
¶ "Adieu," *A Season in Hell*.

"the impossible." All his projects reveal a desperate desire for social conformity, a pathetic effort toward normalcy, and their failures constantly bring home to the seeker of morality the "impossible" within him.

Marrying was for Rimbaud an idea like any other, a whim. He took a wife in Abyssinia[44] as he sent for the best precision instruments—with rather vague purpose. They lived for a few months of 1884 in Aden. She was tall and slim, "rather pretty . . . not very black," dressed in European style, smoked cigarettes. She spoke little French, and Rimbaud himself "talked very little." This Abyssinian woman without name or face, both shy and silent, would only go out with Rimbaud evenings, into the dark streets of Aden. "Funny couple."* Then Rimbaud suddenly sent her back to her family. He gave her a few talers and put her in a dhow. "I had this masquerade before my eyes long enough."† He went on to other things. A much better impossible idea:†† guns for Menelik.

In Harar, "women made up two thirds of the total population of the city," observed Paulitschke. "They took part in all the current amusements of the country." From time to time, a young Galla would run singing through the city. At this signal, the women would assemble on a square and, undressing down to their belts, "would go into very violent choreographic exercises. Many did not leave before collapsing in exhaustion." Rimbaud might have read, back in Charleville, in the 1860 issues of *Le Magasin pittoresque* (*The Picturesque Magazine*), that Harar is "notable for its fertility and the beauty of its women."[45] I see them arrive from the neighboring hills, in rags, luminous, with supple and swift steps, their shoulders strong from pounding durra; and, upset by their eyes which I cannot hold, by the small grain of gold some wear in their nostrils, I pass them, trying to take

* The "Mad Virgin" and "Infernal Husband" of "Délires" I, *A Season in Hell*.
† To Augusto Franzoj, September 1885.
†† 1870: "woman or idea."

with me the smell of their smooth, brown skin, the odor that Flaubert smelled on Rutzchuk Hanem's breasts in Esneh.

Rimbaud may well have known women or have taken occasional rests. In the course of his vagabonding, he may for a few bars of salt have possessed the perfumed body of a courtesan on a bed of leaves or fur.

But he wrongly conceived of marriage (as of final peace) as an ideal social value that he could approach only at the price of strenuous work—that is, at the unconscious price of destroying himself. "You need an income to marry."* Hence woman was for him not so much unknowable as inaccessible.

Action being connected with movement, and movement with freedom, it is his identity he preserves by associating woman with ultimate rest: He bars any idea of an *other* and returns to his fatal loneliness. This is a matter of the deep identity of Arthur Rimbaud, not that of an Abyssinian Rimbaud in contrast to the one who declared "The company of women was denied me"† but, at seventeen, whispered to Nina "Tonight? . . . We'll take the/White road that runs" while Nina interrupted his dream: "And the office?"†† It is the identity of "the infernal Husband" who said of women that "they cannot help wanting a safe position,"§ of the man, finally, who in 1890 asked his family: "Could I come home and get married next spring? . . . Do you think I could find somebody who would agree to travel with me?"‖ His mother no doubt replied that he should come back and settle down. Marriage seems to Rimbaud a chain, a noose. He immediately rectifies: "When I spoke of marriage I always wanted it understood that I would remain free to travel, to live abroad, even continue to live in Af-

---

* December 30, 1884. And on April 21, 1890: "I have, alas, neither time to marry nor to look for a wife."
† "Mauvais Sang" ("Bad Blood"), *A Season in Hell*.
†† "Les Reparties de Nina" ("Nina's Replies") (1870?).
§ "Délires" I, *A Season in Hell*.
‖ Harar, August 10, 1890.

rica."* Could he have remained himself, free, and made happy some Ardennais peasant woman choking in her corset on Abyssinian trails or in the dhows of Aden! "I would have to find someone who would follow me in my peregrinations." This was one year to the day before he died. It was one of his Abyssinian subjunctives, a return to the beautiful uses of the language he used to "flog" and, in the same moral movement, the Rimbaudian mode of "the impossible." Finally, a year later in Marseille, "completely helpless, whimpering,"† Rimbaud feels this impossible within himself and can howl his failure to love: "Just when I had decided to go back to France this summer and marry! Adieu marriage, adieu family, adieu future! My life is over, I'm nothing but an immobile stump."††

His true companion had always been Nature—their first union, their communion, going back to the poem "Soleil et chair" ("Sun and Flesh")—Nature, which he loved physically ("I have felt something of her immense body"§), which he made come alive, in which he could get lost. Nature with which he was smitten and distracted, where he found his freedom and solitude.

> *I'll not speak, I'll not think:*
> *But, boundless love in my soul,*
> *Like a gypsy, I'll walk far, very far,*
> *Through Nature—happy as when with a woman.*‖

Necessarily alone, ferociously alone. If he got married, it was to the steppe or savanna, as the Doge was to the sea.

---

* Harar, November 10, 1890.
† To Isabelle, Marseille, July 10, 1891.
†† Ibid.
§ "Aube" ("Dawn"), *Illuminations*.
‖ "Sensation."

7
INNOCENCE

Thus, Maldoror, you con-
quered Hope.
—Lautréamont

All that was left for the lone wolf was to ruin himself in action. The country was admirably suited for this.

The stretcher on which the sick Rimbaud had himself carried from Harar to Zeila arrived yesterday by plane from Addis Ababa, faithfully reconstructed.

Today we have an early appointment with some camel drivers. They are going to play themselves, accompanying the stretcher through the steppe, for a sequence of *The Fire Stealer*.

The meeting point is a large pepper tree in a courtyard in Harar. We are there at six o'clock sharp, but nobody else is. . . . At noon, still nobody. All buttons have popped off the pants of patience. I keep thinking of Rimbaud's twelve months' wait in Tadjoura. . . . Finally, toward one-thirty, the camel drivers nonchalantly dribble in. The misunderstanding is laboriously cleared up. It is the same one that ruined the American Bay of Pigs invasion: "Six o'clock" in Harar means "noon" since the hours—as we knew—are counted from six o'clock on.

Then, from custom and for the fun of it, our extras start renegotiating their pay, even though it was fair and paid in advance. One of the camels has collapsed on folded legs, its quivering lips drooling a saliva foamy like shaving cream. It will not get up again. We must pay damages to the owner, who refuses to leave. "The smallest enterprise in Africa is subject to mad obstacles and requires extraordinary patience,"* wrote Rimbaud. "It really takes the patience of Job to accomplish anything whatever in these cursed countries": This complaint could be signed by Rimbaud, but was addressed to Zimmermann by Ilg.[1]

With outstretched arms, raised hands, and joined thumbs, Charles Brabant is trying out "frames"; turning on his heels, he "narrows" or widens his field of vision—the screen between his hands, a gestural sketch—dancing all by himself on top of a mound right in the sun, right in the desert.

The camels with their pretentious, stupid faces are "camped." The hair on their thighs comes in tufts, like a moth-eaten rug. They gorge on flowers, then finally, distracted but solemn, move out in the steppe. Now and then a driver pulls back a camel's head and spits tobacco juice into its mouth.

"Motor, we're shooting." The ships of the desert precede the covered stretcher, along with a tribe of very black, half-naked Issas armed with old St.-Étienne rifles, followed by a few goats. Our caravan, formed at Diredawa, slowly strings out before our eyes in the direction of the Red Sea.

In the land of the sovereign sun with the paradoxical pleasures of a furnace, where the cameraman sees the photoelectric cell go crazy as he comes close before the shot, where the lighting technician must do his work against the grain—and produce dark—the "overexposed" images on the film are threatened by whiteness, the white page of a book menaced by torpor. Here, where the senses reel in the phys-

*Letter to his family, Tadjoura, January 31, 1886.

ical test of the sun, I could not say if God is dead or was so for Rimbaud, but I know that Rimbaud was all his life a man of light, both mythic and optical. Squinting and shading our eyes, we are following the caravan of the "son of the Sun," which seems as if it could never stop except in a dissolve, a confusion of sun, as if the dying Rimbaud in his delirium a few months later would hand on the task: "I'll be under the ground," he will say to Isabelle, "and you'll walk in the sun."*

In action, you catch your meals on the run, from haversacks as the cyclists of the Tour de France do—crackers and zebu yogurt. You catch a few winks in a ditch while the camera is recharged. "Sleep in a nest of flames."† The Issas have crouched down and refuse to get up again. Their old wooly- and white-haired chief negotiates endlessly, refuses to "work the whole day," demands additional refreshments. The shooting is interrupted. Issas, Gallas, Ethiopian soldiers on surveillance duty, animals and men are scattered over the plain, immobile. Everybody waits for the cloud of dust on the horizon announcing the approach of the beverage truck. People who have spent a few days in the desert tell how water quickly becomes a hallucinatory obsession.

> *In the artless sun*
> *What does man need? To drink!*
> *—No: die by alien streams.*††

Rimbaud, whose poems show his obsession with thirst ("Weeping, I saw gold—and could not drink"§), and who had experienced it (in June 1872, in Paris, he is "thirsty enough to be afraid of gangrene"), must really have suffered

---

* Isabelle's notes, Marseille, October 4, 1891.
† "Nuit de l'enfer" ("Night of Hell"), *A Season in Hell*.
†† "Comédie de la soif" ("Comedy of Thirst"), 1872
§ "Délires" II, *A Season in Hell*. "To say I didn't care to drink!" ("Larme" ["Tear"]).

from it in this country where he would travel with only a *guerba* of water and a ball of dried dates with butter. It was even worse on his arms expedition to Shoa, where for a long stretch of time he had only a little yellow, brackish water to dole out to his thirst, a thick liquid mixed with goat hair, carried in skins covered in and out with rancid grease and bounced on camel back in the torrid heat.[2] It is tempting to see here the symbolic passage from creation to aridity, from fertile moisture to real dryness. However, the poet already felt a bitter, burning, desiccating thirst, a thirst for alcohol and fire ("And my veins are cursed/with an unhealthy thirst"[*]), a thirst, wrote Maurice Blanchot, that could only be quenched, by the "arid flame and poison"[3] of firewater. In Abyssinia, dryness seems to attain Rimbaud's very body: He speaks of his hair as a "powder puff." Merciniez describes him as "tall, dried up," Righas, as "skinny, dried up."[4] Both his body and soul are tending toward absolute hardness. In the land of salt (the salt of Lake Assal), Rimbaud returns to the soil—not a nourishing, maternal peasant sod, but a dry, hard soil covered with dust. Here, "the pebbles resound"[†] as in his old poem. Every step resounds on the stony ground. An explorer stopped to note: "Climbing the rocks I was astonished to hear them ring like brass under our feet."[5] Every step is a consonant, every breath a vowel, walking a lost tale. A tale of the body told by the ground. Rimbaud is thirsty for stones, has within him a potential for turning-to-stone: "The last expedition has exhausted me so much that I often lie in the sun, immobile like an unfeeling stone."[††] Here lies Arthur Rimbaud on a stone in the sun, dead-tired. Even through his growing obsession with cold and humid climates, we can feel Rimbaud's craving for this desiccating heat expand into a coherent, global refusal of water, rain, the mother, creation, into a passion for dryness

[*] "Chanson de la plus haute tour" ("Song from the Highest Tower"), May 1872.
[†] "Michel et Christine."
[††] After the expedition, end of 1886, beginning of 1887.

and the lethal banquets ordered in *A Season in Hell:* "Eat the pebbles we break,/the old stones of churches."*

Even more than the "Comedy of Thirst," Rimbaud celebrates "Feasts of Hunger":† "My hunger is for bits of black air;/For ringing sky;/ . . , For misery."†† This ringing inner feast of 1872 is realized in Abyssinia, where Rimbaud's only remaining taste, "for earth and stones," demonstrates his refusal of (and even more his disgust with) universal ideas, where he attains dryness within himself, a mental and somatic dryness that confounds being-in-the-world with geological being-there. A position that would seem to say: There is this and nothing more, if it were not a torment, a mouth full of earth, a shipwreck in the desert.

Our caravan took off again, with the camera passing from one end to the other as long as the sun was up. I felt it approach and recede within me like another *Bolero* of Ravel's, long and intense as the solar day, with full percussion battery toward three o'clock in the afternoon when Rimbaud's stretcher went by, but a bolero I would like even more if it started over at its culmination, then dwindled *decrescendo* into silence.

At nightfall we abandon the stretcher and other now useless materials where we are, as NASA did on the moon.[6]

Experience of fatigue in the land of boredom. What Rimbaud endured for ten years under the worst conditions, we began to get a taste of within forty-eight hours, out of breath, at the end of our tether. Yesterday, the historical rifles we had distributed to the Issas seemed suspect to the Ethiopian soldiers that guard the town gates and appear suddenly on the roads to check papers and search cars. We were held all day in a caserne surrounded by miradors,

---

* "Faim" ("Hunger"), *A Season in Hell.*
† "Dinn! dinn! dinn! dinn! my pasture the air/ . . . the meadow of sound!" ("Fêtes de la faim" ["Feasts of Hunger"], 1872).
†† Ibid.

questioned by hostile, pettifogging officers—our perfectly valid passports in the hands of illiterate, decorated, and armed soldiers, our cameras confiscated, reels of film destroyed. Waiting for the embassy to intervene on our behalf, I remembered Rimbaud's troubles: "While our stock is sequestered, our capital eaten up by caravan costs, our personnel subsisting indefinitely at our expense, our materials deteriorating, we wait."* Tonight, our two cars are sitting on a dune all by themselves. We notice that the Issas who come to draw their pay line up again to get paid a second time. They are suddenly "numerous as hair on the head," as the Ethiopian saying goes, and now demand "considerable *baksheesh*."† Fever mounts in Diredawa. The Issas, nostrils flaring with anger, start rocking the two Land Rovers. Lapizo, the "eye of Moscow" officially in charge of supervising the filming, begs; "Don't try to bargain them down, I'm still of use to the Revolution." We jump into the Land Rovers that take off in a whirlwind, pursued by the howling tribe hurling stones. Our vehicles skid. The Issas are gaining on us. The Land Rovers just barely manage to escape them, needing all the power of their four-wheel drive to get out of the sand of the wadi. Packed upright in the cars, we soon reach Diredawa. In the distance, the tribe still hooting and running. But nomads do not leave the desert.

Rimbaud was an armed poet. The preceding episode brought home to us that the man of action must constantly see to his defense. But weapons were with him all his life: In 1870, in Douai, he enlists in the National Guard—manipulating a broomstick by way of a rifle—and drafts a letter of collective protest like Gorju in *Bouvard et Pécuchet:* "They must be given arms at any cost."†† In London he "takes it

* Rimbaud and Labatut to the minister of foreign affairs, Tadjoura, April 15, 1886.
† Ibid.
††Protest letter to the mayor of Douai, September 20, 1870; the word "arms" occurs six times.

into his head to buy sharp rapiers for dueling in the manner of German students!"[7] In 1876, in Rotterdam, he is signed up for Batavia in the Foreign Legion; in 1878, in Lacarna, waiting for a dagger that does not arrive: "This is agonizing."[*] In Cyprus, 1880, on horseback with bare torso, rifle in hand, like Cochise. . . . Quartered in barracks by the sea, his favorite amusement there is to lie in the sand between two swims and blow the gunpowder he was to explode rocks with. In Aden, in November 1880, as he gets ready to leave for Harar: "One must be armed to go there."[†] And finally, he crosses Abyssinia at the head of a caravan transporting two thousand rebuilt rifles from Liège.

Horace already told his contemporaries that crossing oceans will at best change the sky, not your soul: *"Caelum mutaris, non anima, per mare currens."*

I remember Charleville two weeks ago, when Charles Brabant drove his DS Citroën into the park of the station square. Camera pointing out the door, we circled the kiosk for a good ten minutes, time enough to recite the poem "To Music" under my breath. We were doing more than shooting a film! The very sprockets made us hear the oompah of the band. The kiosk turned into a merry-go-round taking us back to 1879, to the crowd of "wheezing bourgeois" that "the bums laugh at." Turning around the text, surrounded in turn by the poem, caught in the music box, we saw Vitalie Cuif seduced right here by the uniformed captain. Staggering out of the poem, I heard the band break into "Le Rêve passe" ("The Dream Vanishes") or "Le Diable au corps" ("Devil in the Flesh"), those infantry marches that must have represented power, adventure, holidays, circus, the colonial dream, for the young man, as for the children running after the music. . . .[8] The image of the soldier who abandoned him is burned into the memory of the boy who secretly

*Without date or place (Cyprus, April 1879?).
†Aden, November 2, 1880.

wrote at ten: "My father was an officer in the king's army."* Rimbaud himself was a strange captain dreaming of several armies, authoritarian and rebellious, recruiter and corrupter, conquerer and deserter. But he had a destiny; he could never have built a military career. He enlisted in order to desert. His projects of joining the Spanish, Dutch, and American armies—like so many dream uniforms to copy his father even to desertion—could only lead to failure: syncopes in his life, experienced in terms of individual adventure, but contradicting his constant hatred for the collective values of the army,[9] his contempt for *"patrouillotisme,"*† or "patroliotism," and the antimilitarism he flaunted before the Prussians who occupied Vouziers.

In 1873, Rimbaud had shouted: "General, you are a nigger."†† Abyssinia did not lessen his antimilitarism, which had intensified to a general refusal of society. On the contrary, this sentiment grew ever stronger, culminating in the poignant scene on August 23, 1891, which Isabelle reports in spite of herself, not daring to understand: feverish, drugged, his leg amputated, waiting for his last Paris–Lyon–Marseille train at the station, Rimbaud "had a momentary fit of extraordinary and harrowing laughter at seeing an officer in uniform."[10] This uncontrollable laughter of the cancer patient is the most authentic moment of Rimbaud's life. It shows his deep and unchanged personality as it is—not only in regard to an officer who may have reminded him of his father, or the flagrant ridiculousness of the army. In the early morning of the same day, the Attigny stationmaster on his miniature platform had triggered the same sardonic laughter. This is the uncontrollable, convulsive, tragic, ridiculous laugh of Arthur Rimbaud, the free man who sacrificed his life to an escape from the absurdities of the bourgeois world,

---

* "Le soleil était encore chaud" ("The Sunset Was Still Warm") (1864).
† To Georges Izambard, Charleville, August 25, 1870.
†† "Bad Blood," *A Season in Hell.*

an escape from mediocrity—and who had forgotten in his remote adventures that it could still exist *to this degree*. And if the dying man knocked about in the train from Paris to Marseille, crossing France for a last time in the most atrocious physical and mental pain, did not laugh at himself up to his death, then he had to stifle this "extraordinary" and incommunicable laugh, perhaps the first laugh of the twentieth century.

Aside from the army that attracts and revolts him, the need of weapons certainly symbolizes Rimbaud's identity. "The tools and weapons" he demands in "Bad Blood" occur all through *A Season in Hell* like so many means for action and signs of energy. Whether they express from the start the poet's aggressiveness and desire for destruction ("I armed myself against justice") or rather a wish to protect himself against fear ("armed with ardent patience"), the ending note of this "black book," the real and imaginary weapons point to a negative will to order—and it is in these terms that Rimbaud speaks in Abyssinia of the son he would have liked to raise in his fashion, to "arm"* with the best possible education.

A drawing by Verlaine shows Rimbaud in 1875, with glasses and cotton sleeve-protectors, "screaming at his subordinates in some atrocious language."[11] This is one of Rimbaud's modes of being: beside himself. "I appeal to your disgust with all and sundry, your perpetual anger against every little thing," Verlaine writes him from London that same year.[12] Rimbaud hits back for his wounds. But at a deeper level, his aggressiveness seeks an object in order to exist, his weapons are in search of a reason to be, so that he could exist through this aggression and loss of self.

On one occasion, when he had run away from home to Charleroi and been taken in by M. des Essarts, Rimbaud, who wanted to become a journalist, was thrown out for insulting all the politicians of the time, "right and left—but

*Harar, May 6, 1883.

especially on the right: X, the dirty cad . . . , the mealy-mouthed Y . . . , Z, that insect."[13] The rebellious poet scared his teacher Izambard: The letter of the *voyant* was a crossing of arms, hooting the "old imbecils" and "innumerable idiotic generations," while "mad anger [pushed him] toward the battle of Paris."*

A melancholy man, who complained of deriving little profit from his travels, was told by Seneca: "I am not surprised: you traveled with yourself." (Which is also what Ginsberg told me in Roche.)

Traveling with yourself: Rimbaud *takes himself along* to Abyssinia. "In difficult moments he became overly rude," notes Bardey, "and threw out slurs at random, like 'that dirty country, X . . . ! the idiotic Y . . . , that imbecile of a Z . . . !' not to place himself above them, but simply from a mania."[14] His "calm and charming" letters (as his brother-in-law, Paterne Berrichon, calls them![15]) are chockful of the same kind of meekness toward his contemporaries. Rimbaud can only dream of wounds and bruises faced with "Labatut's dirty whore,"† some "dirty Greek,"†† the Bardey brothers, "those beasts,"§ or "those —— servants of yours." He gave the same treatment to countries and individuals: the Egyptians: "a heap of curs and bandits";‖ the English: "their Gordon is an idiot, their Wolseley an ass."¶ And the universe "gets it" because of humanity: "Harar is surrounded by brigands";** Obock is "an atrocious colony, colonized by a dozen buccaneers."†††

Rimbaud is hard, his tongue cutting. Bad moods turn into action: The "heartless man" does not control himself,

---

* May 13, 1871.
† December 20, 1889.
†† April 30, 1890.
§ October 22, 1885.
‖ February 15, 1881.
¶ December 30, 1884. We already heard that the Europeans there were just "a few idiotic business employees" (April 14, 1885).
** November 7, 1881.
†††April 14, 1885.

he explodes. Getting mad at his guest in Harar, Jules Borelli, he hands him a broom and demands he sweep the
house.[16] He kicks and terrorizes the dogs that come and piss
on the stacked pelts in his store. Monsignor Jarosseau claimed
that he poisoned two thousand of them![17] Savouré writes to
him: "It seems people now call you Rimbaud or the terror
of dogs." Brémond, who knows and fears him, also makes
fun: ". . . as long as you don't go poisoning all the dogs of
Harar, including hyenas, sheep and even Greeks." When he
is ill, finally, he proves a poor patient. He takes to his bed,
but from it orders his employees about through a window:
"I set up a bed between my cash register, my ledgers, and
a window from which I could supervise the scales in back
of the yard."* Arthur Rimbaud's "meanness" (his nickname, *Kerani,* "Meanie," in Aden) came out of an old, un-
remitting anger (the *hiraregna* Ato Chami referred to: I'm
willing to believe he scared the Harar kids!), an anger that
grew and grew till he could send Savouré the letter of April
1890 ("You'll never have had anything, nothing, absolutely
nothing, nothing of nothing!") An anger he carried all the
way to Marseille (a surgeon of Conception Hospital tells his
family in a still unpublished letter of admitting this bizarre
person whose behavior he finds hateful[18]) and which, if the
other world has not appeased it, might by now fill the cosmos! But whence did it come, this anger—or, rather, does
it have a single root? Germain Nouveau homes in on our
"absolute ignorance of 'what' makes Rimbaud angry." And
Verlaine observed "his unconscious anger at the why."[19]

His nerves raw, taut like cables, Rimbaud was always,
we might say, in a state of *legitimate offense.* By his manner
of always defending himself, he seems to insist that the
aggression does not come from him; he constantly protests
his innocence. Lacan has recognized protestations of innocence as "the subject's most characteristic form of expression in Western society."[20] But Rimbaud's denial is different

*To Isabelle, Marseille, July 15, 1891.

from the claim of the individual not to be responsible for the horrors of the world he lives in. Neither does it resemble the ancient version of the claim to innocence, the negative confession recited before Osiris, the forty-three articles of the prayer of the dead ("I have not slandered God"; "I have not extorted taxes from a peasant"; "I have not robbed a widow!"). Rimbaud is absolutely pure, that is, outside all relationships; pure of the communal crime on which society is based, of corrupting institutions and the "black" values of the West: "Judge, you are a nigger; merchant, you are a nigger." Church, army, and judiciary trigger only revolt in him, patricide as deliverance: "I armed myself against justice."* He has been purged of the sin of being—"criminals are as disgusting as eunuchs; I am intact and don't care."† All his life he pursues a crime he has not committed. The ideal Poet, defined as Seer, is "a great criminal."†† Crime, the dreaded, radical act of freedom, the dream of glory and insolent defiance, keeps him from capitulating to love, which would mean surrender to God, integration in society. Crime purifies the hands of the poet, proud and more alone than God. It is his act of innocence.

The idea of crime obsessed the young Rimbaud, who insisted in Paris that "it was important to kill Cabaner" and in Charleville explained the need to exterminate the "nuisances":[21] "I would not hesitate, if need be, to have recourse to assassination and would feel divine pleasure in contemplating my victim's agony." It haunted the punk who threatened Lepelletier with a dessert knife, stabbed Verlaine's thigh and hands, wounded Carjat with Verlaine's sword stick.§ It haunted the *voyant* who frightened the "Mad Virgin" ("Oh, those days when he walks with an air of crime!"),‖ who flaunted his wild pleasure in defilement ("from my window I see . . . a pretty Crime whimpering in the

---

* "Jadis . . ." ("Once . . ."), *A Season in Hell.*
† "Bad Blood," *A Season in Hell.*
†† To Paul Demeny, May 15, 1871.
§ November 1871; January 1872.
‖ "Délires" I, *A Season in Hell.*

mud of the street"*) and enjoyed his depravity ("I lay down in the slime. I dried myself in the air of crime"†). At the end of *A Season in Hell,* with crime a failure, he still protests against his downfall and reaffirms his innocence: "With what crime . . . have I deserved my present weakness?"††

Then Rimbaud tries to live, pursuing his education as an innocent victim. According to Ottorino Rosa, he accidentally killed a worker by a stone thrown in self-defense, which was the reason for his sudden departure from Cyprus.[22] In Abyssinia, "far from the old assassins," he came to know the hopes and appetites for suffering of all emigrants. "He was a bitter and irascible man," Borelli remembers.[23] He felt he had not accomplished anything. But let somebody—anybody, perhaps because he is anybody—try to treat him as an inferior, and Rimbaud starts a quarrel. It is a mistake to *seek him out,* in the wider sense of the term. In these sparsely populated countries, the altercations multiply, as if his defensiveness demanded more frequent sallies, as if his identity were more fragile, more threatened. "After quarrels . . . with the paymaster and his engineer,"§ Rimbaud speaks of "disagreeable dealings with the administration," ‖ recriminates against "the pure and simple swindling"¶ that he is victim of. "And anyway . . . these people are skinflints and crooks, good for nothing but exploiting their employees."** He quits the Bardeys with a row and a loss: "I quit my job in Aden after a violent row with those disgusting blackguards who think they can make me a beast of burden forever."†††[24]

* * *

* "Ville" ("City"), *Illuminations.*
† "Once . . . ," *A Season in Hell.*
†† "Matin" ("Morning"). Cf. "What have I done, I thought, to be thus, in all ways thrown back on the impossible?" (Georges Bataille, *L'Impossible, Complete Works,* Vol. 3, p. 154).
§ Aden, August 17, 1880.
‖ Harar, September 2, 1881.
¶ Aden, January 22, 1882.
** Ibid.
††† Aden, October 22, 1885.

Rimbaud, who always had a police file[25]—in France, Belgium, England—had to appear before the municipal police of Aden for assault and battery in 1883. He had slapped the shopkeeper Ali Chemmak.* Arab witnesses had laid hold of Rimbaud to permit the said Ali to repay him in kind, hitting him in the face and tearing his clothes. He also came to know the Abyssinian courts. In 1887, Rimbaud pleaded before Menelik his case against the leader of his caravan,[26] who was defended by "the formidable bandit Abou-Beker."† A few weeks later, in Ankober, Labatut's widow sued him before the *azzaze,* the local judge. In the course of these improvised court sessions (which the cantankerous Abyssinians loved, arguing violently, their *chemma* thrown over the shoulder, supporting their claims with bets and swearing "on Menelik's death" that they were telling the truth), the widow Labatut, with the help of the French traveler Hénon and two old Amharan lawyers, fought tooth and nail. "After hateful debates where [he] had now the upper now the lower hand,"†† Rimbaud obtained from the *azzaze* a warrant of seizure to the dead man's house: He found "only a few old shorts which the widow grabbed with fiery tears . . . and a dozen pregnant slaves."§

"I am out of my element, sick, furious, stupid, upset." This as far back as August 25, 1870, in a letter from Charleville! Foretelling of certain failings. Having given up literature and all commerce with symbols, Rimbaud finds— and loses—himself in a Reality without beyond, every religious, cultural, and emotional tie cut by "his well-formulated vow of independence and high scorn for any adhesion to what he did not like to do or be."[27] He heads for open nature, for immense distances where nothing is named or deserves to be. He disappears and blends in; the dryness of

---

* To M. de Gaspary, Aden, January 22, 1883.
† To M. de Gaspary, Aden, November 9, 1887.
†† Ibid.
§ Ibid.

the soil invades his body, the thirst of the ground becomes his own hardness. We might say he found the most arid land to consecrate his own aridity. "Pure, for having purged all disgust," Tristan Corbière would say.[28] Worn down by the climate and his activities, resigned to the worst, violently preserving his solitude, he stresses the silence inside himself to the point of muteness. He slowly learns the values of the desert, waiting and endurance. His chances to overcome his disillusionment get slimmer. When the *voyant* had become aware his enterprise was in vain, the appeal of crime took the form of longing for the delights of damnation, of liberating transgression: "A crime, quick, that I may fall into nothingness, as decreed by human law."* The desert did not disarm Rimbaud. Anger is a state of the body, a way of turning one's arms against it, to be done with it. "Everyone carries his corpse inside himself," said Roger Gilbert-Lecomte. Rimbaud kills himself working, marching. Back with earth and sun, he will have sought out the place where his life would be worn out. His only real crime is perpetrated against himself; he runs to his ruin, pure ruin, in wandering and despair. . . . Read "May Banners" word for word, as if this poem had become fully real in Abyssinia:

> *It's alright for the seasons to wear me.*
> *I surrender, Nature, to you*
> *Both my hunger and all of my thirst.*
> . . . .
> *I have no illusions, on nothing;*
> *You smile at parents if you smile at the sun.*
> *I want to smile at nothing;*
> *But let my misfortune be free.*†

On the road to Harar, at dusk, we come across a small railroad station lost in the savanna, flying one of the rare

* "Night of Hell," *A Season in Hell.*
† "Bannières de mai," May 1872.

French flags here. A marabou guards the top of the tall tree opposite. The traveler begins to miss home, sweet home. Charles says we have to go back to the Ardennes and film his "tobacco road" to come full turn.

"When are you leaving again?" "As soon as possible," replies Rimbaud (legs stretched under the table, a hat, a big glass of brandy—in a drawing by Delahaye).[29] Leaving. With each new departure, a new chance to exist. Once you start traveling, you never stop. After the mountains, more mountains. But "the forgotten fatherland is hard on its terrible sons," writes Verlaine, evoking the fugitive, the prodigal son. Even his "Drunken Boat" heading into the storm had known nostalgia: "I miss Europe with its old parapets." Later, on the shore of the Red Sea, Rimbaud misses his "black-current river." His dread of being fixed, held, imprisoned, his will to forget and the call of the unknown sometimes fuse with his fear of "disappearing among these peoples."[*] The need for refuge is a constant with Rimbaud (see the inns in his *Poems*), and his chronic project of returning "to France next fall"[†] shows his longing for rest ebbing back to his point of departure: a *catabasis*. Both Ovid and Kerouac have connected travel with the theme of regret, and departure calls for return in the cyclical figure of travel (voyage, periplum) that the great travel books have described from the beginning: stories of return like the Exodus from Egypt, the *Odyssey* leading home to Ithaca, or the Persians groaning like ghosts on returning from Salamis. The circular escapades of Rimbaud, who went home to Charleville every winter and in Abyssinia felt the desire to go back to his country, seem to copy the movement of "enclosure" we find in his work, "the limit of departure . . . and its annulment."[30] There was the evening in summer 1879 when

---

[*]Harar, May 6, 1883.

[†]"I'm counting on seeing you in France next fall, before the winter of 1886–1887" (Tadjoura, December 10, 1885). Rimbaud plans to "go back to France to buy stock" (Aden, November 18, 1885), to find a wife in the Ardennes, to take part in the World's Fair, and, finally, to "take care of [his] health in France" (Aden, April 30, 1891).

he joined Millot and Delahaye in a little café on the Place Ducale, wearing a new suit, sure sign of imminent departure. "All evening he was unusually merry. At eleven he left us—for good. He only came back to Charleville twelve years later, in a coffin."[31] "Going back would mean burying myself,"* he wrote in Arabia. And the man who associated Europe physically with cold and symbolically with death ("I can no longer go back to Europe; first of all I would die in winter",† "If I come back, it can only be in summer"††), who longed for an everlasting summer, would find cold and rain in summer 1891 in Roche—a rotten summer that year—and then his death on a tenth of November, in winter: return to the native land, the point of departure, the point of failure.

However, symbolically the loop does not close. Once having left, Rimbaud could not return. For one thing, he had not reached his inaccessible goal—he never considered himself rich enough ("saved!"§) to live up to his hope of a glorious homecoming. "And then, what's there to do in France?"‖ Nowhere does he allow himself to stay. Like a swimmer who ventured too far out and is carried off by the sea, Rimbaud felt he could not return to his hometown, where he thought nobody any longer remembered or cared for him. The current had pulled him to the other side of the mirror, and he no longer recognized himself: "I would be a stranger in France."¶ And the break with Europe had gotten more pronounced, had attained even his language: "Every day I lose more the taste for the climate and life-styles of Europe."** The classical return-cycle is played out as a spiral of no return: In Abyssinia, Rimbaud thinks of going back

* Aden, October 8, 1887.
† Cairo, August 23, 1887.
†† Aden, January 15, 1885. Or June 23, 1891: "What would I do, where would I stay? If I came to you, the cold would chase me away."
§ "Bad Blood," *A Season in Hell*.
‖ Aden, October 8, 1887.
¶ Ibid.
** Harar, May 6, 1883.

to France; when he does return, "he has but one idea: to leave."[32] In Marseille, "definitely reduced to being an ex-patriate,"[*] he dreams of Harar: "I hope to return there . . . I will always live there."[†] It is finally Harar that takes on the name of the inaccessible place; Harar becomes impossible: "Shall I not find a stone to lay my head on and a house to die in?"[33] he asked Isabelle. There was no place for Rimbaud: He would die writing to the director of the Messageries Maritimes shipping line. His last words, dictated with his last glimmer of consciousness, spoke of infinite departure, of impossible return: "Let me know at what time I shall be carried on board."[††]

We get back to Harar at sundown. Our caravan of Land Rovers is spread out on the long winding road in front of the purple mountains. Out of curiosity we stop before the "Makonnen" School, whose courtyard is plastered with huge realistic posters on which healthy peasants, workers, and soldiers resolutely look toward the radiant future rising on the left, the side of the garden. Before the polling place closes, our cameraman takes a few shots of veiled women dropping their ballot in a small basket under the photos of the candidates. These citizens freely make their choice on aesthetic principles—"by the face," the only possible choice when all candidates are of the same party. Lapizo, who has "accompanied" us from Addis Ababa, comments with conviction on this gesture through which the masses take charge of their destiny. According to Fidel Castro's formula, Ethiopia is one of the third world countries with the chance to pass without transition from underdevelopment to socialism—that is, straight to poverty, the suppression of their few freedoms and the pillage of their country by Big Brother.

As the Rovers take off again, Lapizo shouts that "Rim-

* Marseille, June 24, 1891.
† Ibid.
†† Letter to the director of the Messageries Maritimes, Marseille, November 9, 1891.

baud was a capitalist," and our discussion gets lost in the fields. Rimbaud admitted as much: "Who could harm me who have nothing but my person? A capitalist of my kind."* But the *Communard!* The author of a communist constitution![34] Verlaine, who knew a thing or two about it, abandons him to public obloquy: "He joins merchants trafficking in Aden . . . one might say in bourgeois terms, he *settled down*" (Verlaine's emphasis).[35] The failure of his utopia— "to change life!"—a failure that has nothing in common with that of another utopia, Breton's "transforming the world" (two "passwords" that Breton joins in a staggering amalgam), this failure of the impossible breaks all communal impulse in Rimbaud, vows him to his essential solitude. But here the political tribunals rear their head: "Arthur Rimbaud, you wrote *ironically,* did you not: 'Merchant, colonist, medium?'† And now you have *become one.* We judge you unworthy of your poems."[36]

He had gone through it all at great speed. In May 1868 he addressed verses to the Imperial Prince, then cheered the September Fourth Republic. Six months later he was a sympathizer of the Commune—and soon after left the "Western morass."†† Same speed, same getting out of politics in his texts, which we might color from pink to purple (from "Le Forgeron" ["The Blacksmith"] that Verlaine thought "much too *democsoc*"[37] to the red-and-black of "Bad Blood").

In Abyssinia, Rimbaud will no longer get "mixed up in political affairs,"§ of which he had once expected salvation. However, at the beginning of his stay he kept up with the news, commented on it. He was no longer a "Seer," but he was lucid—enough to deplore the "stupidity" of French politics: "No other nation has a colonial policy as inept as

---

* Aden, April 15, 1882. Or Aden, January 15, 1885: "Don't think I am a capitalist . . ."
† "Ce qu'on dit au poète à propos de fleurs" ("What Is Said to the Poet in Regard to Flowers"), 1871.
†† "The Impossible," *A Season in Hell.*
§ "Bad Blood," *A Season in Hell.*

France," which wastes "its money in pure losses in impossible places"*—like Obock ("a coal depot"† "colonized by a dozen buccaneers"††), instead of Djibouti whose future he foresaw.[38] He regrets that France fixed on the barren Red Sea coast instead of advancing "toward the plateaus of the interior (Harar) which are beautiful country, healthy and fertile,"§ that France got stuck in Tonkin‖ ("a miserable region impossible to defend against invasions"¶) instead of establishing itself in Madagascar. A shrewd observer of the European rivalries in the Horn of Africa, which had become a strategic stake with the opening of the Suez Canal in 1869, Rimbaud criticized likewise the "absurd policy"** of the English and the advances of Count Antonelli,††† the most eminent Italian diplomat whose prodigality toward Menelik (ten thousand rifles to be used against Emperor John)[39] ironically helped drive out the Italians in 1896. Or again, he deplored the French government's "taste for renunciation," which Bismarck had noticed and exploited in 1880. To judge by his ironical synthesis of fresh information on the covert war between Menelik and Emperor John that he sent to the *Bosphore égyptien,* combining this with the commentaries he could have made on Menelik's subtle game with the three European nations, our erratic Rimbaud would have made a perfect correspondent for the journals that refused his articles.

"Racist, colonialist!" they cry in the Café du Commerce.[40] Rimbaud, who now left it to others to take charge of humanity,§§ was simply reacting—for some time still—as

---

*   Tadjoura, December 30, 1884.
†   Aden, October 7, 1884.
†† Aden, April 14, 1885.
§   Tadjoura, December 30, 1884.
‖   Aden, May 26, 1885: "France is in a ridiculous position in Tonkin."
¶   Tadjoura, December 30, 1884.
** Ibid.
††† To Jules Borelli, Harar, February 25, 1889.
§§ The poet is "in charge of humanity, even of animals . . ." (To Paul Demeny, May 13, 1871).

a French national. Do we need to recall that colonialism was from the start espoused by the Left also, that it was meant to export "progress" and the generous ideas of the Revolution, including education and human rights? We are approaching Harar, and I am not going to stop and answer people who *don't understand that they don't understand* and for whom, as La Bruyère said, "to speak is to attack,"[41] as with that African tribe that has only one word for "talk" and "fight." Superficial minds, owners of "truths," narrow-minded prosecutors will not be able to see Rimbaud's *innocence:* Like the alternating effusiveness and violence in his poems, Rimbaud's aggressiveness and altruism in Harar are forms of innocence.

I am struck by one particularity of this "absolutely peaceful and totally apolitical man," as Scarfoglio describes him.[42] At the time of Rimbaud's wanderings in Africa and Arabia, France is going through one of the most virulent ideological fevers of its history. "Revenge!": Déroulède sounds the charge against Prussia, missing no occasion to climb the statue of Strasbourg on the Place de la Concorde until death strikes him, symbolically, in August 1914, a few weeks before the outbreak of the war he had called for to his last breath. Nationalism, bruised in 1871, becomes rampant in the 1880s and will be quenched only by carnage. "Heroes of Valmy . . ./We left you sleeping with the Republic/. . . the de Cassagnacs remind us we are not done with you!"* wrote Rimbaud in the Mazas jail in 1870. The same Paul de Cassagnac rages in the paper *L'Autorité* (February 21, 1891): "We have an open wound in our side, a wound that will never heal and that we do not fear to keep bleeding in fierce hope of healthy reprisals." From this open wound, Fustel de Coulanges and Ernest Renan derive their theory of the nation. People in the most remote villages rush to read the *Almanach du drapeau (Flag Almanac).* School re-

*"Morts de quatre-vingt-douze" ("The Dead of '92").

ports picture black clouds in the East. In 1885, Macé writes a preface to a *Rifle Manual for Grammar and High Schools and Citizens' Reserve.* On the last day of classes, often after having read Daudet's "Last Class," the teachers would write on the blackboard: "Child, you shall be a soldier." The rise of nationalism—and the anti-Semitism that goes with it, as we know—poisons the intellectual life. Rémy de Gourmont loses his job with the National Library for writing in his article, "The Patriotic Toy,"[43] that he was not bothered by the loss of a province or two and that the attitude of the revenge-criers seemed "indecent" to him. Petitions circulate. But not all "intellectuals," as Clemenceau will call them during the Dreyfus Affair, are vigilant. Mallarmé votes for Boulanger in 1886. Already in 1875, on leaving jail, Verlaine had written Rimbaud: "The Church has created modern civilization, science, and literature. The Church has in particular created France, and France is dying of having broken with it. . . . I am surprised that you don't see this, it is striking."[44] In 1884 (the year Rimbaud writes, for example: "For I personally don't know where I'll be led to next, by which roads, where, why, and how!"*) appears *À Rebours (Against the Grain),* the great book of this generation. In it, Huysmans shows a Des Esseintes (in whom everybody recognizes himself) disgusted with a world of "bullies and imbeciles," escaping "anywhere out of this world"—a world that Léon Bloy vomits in *Le Désespéré.*

"Send me any old newspaper so that I know what goes on," Rimbaud asks at the beginning of his stay in Harar, on May 4, 1881. But soon the "different man," "the stranger" he becomes, loses all interest in the news "over there." "You give me political news. If you only knew how little I care! I haven't touched a newspaper in more than two years. All these debates are incomprehensible to me now": Harar, May 6, 1883.

Yes, this is what strikes me as we get back to Harar:

*Aden, May 5, 1884.

Rimbaud in Abyssinia was *unscathed* by ideology. He remained fundamentally *pure,* in the way the Greeks opposed the man of the city, the political animal, *politikos,* to the marginal, the madman left aside: the *idiotikos.* Rimbaud the idiot. He never talked about the blue border through the Vosges Mountains, never thought about it either. He remained the only member of his party: the party of "free freedom."

It is night when we reach Harar. After a long day in the sun, the whole crew falls into bed as one, with crossed arms. But the hyenas are coming out of the forest that borders the *ouébi,* rending the night with their cries, and the dogs bark after them. We filmed them cowering back from the blinding light of the projectors; we saw their reddish, bloodshot eyes, flecked with little green spots of decay. "The only way to scare them off if they come too close, is throwing firebrands at them," Bardey noted.[45] Disgraced animal, the hyena is a beast of the dark. In certain tribes it was claimed that white men had hyena blood. Rimbaud heard their morbid cries so often they must have fed his despair. " 'You shall remain a hyena,' cries the demon" at the beginning of *A Season in Hell.* "All action flatters the hyena within us," says Cioran. . . . The Harar sun is too strong for reflection. It is at night that you think, when the hyenas' laughter keeps you awake and carries off all conclusion.

Sitting alone on my backpack by the narrow rails that run straight to the horizon, I wait for the Franco-Ethiopian Railroad. The landscape trembles with heat.

On our first day, leaving Addis in the morning, we arrived in Diredawa at nightfall. In the opposite direction, the train coming from Djibouti is announced for noon—ideal hour for shooting my sequence of "the explorer arrives in Harar" in the picturesque Diredawa station. The rattletrap slowly appears toward one-thirty. At the curve, I run along and climb up on the step, hanging on to the outside of the train (as with Indian buses, there are nearly as many black travelers clinging to the outside of the cars as are inside, crowded together with various sheep). The train pulls into the station packed with an incredibly dense and multicolored crowd. Among them, our technicians with tripod, cables, and camera, trying to run and find a good angle. I look for my friend Sancerni, who is supposed to meet me in the mob. We are to "link up," maintain continuity with the preceding sequence in all the details specified in the script. But for us, this fictional meeting, Sancerni's fraternal welcome, means good-bye. Charles Brabant lifts his two thumbs above the press. A sign of joy: He got a good shot of the arrival. An hour later, the end of our stay, new departure, we are leaving. But in a certain sense, *I can't leave, can't get over* Harar. And I have chosen never to go back there—except in these infinitely repeatable images.

8
LITERATURE

Regrets on which to
build a hell
O that an oblivious heaven
would answer my prayers
—Apollinaire

Seen from the plane, the Dankali Desert is a brown and black surface, with cracks as in a Cranach painting. Now we are above a dark green Shoa, at an altitude of ten thousand meters. Lapizo touchingly does not recognize his country, like the peasant in Malraux's *L'Espoir (Man's Hope)* who takes his first airplane. By the time we have had a cough drop, a cigarette we are in: Addis Ababa—a four months' march for Rimbaud.

The Hilton: "Welcome," say the stylish porters barely skimming the rug. Jazz in the elevators, turkey cries in the lobby. In the "American Bar," the "Gentleman from Cocody." From my room on the twelfth floor, I have a view of the natural thermal swimming pool filmy with sun oil, where Marshal Idi Amin Dada is snorting, fiercely guarded by paratroopers in camouflage uniform.[1] On the lawn, in the sun, twelve Germans in white shirt and tie around a conference table with pitchers of orangeade. A picket fence separates this luxurious rabbit hutch from a shantytown built of corrugated iron. On the dirt road, a few women slowly carry sacks to the huts. Pure air, snatches of voices from both sides.

Under the tall pepper tree in the garden, this side of the fence, I encounter a successor of César Tian and Riès, from Marseille also, plump, in white shorts.[2] We have nothing to say to each other, but I think of that other industrialist, M. Besse, who was eighty and a millionaire when he told Philippe Soupault how he had been able to put Rimbaud's ideas to work.[3] All Rimbaud lacked was consistency. He always complained of not filling his piggybank: "The years go by," he wrote, "and I've no savings."[*] He always lacked a penny to make a pound. "I would like to send you at least 10,000 francs, but as business is poor . . ."[†] A rolling stone gathers no moss: "Business is bad . . . if you have only a small capital here, chances are you will lose it rather than see it multiply; because you are surrounded by a thousand dangers, and if you want the least bit of comfort, the cost of living is more than you earn."[††] In December of the same year, "business is very bad."[§] But he concedes: "I have now 13,000 francs in hand"—a sum that his posthumous brother-in-law will with exasperating bourgeois solicitude transform into 40,000 francs,[4] as Marcel Coulon was able to uncover.

Going again over Rimbaud's letters riddled with figures, I add up columns in the margin of my note-and-account-book. In January 1885, Rimbaud has 13,000 francs[‖] and worries about not augmenting his capital: "My profits . . . cover no more than my miserable appointments." In April 1885, since he does not *"spend one penny,"* (Rimbaud's em-

* Aden, January 15, 1885.
† Aden, July 10, 1884.
††Aden, September 10, 1884.
§ Aden, December 30, 1884.
‖ Aden, January 15, 1885: "My capital is now 13,000 francs and will be about 17,000 by the end of the year. It will have taken me five years to amass this sum. . . . My work here consists in buying coffee. I buy approximately two hundred thousand francs' worth a month. In 1883 I had bought more than 3 millions' worth . . . i.e. an average of three, four thousand francs' worth a year: you see employees are poorly paid everywhere."

phasis), "I still have 14,500 fr[ancs] in hand," which multiply in spite of all. In September, "the small capital I have (16,000 francs) is losing its value because it is in rupees; all this is awful." Then a bout of feverish excitement: The arms caravan for Menelik is to be a gold mine and double his investment: "If my partner hadn't died I would have made about 30,000 francs,* whereas . . . I come out of the deal with a loss of 60 percent of my capital and a month of atrocious fatigue."† But his little nest egg in foreign currency is safe: "I find myself, after two years of strenuous effort, with the 15,000 francs I started out with."†† With this adventure, his projects for getting rich quick have gone out the window. Rimbaud tightens his belt heavy with gold coins and lives on his margin of profit as Catoblepas did eating his feet: "If business is not brilliant . . . at least I'm not losing."§ He cautiously proceeds along the lines of war economics: "I'm doing better than my business which is lots of trouble to little avail. . . . My capital is not growing; I think I am sliding back rather than advancing."‖ A hardworking retailer, he amasses stock and lives now "without hope of being a millionaire soon."¶ People coming here are in no danger of becoming millionaires—except in fleas."** His mother who, for a change, understands him very well, groans in chorus. La Bruyère said that "nothing is more stable than a mediocre fortune." Rimbaud? A merchant who wanted to get rich and did not succeed: This is what book after book repeats. However, aside from money itself not being his goal, the way Rimbaud keeps stressing the bad side of his deals makes us forget his assets: At the sudden liquidation of his accounts in April 1891, he receives from César Tian a draft

* To his family, Cairo, August 23, 1887.
† To M. de Gaspary, Aden, July 30, 1887.
††In fact, he substantiates later, "sixteen thousand and some hundred francs in gold; it weighs about eight kilos" (Cairo, August 23, 1887).
§ Aden, October 8, 1887.
‖ Harar, January 10, 1889.
¶ Harar, August 4, 1888.
**Harar, May 18, 1889.

on 37,450 francs-or. "A small fortune," César Tian will say to Savouré, which at the current value of its weight in gold represents a substantial pile of more than a million francs Fabius.[5] Like Seneca, the man of 80 million sesterces, Rimbaud was *touching his goal* after a decade of enormous efforts—at the moment of death. We cannot help hearing his final balance, his *settled* accounts, his wealth in the delirious inventory of his last breath:

ONE LOT: ONE TOOTH ONLY.
ONE LOT: TWO TEETH.
ONE LOT: THREE TEETH.
ONE LOT: FOUR TEETH.
ONE LOT: TWO TEETH.*

11 518,8
115,3
————————
11 633,11
Arthur Rimbaud
June 1, 1886

Addis. The Néfassié district, meaning literally "the Girls Who Talk to the Wind," so called in memory of the first telephone company set up by Menelik, who was a telecommunications enthusiast[6] (after having received the visit of a stranger, he liked to the phone to call back the visitor on his way home). I spend a long time bargaining for prayer books and healer's manuals written in the Ge'ez language, red-and-black manuscripts with wood covers, whose beauty is even enhanced for me by their being incomprehensible. On the symbolic level of exchange, I buy words and think of Rimbaud's silence, his giving up literature: Words had been gold, they turned into silver.[7] Rimbaud switched among currencies—rupees, talers, dollars, francs in gold—as he

*Marseille, to the director of Messageries Maritimes, November 9, 1891.

changed among the various languages he continued to learn:
Arabic, Amharic, Oromo, Galla. . . .

The symbol (*sym-bolon* coin that represents the bond between word and thing, their mythic unity) being broken,
Rimbaud transfers the word's power to transform and communicate onto money. He passes from searching for mythical gold in poetry★ to silver "scraped up" in reality—but
silver with a *symbolic* value (standing for rest, salvation, Indian summer): This symbolic value is the *continuity* of an
abstraction always searched in "the unknown," always inaccessible, the reality of the paltry dream[8] ("If ever I have
some money"†). Leaving the materialistic Occident (if he
had not already left it by way of poetry) for reality, for the
Orient of his childhood dreams, Rimbaud does not reach
the supreme stage—the alchemist's work turns black, the
searcher for gold gets lost. The money belt that weighs down
his haunches stands less for the tangible realization of a
longing repeated in the poems than for the pursuit of "the
impossible" that regenerates from its very failure—the goal
within reach and yet inaccessible: "Crying, I saw gold—and
could not drink."†† "In comparison to his failure, his poetry hardly gets off the ground," says Bataille.[9]

Was he "never again to care for words? We cannot admit that," spouted Paterne Berrichon, docile follower of Isabelle's official theory.[10] As the poet's fame grew, certain
witnesses (Monsignor Jarosseau, Françoise Grisard) began to
remember that Rimbaud was writing in Harar. "We had no
idea that he was a talented poet," Savouré makes clear, though
he had seen Rimbaud write "day and night at a rickety table" in November 1888.[11] Bardey, consulted after four editions of Rimbaud's works in 1897, remembered that "he

★ Gold chain, golden sparks, golden laundry, golden slope, golden dawn, golden
  liquid, gold star, golden boat (*A Season in Hell* and *Illuminations*).
† "Le Pauvre Songe" ("The Paltry Dream"), "Comedy of Thirst," 1872.
†† "Alchemy of the Word," *A Season in Hell*.

regretted having despised all that . . . and secretly prepared
. . . a comeback in the world of literature. He also read and
wrote constantly. We did not know what he was writing."
But we know what he read! And with bookkeeping, about
twenty correspondents, some stray impulses toward travel
writing or paid articles, Rimbaud had plenty to keep him
busy at his table during the long African evenings, enough
to arouse the curiosity of the Europeans surprised to see
anybody wield a pen in these parts. In his work *Nell'Harar,*
Robecchi-Bricchetti mentions Rimbaud's literary past,[12] but
the vagueness of the terms describing Rimbaud's writing allows us to doubt that he learned about it from the concerned party, if we can call him that.

It is only fair to recognize Verlaine's intellectual courage
and literary lucidity in publishing what works of Rimbaud's
he could gather. He was certainly the first to understand
their importance, jilted and humiliated though he had been
by their author. In the preface to his book *Les Poètes maudits,*
he was also the first to speak of a logic and necessity of
Rimbaud's abandoning poetry. "If M. Arthur Rimbaud by
chance gets to see these lines, we hope he will know we do
not judge people's motives and be assured that we entirely
(if with black sadness) approve his abandoning poetry, provided, as we do not doubt, that this was a logical, honest
and necessary step for him." Rimbaud never got this message, this commentary that says everything in three words.
In 1886, publication date of the *Illuminations,* he did receive
a book from Europe: an Amharic grammar.
    "He had certainly given up on everything and his old
ideas (if he ever held them otherwise than in words)," stated
Jules Borelli.[13] But it was precisely because he had, at least
for a time, believed in words and the mission of poetry, that
he withdrew from all communication. This experience had
been but a brief episode in his life, spectacularly fertile,
comparable to the life of the agave, the flower also called

aloe, which blooms once only, with flower clusters up to ten meters, and then dies. It is vain to hope for a rerun of the mystery. "I suppose," wrote Mallarmé, "that hoping for work from his mature years only hurts our exact interpretation of an adventure unique in the history of art."

From then on, there is a long line of hoaxes and nuisances: decadent pastiches that were in vogue in the 1880s, forty thousand lines of Rimbaud's allegedly found in Abyssinia, but never published[14]—in which I take pleasure recognizing the forty thousand francs his brother-in-law credited him with—some unpublished long poem that has not come out of the box where M. Carlo Zaghi found it, down to the verses chanted by Ato Chami. It is as if these spurious poems were to compensate for the lack we feel because Rimbaud's work is so slim, for our frustration with a genius whose capacities seemed unlimited. Moreover, they register a collective *protest* against a promise not fulfilled. "Why," asks Maurice Blanchot, "why does it seem so surprising that a mind with a talent for letters should turn his back on literature and lose all interest in an activity he excelled in? That this kind of refusal seems scandalous, only shows how incommensurate a value we attach to the writing of poetry."[15] We will not forgive Rimbaud our stupor at his not completing a body of work, denying even those strokes of lightning that still fascinate us, not smelting his intuitions in the reassuring mold of literature that would make them intelligible, refusing the role of the writer, and truly exemplifying a limit against which any society must protect itself to survive. It is a scandal that makes me feel dizzy and menaced as I begin sketching this book in the land where he stopped writing, a scandal that would forbid all writing on Rimbaud if his silence were not, as much as his poetry, *inimitable*.[16]

It remains a unique event in the history of literatures that the man who had raised poetry to a new perfection should abandon it. "Logical, honest and necessary," that abandonment has in the course of time become *the question that is not examined;* it is too mysterious, too hot. Breton thought so in one of his ramblings: "If I have caviled as little as possible at the reasons for Rimbaud's poetic renunciation, it is not that I am not interested, far from it, but it has become nearly impossible to sort them out."[17] So we prefer to avoid this "classical" question that in the end raises the problem of the power of writing. We prefer not to take up the challenge of *A Season in Hell:* "Try to tell of my fall and my sleep."*

Rimbaud did not cheat. He fused with poetry. "My fate depends on this book."† Nobody took in this power. He first knew lack of success (Banville rejected his submissions to the *Parnasse contemporain*), then immense disappointment on discovering the Paris poets of 1871. When he returned to the Latin Quarter in 1873 with six copies of *A Season in Hell,* he was cut by everybody. (His bad reputation was solidly established, and he was held responsible for Verlaine's imprisonment.) He could not help feeling disgusted, which is what he had so carefully prepared for. Only Germain Nouveau spoke to him.[18] And on Place de l'Odéon, a brother in spirit. . . . If back in Roche, according to Isabelle's memory, he threw the few remaining copies of *A Season* into the fire,[19] this auto-da-fé signals the end of his literary career:[20] This "book of one of the damned"†† tossed to the flames is an apotheosis of disgust, his most certain act of purity.

> *The world is vile;*
>
> . . . .
>
> *Live and leave your obscure*
> *Misfortune to the fire.*§

* "Morning."
† To Ernest Delahaye, "Laïtou" (Roche), May 1873.
†† ". . . dear Satan . . . let me tear out for you these few, hideous sheets from the notebook of one of the damned" ("Once . . . ," *A Season in Hell*).
§ "Age d'or" ("The Golden Age").

The admiration and fascination that Rimbaud's renunciation inspires have no doubt to do with the fact that the ability to write (which he possessed like nobody else) does not interest him. It only leads to beauty—in the sense that Nicolas Poussin had very early given to aesthetics: "The aim of art is to please." Rimbaud also despises painting that only leads to *"contemplostate"*: The creative *faculty* alone interests him. Rimbaud's disillusionment goes much deeper than the modern disillusionment with the *capacity* of words ("What can literature do?" asked Sartre. "Next to a dying child, *La Nausée* carries no weight"): The *voyant* had, after Novalis and Michelet, expected a rebirth of the world from language! The theme of Medea could be seen in the burned chapbook of 1873, of supernatural powers destroyed by a collectivity. But the poet's fundamental disappointment is of a different order. It is the Promethean fall of the poet who comes to see the vanity of his enterprise: In short, Rimbaud gives up poetry when he admits to himself that a steam turbine has more of a chance to affect reality than "a thousand antitheses with sweet vignettes and frolicking cupids."*

So the creative period is clearly opposed to the Abyssinian one, to Harar as symbol and synonym of silence, of aridity; but it already presents the same form—is the matrix—of the "impossible" that forever drives Rimbaud, in Java, in Stockholm, in Africa, or in Arabia. Moreover, poetry seems one project among many in Rimbaud's life, the most sublime, the only one addressed to us—but still one among a hundred others, all with the same kind of absolute demand, as unfulfillable as "a summer of fifty years of uninterrupted sunshine," the same radical continuity of instability, of love of aporia. Poetry was a road taken, but *retraced* like so many others, brief or ludicrous.

Leaving "the Girls Who Talk to the Wind," it occurred to me that silence is already contained in language, that all

* With these words he presented his poems to Demeny on June 10, 1871.

words intrinsically hold reasons for forsaking them. I am not speaking of giving up at the difficulty of all communication, of the silence threatening every word we put forth, but of the secret movement within language that leads any demand for truth toward silence. Walking the long avenue up to the Town Hall, I remembered some shreds of a theory I developed as a young man to explain the lightning blaze of Rimbaud's poetry. What intrigued me was . . . the *chevilles* (the "hinges," as the French call padding for the sake of rhyme). Our classical verse forms with their constraints of rhythm and rhyme make them inevitable. "It is unfortunate for our poetry," said Chamfort, "that as soon as we see the word 'man' at the end of a line, we can be sure that the next verse will end on 'what he can' or 'his life's span.' "[21] Even the best-crafted padding remains discursive (of what I called "noetic" order), a persistence of the other genre, prose. Rimbaud, the Seer, disdained "rhymed prose":* Narrative equals impure. "Hinges!" This carpentry term also points to the labor that a fixed form (quatrain, sonnet, etc.) imposes: what Valéry called the double labor of emotion followed by formal elaboration, the anvil that turns the poet into a liar or mere craftsman. After the enjambments of "The Drunken Boat" (daring for their time, or trying to be), emotional necessity and the demands of his poetic material had led Rimbaud to free verse by 1872 ("Marine," "Mouvement"). Here emotion receives its exact form. In free verse, which eliminates all padding, there subsists a form, a vestige of classical verse. It marks a transitional period. The few constraints it still imposes disappear in the *Illuminations,* where the poetic matter *(hyle) immediately* finds its necessary form *(morphe).* This third stage in the dialectic of language, where working time coincides with emotion (time of the "walk-murmur"), is no longer "prose," but *pure poetic matter* dissolving all constraining form, a liberation of both through their fusion in the momentary truth of emotion (a "hyle-

*May 15, 1871.

morphism" that owes nothing to Aristotle though he coined the term). It joins the pure creation of the Greeks, the *poiein*.

This rapid moving toward greater depth in his language seemed even to recapitulate the main phases of the history of French poetry, in the way we see meteors flash by with dizzying speed at the end of a planetarium session—when the film of the stars accelerates under the dome. Like the herd of stars, poetry by itself would have slowly moved from "form" toward "matter," from the discursive, rhymed prose of the eighteenth century (epic or narrative phase, "noetic" poetry) via Romantic lyricism ("hyletic" phase) to the modern "hylemorphic" period (certain Surrealist texts, Char, Perse), which derives genealogically from Rimbaud. This "theory," which now makes me smile as I walk along, shows a quite Hegelian conception of language as the center of the world, poetry as the center of language, and Rimbaud as the center of poetry: a lover's theory. . . . I shall hold on to its conviction that the *voyant*'s need—"to find a language"—attained a new form (independent of Baudelaire's *Petits Poèmes en prose*), a new relation of mass and momentum, as the physicists say, a semantic condensation,[22] a grip on the *untouched*. In this sense, most of the poems of the *Illuminations* would come after *A Season in Hell:* And after this experience all other writing would have meant regression to Rimbaud. "Only true discourse makes authentic silence possible," says Heidegger.[23] Poetry occurs less in what is being said than in its passing through language all the way to silence, the beginnings, the inaudible. The greatness of this poet is not that he fell silent, but that he *arrived* at silence: Rimbaud's work was not abandoned, it is complete.

At the end of the *Illuminations,* Rimbaud felt this silence within himself: Harar is everywhere, in everyone. My path has led me to the market of Addis, the largest in Africa, but I see only Rimbaud looking for Menelik in Ankober. The "reasons" for giving up poetry, whether "necessary" or just sufficient, do still not explain why he *really* sought out Harar.

Daniel-Rops offers a comical hypothesis of the giving up: "If he fell silent, it is definitely because he was unable to reconcile the antagonistic directions implied in, the horizontal and vertical going beyond the theme of the city."[24] Obviously, Rimbaud did not call a press conference, as some people would today, and declare: I have decided to give up literature and I'll tell you why. . . . But he did tell; very clearly, in one word, to Isabelle: "because it was evil."[25]

It is in ethical terms that we must understand Rimbaud's renunciation. The theoretical conceptions of the *voyant,* the Seer—the only ones Rimbaud formulated—signaled an event. But they were ephemeral and, though pervasive in *A Season in Hell,* not applicable to his entire work, at least not to the part before 1871 and some of the *Illuminations.* But above all, in considering only the abstract intentions we would neglect the essential tie between poetry and life. The episode of *voyance* was first of all an experience, a practice. "He was not a man to be satisfied with theories," said Delahaye.[26] In order to reach the beyond, the new, Rimbaud thought he had to strip his thought and actions of all conformity that society instills in the individual to neutralize him. He thought he had to prepare the terrain of his sensitivity, "make [his] soul monstrous."* Enid Starkie realized that the "wallowing in the gutter"† necessary for *voyance* has always been underestimated: We must understand in the most literal sense the "immense disordering"†† the *voyant* imposed on himself. The only means to "make [himself] a Seer"§ was to

---

* To Paul Demeny, May 15, 1871.
† To Georges Izambard, May 13, 1871: "I wallow in the gutter as much as I can. Why? I want to be a poet and am working on making myself a *voyant* [a Seer]. . . . It's a matter of reaching the unknown by disordering all the senses."
†† To Paul Demeny, May 15, 1871.
§ To Georges Izambard, May 13, 1871.

risk everything without calculation—drugs, homosexuality, aggression, cultivating crime: "None of the sophistries of madness—the madness that is locked up—was lost on me." "Morality is a weakness of the brain. . . . As for me, I've loved a pig."* We would have to be strangers to the Rimbaldian alchemy not to recognize Verlaine[27] (or to see *only* him) in the "Mad Virgin"† of *A Season in Hell,* not to *witness* one of their scenes in this *Illumination*: "I lay down on my straw mat. And almost every night, as soon as I was asleep, my pitiful brother would get up with a sour mouth and eyes starting out of his head—just as he had dreamed to be!—and drag me to the room screaming out his dream of idiotic grief."†† Likewise, "the nightmare of constant stage-managing" Verlaine remembered in the poem called "Explication," and its various echoes—to Rimbaud: "Your memory, chockful of obscenities"[28]—allow us to imagine the intensity of "the rages, debauch, madness"§ that the Charleville boy turned to.

Yes, boy, basically. "Tropmann child!" cries Lepelletier.[29] *Infans,* "the one who does not speak," purity enacted, "the sad crouching child" of "The Drunken Boat," the boy who makes love to the summer dawn.‖ All his debauches and crimes amount to, after all, is poems, a worried mother, police alerts, a tormented adolescent sexuality acted out in men's rooms, without the maturity of Baudelaire's *Flowers of Evil.* Or the kind of excess in which all "not too serious" teenagers find their world of sensation.[30] "I imagine some angelic parent or relative awakened nightly by him crawling home on all fours, puking (I know what I'm talking about!) and other anti-toilet-training exploits."[31] We recognize Verlaine remembering Rimbaud. The wallowing was mostly a wallowing in dirt, shaking off his lice at Banville's house,

---

* "Délires" II, *A Season in Hell.*
† "Délires" I, *A Season in Hell.*
†† "Vagabonds," *Illuminations.*
§ "Bad Blood," *A Season in Hell.*
‖ "Dawn," *Illuminations.*

or the cynicism of the anecdote of "Cabaner's milk," which his biographers blush to tell.[32] Scatology and transgressions, treacheries, funny and silly provocations. . . . *Rein beau, vers l'aine,* this pun on their names ["handsome loins, toward anus"] gives us the tone. Ringing the consonant changes from purity to perversity, Mallarmé speaks aptly of "perverse and proud puberty." But as always, Rimbaud went very far in this enterprise (at least *in his own eyes,* which is what counts): "My health was in danger. Terror overcame me."* He had terrorized his friends to the point where they did not dare name him except by hypochoristic detours around the taboo: "the Senegalese, Him, Thing,"[33] reticent to name the "nice little rimb."[34] His name was as it were obscene, not to be touched: "Rimbaud (why should I be afraid to write his whole name?)," Germain Nouveau ventures.[35]

Parabolic failure of a sixteen-year-old "monster." Thinking of his "filthy memories" of Paris and London, Verlaine agreed that "it was evil." Thus Rimbaud, in his poems as in his letters from Africa and Arabia, is a constant reminder that the most daring adventure may be nonetheless trivial, and that the freest poetry will not save us from either contradiction or a humdrum life. In fact, few artists have enacted the contradictory principles of desire and reality with anything like Rimbaud's fury, until both turned on him. At which point, "fed up with being an obscene machine" (Verlaine, "Explication"), Rimbaud turns his back on *us* and goes off. "Sorry to have fed on lies. And now let's go."† As Fénéon placed the *Illuminations* "outside, and no doubt above, all literature,"[36] Verlaine took up the phrase "to put the man somehow outside humanity, his life outside and above ordinary lives. The work so gigantic, the man so free, his life so proud, so proud that we never heard from him again."[37]

*   *   *

*"Delirium" II, *A Season in Hell.*
†"Adieu," *A Season in Hell.*

"Far be it from me to judge his past as a *poet*," testified one of his first employers, Maurice Riès, in 1929, "but I can state with all my conviction that he was a *businessman with a passion* . . . who in conversation always expressed satisfaction that he had left behind what he called the pranks of his youth, a *past he abhorred*" (Riès's emphasis).[38] The passion of the walker, of the "considerable traveler," as Mallarmé called him, was to make his life over; for example, as a merchant without past, without memory, a merchant with a passion to forget, taking his quickest possible distance from "the horizon where the other collapsed."* When we hold the picture of the long-haired poet (whom Lepelletier nastily called "Mademoiselle Rimbaud" in 1871) or the angelic portrait Carjat gave us against the mummylike figure of the Abyssinian Rimbaud with his short gray hair, we cannot help seeing a contrary and equally rabid need to deny his former body—as if he lost his "forget-me-not-blue" eyes by stopping to write and took on eyes gray as a blind man's in the sun. Rimbaud's eyes are certainly a mystery.

He seeks himself and flees himself with a fierce determination to forget the past: "better Aden, even Aden, than elsewhere, Aden where I am unknown, where I'm completely forgotten."† Rimbaud blacks out his past as if trying to scrape off a low birth. "In spite of our long hours together," writes Jules Borelli, "I never asked him about his previous life, and he never spoke about it."[39]

On a few rare occasions, however, he let himself go far enough to confess his disgust with "all that time wasted for nothing," as he already wrote to Delahaye in March 1875. An Italian colleague, Ottorino Rosa, will remember: "In Harar, we often went on long trips of several days. . . . Very rarely did he speak of his past and even less of any poetical work. . . . Occasionally, however, he alluded to the vicissitudes and circumstances of his life. . . . I knew

*To Paul Demeny, May 15, 1871.
†Aden, September 10, 1884.

he expatriated himself in 1880 from disgust with the bohemian life he had led [in France]."[40]

But determination to forget does not give the power to
forget. Rimbaud had a good memory, even a "nasty" one,
that kept persecuting him in fits and starts.

In distant America, at the same period, a legendary young
bandit decided after many misdeeds to leave the United States
and go straight. Whenever Butch Cassidy turned around, he
would see dust raised by the mysterious riders always on
his heels, day after day, at the same distance. Symbolic image of the impossibility of returning to order, of fatal punishment, of irreparable destiny, these riders also tailed the
"supposed tradesman," and the past finally caught up with
him in the form of an unstamped letter addressed simply to:
"M. Arthur Rimbaud, in Harar," which has come down to
us as miraculously as it reached him. "We can assume,"
Mallarmé will write in 1896, "that the concerned party received the news of his fame with a proud lack of interest."
Laurent de Gavoty wrote him from Marseille on July 17,
1890: "Monsieur and dear Poet, I have read some of your
beautiful verse: this is to tell you that I would be happy and
proud to see the head of the decadent and symbolist school
contribute to *La France moderne* whose editor I am."

Alfred Bardey, taking a cure in Vichy toward the end of
1883, learned to his surprise that Rimbaud knew the poet
Verlaine . . . and well enough to use the familiar *tu*. Then,
on the boat of the Messageries Maritimes back to Aden,
Bardey met a journalist from *Le Temps,* Paul Bourde, who
was going to Tonkin as a war correspondent. An old classmate of Rimbaud's at the Charleville high school, Paul
Bourde told Bardey that his manager's poems had a certain
success in the Latin Quarter.[41] Bardey, all excited, gave
Rimbaud the news and heard in reply: "Absurd, ridiculous,
disgusting!" "Cleansings!" Rimbaud was to throw out to
Maurice Riès: "Those were only cleansings!" As far back as

December 1876, his "I'm no longer involved with that" had stunned Delahaye when he asked about Rimbaud's literary activities. To another classmate, Ernest Millot, who tried to bring up Verlaine after the Brussels trial, he said: "Don't stir up this heap of muck, it's too vile." Then in Roche, in 1891, to Dr. Beaudier asking the same question: "That really matters, shit on poetry." Bardey tried to talk to him about London: "My stay there? A period of drunkenness. . . . But don't talk to me about artists, I've known enough of those birds." Bardey will in turn understand: "He was aware he had ruined his life"; as Monsignor Jarosseau had understood: "I knew M. Rimbaud in 1882 and 1888 . . . he realized he had ruined his life with flights of the imagination that pushed him to glorify evil." As Rimbaud himself will say in his hospital room *about his life in Harar,* for he did not stop denigrating himself: "It's being pigheaded that spoiled it all."*

"The scrupulous honesty" that Maurice Riès and all the other Abyssinian witnesses mention, his austerity, and severity against himself bear out "his immense desire to redeem the past," which Isabelle noticed in Marseille. Rimbaud's life in Abyssinia seems an expiation of the "blameworthy excesses" Verlaine mentions in "Laeti et Errabundi," of the "unsated passions/insolent, out of bounds—limits transgressed beyond the pale." We might say Rimbaud felt an overwhelming desire to redeem, to *buy back,* less with money than with his person: He searches for a morality at all costs, without achieving peace, rest, or *respectability.* Even in his last moments, the riders are still there. According to Freud, the desire to break a taboo entails "shows of repentance, efforts toward expiation."[42] These efforts, it seems, won out over all others.

"One never recovers from a wound,"† he had written.

*July 15, 1891.
†February 15, 1891.

He had taken care not to succeed. His dream of paradise was left intact. This hope made his life as difficult as he could wish. "I suffer terribly from life": wrote Antonin Artaud from Abyssinia.[43] Like him, Rimbaud—who was obsessed with the idea of suicide in Marseille—proceeded in his own fashion to the "previous suicide" Artaud will talk about, "a suicide that makes us retrace our steps, but on the other side of existence," which leads him into a painful and inevitable accumulation of failures, until his premature death.* Whether his ambition is to change life, whether he pursues a new commercial enterprise, the opportunity to be recognized as an explorer by the Geographical Society, the intention to write a book on the Gallas or his many journalistic or scientific projects, Rimbaud is unlucky to the point where we suspect he had a knack for always finding the same situation, same fatal setback, as if his failures were always already waiting for him. As if he complied with fate, the Greek *moira,* to its inexorable end, or rather with the Latin *fatum* of a word, of an "it is written," which he fulfills on his own, "always ahead," says Verlaine, *"with his mind made up to die."* [44]

"The itinerary goes first of all through the word. Through a destiny in writing, if not the destiny of writing itself—but writing accomplished, i.e. fulfilled, come to its limits in a breathtaking advance, and exhausted by its own excess." [45] This destiny, which Roger Munier defines as accomplishing an itinerary through the word, compels recognition as the key word of Rimbaud's life—the *fatum,* with the same etymological root as *enfant,* "child": *to talk.*

I went several times to Conception Hospital, in the atmosphere of this poem by Louis Brauquier, that a friend in Marseille copied for me:

*May 21, 1891: "I doubt I'll wait"; June 24, 1891: "Death would be preferable"; June 29, 1891: "This time I'll know to get rid of this miserable existence"; July 10, 1891: "Life is of no account!"

And the night glides over the street lights.
Distant sirens smothered in fog.
A newsman hawking his paper.
Back from Africa, Rimbaud died tonight.

In this place of departure and falling due, where the tireless walker tried one last time to get up—"I get up and hop a hundred paces on my crutches and I sit down again"*—I am struck again by the bad luck that hounded Rimbaud all his life: this mother . . . the war . . . even meeting Verlaine, which helped neither of them. Why could he not have met Nietzsche![46] Instead of "laboring like a donkey,"† he would have seen the performance of *Parsifal* in Beirut on July 26, 1882, would have met Wagner and Lou Salomé! Irreversibility of this word. His bad luck does not give out: Abyssinia! . . . the deaths of Labatut and then Soleillet . . . thirty-seven years of missed opportunities, of trouble, all conceivable kinds of trouble. "I don't have any luck!"†† And his knee keeps swelling: "I'm in bad shape, very bad shape, I am reduced to a skeleton by my sick left leg which has become enormous and is now like a giant pumpkin."§ His pain is such that Rimbaud mistakes its location—it is his right leg that is to be amputated. A poet: one who does not know which of his legs is being cut off. Poetry too has its martyrs. And even a century after his death, ill luck still dogs him: In our dictionary of accepted ideas, the fallen angel of Abyssinia remains discredited, a "merchant" trying to "get rich," an "arms runner," "traitor," "slavetrader," a "bored" man sending "boring letters"—all indelible clichés of middle-class thought, his ultimate misfortune, the only one without interest. "Character is destiny," said Novalis. Rimbaud's character amounts to a certain manner of blam-

---

* Marseille, July 15, 1891: "Perhaps it is my destiny to become a *legless cripple!*" (Marseille, July 2, 1891).
† Aden, May 10, 1882. See also the letter of July 10, 1882.
†† Marseille, June 17, 1891. "I have no luck!" (Cairo, August 23, 1887).
§ Marseille, May 21, 1891.

ing the universe, but *taking it out on himself.* We are tempted to protest against the fatality of this word that always removes the multiple object of Rimbaud's quest at the moment he is about to reach it,* like the beginning of wealth that should have allowed him to take a rest. Even this he cannot touch: "I have not been able to touch the money."† One "is deeply sorry to think," as the unsummarizable Colonel Godchot said with feeling,[47] that the dying man, lonelier than ever, hitting the bottom of despair, did not know anything of his glory to come, of which he had dreamed so much once. Last sign of his destiny: Rodolphe Darzens's visit. A passionate admirer of Rimbaud's work, this young man had edited a collection of it under a title borrowed from Coppée, *Le Reliquaire (The Shrine),* published by Lautréamont's publisher, Genonceaux, in November 1891. As much as I tend to dream that Rimbaud might have been able to see *A Season in Hell* on our bookstore stands, Darzens wanted at all costs to meet his hero and hand him his book. He found out that the poet had been transferred to Marseille. He rushed to Conception Hospital. When he got to the poet's room with a copy of his *Reliquaire,* Rimbaud was in a coma. It was the eve of November 10, day of his death: Rimbaud was not to see even a glimpse, not even symbolically, not even a fragment of his budding fame, his first sign of posterity. He never even knew that he was Arthur Rimbaud.

*"At present, I see it is impossible" (Marseille, June 24, 1891). "Impossible to take a step!" (Marseille, June 29, 1891).
†Marseille, May 21, 1891.

9
REALITY

People do not understand how
that which is at variance with
itself can also be in agreement:
There is harmony in opposing
movements, as in the tension
of bow and lyre.
—Heraclitus

What if Rimbaud knew the poetry of the real, if he lived
poetry? This question has preoccupied me from the start; it
is the starting point. Words not being tied to things, they
do not open onto the world. Language as mediation comes
between man and nature. Only by eliminating this mediation could man return to an earlier harmony, regain an *immediate* relation with nature, and finally return to a "primitive
state." To this end, "there is basically only one means: to
purify yourself of the law of language and decisively go beyond the domain of words and discourse."[1] Outside the
symbolic order, outside communication, Rimbaud could have
found in Abyssinia the lost unity of imagination and reality.
In logical pursuit of his object after the failure of *voyance,* he
could have *realized* poetry in the "power of the diverse."[2]
"Does the imaginary grow weaker or stronger when it con-
fronts reality?" asks Segalen in *Equipée.* "Could the real not
also hold great savor and joy?"

"The will to live a poetry in action,"[3] which drove
Rimbaud *already* in his creative period, does not authorize

us to distinguish the poet and *then* the man of action. But it is tempting to consider Rimbaud's activities after 1875 or 1880 as a form of immediate poetry. Then he would have known his "golden age" during the time without writing: "my eternal life, not written, not sung,"* "something like Providence, which we believe in, but which does not sing."† Solitude and freedom, the physical momentum toward open space—and the very concrete handling of bales of coffee or transport of skins—would have formed the poetic raw material. "He was a true poet, he had no song," says Tristan Corbière in *Les Amours jaunes (Jaundiced Loves)*. "The poet in action is the explorer," Duncan Forbes assures us,[4] and Taylor, comparing Rimbaud's with Segalen's experience, sees "Rimbaud led by thirst for the absolute to turn his back on literature and pursue his quest in the desert. . . . When one goes far beyond the limits, where there are no more colors, sounds or smells one could identify, nor any qualities that could be expressed in words, the real and the imaginary fuse, and there is no reason for poetry to exist as a separate activity."[5] Poetry without a trace, poetry as a state of mind, this is what Tzara and the Dadaists were first to salute in the Abyssinian Rimbaud, one of the poets in whom Tzara could discover "violent contempt of accepted ideas, an intuition that the world is *poorly made* . . . who allow us to glimpse the coming of a new world without disorder, where beauty can be seen and life lived. . . . [These poets] suffer the suffering of all mankind whose infinitely sensitive stakeholders they are."[6] Distractedly opposing poet *(der Dichter)* and fugitive *(der Flüchtige)*, Hugo Ball acclaimed Rimbaud's "flight from European decadence, his acute instinct against softness and hypocrisy,"[7] whereas Huelsenbeck's *En avant Dada* treated all writers as *Germans* "who never live fully: yes, Rimbaud fully understood that literature and art are very suspect—that, on the contrary, it is easy to live like a pasha."

*"Age d'or" ("The Golden Age").
†Sketch of "Alchimie du verbe."

And all the pillars of the Cabaret Voltaire join Huelsenbeck in seeing Dadaism (Dada is nothing! but Dadaism . . .) "as a philosophy that goes beyond art to issue into life, as Gauguin and Rimbaud have done before us." This idea is also the backbone of Antonin Artaud's entire work—culture is not written—Artaud who in his *Messages révolutionnaires* uncovers "the hideous imprisonment of poetry in language" and proposes to "find the secret life of theater as Arthur Rimbaud had known to find the secret life of poetry."[8]

Before Tzara and Artaud, Isabelle had already claimed that "poetry had never abandoned him."[9]

Abyssinia and Egypt are a constant spectacle. You cannot take in everything with your eyes. Walking through the huge *mercato* of Addis Ababa, giving the slip to the movie camera, which is swept off in the crowd, I thought of Arthur Rimbaud's camera. With these buffalo-hide shields, these harnesses, parchments, ostrich eggs from Ogaden, objects made of porcupine quills, but even more with these "strange races,"* these unexplored regions, the poet who once considered the title "Photograph of Times Gone By"[10] could have put together a prodigious collection of images. "I mean . . . to make a curious album out of all this."† The apparatus he had delivered in 1882 was one of the first objects of our century to set its tripod on this unknown world. Photographs by Arthur Rimbaud. Nadar in Harar! Carjat's second death!

Having stayed on in Harar with only Rimbaud, Pinchard wrote to Bardey on January 8, 1881: "A photographic apparatus would be very useful here; there are so many interesting things I could send on to you." Although photography was already sixty-four years old—Nadar had even already carried it to unsurpassed perfection—the idea came

*Letter to his family, Harar, May 6, 1883.
†Aden, March 15, 1883.

to Rimbaud the African as slowly as the actual camera. And when Rimbaud finally, with his enormous apparatus with metal plates, moves through a herd of ostriches—which every chief of a clan treats as sacred animals—or walks through the crowded markets where great numbers of cows and goats are slaughtered, cut in two and hung up on hooks, photography is for him only a quick way of making money ("Everybody wants to have his picture taken: I'm offered as much as a guinea per photograph"*) and a curiosity for its own sake, one of the technological novelties that fascinated him. (Possibly Charles Cros had talked to him of his color research in 1871.) What does he take pictures of? Himself, three times. Some views of Harar, an Abyssinian rider, a coffee trader, Sotiro in the jungle. Bardey, taking his cure in Vichy, thanks him for the "somewhat out of focus photos."[11] Photography was for him only an *intention* toward the world. "Those are of no interest,"† he admits of his portraits. Then promises curiosities in procrastinating terms: "I'll send you curious things";†† "I'll soon send you successful ones";§ "I could send you really curious things."‖ He will not send them. He will not see them again. "To my great regret I've sold the photographic apparatus."¶ Bad weather, bad times, bad reasons. "That was a good idea I had,"** he had written a few months earlier. An idea indeed, like the piano, the Abyssinian wife, telegraphy, all suddenly abandoned. The only "curiosity" was himself. The man of action made fun of the photographer Bidault in a letter to Borelli: "He only lives in contemplation."††† In

---

*   Harar, May 6, 1883.
†   Harar, August 26, 1883.
††   Harar, May 6, 1883.
§   Harar, May 20, 1883.
‖   Harar, August 26, 1883.
¶   Aden, April 14, 1885.
**   Harar, May 20, 1883.
†††Harar, February 25, 1889: "Bidault . . . has not yet been able to place his collection of photographs of the country which is now complete."

1871, in the Parisian bookstores, Rimbaud disdained the "fastidious rustling of photographs";* now he repudiates the "curious things." Even in the modest successes among his pictures, the world remains distant. Reselling his camera, Rimbaud economizes on the real objective—and giving up photography seems a *renewed* forsaking of the world in an ultimate mode of communication.

Rimbaud's silence seems inconceivable—everybody seems to exclaim: "he couldn't do this to us"—and the idea of a "poetry of the real" exorcises the radicality of Rimbaud's giving up by making it an aesthetic project: "We propose to show," writes a follower of Derrida, "that Rimbaud's silence was not total, that the writer continued in a certain way to search for the language he had glimpsed for a moment, that he searched Africa for a pagan language."[12] Verlaine, from 1888 on, pictured Rimbaud as a poet "thirsty for, drunk with" the world, "the poet who takes his distance from a well-deserved notoriety, renouncing the admiring caresses of the elite, again to follow, to live his dream—through the world, through things and people avidly watched, devoured as it were."[13] The evidence of our Abyssinian trip, which put us on location, which let us live and see this exteriority, tells me on the contrary that Rimbaud's correspondence is all interiorized. "Things avidly watched"? We only have to see them to realize that Rimbaud did not talk about them. His correspondence takes comfort from incredibly much that is *unsaid.* And the unsaid is *such* that I ask myself if it is not even unseen.

Once, only once, did Rimbaud stick his head under the black cloth of the dark box in order to look at the world: on crossing the St. Gotthard Pass. A world all white. He as it were took an all-white photo and sent it to his mother, one of his most beautiful letters, dated a Sunday, November

*To Paul Demeny, April 17, 1871.

1878: "Impossible to take my eyes off the white nuisance."*
He describes himself in snow up to the knees, head bent,
"eyelashes and mustache turned into stalactites, ears aching,
throat swollen," walking into the wind, into this white world.
Two kinds of black lines: "the telegraph poles," only visible
sign of the buried road, and "the shadow you are of yourself." A world like a Japanese print. World of silence where
he marches on, hearing other travelers call in the fog. Desert
or snow, a blinding world, covered, sheeted, immense and
pure. Drawn in chalk. At the high point of the letter, the
culmination of his vision of the world: "Here we are! not a
shadow above, below or around . . . no more road, cliffs,
ravines or sky: nothing but white to dream, to touch, to see
or not."†

Arthur Rimbaud—the only "writer" who had "corresponded" with the Negus—was certainly among the huge,
delirious crowd that gave Menelik, victor over Harar, a
triumphal welcome in Entotto, the new capital of Abyssinia, in March 1887. About this historical event that had
been announced three weeks in advance, this glorious return
worthy of Germanicus' return to Rome at which Tacitus
makes us *feel we are present,* Rimbaud has one whole sentence to say: Menelik "entered Entotto, preceded by a band
blowing their lungs out on the Egyptian trumpets they had
found in Harar, followed by his troops and booty, among
which two Krupp cannons, each carried by eighty men."††
He was not part of the festivity. Of his encounter with the
future emperor a few days later, he says nothing, except
that he tells M. de Gaspary the "disastrous conditions" of
his negotiation. To imagine what this interview was like,
we must go to the account of Achille Raffray, who got it
from Emperor John in 1875:

---

* To his family, Genoa, November 17, 1878.
† Ibid. Or again, twelve years later, from Harar: "Deserts . . . without roads"
  (February 25, 1890). And "deserts of snow" in "Génie" (*Illuminations*).
††To *Le Bosphore égyptien,* August 20, 1887.

The reception had been very solemn. The king was crouched like an idol on a bed covered with rich rugs at the back of a vast tent. . . . The Ras stood forming a circle around him in their gold crowns and long, red, gold-embroidered silk robes; behind them a crowd of lords and warriors, spears in their fists, shoulders ornamented with *lebdé*, swords in their belt, shields on their arms, bare-headed, with newly braided and buttered hair. Nothing was left out of the tableau, not even the traditional lion of the Ethiopian emperors. He was there in the flesh, perfectly free, lying at his master's feet.[14]

THE GALLAS, by J.-ARTHUR RIMBAUD, East-African Explorer, with Maps and Engravings, Supplemented with Photographs by the Author; Available from H. Oudin, Publishers, 10, rue de Mézières, Paris, 1891.[15] What a lost—and impossible book! It was the idea of a January 18. He had written to his "dear friends": "I am going to write a book for the Geographical Society, with maps and engravings, on Harar and Gallaland. I'm having a photographic apparatus sent from Lyon . . . and will bring back pictures of these unknown regions."* And, in stride, he tells Delahaye of "Harar and Gallaland which I have explored" and of "the instrument which will allow me to interleaf pictures of these strange areas in the work."† Learning that Monsignor Taurin was planning such a work, Rimbaud exclaimed: "I too am going to write one and cut the ground from under Monsignor's feet!"[16] These statements confirm (as if it were necessary) the opinion Rimbaud always had of his *capacity*. He has no doubt of it if the *stakes are real*. "I am traveling in Gallaland."†† A lot of good it does us. He could have told in this book about "the training of a troop of elephant hunters"§

* Aden, January 18, 1882.
† Aden, January 18, 1882.
†† Aden, January 22, 1882.
§ Ibid.

that he had undertaken; all we know about it are two dry sentences to a certain Devisme.[17] The abandoning of this projected illustrated volume follows the same curve as that of the camera put aside, boxed up. If you lose your taste for Europe, you also by and by lose interest in the "here" of Galla. He could write or take pictures, but he finds nothing to say, nothing to see: "Don't be astonished if I hardly ever write: the main reason is that I never find anything to say. For if you are in countries like these here you have more to ask than to say! Deserts . . . without roads . . . : what do you want me to write from there? That one gets bored, annoyed, stupefied; that one gets sick of it, but cannot give it up, etc., etc.! That's all, all that one can say, then; and since that does not amuse anybody, one must be silent."*

From Europe to Arabia and Africa, Rimbaud goes "from the same desert to the same night"† "Drunk with the world"? The error of Verlaine (and all the *others*) is much less surprising than that Rimbaud should "never find anything to say." For the learned scholars of the Geographical Society, Abyssinia was the land of *men with tails*. The very honorable Antoine d'Abbadie, who traveled for several years in Abyssinia, was looking for these men the Galla sorcerers had mentioned to him, "strange, strong, heavyset beings with a caudal appendix one span long," whose skeletons were put at the price of a million francs. Alfred Bardey had promised him to ask around. All travelers in Abyssinia "found things to say," "really curious things." "En route, everything astonishes me," writes Bardey, who brings back a voluminous travel book, *Barr Adjam*.[18] Rimbaud's "boss," at twenty-six, took the boat to India by himself in 1880, from Aden to Bombay, and was interested in the "stupefying vows" of the Hindus: One man had vowed to walk without stopping, another, to keep one arm always lifted. "After a few years,

*Harar, February 25, 1890.
†"Morning," *A Season in Hell.*

the extremity is atrophied, shriveled and can no longer be lowered." There were men whose fingernails had grown through the fist they had decided never to open. In the zoo, he was troubled by a big Malay orangutan prostrate with despair. The animal had gone through terrible fits of fury and now was dying because he could not stand being separated from his mate, these big monkeys living only in couples. Valuable in themselves, Bardey's *Souvenirs d'Afrique-Orientale* tell us what Rimbaud saw, reveal what he left unsaid. During his first years in Harar, Rimbaud saw the Egyptian garrison, "a detachment of cavalry wearing tall chenille caps and polished copper armor," with two hundred Bachi-bouzouks (Albanian irregulars) and a Sudanese bugler who used to play Gounod's *Faust*. He saw Galla chiefs dragged by force to the mosque, dressed in *gandourahs,* then chased out of town with artillery salvos meant to terrorize them into keeping the faith. He watched feasts of the Sudanese Askaris who would dance and sing, armed with clubs, but otherwise almost nude, their bodies painted with white zebra stripes, faces "disfigured by chalk circles around eyes and mouth." Among them he must have noticed the men with tails, "a few heavyset Negroes who, with the horizontal white stripes, look almost as broad as tall," says Bardey, "and whose posterior was decorated with a short cow tail."

In the mob of the Addis *mercato,* the coffee district reminds me fleetingly of the Harar market, the *faras magalah,* which in comparison seems like a small, colorful market in Provence, where I imagine Rimbaud walking through without a look at the women with yellow *wars*-powdered faces, asking the Guragué and Galla merchants the price of their wares. I see him talking to the women that Provost describes, "sitting by their merchandise . . . protecting their profiles of Giotto madonnas under parasols of rushes, hair braided in countless dense, parallel braids that make their brown heads look like melons."[19]

*   *   *

Rimbaud spent his time distributing and receiving "gifts," exchanges indispensable for any transaction, especially with the *ogas* (*oughaz*), the tribal chiefs: "The little we brought back from there [Ogaden] cost us a great deal; almost half of our merchandise had to be distributed as gifts to our guides, *abbanes,* hosts wherever you looked and on every trail."* He no doubt received Ethiopian magic scrolls, *dabtaras* (at least he constantly saw them), which were for centuries the only images people of this country saw: beautiful paintings that could be by Klee, *and with healing power.*[20] Nothing is left of this great Abyssinian potlatch, not a single object, not a word. Bardey was a collector, a veritable ambulatory museum. Already in 1881 he was "encumbered by shepherd's crooks, bows and quivers with poisoned arrows, iron and ivory bracelets, Somali vases inlaid with shells, baskets from Harar." He owned one of the rare inkwells of the country. His brother also sent him books in ancient Arabic containing "information about the country quite unpublished elsewhere," and, preserved in a tin of alcohol, the head of an unknown species of bird. Later, Bardey let go of some of his most cherished objects (the weapons of Emir Abd el-Chakour) and gave them to the Cairo Museum.

Failing to write a work on the customs of the country, Rimbaud could have described some of the situations he was in. Several times, in the course of solitary expeditions, he was the first white man the women encountered: They would feel him shamelessly, trying to see if his skin was also white under his clothes. . . .

Except for saying that he is frugal, Rimbaud never speaks of his food (basically durra, sesame, barley, which always smelled smokey, like the green coffee beans cooked in but-

---

*Harar, December 10, 1883: "And the Oughas has personally received from us some hundred dollars' worth of gold abbayas, immahs, and presents of all sorts, which however have sincerely attached him to us, and that is the only good result of the expedition."

ter). Yet he must have been welcomed according to current Galla custom: The chief, the *guerade,* chooses (with his fingers, of course) the best morsels and puts them in his guest's mouth. The pepper taking effect, every guest starts gasping for air: This is the moment the *guerade* seizes to push into the open mouth a piece of chicken stuffed with egg that he pats in with his fingers.

Why did he not even give his mother and sister some fleeting impressions, as Michel Leiris will do, of "the nobles coming out of mass surrounded by rifles, women chattering on their way to the well . . . muledrivers teasing the girls in the mead houses, wakes with heartrending lamentations and tears on command"?[21]

Why did he not tell (this from another postcard to Delahaye) about the violent tournaments called pole games, in which Bachi-bouzouks and Egyptian horsemen would rush at each other from the two extremes of the *faras magalah,* trying to unseat each other with long poles!

In a letter to Jules Borelli, he is supposed to have described the Guerris, the large neighboring tribe that lived by raising camels (Bardey bought from them), and the Nollis-Gallas that he and Pierre Mazeran visited in April 1881 without guide or escort. He could also have given his impressions of the *guébeur* he saw, the royal feast the king of Shoa gave for his soldiers, his *ouatadeurs*—literally "those who sleep outside." The soldiers greedily fell on the raw *brondo* of beef while the king was hidden from sight by *chemmas,* held by servants, so that he could eat without worrying about the "evil eye."

To Alfred Ilg, who appreciated his caustic manner, Rimbaud is said to have commented in his fashion on some episodes of daily life in Harar: When the Emir Abd el-Chakour wanted to spit, the fanatic Muslims of his entourage would compete to receive this humid and precious homage of His Highness on their face. . . . Seeing their first white missionaries with long beards and large tropical helmets, the

Somali girls would hide the lower part of their faces with their hands, as if they had lifted the *shador*. Bardey told Rimbaud with a good laugh of the fathers' first trip on a sambuk: Because of their presence, the Somali *bahris* raised their heavy veils, outdoing each other in invocations of *"Allah ouaded!"* ("God alone!") "Our fathers in their white cassocks, the black Somalis and the praying Somali women on the old kind of sambuk formed a picture one could date from the year 1000," writes Bardey. Since Menelik took away from Makonnen all the presents he had brought back from Italy, Rimbaud was able to see hanging in a Harar bazaar the parasol Queen Marguerite had given the Ras. . . . He is said to have made fun of Sotiro (whose meekness made him a natural target) when his Greek partner, who was very nearsighted, left with the blunderbuss Monsignor Taurin entrusted to him. In the holy city of Harar, the memory of many Sufis is still honored today: A discreetly consecrated corner or stairway marks the place where they lived. It is the women who keep their memory alive, from mother to daughter. There are still Sufis today, practicing a specific Harar interpretation of the Koran. They lead an apparently "normal" family life, but spend most of their time in solitary prayer in their *geb*. In his ten years there, Rimbaud could not help knowing about the Sufis who were more numerous at the time: He wrote not one word.

When he wanted to tell how difficult his life was, Rimbaud could tell M. de Gaspary about the sentences passed in the *Divan* (held on the ground floor of Raouf Pacha's house, where Rimbaud lived on the second floor): two bandits sentenced to death, bastinado for thieves. It is also astonishing that he did not speak of the effects of famine and plague: Rimbaud picked up corpses at his doorstep—in 1881, the city mourned twenty dead a day, forty on days of rain. Rimbaud distributed green durra sticks to the starved *meskines* (poor) who were begging at the depot with *"Allah*

Kérim! Allah oudj Allah!" ("Mercy for God's sake!"). He also learned that the Niam-Niam, a Sudanese Askari tribe, were reduced to eating their children.

"The formidable bandit Mohammed Abou-Beker, enemy of the European traders and travelers in Shoa,"* whom Rimbaud had reason to complain of to de Gaspary; this all-powerful sultan of Zeila, who sued him before Menelik in November 1887, without whose permission no caravan could take off, who complicated Rimbaud's life for ten years, who (at the head of his innumerable family) managed the large enterprise of the slave trade, this much feared Abou-Beker (with whom Rimbaud, in spite of everything, had to drink the obligatory, ritual cups of coffee) we finally get to see— thanks to Bardey:

> We are having our first interview with Abou-Beker. He is an old Dankali, thin, of medium height, with the very black face, straight nose and rather thin lips of his race. Hair shaved off in front and a short gray beard frame a face with almost constantly shifting eyes. He is sitting on an *angareb* woven of strips of raw skin, dressed in an Arabic *gandourah* of doubtful white, a *chamah* (an enormous white muslin turban) on his head. His left hand is telling his Muslim beads, while his right again and again takes a little wooden stick out of his turban . . . to use as a toothbrush. After each brushing, with a little whistle from between his teeth (still good in spite of his age), he spits out a gob of spittle without caring where it falls." [After the customary *Salam aleikoum,*] "he claps his hands and tells the Dankali servant who comes running from the next straw hut to bring *el boun,* the coffee. . . . Abou-Beker's eyes never meet ours. He watches us on the sly. We tell him we want to leave for Harar with our *gaflah* in eight days. Every time we mention the date, he replies *"Inch Allah!"* This is every good Muslim's reply to any state-

*Aden, November 9, 1887.

ment, but in his mouth we understand it to mean "If *I* please." He avoids committing himself by following each of our statements with his *Inch Allah,* along with two or three gobs of saliva that sometimes come rather near us.

"I find nothing to say . . ." And the untold fauna and flora! This suddenly struck me when our cameraman let me watch an eagle through his reflex. (Immediate cinema with hairlines on the image.) The eagle was circling in the Harar sky, hovering very high up for a long time, then swooped down on a prey like lightning and disappeared from my field of vision—a rabbit, no doubt, commented Father Émile on the terrace. Reading his letters, one might forget that Rimbaud lived among animals of all sorts.* In Abyssinia, Lebrun writes in 1856, "birds of prey like vultures and eagles are very numerous whereas there are few songbirds. The country is infested with serpents that grow to prodigious proportions."[22] In the high grass of the vast prairies, Rimbaud, like Bardey, saw green turtles that would hardly bother to withdraw their heads even when you hit their very round shield, and whole legions of calm black boars with large heads and tusks. He had gone to Balao on April 15, 1881. The night before, Bardey had watched on the rocks some "large monkeys with big manes and long doglike snouts." The camel drivers would point their spears at bustards, of whom he most often saw only head and neck, and sometimes, in the evening, they invited him to share their very spicy ragout of giant rat.

When he gets to the Red Sea, Bardey contemplates "innumerable white gulls at rest in the distance, forming immense daisy fields." On the way back, Rimbaud must like Bardey have stopped his caravan on seeing the bush strangely yellow, and then have gone through the dense sheet of yel-

---

*The only thing Rimbaud (according to Sotiro?) wrote about ostriches is that "the ostriches travel in caravans after the camels. They are nearly as tall" (*Rapport sur l'Ogadine,* 1883).

low-and-black-striped crickets that covered all vegetation, but opened and reclosed under the camels' feet. He heard the tam-tam announcing a cloud of grasshoppers that would rapidly darken the sky for a night of pillage. "Grasshoppers as big as shrimp," writes Bardey, which come down like "black snow . . . while fires are being lit in the fields they threaten."[23] I remember copying this last phrase in Paris, in the National Archives, with Pierre Petitfils. The handwriting is that of Arthur in 1870, but the report on "the grasshoppers" is by his father, as if Captain Rimbaud were describing in his stead, forty years earlier, from Sebdou in Algeria, what his son would not write.

Suddenly, the world appears in one detail: "The coffee shrubs are ripening."* A country in three words. "All of Abyssinia," wrote Doncourt in 1886, "smells of roses, jasmin, lilies and carnations that cover the fields."[24] That year as any other, nothing about flowers or smells from Rimbaud, not a single lily. "After a sixty days' trek through an awful desert,"† he crosses the Itous Plateau with its "magnificent pastures" and "splendid forests." This is all the readers of the *Egyptian Bosphorus* will get to hear, not the song of the camel drivers as they go through the forests. On the St. Gotthard too, "the mountain [was] marvelous."†† I can see, against the light, Rimbaud's long caravan moving "along the crest of a chain of hills"§ in 1887. In a hurry, he describes nothing, but scribbles a few elliptical phrases on his return: "In Bedouin country, in Konella, or warm earth. Brush and woods peopled with elephants and wild beasts . . . marched along the elephant trail." ‖ Opening this letter, Bardey, who was as enchanted by Ethiopia as anyone who ever ventured there, must have remained hungry. When Bardey mentions "luxurious vegetation" (as Rimbaud does

* Harar, November 7, 1881.
† To *Le Bosphore égyptien*, August 20, 1887.
†† Genoa, November 17, 1878.
§ To Bardey, Cairo, August 26, 1887.
‖ Ibid.

also, thinking of Harar in Aden: "a luxurious vegetation"*),
he adds a picture: "Thickets of bush alternate with woods,
prairies with high grass and an occasional isolated big tree."
But Rimbaud does not stop and look. All he finds to say is:
"beautiful woodland," "magnificent forests," "beautiful
mountains," "splendid valleys," "panorama."† His Abyssinia seems to be in the image of the plain changing with its
three names he knew well: the land that first denies (Dah-
elimalah, "sterile and uncultivatable land"), then absorbs him
(Dalah, "when you pass you are a friend"), and finally
withdraws and disappears (Maleh, "gone, I no longer know
you"). His Abyssinia seems the improbable land beyond him,
like the "splendid cities"†† he always searched for, and really
saw in the desert—and of which Bardey speaks for him:

> Turning, we issue onto a narrow platform overlooking
> the great plain of Mandao that stretches endlessly to the
> north. Well on this side of the horizon, which is fuzzy
> with a light haze of heat or dust, we see an agglomoration
> of white Arab buildings crowned by a dome. Surprised,
> I ask Mohammed: "Zeila?" But he replies, *"La! La!"* ("No!
> No!"). And I realize that it is only a mirage, since Zeila
> is still eighty kilometers off. Yet the mirage is in the di-
> rection of Zeila, and its dome resembles the *koubba* of Zeila,
> only larger. As for the surrounding buildings, they are
> more numerous than in Zeila where, beside the Somali
> straw huts, there are only two white houses. So it is not
> an image of Zeila, but of another town, farther away. For
> the original of this Arab city, so neatly sitting a few ki-
> lometers before us, is certainly not in Somaliland. Mo-
> hammed has often seen mirages, but he will not venture
> any explanation. *Allah akbar,* God is great!

---

* Aden, January 15, 1883.
† To Bardey, Cairo, August 26, 1887.
†† ". . . armed with ardent patience, we shall enter the splendid cities" ("Adieu,"
  A Season in Hell).

In Harar as in Charleville, Rimbaud often disappeared for a long time without sending any word. Bardey would be worried: "After two weeks without any news, Rimbaud comes back, very tired. He has to take to his bed and for a week is sicker than when he left. There were times when he thought his hour had come." If Rimbaud disdains the picturesque, if he seems not even interested in customs and country, he also never speaks of the dangers he is constantly in, which is the most surprising thing to remain untold. "I do not disregard the dangers; I do not ignore the strain of these expeditions."* But in order to imagine them, we must know that no camel or mule ever made the trek from Harar to the coast more than once: They died en route or had to be slaughtered on arrival. In ten years, Rimbaud covered this distance about ten times, on foot, without roads.[25] At the end of the trek, the Galla donkeys, *dèbres,* would be exhausted by loads larger than themselves and no longer able to bend their stiff legs. He would see the owners holding them by the ears and burn their joints with red-hot knives straight from the fire. At the slow pace of the caravan, accompanied by Somalis with extremely long legs, leading a "theory" of camels (up to sixty, each carrying two hundred kilos of coffee or skins—yet the camels arrive at their destination within fifteen minutes of schedule), Rimbaud would encounter children bloated with typhus or eaten with leprosy, would daily run the risk of all sorts of illnesses, and for ten years defied murderous sunstrokes. Then there were the "transport worries" that wore Bardey down: "The caravans took over a year to leave the coast. The first thing one needs is Abou-Beker's goodwill. . . . You also have to reckon with camel drivers who only follow their own head and the tribes whose territory you want to go through." Achille Raffray, who in 1876 had wondered "why all the commercial enterprises in Abyssinia had failed," was quick to see that there were simply "no means of transportation

*Aden, November 18, 1885.

and no roads* from the center of the country to a port."[26]
On narrow and steep paths, Rimbaud would see his pack
mules hesitate and, in a panic, try to bite through the ropes
of their loads, which risked dragging them down the cliffs.

Rimbaud's "Studies in Merchandise" were numbered,
like symphonies. In the seventh, he names a forest with an
enchanting name (I would have liked to take a stroll in it,
but it no longer exists): "Four or five hours from Harar
there is a forest (Bisédimo) full of wild beasts."† In Harar,
you had to think of your own safety first. There were animals everywhere, in the plains, the forests, the towns. You
had to know them to survive. "At the moment the enormous red sun was about to set," Bardey saw "four black
jackals come out of a clump of shrubs"; another time, lions
fighting over a cow by moonlight. Lions would follow the
traveler in the desert at a distance while he was marching,
but the moment he fell they would be on him and tear him
to pieces. It is inevitable that Rimbaud must have had *his*
encounter. Bardey felt as if electrocuted by his:

> I see a bright reddish mass. . . . At first I do not realize
> what it is; then, suddenly, I feel completely empty, my
> blood frozen. I slowly move on, veering instinctively
> toward the right. . . . I try to reassure myself thinking:
> it's a calf, it's a calf. . . . I continue to move away slowly
> like somebody who wants to see nothing, know nothing.
> I left the camp in a moresque (a jumpsuit of Madras silk
> with big red palms) and have only one cartridge in my
> rifle. . . . Many things have passed through my head
> during the fifty steps since I saw the beast. . . . Two
> Askaris have knelt down and fire stupidly. The lioness,
> who does not seem to notice, disappears behind some

*"The problem is that we are sixty leagues from the sea" (Harar, February 15,
1881).
†"Septiéme Étude de marchandises," 1883.

rocks, without running, to reappear again a bit farther off
. . . and Ephtimion saying again and again, "*Come e
maestosa* ["how majestic she is"].

For ten years, animals spelled death to Rimbaud: He saw
a sick woman devoured by a hyena "as big as a donkey."
The camels that collapsed en route were divided among the
Somalis who cut the meat into nut-size pieces and sun-dried
them in a hammock, like figs. Perhaps he too had Bardey's
"morbid curiosity" to look into the eyes of a dying goat for
the last landscape the animal saw before dying. One of the
Abyssinian plains is called Mandao: "fool who stops here."
Allah akbar!

From Paris, the secretary of the Geographical Society
warned Rimbaud in 1887: "The country you are thinking of
exploring is very dangerous for Europeans." Combes and
Tamisier, who traveled in Abyssinia between 1835 and 1837,
reported in the *Magasin pittoresque* the "great perils" of the
road to Zeila, where the Arkeko tribe "sheds blood for the
fun of it, without reason or hatred." Rimbaud did not carry
a tube of strychnine like Lucereau, who preferred killing
himself to agonizing among lions; nor cyanide like Achille
Raffray, who was ready to kill himself rather than suffer
castration; nor flares, which Bardey started carrying after
some warriors had tried to stone him, their first white man,
helmeted on horseback—and after he began having "nights
of anxiety" and days in which he felt pursued by hundreds
of silhouettes. . . . Arnoux, a Frenchman arriving from
Obock, was assassinated in Shoa in 1883. On August 12 of
the same year, Pietro Sacconi, an Italian merchant in Harar,
met the same fate on a visit to Ogaden. Barral's caravan was
massacred in April 1886. Chefneux, who went to identify
the bodies, could recognize only a tooth of Barral's wife
glittering in the sun. In 1896, Vignéras came to inspect "the
corrie where the caravan of the merchant Eloy Pino was

attacked in 1890, in the middle of the night."[27] Returning "haggard and ragged from his trip to the Guerris," Lucereau got off his mule and said to Bardey: "I would not make another trip like this for 100,000 francs." Afterward he wrote Bardey in a quite Rimbaldian tone: "And if something happens to me, a curse on the five hundred devils on the other side of the Arussis." Lucereau was killed by the Itous Gallas at Warabeili in December 1880. By the time Bardey found his body, the lions had torn it to pieces. In order to survive ten years of constant travel and expeditions, Rimbaud had to overcome fear, be very well informed, adapt to custom, be infinitely patient and diplomatic, *inured to hardship*. Lucereau was too ambitious and inexperienced. Rimbaud severely criticized Sacconi, who paid with his life for his contempt of the natives, "whose manners, religious customs and laws he flouted (from ignorance). . . . [He] went about in European dress, ate ham, had little drinks right in the council of sheiks . . . pushed his suspect geodesic sessions and cranked his sextants, etc. at every step of the road."* Rimbaud is not ignorant of the dangers: They attract him (when he plans to leave for Tonkin the country is at war)—to the point where one asks if Africa did not answer to a death instinct in him. We cannot approach Rimbaud's Reality except by deduction. He went through Abyssinia in silence, as if these strange countries were like the market where Gallas and Somalis stopped their war long enough to trade supplies they needed—without exchanging a single word.

In the *Magasin pittoresque,* Rimbaud could have read an article on the explorer Stanley by his schoolmate Paul Bourde: "The cannibals were shouting from one bank to the other: *Bôo! Bôo!* Meat! Meat coming our way!" Delahaye sketched for Verlaine a "Kaffir Rimbaud," sitting crowned amid drunken blacks. And in the *Album zutique,* Rimbaud had lampooned François Coppée by having him read *Dr. Venet-*

*Harar, August 25, 1883.

ti's Treatise on Conjugal Love. This astonishing *Traité de l'amour conjugal* by Dr. Venette[28] (Latinized to "Venetti" in the poem, for the sake of rhyme) also spoke of Kaffirs "who glory in cutting off their enemies' members." If Rimbaud did not encounter the cannibals of his childhood reading in Ethiopia or Kaffraria (for the Arabs, all black countries south of the equator), he did actually see "Shoa soldiers [bring back] the testicles of all the *Franguis* in Harar."* He went through territories of the Danakil whose customs demand that they adorn their body with as many such ornaments as possible before taking a wife. And on his return from the daring foray into Bubassa, Rimbaud told Bardey that he (and his two strong Galla bodyguards) had several times "separated fighters at the moment when the defeated were about to undergo the usual mutilation."[29] A few years earlier, Achille Raffray had quickly localized his dignity—and escaped suicide and mutilation by a hair. More recently, Monfreid had seen a Bedouin draw his double-edged *djemba* and appropriate a dead warrior's virile parts, "whose skin he put on his right arm as is the custom of his tribe. It is a rare Bedouin who does not wear several—every defeated enemy is commemorated by these insignia."[30]

The few Europeans were exposed to such intense danger that one understands (and almost shares even today) the sentiment that Rimbaud must have had, and that overcame Bardey when, back in Arabia, in the Aden harbor, he saw the great ocean liners of the Messageries Maritimes. "The rows of lit-up bull's eyes illuminate" the night, he wrote. And while Bardey's felucca rounded the prow of the packet, there came from one of its salons a tenor voice singing a French opera tune that "quite thrills me." The ship reminds the adventurer of comforts whose very idea he had forgotten and by contrast brings home how strange and destitute a life he has led the last ten months (ten years for Rimbaud). This liner that "illuminates" the night becomes the symbol

*To the *Bosphore égyptien,* 1887. "Franguis" or "farengis," foreigners.

of a return to "normal" life—which he, Bardey, will be able to do: "I am happy to think that it will soon be my turn to go back to a normal life, to France, my family and the civilized world."

"If Europeans and their caravans were massacred and robbed at that time, [Rimbaud] was never the object of any ill will, even from the most feared tribes. . . . So that he came to know regions in Shoa, Godjam and Kaffa never seen by anybody."[31] Taking Paterne Berrichon literally, and considering how much Rimbaud left unsaid, one might indeed end up asking if the "supposed tradesman" did not live in "regions never seen by anybody," in a country other than where I came to look for him, a country of which there are no maps. . . . But the reality of the set (our stay on the fertile plateaus of Harar, in the Diredawa desert) and the intense witness of the actors (Bardey in particular) make me think Rimbaud lived an extraordinary life in Abyssinia, and not so long ago, strictly speaking. Another stroke of bad luck: This reality cannot be inferred from reading his letters. So what Rimbaud left unsaid is at the root of the contempt in which the homebody commentators of our era still hold the Abyssinian: From the railings of their civilized liner they spit on the stranger in his felucca and treat him as "bourgeois!"[32]

The "great savor and joy of the Real,"—Segalen's lived poetry. Not really . . . "What do you want me to tell you . . . of the country I abhor?"* We can trace back to the Nietzsche of *Joyful Wisdom* an overestimation of the Dionysiac, a "return to the *Lebenswelt*" characteristic of the last stages of phenomenologies. Rimbaud conceives of innumerable worlds ("the world is full of countries"), whereas he is not concerned with the unique real world that attains him in all his existence. Does he say nothing about Ethiopia because he is writing to his mother? No—he writes only to

*Harar, July 22, 1881.

his mother because he has nothing to say. His capacity for practical adaptation does not keep him from living in complete abstraction, from deferring till later, till the hour of rest, the contemplation of the world. It is ideas that excite him: A mountain suggests the other side; the sea, shipping out; the desert, adventure—everything beckons beyond. But the "here" of landscapes and customs he does not look at. What we might have seen of Abyssinia went down inside him like the big ship with marvels of the Orient that was to come to the World's Fair in France, but was wrecked in the Red Sea. "Rimbaud was never able to accept life as it comes," writes Enid Starkie. "He found its conditions unbearable and hated it for not being as he had imagined."[33] We can feel him breathless with trying to fill some shifting *emptiness,* a missing word, the always searched and unfindable secret, which is a secret only for remaining so. But the earth is silent. And Rimbaud marches on. He is the Fool of the tarot card whose knee is bitten by a dog: His road to rest is constantly blocked by thoughts that keep him from taking it. Here in Abyssinia I have come to understand the remarkable letter Verlaine sent Delaháye from London in 1875: "one who deep down is positively closed, blocked on many sides, and whom *only* fierce egoism disguises as an individual more intelligent than his turn."[34] When Bardey left Abyssinia, he took a little sack of red earth with him. Rimbaud, on the other hand, had perhaps not noticed the Southern Cross just above the horizon.

So, after failing to transform Reality through poetry, Rimbaud *failed to see Reality.* If he had been unable to change the world with words, one might have thought he would try to change it with his hands. But he was never in the world. In the snowy Ardennes, he was already in the desert. In Abyssinia, he knew the "white nuisance."* Rimbaud was always in Abyssinia (or perhaps never). I remember a walk

*November 17, 1878; cf. above.

through Rome with Gabriele-Aldo Bertozzi:[35] We believed that Rimbaud had spent a month in this capital in September 1877, but were unable to imagine *any* trace of the poet in the city, real or dreamed. He had written a poem with the subtitle "Seen in Rome," but that was long before he got there.[36] Rimbaud did not speak of Java either. But in the jungle he met Antonin Artaud, and they said to each other: "All writing is swinishness."

Given the "splendid valleys" and "magnificent forests," we might think Rimbaud simply kept everything to himself.[37] But the astonishing, repeated "I never find anything to say" forces us to consider what is unsaid as a form of not-seeing. His poems as much as his letters from Africa and Arabia are a discourse on how little reality there is. If experience is inseparable from writing for him, it is inner experience. Rimbaud in Abyssinia always sees the world as pure immanence, but remains an idealist—all he actually sees seems without interest when looked at through an Idea formulated in multiple projects and never realized. In the catalog of a photographic show in Charleville in the 1950s,[38] André Dhotel, among a whole library of commentaries, is the only one to remark simply and justly: "The village of Roche . . . is a green hole. But it is a strange omission that a hiker like Rimbaud did not on occasion notice the perspective of the valley that, some two hundred miles from Roche, rises beyond Voncq into steep limestone and forests." The unseen was the condition of *voyance:* it was in an attic, rue Bourbon in Charleville, that the "Seven-year-old Poet" dreamed "amorous meadows where swelling light . . ." It was on the banks of the Meuse that his "Drunken Boat" became a vision:

> *And I've seen some things that men claim to see!*
> *I've seen the low sun . . .*
> *I've dreamed of green night . . .*
> *I followed . . . the swell . . .*

I struck . . . unbelievable Floridas . . .
I've seen fermenting swamps . . .
I've seen archipelagos of stars!

Then the Seer disciplined his faculty: "I became an adept at simple hallucination: I saw coaches on roads in the sky, a living-room on the bottom of a lake . . ."* He loved "the absence of descriptive abilities in a writer"† and reproached the "fourteen times execrable" Musset with having missed "visions behind his gauze curtains."†† Reality is not absent, it is a starting point. "I very frankly saw a mosque instead of a factory."§ But the eighty mosques of Harar he frankly did not see. They lay dormant, exiled in a bottomless night, transcended by the hope of a "future strength"‖ that always drove Rimbaud.

* "Alchemy of the Word," *A Season in Hell.*
† "Once . . ." *A Season in Hell.*
††To Demeny, May 15, 1871.
§ "Alchemy of the Word," *A Season in Hell.*
‖ "The Drunken Boat."

10
THE MIDDLE TERM

If one tightens the bow over-
much one only increases the
emptiness in the middle.
—Geronimo, *Memoirs*

If the poet did not find poetry in Reality, could we not at least oppose "poésie" and "Papuasie," as Léon-Paul Fargue would say? A solution seems to appear in the definite continuity between literature and technical manuals, between the two so-called *voyant* letters and the letter published in two successive issues of the *Bosphore égyptien,* between literary expression and scientific knowledge. The double Rimbaud resurfaces: one absorbing the public library as well as Izambard's, the other telling Millot on the eve of his final departure that "books . . . are only good to hide leprous old walls" [1]—and then ordering treatises on hydraulics or trigonometry. However, the two opposing poles are joined in Rimbaud's lifelong asking for books and are part of the same and most constant intellectual passion of Rimbaud's: Science (in the wide sense that encompasses the humanities, the *sciences humaines*).

"I am the scientist in his dark armchair."* For Rimbaud as for Charles Cros, science and poetry are not just two

* "Childhood" IV, *Illuminations.*

simultaneous or even complementary activities—nor would it be sufficient to introduce a scientific vocabulary ("telephone poles" or "Metropolitan")* into his poetry. They have objectivity in common. It is the poet who should be "the supreme scientist."† The Seer's experience was not oniric or delirious, but a "reasoned" disordering.†† Rimbaud despised subjective poetry and tried to restart the "discarded, but still steaming locomotives" of the "early Romantics"§ in the name of a "scientific" conception of literature: Since words are linked to things, a new language can change our lives. "The poet would give more . . . than mere notation to *the march of Progress!*" ‖ he insists. "He would truly *multiply progress!*" (Rimbaud's emphasis.) Science was the great idea of Rimbaud's century. What was "new" tended to be associated with the idea of "better" (an ideological mutation hardly weakened today), and Rimbaud always asked for the best or the "newest." While working on *A Season in Hell,* he wrote to Delahaye: "If you can send me the newest catalog, do so";¶ from Aden, in 1881: "I would like to know about all the best . . . instruments manufactured";** in Marseille, he asked Maurice Riès "to have the most perfect possible artificial leg built."[2] "We must be absolutely modern!"††† The young poet greeted the future with a revolutionary enthusiasm that betrays his dreams of power and glory— "Science, the new nobility! Progress. The world is advancing!"§§—and his haste to be done with the old world: "Science is too slow";‖‖ "My mind . . . Get going! Ah! Science does not move fast enough for us."¶¶ Modern science

* What One Says to the Poet on the Subject of Flowers" and *Illuminations.*
† "Lettre du voyant," May 15, 1871.
†† "Lettre du voyant," May 13, 1871.
§ "Lettre du voyant," May 15, 1871.
‖ Ibid.
¶ May 1873.
** Letter to M. Bautin, January 30, 1881.
††† "Adieu," *A Season in Hell.*
§§ "Bad Blood," *A Season in Hell.*
‖‖ "Lightning," *A Season in Hell.*
¶¶ "The Impossible," *A Season in Hell.*

(mocked by Nietzsche for its "goal of as little pain as possible") tosses out resignation and submission along with ignorance, champions the project of everlasting happiness that successfully competes with the promises of religion— "Nothing is vanity; onward to science!"*—and joins the various socialist utopian currents. (In "Ouvriers" ["Workers"], Rimbaud deplores "the horrible quantity of strength and knowledge that fate has always kept from [him].")

Like poetry, science, or what amounts to the same, the idea of poetry-as-science, carries Rimbaud "forward": at sixteen, "we must get to the unknown";† at thirty, he goes to "traffic in the unknown."†† The form of the unknown varies (it seems even more exalting in Abyssinia), but it always remains unreal or ideal. What matters is the *searching*.

"In an old *passage* in Paris I was taught classical sciences."§ Is Rimbaud referring to the Passage Choiseul, where he met the Parnassian Poets? But if "he gave himself to science,"[3] according to his sister's memory, it was to a global conception of knowledge without separate disciplines or specialties, an analogical, non-"categorical" conception similar to that of the great oriental scholars Avicenna or Ibn Arabi, who were astronomers, physicians, mathematicians, and alchemists at the same time. "He pretended to know everything, commerce, art, medicine,"‖ groans the "Mad Virgin." The scientism of his era is perhaps responsible for the notion of absolute knowledge in the *voyant*'s idea of science, but God is not his concept for what science does not yet know and for which Comte's positivism substituted the religion of humanism. The poet-scholar steals supernatural knowledge and power to defy God. "Science, violence!" allow us "to bury the tree of good and evil in the dark, to deport the tyranny of honor, so that we can bring forth our

* "Lightning," *A Season in Hell*.
† To Izambard, Charleville, May 13, 1871.
†† Harar, May 4, 1881.
§ "Vies" ("Lives") III, *Illuminations*.
‖ "Délires" I, *A Season in Hell*.

very pure love."* In his curriculum vitae, the fallen angel presented himself to the American consul in Bremen as a "teacher of sciences and languages."†

The "Philomath" (the "lover of knowledge," as Verlaine called Rimbaud, who appreciated it[4]) who will ask Delahaye to consult "an expert, a professor of mathematics"†† to buy the instruments he has requested, also asked him "a little favor" in 1875: "Can you tell me briefly and precisely—what is required for graduation, the *bachot* in science, classical and mathematical division, etc.—You must tell me the level required in each subject: math., phys., chem., etc. and then immediately the titles of the books used in your high school (and how to get them)."§

Elsewhere, in East Africa, ideal terrain for the meeting of explorers and disciplines, Rimbaud's wanderings take on the sense of research—"I venture out only with full knowledge."‖ They are also the disorderly quest for identity of a scholar who has turned from magic to applied sciences. Avid for knowledge—he wanted his Abyssinian wife to go to school in Europe—Rimbaud orders the most recent scientific instruments¶ and keeps his faith in the progress and power brought by science, a faith he projects onto the son he will not have, and who represents what he would have liked to be, a man "after [his] own idea . . . with the most complete education one could get in this time," his Other-Self, not a figure of impotence, but also of "the impossible"—"a renowned engineer, a man rich and powerful through his knowledge."**

* "Morning of Drunkenness," *Illuminations.*
† May 14, 1877.
†† Aden, January 18, 1882.
§ Charleville, October 14, 1875.
‖ Harar, November 7, 1881.
¶ "*A travel theodolite. . . . A good sextant. A Cravet compass, with a level . . . a collection of 300 mineralogical samples. . . . An aneroid pocket barometer. A hemp surveyors' tape. A mathematics kit containing: a ruler, a T-square, a protractor, proportional compasses, decimeter, drawing pens, etc. Drawing paper*" (Rimbaud's emphasis) (Aden, January 18, 1882).
** Harar, May 6, 1883.

Among the scientists he met are particularly an engineer in Cyprus who is mentioned twice in 1878, the engineer Ilg, the medical doctor Traversi, and the explorer Téléki. Jules Borelli admits generously: "He traveled for his business, I, for Science and curiosity. Science would have been much better served if our roles had been exchanged!"[5]

What is left then of Rimbaud the writer? Dashes into projects, projects without dash. All afternoon I was lost in the *mercato* of Addis, as one can get lost in a great festivity without even taking part. I thought of the book Rimbaud did not write, the photos and engravings for which are still here, scattered all over the neighborhood where eucalyptus coal and acacia wood are sold. Burned in a thousand fires, they give Addis Ababa its evening smell.

"He told me he was preparing beautiful works," Françoise Grisard confirms.[6] No doubt it was the project on the Gallas, a few scattered parts of which must have found their way into the *Report on Ogaden* (and perhaps into the letter to the editor of the *Bosphore égyptien,* a book edition of which, on thick paper, tries to make up for a lost work with a fancy title: Arthur Rimbaud, *Voyage en Abyssinie et au Harar* [Paris: La Centaine, 1928]). The *Report* and the letter, Rimbaud's only publications in Abyssinia, do not make us expect a thrilling testimony like Bardey's *Barr Adjam,* but rather an outdated work like Soleillet's, where experience is filtered through didactic intent, or a sepia souvenir like the essay by Borelli, who was for a long time the best-known French "writer" in Ethiopia.

The work Rimbaud dreamed of in 1882 was transformed into a few articles sent to newspapers in 1887, during the strange Egyptian episode of his African life. "I have written up my travels in Abyssinia for the Geographical Society. I've sent articles to *Le Temps, Le Figaro,* etc. I also intend to send the *Courrier des Ardennes* some interesting stories from my travels in East Africa."* These articles con-

*To his family, Aden, December 15, 1887.

dense several Rimbaldian constants: whim, travel and science, an old leaning toward journalism that Izambard had witnessed to his cost,[7] hankering for renown and recognition. Sent to newspapers the poet used to despise, they represent even more his desire for *inclusion,* in the double sense of publication and return to normalcy. Once they had landed in the wastebaskets of the press, they took on a symbolic dimension: the society that has ignored and rejected him, missed occasions, persistent bad luck, stubborn silence—a lost image of Arthur Rimbaud and his castles in Abyssinia. Afterward, Rimbaud quickly builds up other projects. All absorbed in his business, he soon no longer has time . . . to write to *Le Temps:* "If I were not settled here I would send *Le Temps* interesting details on the economic situation of these countries . . . and the manner in which Menelik sends his creditors to hell! But let's pass over these disgraces!"* Simultaneous translation: "If I had the time I would live!" General grammar of the project: from past ("I've sent") to conditional ("I would send"), and return to silence.

Reality vanishes at the least doubt, inkling of improbability, or fit of anxiety. The work planned and abandoned, the articles that end in the wastebasket, the unfinished or never begun travel writings, the papers he burned at his final departure, are only fragments of a consciousness off course. They resemble the illegible books he received one day: Bottles of ink had broken in the trunk; "All the books were bathed in ink."†

"The mail is getting organized—small packets of letters are put in sheepskin pouches,"[8] writes Rimbaud in 1881. Did the poet in spite of himself compose an epistolary work, now collected, after his *Poems*? "But can we call them literary productions," asks Jean-Marie Carré, "these dry, prosaic reports with their strict and naked precision, without

*To Ilg, Harar, October 9, 1889.
†To his family, Aden, January 22, 1882.

personal traits, without voice? We are very far from the 'Alchemy of the Word.' There is an absolute detachment, a radical indifference to form."[9]

Alfred Bardey himself was "disappointed"[10] by his old associate's letters when they were published. The syntactic and thematic components of Rimbaud's African correspondence are repetitive to the point where it would be easy to fabricate any unpublished letter:

> Dear friends,
>
> I have not yet found the occasion to send you a letter. Tomorrow, however, I will entrust this to somebody who is going to [Zeila]. Be so very good as to reply and send me what I am asking, for I need it all badly. I am still employed here. The weather is very good now. In a few days I shall leave for a deal in ashlar and limestone from which I hope to make some money.
>
> More soon.
>
> A. Rimbaud

But Rimbaud already anticipated his own pastiche in the paragon of a letter mailed from Limassol (Cyprus) on June 4, 1880. A letter quoted too often. It precedes all the African and Arabian correspondence, and its expandable model[11] will change according to periods of hope, resignation, or distress. Rimbaud's letters are in the image of their sender, as dry as Calamata figs. But they are "yearned for" by his mother and sister or, rather, the female family complex, the "dear friends." They are echoes of the preoccupations (money, health, climate) of these imagined readers by whom Rimbaud does not feel sufficiently loved to make his letters *necessary*. They are written, as it were, at a distance to the second power. Their brevity, the haste in which they were written, seems in inverse ratio to the physical distance: "The desert to be crossed twice doubles the postal distance."* A

---

*Harar, July 22, 1881.

correspondence shrinking like Balzac's *peau de chagrin,* further abridged by family taboos, the mutual consent not to mention certain people (father, brother, the past), to *be silent* about the essential. Rimbaud is stingy with his words; he economizes on the detailed informations he is asked for; his notes have more contact function than exchange value. They are written *in the margin* of his activities—and only when there is a problem—in conditions of boredom or fatigue, impatience or detachment, which give them a turn quite different from his daily life. Letters without effigy, they are above all written with the proud indifference to literature of a man who considers himself alone and definitely forgotten.

Outside any aesthetic project, unvalued, do these messages then have only historical interest?[12] "Two thirds of what we can know about Rimbaud in Abyssinia comes from the correspondence," Pierre Petitfils observed rightly[13]—even though it does not tell even a thirtieth of his reality. . . .

Mallarmé's writing for his society ladies (when he assumes he will be read) is sometimes boring and painful. But aridity can have its own beauty. "I shall buy a horse and leave."* I used to think with (or because of) Blanchot that these letters were of "poor quality."[14] Now, rereading them in Ethiopia, their "banality" seems a bait: all of Rimbaud's letters have a "quality" of their own. Two volumes, yet! On one hand, the *Lettres de la vie littéraire, 1870–1875,* collected and annotated by Jean-Marie Carré; on the other, the *Lettres d'Égypte, Arabie, Éthiopie,* introduced by Paterne Berrichon. Then, corrected and augmented by a third volume, the *Correspondance 1888–1891,* edited by Jean Voellmy.[15] For a hundred years now Rimbaud's letters have as it were *appeared in court*—used for two purposes they in no way satisfy: documentation and chronology. A web of multiple contradictions—a literary procedure par excellence—Rimbaud's correspondence is a game of pick-up-sticks.[16] All the

---

*Harar, May 4, 1881. Dry sentences in *A Season in Hell*: "My day is over; I'm leaving Europe," etc.

letters refer to episodes of a life forever on the move that we have trouble imagining today.[17] A letter like the one from Charleville in 1871 with a list of books he would like to resell is just about completely without interest. But the crossing of the St. Gotthard!* This letter is as valuable as one of the *Illuminations*. Or the unsettling letter dated Harar, May 6, 1883, to the *Bosphore égyptien,* a historical document under its frozen epic veneer. The extraordinary tale told to the consul,† of the winding up of Labatut's caravan in Entotto, a tragicomedy in dazzlingly effective language. "Philosopher that you are, tell us what is going on," asks Ilg,†† who does not hide the pleasure he takes in reading Rimbaud's letters. If the correspondence to the second group of recipients—businessmen—differs tonally from the "letters to his family," the whole is not "without voice." On the contrary, aside from dreams of travel and getting rich, aside from his many projects and fierce independence, every page varies according to his impatience ("finish up, will you please finish up!"),§ rage (against Savouré), irony (at Brémond who sells "sculptured oysters"‖), distress or despair (when the depot is dissolved in 1884): a *tone maintained* till Marseille where Rimbaud ("impotent, miserable, any dog in the street will tell you"¶) dies dictating—what a letter!

His letters remind me of the postcards we traditionally send on trips and which arrive after we have already returned. Tonight, I am without words. . . . Too much reality. I must allow the images time to come. The time, not to "realize" what is happening to me, but to "derealize," "defamiliarize" it, as if certain dreamed-of countries—the Orient, India, China—held so much Reality that they dumbfound us. Suddenly Rimbaud's letters seem incompre-

* Genoa, November 17, 1878.
† Aden, November 9, 1887.
†† Boulluk, July 17, 1890.
§ To Ilg, February 20, 1891.
‖ To Ilg, July 1, 1889.
¶ To the director of the Messageries Maritimes, November 9, 1891.

hensible to me in printed form, and on "Bible paper" yet (as the French call India paper)! They regain their power "as soon as one travels a bit in the Ethiopian countries,"* which they cannot be separated from. Rimbaud's letters do not belong to belles lettres: We would need to keep them in manuscript and know how to speak them, give them breath. Under the title *Complete Works* (which they render absurd), they now address an infinity of recipients, still calling to each one in a singular, existential relation. Camus, in *L'Homme révolté,* says: "In order to keep the myth we must ignore these decisive letters. They are sacrilegious, as truth sometimes is."[18]

Business notes? The other dealers' letters, Brémond's or Savouré's, are the kind that we have replaced with telephone and fax. They have none of the speed, energy, moods, thematic frames—or the vibrancy—of Rimbaud's letters. But the paradoxical—not literary—beauty of this correspondence and the Rimbaldian constants of its structure still do not give us the possible *remainder* of poetry, its persisting traces: Indeed there are some.

Short sentences, signals: "Coffee fluctuates . . . ,"† "Rupees are dancing . . ."†† Like an Egyptologist dusting a scroll with a brush, Agnès Rosenstiehl[19] has managed to isolate poetic fragments in the African and Arabian letters, brief moments of poetry *rising up* in Rimbaud. Scattered bursts barely dimmed, impossible to make into a coherent text, to recompose (except perhaps by placing each on a blank page in the manner of Georges Schéhadé's anthology of one-line poems[20]), these scattered fragments are fascinating like unearthed lines of a story we will never read:

> . . . and the Djanos of the Shoa embassy floating on the planks.

* Cairo, August 26, 1887.
† Harar, March 1, 1890.
††Harar, February 5, 1891.

We are in our spring baths; skin glistening, stomachs sour, brains fog over . . .

. . . strangle the cashiers and break the registers.

The elephant hunter caracoles endlessly in the ravines of Darimont; he'll end up here when he's done drying his *votris Kys* of pork and preserved milk among the Guerris and Bartris . . .

. . . the beautiful big yellow dogs with the familiar story.

. . . behind him, the frenetic widow's burnous snaking along the precipice.

The essay Rimbaud intended for the Geographical Society (the *Report on Ogaden*), leaves out these glimmers, eliminates these contrasts. An alert consciousness of writing (for publication) imposes attention, a challenge and at the same time repression—of the madman inside him (an effort toward normalcy). In the letters, where autocensorship tends to relax, there can be strokes of lightning; the formulation comes, as if by accident, a skid or slip. Expression overflows communication. Rimbaud forgets himself, finds himself. Immediately and of his own will, he takes himself in hand again and brings the fragments back into the order of the sentence, down to earth. Reflex action of the code, prose technique. Metapoetics of the fragment, the letters from Africa and Arabia show rather the reverse of creation:[21] They would be to poetic matter what the incision in a copper plate is to a relief print. A prose in negative, black *Illuminations*. *A contrario*, the *Illuminations* show only poetic matter, eliminating all narrative dross. In Abyssinia, Rimbaud puts on hairshirt and mask. A letter from Harar means the mask of Borelli with Arthur Rimbaud's blue eyes.

★ ★ ★

"We haven't had any news of the grrrreat diplomatic mission," Ilg writes to Rimbaud. "I expect interesting details, you tell such a good story when you want to."[22] "We used to gather to read his letters," Savouré remembers, "and it was always a real pleasure party." For example, Rimbaud had indeed given his version of the Italian epic in Massawa: "They will conquer all the volcanic hillocks scattered in a radius of thirty kilometers around Massawa, connect them by a jerry-built railroad and, having reached these extreme points, fire their howitzers at the vultures and fly a ribboned balloon with heroic slogans. . . . That will be all."* Bardey told Jean-Paul Vaillant that "when we found ourselves in a situation of forced rest, he could talk volubly by the hour. But those moments were rare." It makes one think of the *Wotads* of Rimbaud's *Report on Ogaden,* "scholars" every tribe has, who know the Koran and can improvise poetry. Monsignor Jarosseau, in 1936, recalled "brilliant extempore talks on French literature."[23] A *Wotad* in rare moments. These talks are perhaps what was left of the literary Rimbaud whom Verlaine knew full of "banter and poker-face humor"[24] and whom Robecchi-Bricchetti remembers full of spirit and a truly French gift of gab: *"Aveva spirito, verve et abilità di causerie veramente francese"* ["He had spirit, *verve* and a truly French gift of the gab"].

"He was given to mockery," remembers Ottorino Rosa, "caustic, and liked to find the comic and ridiculous side of people and things."[25] And Savouré: "A poker face. I've rarely seen him very joyful, but he had the talent to amuse his audience with stories and anecdotes told with such funny turns one wondered where he could have gotten them." His irony ever vigilant, his mockery an answer to aggressiveness, Rimbaud's humor[26] is occasionally *disarming:* "Good news over here," he writes from Aden. "Peace and silence on earth as in heaven. The doctors doctorize—and get their wives stolen, at least that's what happened to good old Sig.

*To Ilg, February 1, 1888.

Traversi, they say. He's repudiated the missus and taken his kid away?"* A complaining Arthur with his mother, a laughing Arthur with Ilg, making fun of the Shoa campaign: "I think they left Italy with destination Jerusalem, Bethlehem, Sodom and Gomorrah—because they don't seem to miss any occasion to visit a Holy Place."† Rimbaud throws out *digs:* "Here lies, in Lit-Marefia, Antonelli and his pox . . . Antoine Brémond giving suck to his infants in Alin-Amba . . . the tanner Stéphane asleep in the gutter in front of the house."††

Did he not use to have his "old portion of divine joy"? Every now and then he gets a certificate of merriment. "He burst into laughter, as he often does, silently, softly," said Verlaine.[27] "And he was an astonishing talker: all of a sudden he'd make us laugh. . . . We'd stop him . . . enough, enough, but he would go on and on," Righas told Segalen. "Your details about Mr. Bidault," writes the austere Ilg, "have given us divine amusement, and I only regret that I can't draw his portrait in your manner, I'd surely be a success. . . . I would also have liked to have the honor and pleasure to be cheered up by you and your good memories."[28] I also burst out laughing when I read his somewhat excessive schoolboy humor that makes a mockery out of Ras Makonnen's reception in Italy for Ilg's benefit: "The Dedjaz left Zeila on the third for Naples and Rome. The twenty-four cannons shots fired in his honor as he got into the train gave him acute diarrhea, which infected his entire retenue."§ But jokes are quickly forgotten, and none of the laughers in this land of oral tradition (not even Franzoj who stayed a whole year with Rimbaud in Tadjoura) has given us Rimbaud's stories.

* To Ilg, February 29, 1888.
† Harar, October 7, 1889.
††Harar, June 25, 1888.
§ To Ilg, Harar, August 24, 1889.

Rimbaud had a taste for amplification. Cultivating "[his] lip's atrocious irony,"* he used to scandalize his classmates with outrageous stories. Verlaine was in a good position to observe "his extraordinary, precocious seriousness bordering on the sullen, but with sudden flights into very peculiar or macabre fantasies." His favorite word ("atrocious") is as frequent in the letters as in the poems, it must have been in his mouth every day. Hyperbole abounds. The Seer was committed to excess in his disordering. He always exaggerated,† even in talking of *A Season in Hell*: "this book, for which I must still invent half a dozen atrocious stories."†† He still lays it on thick in Abyssinia when complaining of taxes ("a farce that has now turned atrocious"§) or Menelik's regime ("horrible and hateful tyranny"‖). Harar did not cure him of his tendency to disproportion, of the cruel merriment that hides daggers under its smile. "Your usual exaggerations," replies the inoculated Savouré. Rimbaud is always called an "Ardennais," but if we go by stereotypes, he was also a Marseillais for his exaggerations and braggadocio, and because Marseille, great seaport, gateway to Africa and the Orient, limit of the West, is already Egypt, the elsewhere, a copy of Alexandria, the beyond. And Marseille was as much as Charleville the wanderer's rest stop, city of departures and returns, where Rimbaud looked for work in June 1875, where he took the boat for Alexandria in September 1878, where fever stopped him in winter 1879, Marseille where he must needs die.

"Holy . . . the mask you gave us."¶ Could it be that Rimbaud's true face is the mask behind which he imagined

---

* "Le Juste . . ."
† ". . . first communion is held at the hundred thousand altars of the cathedral" ("Après le déluge" ["After the Deluge"], *Illuminations*).
†† To Delahaye, May 1873.
§ Harar, August 26, 1889.
‖ Harar, September 7, 1889.
¶ "Morning of Drunkenness," *Illuminations*.

his return? "By my mask I will pass for being of a strong race."★ "I had a good laugh, I assure you," Alfred Ilg comes back at him. "I see to my great pleasure that behind the terrible mask of horrible severity, there hides a good humor that many would envy you." And Bardey: "He could never get rid of that poor, mean, satirical mask which hid the true qualities of his heart."[29] However, passing time accentuates Rimbaud's grimaces. "Well, by dint of groans and grimaces . . ."† "You have no idea what grimacing, screaming and clowning it takes to shake loose a few hundred talari."†† Even "Menelik made some grimaces."§ In life-as-work-of-art, the grimace points to both theatricality and otherness, but theater calls for a spectator, and this triangulation is absent from Rimbaud's texts. It is in internalized dialogues, of the "Mad Virgin" and "Infernal Husband" especially, that the comedy or drama of the Other is played out, a re-presentation, theater and its double, a polylogue ruined in possession.[30] Soon the severity of the Abyssinian Rimbaud no longer hides any fleeting good humor. His alacrity turns grimace; his face tends toward the truth of the mask, as at the end of "Delirium" in *A Season in Hell,* when "he gave a long, horrible laugh." All that remains of the laughs and stories, whose content has vanished in distant echoes, is the grating of a bitter and bruised sensibility. "A white ray from high in the sky blots out this comedy."‖ Once the mask falls: a wolf's face.[31]

At least we think Rimbaud kept his "gift for languages" that Mallarmé had noticed,[32] the languages "he collected, having sworn off all enthusiasms for his native one." In hope of "finding a language,"¶ the *voyant* "ex-pressed" language as one presses juice out of an orange, combing the dictio-

---

★ "Bad Blood," *A Season in Hell.*
† Harar, October 7, 1889.
†† Harar, September 7, 1889.
§ Aden, February 1, 1888.
‖ "Les Ponts," ("Bridges"), *Illuminations.*
¶ To Demeny, May 15, 1871.

naries for rare words, for unheard-of associations. "Which language was I speaking?"* He "disordered" even *its* sense, cultivated dialect[33] and slang deformations, mutilated his language. "His conversation was spangled with slang and literary quotations, quite witty by the way, unless he sank into stubborn silence."[34] Verlaine's "Dizains" caricature his *"tourisses"* or *"artics,"* his preferred "Parisiano-Ardennais accent," where dreaming of a business is drawled out as *"j'rêve eud négoce."* Then Rimbaud gives up. "No more words!"† Verlaine: "You are no longer good for anything: your words/ Have died of slang and sneers." *"I can no longer talk!"* †† He had tried to "invent . . . new languages";§ he learned others, perhaps pursuing a chimera of "supernatural powers" ‖ in the scholar who can speak to the greatest number of people. Rimbaud, whom his mother made recite Latin verses by heart, locked himself in, mumbling the raw poetry of English, German, Italian, Spanish, modern Greek, and Arabic vocabulary lists. "M. Dubar is very satisfied with Rimbaud, who knows enough Arabic to give orders, which gets him the respect of the native personnel," Bardey noted when Rimbaud arrived in Aden in 1880.[35] "One of the best speakers of Arabic," Savouré remembers.[36] Everyone who met him confirms Robecchi-Bricchetti's verdict that he was "polyglot."[37] Every language is a travel project for Rimbaud, means so many directions abandoned after a few months, a few hundred words. He disposes of rich vocabularies, as a bank teller keeps foreign currencies, with a sense of poverty. His languages lead him into a labyrinth. "Alas, what good are . . . these languages that we stuff our memory

* "Bad Blood," *A Season in Hell.*
† Ibid. "I loved . . . old fashioned literature, Church Latin, erotic books with bad spelling, the novels of our ancestors, fairy tales, children's books, old operas, silly refrains and artless rhythms" ("Alchemy of the Word," *A Season in Hell*).
†† "Morning," *A Season in Hell.*
§ "Adieu," *A Season in Hell.*
‖ Ibid.

with."* He had once thought with La Bruyère that "languages are the key to knowledge." Then, heeding the call of the Orient, Rimbaud retraces the history of writing against the stream, loses himself in a multiplicity of languages to the point of losing his origins, forgetting his native tongue and feeling a stranger to himself: "I'm losing my taste . . . for the languages of Europe by the day."† He finds himself on the side of the "strange races" with the most languages and the *least* to say, on the side of Ethiopia until silence.

Rimbaud is taciturn like an Indian: "He came into the tent, sat down without saying a word for half an hour and left."[38] Like Borelli, Bardey knew him "usually taciturn," and Ilg likewise described him as "taciturn, reserved, not looking for companionship." Already in Paris, he seemed to open his mouth only for insults, replied in monosyllables to Charles Cros, and shut off his mother's questions about his "pagan book" in Roche, 1873: "It says what it says, literally and in all senses." But in Abyssinia his anxiety mounts, to the point where he fears a *trap* back in Marseille. Ilg promises to "drive out his baleful ideas"[39] and is clearly unaware of the irony of his repeated injunction not to worry: "Ne vous faites pas de mauvais sang."[40] In most of Rimbaud's letters, we find the abbreviation "etc." (the first "etc." appears in 1875, at the end of his last dated poem, no doubt the last written††), which implies his haste and his giving up, like the little characteristic gesture that surprised Bardey: "He talks little and accompanies his short explanations with small, cutting gestures of his right hand, and at the wrong moments." The last word, what is left of the dream, reiterating, with supporting gesture, the end of the dream.

* May 6, 1883.
† Ibid.
†† "Rêve" ("Dream"): "The genius: 'I am Roquefort!'/—'It'll be our death!' . . ./ —'I am Gruyère/And Brie! . . . etc.' " (In a letter to Delahaye, October 14, 1875.)

*　　*　　*

"To me. The story of one of my follies." A first line to
drive one crazy. An insane supplication. Is this "*À moi*" a
cry for help as in "To me, I'm drowning, help!" Or, rather,
a sober "Now to myself." Not to you. My story, as nobody else has lived it. Or a satanic: Come "to me," my little
innocents. Or again: "Now for myself." It is my turn on
stage. The neighbors in Roche-Laïtou, the wolf lair, were
certain, that spring of 1873: He's mad, the Rimbaud boy—
with his punk hair. . . . Just listen to him. Locked in his
attic, wrapped in a sheet, howling in falsetto: "Ah! I'm mad!
. . . I'm the slave of the infernal husband, the one who
ruined the mad virgins." Really ought to call Dr. Beaudier quick.

Like the "dream of idiotic grief" in "Vagabonds," Rimbaud's life in Abyssinia still bears the mark of the Roche
madness: It might even be the only intact *remnant* of the
poet, as his life continues. Like the spring that brought back
the "idiot's gruesome laugh,"* (where we may, in a sense,
literally hear Frédéric and *his* laugh), the long African summer struck Rimbaud with a kind of idiocy—"because though
you assume I live like a prince, I am sure I live in a very
stupid way."† He even fears becoming "completely idiotic"†† in this country. Or again: "in these countries where
one becomes stupid as an ass."§

The Reason of the Enlightenment was replaced by a *praise
of follies,* a luminous madness, bright flare of the "Night of
Hell,"‖ a madness of incandescent intelligence that dissolves
"my two cents' worth of reason."¶ Madman: vague term.
. . . We might as well say, without more explanations, a
theopathic wound. Perhaps madness corresponded, in Rim-

---

* "Once . . . ," *A Season in Hell.*
† May 10, 1882.
†† Ibid.
§ March 14, 1883.
‖ *A Season in Hell.*
¶ "The Impossible," *A Season in Hell.*

baud's mind, to the "moral madness" old Ribot defined as a passing disorder, a "deep perversion of the moral sense" that leaves the intellect intact and may even develop it. Madness did not come to Rimbaud though he invited it: "I expect to become a very mean madman."* The follies he brags about are not diminutive forms of "real" madness, but all the satanic, magical forms to be invented in the revolt against God, in the delirious affirmation of himself as God, both innocent and damned. Rimbaud talks man to man with God. He speaks simply, "like a Christian."[41] He has the language of the damned in his keeping, the language of soul to soul.

Hence "reason" was not an opposite of "madness," but its vector, which he used. "I played nice tricks on madness."† Perfectly lucid. He played with fire, with folly, descending the concentric circles of hell, that of moral and social law first, then by way of the left hand to the basic circles of the spirit and all the way to the central core where his physical integrity was menaced. "I have not forgotten one single sophistry of madness—the kind of madness that gets locked up: I could recite them all over again, I know the system."†† He attained the raptures described by Nietzsche at almost the same time: the joyful lightness, the moments of truly free freedom, and the clown moods inherent in the most elevated states.

Saturated reason-madness, *A Season in Hell* gives us a Christian variant of satori: "quantity of love"§ without a mast, a bloodstain in the desert. Most clever to go destroy himself correctly in Abyssinia, with the impossible desire to regain Reason, reach Knowledge, Salvation, Gold . . . "I am an incurable brute," said Antonin Artaud, "I have felt

---

* "Lives," *Illuminations.*
† "Once . . . ," *A Season in Hell.*
†† "Délires" II, *A Season in Hell.* Or: "Madness, all of whose impulses I've known" ("Bad Blood").
§ "The poet would define the unknown quantity that in his time awakens in the universal soul" (May 15, 1871).

this Void so long, but have refused to throw myself into it."[42] As Artaud will later see his hand continue to "doodle pen-strokes" when he tries not to write, Rimbaud ("I'm getting stupid,"* "I am a brute"†) draws figures in his letters as one would doodle. His invoices are a journal of what has stopped being said. "My writings,"†† he calls them: Sums among the words, letters and figures mixed together, these "writings" are all that remains of Poetry and Knowledge. An idiolect . . . "The *invoice* is all that is left of the voice."[43] The "logical and necessary" giving up of poetry had been an act of supreme lucidity. His intelligence, which he had wanted to endanger or transcend, remained "above average," said Borelli,[44] and more or less useless. He is Arthur Rimbaud entirely—but as if he had excised an organ and seen to its atrophy. As Mallarmé put it, Rimbaud "cut poetry out of his own living body." Rimbaud, the man who once planned a book of *Études néantes* (*Nothing Studies*)[45] draws progressively nearer the Void, draws near it in Harar. The man of action is idle. All his fervent action hides an essential idleness, a *désoeuvrement* in the literal sense of having forsaken an *oeuvre,* a work. "And this is not what's saddest," he said about his boredom. He was afraid of "becoming besotted by and by, isolated as we are . . . remote."§ And under the Harar sun, Rimbaud the idiot, too distant for us *to hear,* was no doubt sometimes overcome by an "idiot's gruesome laugh," by fits of uncontrollable, mad, Abyssinian laughter.

To smile at the desert—"and let my misfortune be free."‖ To die in the desert, defeated but legendary, like Charles the Bold devoured by wolves on a frozen lake. So much does Rimbaud prize the idiocy conjoined with his body, his

* "Fausse conversion" ("False Conversion").
† "Bad Blood," *A Season in Hell.*
†† "I put up a bed between my cash register, my writings . . ." (July 15, 1891).
§ Harar, August 4, 1888.
‖ "But I want to smile at nothing . . ." ("May Banners").

malady of being unique, that he attains in Abyssinia "the holy idiocy of the desert Fathers." Not the first-degree idiocy ("of the old imbecils at school"),* but a second-degree idiocy of giving up knowledge and the self, the truth of nothingness. "Man," asked Goethe, "when will you learn that not to succeed is greatness?" Laughter, pain, suffering on the scale of the desert. "If I complain it is just another way of singing."† But in Harar, Rimbaud stops singing, his song leaves him. "An artist's and storyteller's fine runaway fame!"††

* May 13, 1871.
† Aden, July 10, 1882.
†† "Adieu," *A Season in Hell.*

11

THE SLAVE

Who does not vindicate on
earth his divine portion will
not find rest even in hell.
—Hölderlin

Addis. The palace where the Negus dynasty, the Abyssinian House of Capet, came to its end. Here, the last "king of kings," who used to throw bread balls and gold coins from his Rolls-Royce, is said to have been smothered under a pillow by a rebel officer, like Pope John X by his mistress, or Desdemona by Othello. Not far from the palace, we are crossing a vast fallow garden on our way to the deserted university. Professor Alémé Eshete, who receives us, pays tribute to Rimbaud's historical role in wooden, if impeccable, French: His arms sale to Menelik contributed to the Negus's victorious struggle against imperialism and for Ethiopian independence. . . . Professor Eshete is quoting Berrichon without knowing it: "He was certainly motivated by a desire to put Abyssinia in a position to make sure of its independence and dignity."[1] Our interlocutor, who has a bad cold this morning, deplores, however, that Rimbaud had been involved in slave trade. I might have known: Enid Starkie's *Rimbaud in Abyssinia*[2] lies open on his desk. Our cameraman puts us in the same frame so that my reply will not get cut during montage—but I am sorry that there remains some ambiguity about this unfortunate myth in the film. After the work of Mario Matucci and Jean Voellmy, authorities on the strength of rigor and honesty, we no longer have to prove that Rimbaud was not compromised in the slave trade.

If we care about historical reality rather than myths, if we are not out to defend an a priori image of Rimbaud, whether that of his family's hagiography or of the cynical slave trader proposed by his detractors, analysis of facts is imperative.

Slavery produces revulsion and indignation in any humanistic consciousness, which has developed from abhorrence of servitude. Attitudes were different at the time in East Africa, whose customs we must know. A time-honored practice, slavery here had nothing in common with the Roman slaves crowded in the *ergastulum,* the appalling incidents of deportation, mistreatment and killing at the time of Cortez, or even with the chubby, chained Venuses of the "Slave Market" Gérome painted in Cairo. . . . "The slave's situation," writes Jules Borelli, "is not necessarily as horrible as Europeans would represent it. No doubt they suffer under bad masters, but cruelty is not the rule. The fate of these poor creatures is not enviable and must inspire legitimate compassion, but most often they are not mistreated by the family they are placed with. If they win their master's confidence, which is not rare, they rule the household."[3]

On his arrival in Abyssinia, Alfred Bardey encountered a column of slave women and girls near Farré:

> They were sold by their owners, their parents, or have sold themselves. They are worth ten to twenty talari each. If there are a hundred of them, I could buy the lot for fifteen hundred talari, i.e. seven thousand five hundred francs. Like my companion [Pinchard], I am disturbed, surprised, and not sure that I feel the revulsion one nor-

mally has when there is a question of slavery. To report exactly what we saw, I must say that this caravan does not seem to have anything tragic about it. Most of the girls seem self-assured and give free rein to merriment and mockery—at our address, it seems. . . . A few men, apparently of Asiatic origin, move among them. They are dressed in the Arabic *foutah* that comes down to the knees and is tied with a scarf at the waist. . . . The *djellals* (slave traders) make the women move with gestures and words that do not seem brutal or even very imperative. . . . They obey, not without protest, with laughter and shouts that do not indicate a depressed morale.

Later, Bardey meets another caravan of women slaves: "They are visibly from different tribes. Most of them wear almost new cotton which must be part of the payment for their persons."[4] This was the custom: Rich Abyssinians bought their servants, and entire communities sold their services. Savouré, Labatut, and most of the Europeans had twenty or so bought servants. Borelli himself reports: "I can no longer count my slaves; luckily Abba Djiffar takes care of them."[5] Having renounced their liberty—or having no concept of it—these women and men were not servants, lacking what we consider the dignity of the individual. Neither were they slaves, in the strict Berber sense, by the nature of the treatment they consented to, but rather by their consent to be traded, which illustrates one of the phases of the Hegelian dialectic of master and slave.[6] "I look like a slave trader," Borelli complains. "I try to get them to go back home. They refuse . . ." "They do not want to be emancipated," Provost remarks likewise. "They prefer belonging, being part of the family, to being tossed out under the iron law of modern wage-earning."[7]

The same Borelli will go into more detail with César Tian's son:

This slavery question is far from what is said about it. It takes very different forms in different countries. In Mima, where I lived, the slaves inherited their fields from father to son and were masters of their land. As for corporal punishment, I never saw any. Moreover, you never knew if an individual was a slave or not. But it would take a whole book to tell of all the nuances. And, a matter to think about, the slave is free, works little and always has to eat, because his master does not have the right to fire him.[8]

In 1938, the French, enlarged, version of Enid Starkie's *Rimbaud in Abyssinia*[9] was published. The Irish critic's work (which was then newsworthy because of Mussolini's occupation of Abyssinia) remains indispensable for understanding the rivalry of the European powers for East Africa and the coasts of the Red Sea at the end of the last century. But her chapter, "The Slave Trade," contains the four pages most damaging to the knowledge—and memory—of Rimbaud in the entire history of Rimbaud studies. The hypothesis of Rimbaud as a slave trader, skillfully presented and reinforced by the contrast to the family hagiography, rested on the clay feet of four specious claims.[10]

First Claim

Starkie claims first of all that traffic in arms and traffic in slaves "were inextricably linked."[11] Perhaps she imagined that caravans that "went up" into Shoa with arms would come back down to the coast with slaves or that they accompanied slave caravans as a security measure, or that both were part of one and the same illegal commerce. So Rimbaud, having sold arms, must necessarily have been a slave trader.[12]

However, Starkie pretends not to know what Rimbaud

himself wrote to the Ministry of Foreign Affairs, cosigning with Labatut:

> It cannot be said that there is any correlation between the importation of arms and the exploitation of slaves. This latter traffic has existed between Abyssinia and the coast in invariable proportions since time immemorial. Our affairs are completely independent from the dark traffic of the Bedouins. Nobody would dare claim that a European has ever sold or bought, transported or helped transport a single slave on the coast or in the interior.*

The legal tone—unless it be the roster of denials—does not make this declaration suspect. In Abyssinia, only Europeans imported arms. They did not act as "dealers" (a term that seems used to discredit activities that went counter to English goals), but legitimately, as nationals with full agreement of their governments. The slave trade, on the other hand, was reserved for Arabs from the beginning—monopolized by approximately twelve thousand families, especially Abou-Beker and his eleven sons whose reputation was established in all the communities, but did not take in Menelik. "All the slave traders in the vast kingdom of Shoa are Muslim," wrote the Marquis Antinori.[13] Edoardo Scarfoglio, a journalist from Naples, also observed that "this flourishing trade [was] in Arab hands."[14] And in 1886, A.-S. de Doncourt gave precise details about this traffic "of the Muslims . . . who bring back to Gondar slaves, civet, wax, skins, cardamom with magnificent bark, and finally ginger, in quantity."[15]

Not only can Europeans not be implicated in this traffic, but the Amharas can not either. "One must know what one is talking about, especially if it is a matter of libel," writes the Marquis Antinori. "Everybody knows that Abyssinian

*Rimbaud and Labatut to the Ministry of Foreign Affairs, Aden, May 21, 1886.

law permits buying of slaves, but not selling, and this law is enforced with very severe penalties: minimum, is amputation of the right hand. Moreover an Amhara who dealt in slaves or led their caravans would be a disgrace to the people. . . . In all the markets of Shoa, not a single slave is sold: the law forbids it, and the Amhara populace would oppose it."[16] (Amharas here in the sense of "Christians.")

Menelik had been suspected of being proslavery, notably by Bianchi. Major Hunter even accused him in the Bombay newspaper[17] of selling Gallas to Abou-Beker. No doubt the law he himself passed in 1884, ostensibly banning slavery in his states, could not be absolutely enforced any more than the humanitarian resolutions proclaimed in both hemispheres, but the king and future Negus did succeed in reducing the scourge. "As for slavery, it does not exist in Abyssinia," Vignéras will claim in 1897, "and the trade is severely prohibited; when four slave dealers were recently discovered, they were hanged immediately."[18] But especially in the 1880s, Menelik must have closed his eyes to the Abou-Bekers' doings because he needed them to communicate with the coast. "If Menelik could get away from Abou-Beker," Ilg explained to the English minister in Aden, "no slave would leave the country and . . . this family would lose the influence it has in the region. Without the support of the Abou-Bekers, Shoa would not find any market for its slaves, and Menelik could not import any arms because their importation is illegal in the Zeila port."[19] No caravan, in fact no *gaflah,* could form or travel in relative security without Abou-Beker, the pasha of Zeila, or the very influential Sultan Mohammed Anfani, who thus controlled the import of European products and pursued with impunity their slave trade. "Nothing hurts the king's self-respect more than being called a slave trader," Antinori goes on. "Recently he had his antislavery edicts reproclaimed in the markets and forced baptism on thousands of Muslim who lived among the Amharas. Those who refused were reduced to beggary, forced to leave their country." The suspicion of complicity with Abou-Beker is unfounded: Menelik had simply to handle them with kid gloves. An understanding with the slavers was likewise insinuated against Rimbaud.[20] He, on the contrary, strongly denounced them:

> On all these occasions, the most dangerous enemies of the Europeans are the Abou-Bekers with their easy access to the Azzaze and the King where they slander us, throw off on our customs and pervert our intentions. They set a barefaced example of theft, assassination and pillage for the Dankali Bedouins. . . . But the few Europeans in Shoa and Harar who know the politics and morals of these people execrated by all the Issa Dankali tribes, Gallas and Amharas, avoid their company like the pest.*

Young Lucereau, held in Zeila, did not fail to tell Abou-Beker publicly what he thought of him, throwing out Arabic insults "including that of slave dealer."[21]

The Union Jack floated over Harar between November 1884 and May 1885: The British who administered Thewfik's Egypt were in favor of an Egyptian garrison occupying Harar. When Menelik kicked out Emir Raouf Pacha and the Egyptians in February 1887, England, having lost an important trump, opposed with all its means the influence of Italian and French merchants and diplomats—the French in particular were accused of supporting slavery with the import of arms. Great Britain, which had supported Emperor John of Tigre, had bet on the wrong Negus. . . . When Menelik, his vassal, succeeded in unifying Abyssinia, he favored England's rivals and, suspicious of the young Italian republic, showed particular preference for France: sly logic of the exchequer. "Protestant England," Paul Morand will write, "ennobles itself forever by its initiatives against the

*Letter to M. de Gaspary, Aden, November 9, 1887.

trade."[22] The English had only one abolition of slavery whereas the French had three, plus two reintroductions.[23] From 1884 on, French and Italians could not but subscribe, naturally, to the denunciation of slavery reiterated by Britain, but the latter also saw its fight against French influence merge with its humanitarian preoccupations and hoped to reduce, along with the slave trade, the arms traffic for Menelik's benefit. . . . Shrewd Rimbaud reported that Menelik was very annoyed by the ban on importing arms to the coasts of the Red Sea. Savouré, for his part, addressed a letter to the Ministers of Foreign Affairs stating that "Menelik would always protect the French, especially if we, in exchange for his concessions in suppressing the slave trade, granted him passage of arms which he was still in need of."[24]

So, in order to develop its interests, the French government protected its principles with promises, and thought it could not radically trammel the Abou-Bekers' activities: In Tadjoura, where they assembled the slaves, France had a small garrison. "The local trade is slaves," writes Rimbaud. "From here the caravans of the Europeans leave for Shoa, very small affairs; and we cross under great difficulties because the natives on all sides have turned hostile against Europeans ever since the British Admiral Hewett made Emperor John of Tigre sign a treaty abolishing the slave trade, the only flourishing native commerce. In the French Protectorate, however, the trade is not interfered with, and that is better."* It seems nevertheless excessive to insinuate that France, unable to change the situation, made its peace with the slave trade. Borelli tells that Ibrahim, the oldest Abou-Beker and a notorious slaver, would hide his human herd at the approach of a French ship. The British exasperated the Arabs by insisting on searching all dhows in order to hinder the trade, but an 1887 report from Rome indicates that they sent slaves as "free laborers" to the Seychelles and Mauritius, where they were "ransomed" by their employers. Rous

*Tadjoura, December 3, 1885.

noted that the British "close their eyes to the slave trade in Egypt," and that Arabian slavery, which appears "quite natural" to the natives, "is all in all less hard . . . than the free workers' conditions in the British colonies."[25] Nevertheless, the fact that the *djellals,* the slave drivers, could organize their traffic under the nose of a French sergeant and six soldiers in Tadjoura, constitutes a serious fault in French politics, narrow-minded ("inept") after all. On top of it, the Abou-Bekers proved false friends and robbed French merchants whenever they could. It is likely that Great Britain had a hand in the "mysterious" death of the Abou-Bekers. The construction of the Franco-Ethiopian Railroad was to ruin their power definitively.

The British Foreign Office and the French Ministry of Foreign Affairs multiplied their notes of protest. Every week, France (or, rather, Paul Soleillet) gobbled another dune on the Somali coast. A new treaty was drawn up to regulate the importation of arms into Shoa—which stopped Rimbaud's project to repeat his expedition in May 1888. But the French and Italians did not stop accumulating weapons in their concessions. According to Starkie: "Menelik, to express his gratitude to France . . . had promised to advance its interests in Djibouti."[27] The British authorities began to realize that their interests were hurt by honoring the formalities of a treaty nobody else respected and, not wanting to lose out on the lucrative traffic, abandoned the treaty in 1890 and joined the other powers in supplying arms to the Negus—along with Italy, which was to see the rifles sold to Menelik turned against itself in Aduwa.

Inserted in Enid Starkie's book is a loose pink slip, on which the author apologizes to the sons of César Tian. Starkie had claimed that the latter had also been implicated in the arms and slave trade: "*This remark,*" she herself underlines, "*is not supported by any document; it was simply my personal guess. . . .* To my guess concerning the commerce of arms," Starkie goes on, "I had added the following sentence: 'or perhaps even of Negroes, for the two traffics were inextricably linked.' *This hypothesis is also not supported by any document.*"[28] So, in the beginning there was: "simply my personal guess."

Second Claim

Biographers have credited Rimbaud with prodigious traveling. No doubt, "the man with soles of wind" rides faster than a caravan: "six hundred kilometers which I covered in eleven days on horseback."* At the "automatic pace" of his horses, Bardey takes six days to cover the three hundred fifty kilometers from Harar to Zeila. But, categorically stating her hypothesis (unsupported by fact) of two new arms expeditions in collusion with Savouré, during the end of March and end of April 1888, Enid Starkie follows Rimbaud on a map on a scale of one to one million.[29] She forgets that Harar is only halfway between Shoa and the coast— Rimbaud himself had noted that it took "all in all a month between our coast and the center of Shoa."† She likewise neglects to allow time for crossing the Red Sea—"about ten days in dhows and steamboats (because this is the longest and most boring part)."††—ignores the documents that prove Rimbaud's presence in Aden on April 4, 1888, and in Harar on the third and fifteenth of May; and does not take into account the time needed to organize a caravan—including the hitches mentioned above. Borelli had waited several months on the coast of Obock; Labatut's caravan was immobilized for a whole year. . . . If Starkie had attentively studied even the approximate map of Abyssinia that is the frontispiece of her book, she could have ascertained (as M. Matucci did with the required precision) that it was abso-

---

* Aden, April 4, 1888.
† Cairo, August 20, 1887.
†† Aden, March 29, 1888.

lutely impossible for Rimbaud to organize Savouré's caravan of April 26 or to accompany that of Abou-Beker to Ambos on May 10: unless Rimbaud did as I did and took a plane—along with his 225 camels.[30]

Again, arms traffic does not mean slave traffic; and Rimbaud's "traffic" amounts to a single expedition in 1886–1887 whose difficulties and vicissitudes he has told. On the way back from Entotto, Rimbaud took by himself the new road to Harar opened by Menelik, arriving a day before Jules Borelli, whose geographic observations correspond point for point with Rimbaud's.[31] We learn from Savouré that the attempt to repeat the expedition failed; and Rimbaud, who did not obtain the ministry's authorization to import arms, writes explicitly that he has given up the project: "It's been a long time since the minister's reply arrived, negative, as I had anticipated. Nothing doing on this side and, in any case, I've found something else."* He now thinks of "the gum trade,"† of importing cloth from Sedan.†† His cursed caravans exist only in the biographers' imagination. Such is his strength, and his bad luck.[32]

Third Claim

More and more the detective, Miss Starkie discovers in the archives of the Foreign Office a secret document claiming that Rimbaud accompanied a caravan of Abou-Beker's to Ambos that transported ivory and a great number of slaves: "A French merchant of the name of Remban [sic], one of the most active and intelligent agents of the French government in this region, accompanied the caravan."[33] But we no longer even have to prove that this report is a dead letter. Starkie is unaware that she is referring to an Italian document, the "Cecchi Report,"[34] whose first sentence had been

* Aden, April 4, 1888.
† February 1, 1888.
†† May 15, 1888.

diplomatically censored. "I believe I know, by confidential information"—that is, Cecchi knows by the grapevine. Some sycophant sold the English some information that was reported to Cecchi, explorer and Italian consul at Aden, who on May 22, 1888, sent a report to his superior, Crispi—in which there was talk of "a French merchant of the name of Rembau [sic]"—who in turn transmitted it to the British Services where Starkie was to dig it up fifty years later. But she only quoted what might feed her hypothesis, without reproducing the entire report or asking where it came from. She also passed over the date of the caravan given in the report—May 10, 1888—mentioning only the date the document was registered at the Foreign Office: June 16, 1888— which left readers free to suppose that the report referred to that date. There is no question: The date of May 10 ruins the hypothesis of Rimbaud's presence in Ambos since numerous documents—Rimbaud's letters to Ilg and his family, Ferrandi's notebooks—attest his presence in Harar at that moment. Elementary! So who was this *Rembau*? Intuitively I am not averse to recognizing Rimbaud in the phonetic transcription and the transparent distinguishing marks which could neither have been invented nor designate some improbable namesake. Deductively it is clear that Rimbaud does not fit the particulars of Cecchi's report. But in this Rembau who turns into Remban, in this name that comes to us through oral transmission, through writings in several languages, in broken echoes, repeated without his knowing from mountain to mountain, from confidential report to secret document (and thinking of Ouordji, that Abyssinian plain whose name means "one hears oneself talking"—"a mountain region where news is spread by shouting"[35]), in this name we can literally hear Arthur Rimbaud's *reputation*. His feverish activity and intellectual reputation inspired fear, gave rise to amplification and denunciation.

We also must take into consideration the "prejudice that Anglo-Italian diplomatic correspondence has shown toward

French businessmen."[36] Scarfoglio, who was in sympathy with Brémond and Chefneux—and defined Rimbaud as a peaceable man—testifies to this: "MM. Crispi and Antonelli have always wanted to see conspirators against Italy in these people who are simply honest tradesmen, entirely taken up with their strenuous business. They have used every available means to damage the reputations and interests of these merchants." Likewise Monsignor Jarosseau justly cautions against "the defamatory and slanderous notes which the London Archives record against all French enterprises."[37] Even if the Cecchi Report designates Rimbaud, it is still only diplomatic tittle-tattle. The camels stay, the caravan passes on. . . .

Fourth Claim

In Enid Starkie's four fateful pages, there is one single piece of evidence, the all too famous three lines from a letter by Ilg to Rimbaud: "As for slaves, I'm sorry, I cannot handle that. I have never bought slaves and do not want to start. I will not even do it for myself."[38] Unfortunately, Miss Starkie abridges the passage to make it conform to her demonstration, without troubling to indicate that she is omitting a phrase that radically changes its significance: "As for slaves, I'm sorry, I cannot handle that. I have never bought slaves and do not want to start. I absolutely recognize your good intentions [sic], but will not even do it for myself."[39] Ilg does not reply to Rimbaud as he would to a "slaver." He excludes any secret allusion to the traffic. He clearly does not entertain the idea that Rimbaud had any intention of going into the slave trade. The ethics of research should make a critic recoil from procedures like elision and dissembling, which tend toward falsification. Besides, the quoted passage has no bearing on Miss Starkie's preceding "arguments." This correspondence dates from 1890, only a few months before Rimbaud's definitive departure from Harar, in personal and general circumstances very different from those of 1887–1888, the time of his arms expedition. Out of context—and copied with three errors in two sentences—Alfred Ilg's lines take on the character of haughty reproach, whereas they occur at the end of a long, friendly, bantering letter. Also, the mere fact that Rimbaud was writing to Ilg, whose moral integrity and influence with Menelik he knew well, Ilg with whom Rimbaud had a more than cordial relationship and shared commercial interests, makes unlikely the intentions he is reproached with. "If the poet had had the least connection with the slave trade, he would certainly not have lost his time in a two years' correspondence with Ilg."[40] Nor would the Swiss engineer have stayed friendly with Rimbaud if the latter had been compromised by the trade. In December 1888—the year of the alleged crime—Ilg on his way back from Zeila spent six weeks with Rimbaud in Harar. But his reply of August 1890 is understandable: If he had replied favorably to Rimbaud, he would himself have been guilty of trading in slaves.

Moreover, asking to buy two slave boys is not the same as *selling* slaves, as Starkie insinuates! "Ilg refused to procure him slaves for resale."[41] We must reduce Rimbaud's step to its proper proportions. Being short of personnel, Rimbaud asks Ilg, among other services, to buy him two servants according to the widespread, legal custom of the region at that time. Buying was permitted, as we know. This is the "slave trade" Rimbaud engages in: At the end of his stay in Harar he wants to buy a mule and two slaves, neither of which he will ever have, by the way.

Ilg's first reaction (some months before the letter of August 1890, which seems abrupt) had been to comply with Rimbaud's request of December 1889 by handing it on to Zimmermann—"Zimpy"—manager in his absence. "As for Rimbaud's orders (mule, slaves)," he writes him on January 22, 1890, "do what seems best to you, I think one could without remorse entrust the fate of two poor devils to him."[42]

Rimbaud repeated his demand with insistence and urgency, the habitual imperative of all his obsessions: "I confirm very seriously my order for a very good mule and two slave boys."* The equivalence between mule and slave boys clearly indicates the character of his project. Later he limits his order to the mule, but as always, wants the very best: "Send me also a very *saggar,* very large and strong, young mule, male or female, the best you can find, with a good harness, at whatever price."† Two months later, still no mule. Rimbaud gets impatient: "Do send me the very good mule."†† From these reiterations, we can infer the contents of the lost letter in which Rimbaud renewed his demand, and which got him the famous reply of August 1890. Perhaps Ilg was again in the country with Menelik, as in the preceding December, when he first got Rimbaud's message. He could not take care of it, so that, in November 1890, the mule had still not been delivered. The story is taking a hilarious turn, like one of Robert Lamoureux's hoaxes. . . . Stubborn, a veritable mule himself, Rimbaud implores desperately, as if he were not sure he had been understood: "Please do find me a very good MULE (not a male, *a female*), young, big, very *saggar,* very strong, good at uphill and downhill, etc., etc."§ Abyssinian torpor compounded by the slowness often attributed to the Swiss national character must have exasperated our impatient Ardennais on receiving, two months later, in early 1891, this reply from Alfred Ilg, which must be read slowly: "As for the mule you asked for, there is no way of finding one in spite of all my looking. If I find one I'll bring it along."[43] Investigating the file on "Rimbaud and the slave trade," I find I am telling the story of Rimbaud buying a mule—this is what the file boils down to. . . . Three months later, Rimbaud, who had already in February

* December 26, 1889.
† March 1, 1890.
††April 25, 1890.
§ November 20, 1890.

had difficulty walking, left Abyssinia for good. Did Ilg ever make it to Harar with Rimbaud's mule? I fear this mystery will never be cleared up, unless by a new document.

Any accusation without proof is detestable. Some readers may now think we must suspend judgment until there is positive proof. Two evident observations will allow us to understand that implicating Rimbaud in the slave trade is not only improbable but quite impossible. Between the present office of France-Presse on Tito Road, with its Telex crackling day and night, the French embassy and consulate, the soldiers of the French Camp at the entry into Harar, the Catholic Mission of Harar, the branch offices of Peugeot and Air France, and the cooperating French scattered over Abyssinia, there has naturally developed a village situation comparable to the even closer network of the much fewer* missionaries, explorers, war correspondents, merchants, and diplomats of the last century. Sharing language and origin, the sentiment of being foreigners, and the same dangers, and being deprived of entertainment, they did not fail to talk and exchange news of absent persons whenever they met. "The rare Europeans forced to live in this country for business reasons have no remedy against boredom except getting together as often as possible," wrote Scarfoglio.[44] This scattered community formed a kind of radar impossible to pass unnoticed. There is not the smallest allusion in the private correspondences, memoirs, or testimonies published over fifty years that would allow us to suspect any one of them of being implicated in the slave trade. On the contrary, Savouré, for instance, writes to Rimbaud from Paris of "your loyal sentiments which I know you live by."[45] Of course—worst-case scenario, they could all have been careful to use the same code word, as in the stories where drugs are called "Aunt Alice," and slaves "coke in stock." Or as

---

*"There are barely twenty Europeans in all Abyssinia, these countries here included" (Harar, August 4, 1888).

the old slavers used to speak of "ebony." We could get lost in conjectures. . . . Bardey, himself a man of courage and integrity, who will say of Rimbaud that he had been "sufficiently troublesome ["disagreeable" was crossed out] in his lifetime,"[46] would not have covered up such activity, especially if Rimbaud had been compromised after their contract had been broken. He could have said of his associate what Borelli wrote about César Tian: "I have lived his life, he could not possibly have participated in the trade without my noticing. . . . I know too many people of all kinds on the African an Asian coasts and who speak Galla."[47] A white slaver could not have escaped the village gossip or the nets of history. When Rimbaud intends only to buy a mule and two slave boys, he unleashes fifty years later a European scandal at his expense. *"Two boy slaves do not make trade"* (emphasis added) goes a very British comment.[48]

Further, over his ten years in the country, Rimbaud encountered thousands of natives who, watchful and touchy, with the strong social cohesion of oral traditions, make for another human network. "Is it true that Rimbaud dealt in slaves?" Philippe Soupault asked a Frenchman who had lived in Ethiopia for years. "That is absolutely impossible. Rimbaud lived amid Ethiopians, even with an Ethiopian woman. If he had recruited slaves, the villagers would have shunned him. To live in this country you have to have the trust of the inhabitants."[49] Rimbaud was known to be on good terms with Ras Makonnen, the governor of Harar, and Menelik, the Negus himself, toward whom all information converged and who had his eyes everywhere. "I have a very good reputation here,"* Rimbaud could write his family in 1884 as well as in 1890. Rimbaud, who slept among the animals of his caravans and did three fourths of the trek on foot, knew how to get the respect, if not the affection, of the natives. All who knew him, without exception, agree on this point. It is the one quality he is granted unani-

*Aden, October 7, 1884, and Harar, February 15, 1890.

mously. "He assimilated . . . the habits and customs of the natives," writes Bardey, announcing Rimbaud's death to the Geographical Society in Paris. "All who knew him . . . will agree that he was an honorable, useful, and courageous man."

From Tadjoura, a crucial center of the trade, Rimbaud himself wrote: "Don't think I've become a slave trader."* It would have done to take his word for it.

It is infamous to accuse Rimbaud of having been a slaver.[50] Perhaps taking pleasure in slander is one of the conquests of civilization: The Danakil kill each other rather than speak evil. "Rimbaud is ready to sell Negroes to whoever wants them. . . . The case is closed!" cries the prosecutor.[51] Inconsistency and falsification, ignorance of Abyssinian history and geography, even misunderstanding of Rimbaud's moral project of a return to order, have been stronger than the truth. Ignorance is no argument, said Spinoza.

When Scarfoglio one day told Brémond and Chefneux that Antonelli suspected them of "conspiracy against Italy," they burst out laughing, and Scarfoglio with them. If Rimbaud could have known that the Cecchi Report called him one of the best French agents, and that his biographers would deduce his involvement in the slave trade from it, he would no doubt have responded with his favorite expression, in the manner of Pagnol's celebrated joke about the French Navy.

Without exclaiming with Paterne Berrichon "How many slaves he must have ransomed to teach them dignity!" one wonders where this rumor could have come from, which, ever since 1891, the year of his death, denounced Rimbaud as a "slaver in Uganda"; how Lepelletier could in 1897 settle an old score by insinuating that the poet had turned "slave merchant." And who would join the chorus talking of Rimbaud, "merchant in human flesh?" Izambard! As early as 1898! The old professor makes fun of the poets who claimed

*Tadjoura, December 3, 1885.

Rimbaud, "who thus found himself a Decadent without knowing or wanting it, without having ever spoken or written—just reread him!—the priceless jargon of this school."[52] The Decadents were looking for a master and found him in the man who "gloried in infamy, whose charm was cruelty."* And now we understand why the image of the slave trader came as no surprise: It went with the "crimes" the *voyant* had prided himself on, with his reputation as a hooligan, which was only amplified by echoes like Izambard's sneer: "Thief, assassin, merchant in human flesh" (almost suggesting: why not cannibal as well?). Rimbaud was a priori suspect. A victim of his past, which he had been in a hurry to flee. Like Lord Jim, Conrad's hero, he tried to "rebuild his life" in Abyssinia, tried to escape a long way from himself, only to have fate catch up: so many unexpected misfortunes for the man hoping for impossible purification.†

Our interlocutor, Alémé Eshete, replies between two inhalations that Rimbaud had at any rate been "proslavery." An attorney's dodge, trick up his sleeve: "If we lack proof to make Arthur Rimbaud a slave dealer [so I read in *Le Figaro*,[53] a paper that would search such proof rather than the truth], we are certain that Rimbaud had no scruples [in the name of what, this certainty?] to profit from the trade for his personal use and confort [*sic*]. Do not tell me that a buyer of slaves is morally superior to the seller. Eliminate the buyer: no more trade." Nobody dreams of telling him such an enormity. But our newspaper judge (who refuses to answer a clear *no* to the question he raised: "Was Rimbaud a slave trader?") neglects or ignores the historical circumstances of Rimbaud's African adventure. A European abstaining from buying slaves would not have abolished or even affected this

---

* "Delirium" I, *A Season in Hell.*
† "Let's take to the old roads again, laden with my vice, the vice that pushed its roots of suffering into my side since the age of reason . . ." ("Bad Blood," *A Season in Hell*).

traditional trade. "Rimbaud's asking for two slaves is nearly as natural as a French bourgeois of the period having two servants sent from the country," a reader familiar with Ethiopia tells me.[54] "Anyone who was there at the time, missionaries, explorers, merchants [adds an honest man, witness to the trial] had to have recourse to the only work force available, without anybody having the idea of making them slavers. Rimbaud, who was neither saint nor hero, did like the others, rightly or wrongly. He must not be judged differently."[55] And by what right, in any case, do we "judge" him? In his letter to the Ministry of Foreign Affairs, Rimbaud states his opposition to slavery on Western principles, his tacit and understood approval of paragraph 4 of the human rights bill. If, two years later, he wants to follow custom and buy two slaves—whom he will not get—while his compatriots own several dozen, his fault according to European morality lies in the wish. But what can a single individual do against the customs in force in an empire? Montaigne called it a sign of madness to want to change the customs of a country.[56] Twenty Europeans could do nothing against the weight of tradition and culture, a mentality deeply different from ours, and the highly developed national sense of the Abyssinians. Almighty Menelik himself, hostile to slavery as he was, had to make the best of a bad business. A European merchant was in no position to influence Menelik's politics in an area of this importance; not even Ilg, his "prime minister," was able to do so. Della Vedova observed that "aside from Menelik, there are only four or five men in the whole kingdom who listen to the Europeans."[57] Rimbaud would only have shared the fate of the young Colombian aristocrat in the romantic story by Jorge Ricardo Gomez—South America's Chateaubriand: Back from Europe, this young man pushed his philosophical ideas all the way, fought against slavery, for sexual freedom and a kind of self-administration, only to find himself sentenced to death, and the landowners divvying up his property on the eve of his execution.[58] One could of course boycott—the word appears in the 1880s—a custom contrary to the European conception of remedies, which was proving to become universal. But if the Europeans could not afford financially to abstain from recourse to this ancestral practice, was the essential not their behavior, the human respect that Borelli, for example, accorded his slaves? It was not for Rimbaud, but for the railroad, to abolish slavery.

A vagabond does not own slaves. But it is more interesting to understand that on another, interior, level, the vagabond was his own slave—"since every man is slave to this miserable fate."*

Freedom is not enough: The freer Rimbaud felt in his wandering and the solitude of vast spaces, the less he could get away from a deeper sentiment of being a slave, which he hoped to escape in Harar ("I have no intention of passing my entire life in slavery"†), which he feels again in Aden, in 1884 ("If there were only one day that I could get out of this slavery"††), and which is still with him in 1890, when he seems to surrender ("Here I am, a slave"§). Rimbaud carried a misery principle inside himself. He always considered himself "condemned": "I am condemned to wander"; "I am condemned to live"; "condemned to follow these trails"; "roads I am condemned to take."‖ Even his freest roving takes on the appearance of a long sentence the condemned man serves on the black continent. "So I am to spend the rest of my days wandering in fatigue and privations, with the only prospect of dying to my pain." In his

* Aden, September 10, 1884.
† Harar, May 25, 1881.
†† Aden, May 29, 1884.
§ Harar, March 1, 1890.
‖ May 6, 1883; May 5, 1884; December 30, 1884; November 9, 1887; "whoever would sentence me to marriage" (Aden, September 22, 1880); "a rheumatism in the hips that sentences me . . ." (Cairo, August 23, 1887). In Marseille, his sister will call him twice "condemned" (September 22 and October 3, 1891).

"most abominable privations,"* in his insistence on carrying his heavy gold belt like a penitent until dysentery makes it impossible, in his complaints of stabbing pains in the knee and tightening the bandage, in recording pain in his body, and even in the money he sends his mother, we may recognize a slave's efforts to *buy his freedom*. "Everybody is his own enemy," states Anacharsis, well before the Christian era. If you target yourself, you never miss. What suffering! Rimbaud gave life its entire worth, which is, in sum, life itself. He lived at all costs.

Amazing course from dreams of Eden ("It's true, I was dreaming of Eden!"†) to finding—or losing—himself in Aden. According to legend, Adam was buried there. The Tree of Knowledge would quickly have burned to a cinder: The heat is crushing—"it's always 40 degrees."†† Aden, where it rains about once every five years, was at the time a mere coal depot, delivering ninety thousand tons a year to passing ships. "The dirty old Red Sea is tortured by the heat."§ Aden, where Rimbaud often, as if to point at himself, crossed the "slave island" in front of the famous rock, which is nowadays called "workers' island."59 One section of town is called the Crater, and that is the word Rimbaud uses to evoke Aden: "You cannot at all imagine the place. There is not a single tree here, not even dried up, not a blade of grass, no clod of earth, not a drop of water. Aden is the crater of a volcano."‖ What we associate with the image of the volcano is dryness, a pit,¶ fire, in short, hell: "The sides of the crater keep the air from coming in, so that we are roasted at the bottom of the pit." One might say that in Africa and Arabia Rimbaud lived in Reality his season in hell. "Staying here is getting atrocious

* Cairo, August 23, 1887.
† "The Impossible," *A Season in Hell*.
†† Aden, July 31, 1884.
§ Aden, September 10, 1884.
‖ Aden, September 28, 1885.
¶ Ibid.

again."* "Here one leads the most atrocious life in the world."† "I would like to see this place reduced to ashes."†† "Rimbaud always clamors and complains," wrote César Tian to Monsignor Taurin on March 12, 1890.[60] "If I complain," says Rimbaud, "it is another way of singing."§ But his clamors and complaints, his "perpetual lamentations" ("you must be taking me for a latter-day Jeremiah"||), his songs of despair sound like the groans of the damned in hell.

But what kept him in this place where he suffered so? Contracts? Pieces of paper! He had deserted from armies and known how to leave Bardey (who complained of being faced with the accomplished fact, contrary to their agreement) for other adventures. And if his "business" constrained him more and more, nothing had ever held him (during his African years, Savouré had gone back to Paris, Ilg to Zurich, Bardey to Lyon, Vichy to New York—and Zanzibar is not far from Harar)—nothing held him except himself. The Ardennes mountains were "execrable," but he went back there every winter. The demand of the absolute, the force of the "impossible," the pursuit, not of happiness, but of salvation ("it is evident that I did not come here to be happy"¶) drove him to that fulfillment of his sentence that was the work of self-destruction ("I work like a donkey in a country for which I feel invincible horror"**). Never settled, always on the road, but like a prisoner on parole.

The regions stretching on either side of the Red Sea, Abyssinia and Arabia, where Rimbaud seemed to arrive by chance, became the necessary place for perfecting his suffering, where he always seemed drawn in spite of himself, but

* December 30, 1884.
† April 14, 1885.
††November 18, 1885.
§ July 10, 1882.
|| October 8, 1887.
¶ Aden, May 29, 1884.
**Aden, May 10, 1882.

by himself, as if he had chosen (while accusing others and the whole world), had decided (while complaining) on the precise place for what was to happen to him. "After all, it is most likely that we go where we don't want to go, do what we don't want to do, live and make decisions unlike anything we ever wanted, without hope of any kind of compensation."* "Aden and Makalla are among the hells mentioned in sailors' proverbs," notes Elisée Reclus, quoted by Nizan. Opposite the volcano of Aden where he "suffered so much," the deserts of Abyssinia and the plateaus of Harar form more circles of hell. I think again of the moment when Harar rose in front of us, at a turn of the road looking down on the city, when dream and reality suddenly coincided. Like the first French travelers in 1835, Combes and Tamisier, "we thought we were in Arabia Felix where our fathers' imagination had placed the terrestrial paradise."[61] But for Rimbaud, Abyssinia took on a different meaning, as if the *poète maudit* had been drawn here by the echo of "abyss," *abyssos,* the bottom of the sea, the abyssal land, or by the pejorative meaning the Arabs gave it: Habech, "mixture"; Abyssinia, "land of mixed population"; and Barr Adjam, "land of non-Arabs." As if he found in Shoa, which means "misfortune" in Anamitic and "holocaust" in Hebrew, the only just echo of his adversities. One might say that the names of these countries were waiting for him to find their meaning, and that fate led him to the necessary place, where the outcast Cain finished his days, to the Ethiopia that Voragine's *Golden Legend* calls Myrmidonia, land of cannibals; that the Hebrew Bible calls Cush,[62] after the son of Ham. "I enter the true kingdom of the sons of Ham,"† announced *A Season in Hell.* Rimbaud had in advance traced the curve of his destiny. "I have been of inferior race from all eternity,"†† he once cried—and was to end up in Abyssinia, where the first people en-

* Aden, January 15, 1885.
† "Bad Blood," *A Season in Hell.*
†† "It is quite clear that I have always been of inferior race" (Ibid.).

countered by Combes and Tamisier declared: "We are black. How beautiful your white skin! Our color is that of slaves, we are molded from mud! We are of an inferior race . . . descendants of Ham who was cursed by his father."[63]

He was to end up in Harar, the letters of whose name are scattered through his first and last name, in the land of the Gallas, who grease their hair with rancid butter like the ancient Gauls[64]—"I have the narrow brain and clumsiness in fighting of my Gallic ancestors. . . . But I do not butter my hair"*—the Gallas, whom he wanted to describe and who according to an old book descended from the Gauls.[65] He was to end up in the country the historians called Ethiopia, a word deriving perhaps from the Greek *aitho,* "I burn," and *ops,* "face." So Rimbaud, the Ethiopian, the poet with the burned face, slowly achieved his descent into hell. He soon lost what Dante called *l'arte di tornar,* "the art of turning back," for, as one traveler reports, according to Abyssinian law, once a stranger has set foot on the land he cannot leave again."[66] He came out of it to die, like a miner covered with coal dust from the mine. In the "Arabia Felix" of the maps, he knew the delights of damnation named in *A Season in Hell.* On "these cursed coasts," in "these satanic countries,"† he lived the "real nightmares"†† of a new "Night of Hell."

"I compare this series of trials I have gone through to what the ancients called a descent into hell," Nerval writes in *Aurélia.* It is a descent into himself achieved at a distance. The suffering has only inner reality. Hell means being cast out of his own words by his own will. His wanderings through Abyssinia mean also being lost, a loss of his self, a fall into the inner abyss, a slow consuming of his I in the abyss of infinite regress. The distances did nothing for him.

---

* Ibid.
† Aden, November 4, 1887.
††Aden, May 5, 1884.

Rimbaud did not accept himself: hell is the other (his impossible *I*).

But what was this "judgment" of which we know only the sentence?* Who was the judge? What the offense? Rimbaud lived his wanderings as if he had been exiled, or had exiled himself. Like Adam chased out of paradise, he inflicted *travail*, "work," on himself—in the literal sense of its root—*tripalium*, "torture"—in the hope of redemption. The Seer who defied God through the Word felt no doubt a Promethean form of guilt. An early draft of "Bad Blood"† clearly reveals acceptance of impotence and defeat. Punishment is meted out to the man who thought he possessed supernatural powers. "I am chosen! I am damned!" cries Verlaine's "Bon Disciple," Rimbaud himself, who also said to "The Just": "I am cursed, you know."††

But we hear a child's voice. This very literary, adolescent conception is not satisfactory when we think of the real intensity of Rimbaud's African sufferings. Neither can the feeling of guilt be explained simply by the "monstrosities," the Parisian orgy, the period of *encrapulement,* the wallowing in the gutter he wants to forget, the "second damnation" of poets, as Baudelaire called it: immorality as necessary condition for work of the imagination. In the train of the Franco-Ethiopian Railroad, which stopped in the middle of the desert, crossing Rimbaud's itinerary, I remembered how the fugitive had evoked one of these places: "Our road is called Gobât Road, from the name of its fifteenth station."§ Fifteenth station . . . This caravan term, which we might innocently apply to the train stop in this furnace, brings up the subjective, anonymous *stations of the cross* Rimbaud sought

---

* "So I am to spend the rest of my days en route" (*A Season in Hell*).
† First draft of the fourth part.
†† "Le Juste restait droit . . ." ("The Just Sat Straight . . .") (1871?).
§ Letter to the *Bosphore égyptien*.

in his fatigue and pain. It is striking to what point his *passion,* in the literal and figurative sense, marked his life. His slavish conscience tormenting him in Harar is from the start determined by the words of the Gospel: "I am the slave of my baptism."* The Gospel is "a slave morality" exalting humility and resignation, according to Nietzsche, who opposes it with his "master morality," a cult of pride and strength.[67] Rimbaud's entire life—"it's my baptism, my weakness that enslaves me. It's life, again!"†—is a fight against the bondage that comes with life, before any sin, a desperate affirmation of innocence through suffering, an impossible attempt to redeem a sin he did not commit. Baudelaire had likewise felt stricken by misfortune from adolescence on. In 1854, he wrote to his mother: "I feel my life has been damned from the beginning and forever." As early as 1871, in Charleville, Rimbaud wrote categorically: "I have always been condemned, forever."†† This sense of damnation is not a youthful act tied to the poetic enterprise or its abandoning; it is a given from the start, a given that, for a time, had led him to literature.

This is the deep sense of his perpetual vagabondage: "Here is the punishment—*Forward, march!*"§ We may recognize in this eviction and sentence to march the "roving through infinite solitudes" that Mephisto promises Faust (Rimbaud borrowed Goethe's *Faust* from Delahaye while writing *A Season in Hell*)‖ but not in the sense of a "de-paradisation":[68] Rimbaud never stopped moving and always crossed "the same desert."¶ Can we then truly speak of a "real season in hell" in Abyssinia? Is it less real when written? Is it less internal for not being written (except in the broken echoes of the letters)? For Rimbaud, hell is "the old one, the hell

---

* "Night of Hell," *A Season in Hell.*
† Draft of "Bad Blood."
†† To Demeny, Charleville, April 17, 1871.
§ "Night of Hell," *A Season in Hell.*
‖ May 1873.
¶ "Morning," *A Season in Hell.*

whose doors were opened by the Son of Man."* "I was assailed by the pains of hell," Rimbaud may have read in his Bible with the "cabbage-green edge,"† translated by Lemaistre de Sacy, the only book at hand when he wrote his "Pagan Book," when he *already* experienced "these pains" in fact. Having "always" felt uncomfortable in his skin was all it took to call his unsatisfactory life a "hell" according to the infernal *cogito:* "I think I am in hell, therefore I am there."†† And deciding his life was hell was all it took to make it so, in the "horror [of] this French countryside"§ or "these countries I abominate,"‖ in the "sad hole" of Roche or the "terrible hole" of Aden.¶ Again, a passion for failure does not only characterize Rimbaud "in Abyssinia," but the person already [in 1871] "determined not to do any of what one must do," a convict of freedom who, from 1873 on, "hardly even [thought] of the pleasure of escaping the modern suffering." Hence, no doubt, the *heroic* tone of his writings, his letters of a rushed, breathless, bold vagabond who sings in his misfortune, and the heroism of his poetry. I am in hell, therefore I shall stay there! "So I stayed! I stayed!— and will want to leave many more times. . . . But I'll stay, I'll stay." This was in Charleville, in 1870, to Izambard.

In the evening, the "Rimbaud" bar in Addis Ababa—"I served as a dubious sign for an inn"**—with Delahaye's enlarged portraits of Rimbaud on the walls and telephones on all the tables as in the dance bars of Hamburg. We are eating some peppered meat, *vhat;* and *injira,* the national dish that tastes like a kind of Band-Aid; accompanied by *tej,* the Amharan mead; or *kabikata,* a very strong liquor requiring a

* Ibid.
† "Les Poètes de sept ans" ("The Seven-year-old Poets").
†† "Night of Hell," *A Season in Hell.*
§ Roche, May 1873.
‖ Aden, May 10, 1883.
¶ May 9 and November 18, 1884.
** "Alchemy of the Word," *A Season in Hell.*

stomach lined with asbestos. . . . While we discuss the film's title, *The Fire Stealer,* I think more about fire than about the Promethean Seer, the fire through which Rimbaud escapes us, the two thirds of his work that are lost, *La Chasse spiri-tuelle* (*The Spiritual Quest*), and the "martyr letters" of 1872 burned by Verlaine's wife, Mathilde Mauté. I think of Vitalie throwing the captain's correspondence into the flames, of the Delahaye girls remembering that their mother burned Rimbaud's letters, as if burning his effigy in exorcism of his passage. The poet who offered himself "with closed eyes . . . to the sun, god of fire,"* had this Luciferian destructiveness—"the fire flares up again with the damned."† He himself begged Demeny, as Kafka will beg Brod: "Burn, I want it, and I think you will respect my wish like that of a dead man, burn all the verses I was stupid enough to give you."†† He had also tried out God's judgment by ordeal in throwing copies of *A Season in Hell* into the fireplace of the farm in Roche. Again, having gathered the thirty-two notebooks of Labatut's memoirs, he threw them in the fire.§ He made all the necessary preparations for being misunderstood, pursued in spite of himself by the fire he carried, disappearing into the furnace of the Red Sea. "Live and leave to the fire/The obscure misfortune."‖

". . . a fucking lot of manuscripts, notebooks, etc. he must have left there." Verlaine imploring Matuszewicz to go "right away" to Camdentown (where he had "left Rimbaud rather stranded") is typical for our desire to find Rimbaud's lost, burned, abandoned works.[69] A trunk full of unpublished manuscripts—Tutankhamon's treasure! We know only about a third of his writings (and almost nothing by his own care). For all that is lost, our era has substituted

---

* "Delirium" II, *A Season in Hell.*

† "Night of Hell," *A Season in Hell*: "Do not come near me, I am sure I smell scorched."

††Charleville, June 10, 1871.

§ To M. de Gaspary, November 9, 1887.

‖ "Age d'or" ("The Golden Age").

false leads—like this meretricious bar we are in (or the "Rimbaud" cafés and "dancings" in France). Ethiopia has caught up with the international moment. Soon there will be Rimbaud safaris! Torn down, the poet's birthplace in Charleville, the farm in Roche, the hotel in the Rue des Brasseurs in Brussels; demolished the Café de l'Univers where he used to meet Verlaine, the Place de la Gare in Charleville where a housing complex is under construction with the name Les Assis ("The Sitters"). "The havoc of the walks . . ."* The buildings have disappeared, and a bit of soul along with them, the chance of a sign to capture. Imagination left without support, relation to history lost, we enter Alphaville. True, we have the texts, and that is all that counts—for the sedentary Rimbaldians, the survivors. We won't have the emotion, but we'll have the ideas. . . . Epoch of catalogs. Even printing broaches too much legibility for my dreams, and nothing can ever bring back the emotion I felt at Henri Matarassos's in Nice, reading Rimbaud's original letter of April 30, 1891, to César Tian; or, at Jean Voellmy's in Basel, the facsimile of his letters to Ilg. "A small world, pale and flat, Africa and the West, is going to be built."† Among the concrete of Addis Ababa, where the Amharas lose their customs for a cannister of gasoline or a nylon suit, I miss Harar, the untouched Africa of the Gallas. Back at the hotel, I read Bougainville's account of his reception in Tahiti: a hundred canoes laden with presents, women swimming to meet the boat, bonfires all over. "Everybody came crying *tayo,* which means friend, giving us a thousand signs of friendliness" (1772). Then Diderot was to write a *Supplément au voyage de Bougainville* and reveal the catastrophe that the Europeans' arrival meant for the "good savages." Segalen, likewise, understood that he could not study the Maori, who were dying of diseases unknown in the islands before the arrival of the white man. As for ancestral beliefs and customs, the

*"Phrases," *Illuminations.*
†"Soir historique" ("Historic Evening"), *Illuminations.*

missionaries had had an easy job of erasing them from the memory of a people careless of its past. As if in exchange, Segalen left us his book, *Les Immémoriaux* (*The People Without Memory*). But the immobile Ogadens, the villages we went through in the train, do not inspire pity. The misery is in the modern cities. Pierre Bardey wrote to his brother on December 6, 1881: "What a country Harar is! After eight months in Zeila, it's paradise!" In Harar, where there are no high-rises, discos, or parking meters, we saw Rimbaud's Africa, eternal for a few more years. Paradise. Almost.

12
EGYPT

I know why the volcano is
eruption again,
You touched it yesterday with
your light foot,
And suddenly the horizon was
dark with ash.
—Gérard de Nerval to Nina Glaser

At the top of the long main street of Addis Ababa, silent and cold during the nightly curfew, our metal film cases are piled, catching the first light of morning. The sun is already high in the sky when our plane leaves Ethiopian soil. I am one of those who cannot tear their eyes from this country, who would like to stay on through looking.[1] For a moment, I am the immobile shepherd down there who, smaller and smaller, watches the Boeing write a curve of farewell on his ever blue sky.

Unimaginable Ethiopian map—dark green chasms, immense precipices, high, off-balance plateaus. The great petrified mushrooms of the Sudan, which seem strewn over the savannah, form a geological border between Ethiopia and the flat, pink to khaki desert.

The TWA stewardess is so seductive (Nastassia Kinski's sister?) that all heads are stuck out into the aisle after she passes. The microphone informs the passengers, mostly Ethiopians, that we are going to film, which makes them kneel backward on their seats. With the projectors lit and the tangle of cables, the plane soon looks like a studio on the Buttes-Chaumont. We are shooting the "prologue," and though I feel a ton of sleepiness on my lids I must answer my traveling companion who asks *off* screen where I am going—"To Ethiopia," I am supposed to say, which makes me feel I am going back whereas we are leaving at eight hundred kilometers per hour, sweet lie of movies—and *why*— to which I still do not know the answer. . . .

A wing dips: Khartoum. Turning with the meanders of the Nile, the plane descends toward the sand, at the confluence of the Blue and White Niles. An hour to wish for the Sudan from the windblown boarding stage of the plane.

Between Khartoum and Cairo, we shoot the "epilogue"—all it takes is a change of seats—the "return from Ethiopia" sequence. This time, I am supposed to say what I am "bringing back" from this country. . . . But pulling the beige curtains on the window, I suddenly see Egypt. From the air, you realize that Egypt is nothing but a river, the longest on this continent, between two parallel stripes of greenery and a straight black road. Egypt, *gift* of the Nile, said Herodotus. On either side, as far as the eye can reach, the moon.

We shall land in a few minutes. On landing, the passengers applaud the crew, as in the heroic times of aviation. Where is the Renault bus labeled "Follow Me" taking us? In mid-December, everybody here is in shirtsleeves and dark glasses. A squeaking sound in the cool hall of Cairo's Al Maza Airport distills into "Tico-tico here . . ." Behind the counters, tellers with large eyes change dollars into Egyptian pounds, large worn bills, soft as philodendron leaves.

Since the largest part of the Egyptian population is concentrated in the Delta, a human tide obstructs the airport, as if for an everlasting funeral of Oum Kalsoum. Stuck by myself in this congestion, I have mixed feelings as I see the plane that carries my companions home take off.

After Heliopolis—luxurious, calm—we drive through the overpopulated suburbs of Cairo with their large tan buildings between minarets. Gérard de Nerval's first observation on arriving in Cairo concerned women: "Cairo is the Levantine city where the women are still most closely veiled."[2] Today less faces are hidden behind the *shador* than in Aden or Harar. They mostly wear Western clothes and grow fat after forty. . . . Better represented in the streets, men in djellabas or *gandourahs*, battledress or desert-blue *boubous*, or even in Fifth Avenue suits (the sheiks' cadres) seem to have flocked from all the horizons of the East to the protected city, "the mother of the world." Al Kahira, "the victorious." Busy and noisy, they pass in front of a great Ramses with fixed smile.

Cairo should be approached from the south. If you come from Europe, you think you are in India. But coming up from black Africa or from the southern deserts, you have the impression that you are back in Europe, about to board the ship that fascinated Bardey. This was already Rimbaud's feeling when he arrived in Fatima's city. "Life is European style and rather expensive," he wrote on August 23, 1887, booked into the Hotel Europe. Unmetered taxis, screaming vans, packed buses caught in bottlenecks—a camel crouched in the bed of a truck—all rush by, indifferent to the *sharif*'s red light. Even at night, the city's incessant cacophony and swarming crowds pursue the walker who is after a casual view from any of the great bridges over the Nile onto the slow dance of cutters, feluccas, and floating reflections of lit-up houses on the banks of the river.

Yet the dark brown windows of the tall, modern buildings reflect unchanged images: merchants sitting in front of their shops, on those Islamic stools of carved wood inlaid with fake ivory and mother-of-pearl, bargaining, smoking their nargilehs and chibouks, drinking coffee, worrying large amber beads of huge rosaries. They entice the stranger into khans and souks, endless labyrinths of crowded, muddy alleys exactly as painted by the Orientalists, with languorous, syrupy music sighing from every stand, with the odor of the trade pervading the entire section of town: the souk of spices, the souk of sweets, of coal, cloth, leather, copper, "Arabesque" furniture or metal. Then there is the bazaar of painted plates, of secondhand goods covered with Mameluke calligraphy, the souk of newly fabricated antiques. . . . And everywhere crowds brushing and knocking against you, crowds that seem the denser after the Abyssinian steppes. At nightfall, I am lost and take a rest over perfumed tea in the strange sweetness of a café, a very old, green and mauve place with bead-encrusted pillars, cracked mirrors, sparkling Venetian chandeliers, that I will never find again in this souk. It does not take a great effort of the imagination to see, through the smoke barely cleared by the large fan, Rimbaud's thin and nervous silhouette moving through dark alleys, back from East Africa, with his "shady appearance,"[3] short, gray hair, small, yellow mustache, and ravaged face. I can see his "strange gait" that Savouré commented on: "the left shoulder always way ahead of the right," his white suit, and the belt with eight kilos of gold pulling on his hips. Tired and helpless, "very much weakened,"[*] he threads his way through the mob with a slight limp because of the winding alleys, his heavy belt, and the pain in his hips, knee, shoulder and thighs ever since the difficult expedition to Shoa. What is he doing in Egypt?

"M. Rimbaud is going to Egypt to recover from long strain," writes Alexandre Merciniez, to whom he was brought by the police for being unable to "prove his identity"—a formula strange in any but the legal sense. This was at Massawa, where he landed on August 5, coming from Aden with Djami to cash a draft of five thousand talers on M. Lucardi, an Italian dealer, and another of twenty-five hundred talers on an Indian merchant. After short stops at Suakin and Suez, where he met the French vice-consul, Lu-

*Letter to his family, Cairo, August 23, 1887.

cien Labosse, he arrived in Cairo around August 20. His colleagues Savouré and Labatut dead, free of any contract with the Bardey brothers since October 1885, Rimbaud vagabonds through Cairo in regained independence; wandering and freedom are once again fused and reaffirmed: "I am too used to a life of free wandering"; "I am used to a free life."*

Everything is possible again, but despair lies in wait. Fleeing Labatut's creditors, trying to forget his misadventures, he came, as one says, to turn over a new leaf—on health and the fortune that escaped him. He looks more for work than for rest, making projects in all directions as usual. He deposits his money for six months at the local branch of the Crédit Lyonnais. He goes to see the Marquis de Grimaldi-Régusse, to whom Merciniez, to make up for the blunder in Massawa, has referred him as a "very honorable Frenchman." He thinks of manufacturing war supplies for Menelik.† He plans to go to Syria and import mules into Shoa. He looks in vain for some French merchant to go in on importing gum from the Sudan. Just in case, he proposes his services to Bardey.

After adventures, one needs to write. Right after his arrival he takes up the explorer Jules Borelli's suggestion to go see his brother, Octave Borelli Bey, a rich Cairo lawyer and contributor to the *Bosphore égyptien,* the important French daily of Cairo. In the form of a letter to the editor of the newspaper, Émile Barrière Bey, Rimbaud writes out in one breath the tale of his travels in Abyssinia, which is published immediately, on August 25 and 27.[4] Just picture Rimbaud in the streets of Cairo, buying the *Bosphore égyptien* with his article, realizing for the first time the dream of his adoles-

---

*To his family, August 23, 1887; to Bardey, Cairo, August 26, 1887.
†"Plates, chemicals and materials to manufacture firing caps. I came here to see if something in this direction could be set up" (to Bardey, Cairo, August 26, 1887). Ilg will start a shell factory for Menelik in Basel.

cence, *to read himself.* Everywhere, for two days, Arthur Rimbaud is finally in this form a name in the nameless crowd. His long letter to the editor of the *Bosphore égyptien* picks up on the spirit of adventure and historical-geographical observation of his *Report on Ogaden* of 1883. His style has lost none of its vigor or rigor, even though he has barely written three short notes during the past year. The man who burned *A Season in Hell* and ran through the world, convinced that he would never be read, suddenly believes for the space of a summer week in Egypt, that he can solve his problems by writing. He is asking for a second chance with writing. He also writes to his family every day.* With an introduction by Bardey, he contacts M. Maunoir to obtain a mission from the Geographical Society. He tells the eighteen stages of his expedition to Bardey, who hands the report on to the geographers in Paris, as Rimbaud no doubt hoped: Rimbaud's account will be printed in the "Minutes of the Meeting" of November 4, 1887. Then, having for a moment regained confidence in his known and silenced capacity, Rimbaud writes those articles for the French dailies that will not be printed.[5]

None of these projects worked; or, rather, Rimbaud did not carry out any of them. The secretary of the Geographical Society declared himself "very disposed to help,"[6] but Rimbaud once again let his chance slip. At his return from Egypt, we can feel a loss of ambition. If there ever were two Rimbauds, it was in Harar: After the Egyptian break, comes the Rimbaud of 1888–1891, feverish retailer glimpsed in the Harar markets, giving up any other travel or writing, resigned to make money slowly, taler by taler, the Rimbaud who is going to die. His only deliberate writing plans, the articles and scientific publications he dreamed of, hoped for, in Cairo, were but a last flare-up of ambition, the final return of writing to the land of the crouched scribe—fist closed on his lost brush. "The dream of a supremely beautiful at-

*August 23, 24, 25; the letter of August 26 is lost.

titude was not vouchsafed him," Gabriel Bounoure will write in Cairo. "What awaited him was a round of ugliness and torture—the point of the world where his will and his fate coincided."[7] The paper in which Rimbaud published and which he kept on him, walking through the city of the thousand mosques with his article folded in his pocket, marks the end of his attempt to take up prose on a daily basis—his previous renunciation having already demanded poetry—the end of a desire already weakened to prose, fading into the mystery of hieroglyphs. This was his last week.

He just turned around the corner. I run: nobody. The souk is the one I just came out of. I meet Pierre Petitfils who tailed him discreetly, at a distance, and also lost him. Under his black felt hat and from behind *L'Orient le jour,* he whispers, "Little is known about his stay in Cairo."[8] Rimbaud, or the art of shedding biographers. We trade information. Arrived in Cairo on August 20, Rimbaud writes a daily letter until the twenty-sixth. Then his correspondence is interrupted on August 26 on the note of his "free life." His next letter is dated Aden, October 8. Where was he during those five weeks? On August 23, he had left a rather good address: "Arthur Rimbaud, General Delivery, Cairo (Egypt)"—and his last letter on the twenty-sixth says "in Cairo till end of September." It is the usual address of the "considerable traveler," the man who only passes through, always about to take off.* Antoine Adam, also lost in this labyrinth, claims "he spent five weeks in Cairo."[9] This seems unlikely to me. The deal of the Remington shells Rimbaud wanted to manufacture had no follow-up; and it was not in his nature to stay five weeks in one and the same place ("Here . . . people are too sedentary,"† he writes already on Au-

---

*Brussels, general delivery, July 5, 1873; general delivery at Larnaca (Cyprus), February 15, 1879; general delivery, Limasol (Cyprus), May 23, 1880; general delivery, Aden Camp (Arabia), May 5, 1884; general delivery, Aden Cantonment, November 22, 1887.
†August 24, 1887.

gust 24), especially in this period of instability and feverish idleness. On Tuesday, he writes: "I think two or three months here would make me well";* on Wednesday, his stay has already shrunk to three weeks: "I'm leaving"—"We're not leaving."† Besides, he feels less than ever able to take to "civilized" living again. Egypt seems to be going through one of the long "intermediary periods" that punctuate its five thousand years of civilization. "I'll not stay here long: I have no work and everything is too expensive."†† "Life here bores me and costs too much,"§ Rimbaud repeats, sharing Nerval's disappointment: "What can we expect from this noisy labyrinth choked with advertisements on corrugated iron, from palaces and mosques by the thousand. Once all this was splendid and marvelous, but thirty generations have gone by. Everywhere, crumbling stone and rotting wood." [10] "I won't stay here,"‖ Rimbaud reiterates, though it gets him away from "this year's horrible heat by the Red Sea: 50 to 60 degrees centigrade all the time."¶ Nevertheless, he cannot do without the sun. But Amon-Ra, supreme god of the world's greatest temples, cannot penetrate into Cairo with its somber buildings, where night falls quickly on streets full of smoke and dust. To get some sun, you must get out of town up the hill, to the citadel built on the site of the old Dome of Air. Finally, Rimbaud is one of those beings who die if deprived of freedom, like the okapis: "I cannot stay here any longer because I am used to a free life."** Cairo is not a city of peace and quiet, but of interruption and imprisonment: A stranger is constantly badgered, as by the thieves in the *Arabian Nights,* led out of his way by merchants grabbing his arm. It is a city it seems one will never

---

* August 23, 1887.
† "Bad Blood," *A Season in Hell.*
†† August 23, 1887.
§ August 25, 1887.
‖ August 26, 1887.
¶ August 23, 1887.
** August 26, 1887.

be able to get out of, caught in the chain of taxis always going to the central square. . . . Not a trace. Where could he have gone? Aden? He would not have gone straight back to the steam bath he came from. Syria? He will come back to his project for a superior breed of saddle mules in December, as shown by the astonishing letter of the Vicomte de Petiteville, a kind of real Baron Petdechèvre or "Baron Goatfart."[11] He also thinks of China, Japan.

However, one clue: Rimbaud, having deposited his money with the Crédit Lyonnais, begs his mother to lend him five hundred francs—"I haven't asked anything of you in seven years"*—for the boat to Zanzibar. But since he puts off this trip from October to November, there is no need for him to be in Cairo after September 15, and, rid of his heavy belt, Rimbaud is ready to leave.

The Sudan! One could read in the *Bosphore égyptien* of August 22: "M. Raimbaud [*sic*], French traveler and businessman from Shoa, arrived in Cairo a few days ago. We have reason to assume that M. Rimbaud will not stay with us long, but is preparing to go to the Sudan." The following day's letter to his family confirms: "I'm forced to go back via the Sudan."† Possible story of a disappearance: Rimbaud goes up the Nile to the First Cataract, then crosses the "kingdom of spirits." He reaches Khartoum during September. Not finding "anything to do," faced with the Sudanese blockade, which he will mention in October, he goes back to the coast, straight east. Passing through Massawa, he gives a copy of the *Bosphore égyptien* to Merciniez, who had recommended him, then goes back to Aden, from where he will thank his mother for the money received—which he had had forwarded by the consulate. . . . And yet . . .

The Sudan? It is too hot there, and he has not found a single French merchant to advise or accompany him.†† The

* August 24, 1887.
† Aden, October 8, 1887.
†† Cairo, August 26, 1887.

trip is too long for his budget and too soon for his weakened state. Above all, Egypt is what attracts him and is certainly the only likely direction. So, wandering along the quais,
letting my eyes follow the slow boats on the Nile, and my
mind's eye all the boats Rimbaud took: the steamer *General-
Paoli* from Livorno, the *Prinz van Oranje* bound for Batavia,
the *Wandering Chief* back from Java, and the *Amazone* that
took the dying man back to France, I pursue the fugitive
from Cairo up the Nile[12] (a three-week round trip like Chateaubriand's) all the way to the name "RIMBAUD" in Luxor,
all the way to the Valley of Kings.

One night during those years, Verlaine was heard in the
Chat-Noir, throwing out mysteriously, "He left for
Egypt . . ." All roads led him east, whether to Vienna or
Cyprus, and he had indeed long ago left for Egypt in a dream,
which can be found in his notebook from age ten. This dream
he was able to feed from the libraries with Chateaubriand's
Itinéraire de Paris à Jérusalem, Flaubert's *Voyage en Orient* (1849–
1851), Nerval's account, whose definitive edition came out
in 1850, and with Théophile Gautier who, pilfering Champollion and Du Camp for his *Roman de la momie* (published
by Hachette in 1858) had *seen* the Egypt of the pharaohs
long before he went to visit the buried temples in 1869. "I
am bored on this square,/An odd obelisk out." Crossing the
Place de la Concorde with the obelisk set up by the bourgeois Orleans monarchy "to the applause of an immense
crowd," Rimbaud could have shared "The Obelisk's Longing" of Gautier's *Emaux et Camées,* its wishing to see the
"brother" left behind in Thebes.[13] "It is to the Orient that
we must look for supreme Romanticism," Friedrich Schle-
gel had cried at the beginning of the century, and Rimbaud
found all his basic themes there. Egypt holds the secret of
beginnings, as if thinking had been born with those giants
rising on the horizon of time. In the kingdom of sacred
knowledge, where religion, arts, and sciences were one,

words held the power of life (the symbol ankh carved next to Nefertiti granted her eternal life) and death (Hatshepsut's name scratched in all temple walls to make her disappear). And, after the Romantic impulse, science! The prodigious volumes of the *Description de l'Égypte,* the foundation of Egyptology, had revealed this civilization as a field science could describe and decipher—to a point where the encyclopedic spirit joined that of poetry. Thus Lefébure, vainly trying to take Mallarmé along, went from poetry to Egyptology.[14] At twenty-four, Rimbaud already left in this direction: Marseille and Alexandria hold an antiphonal dialogue among his comings and goings. Getting off in Alexandria in November 1878, he spent a few days in Egypt—"passage to Egypt is payable in gold"*—then tried to leave for the East during the winter of 1879, shipping out to Alexandria again in March 1880—"I found nothing to do in Egypt and went on to Cyprus."† He is again bound for Alexandria in July 1880. At the end of that same year, in Harar, he was able to tell of his passing through Egypt and rekindle his plans by talking with the emir of the city or the French-speaking officers of the Egyptian garrison in Harar. He was still able to dream of the impossible—of settling in the ideal, like Germain Nouveau who will write him, in his "phantom letter" from Algiers to Aden in 1893, that he intends to go and settle there: "I have thought of Egypt, where I already spent a few months seven years ago."[15] But whether passing through or just thinking of it, Egypt seems an unreachable dream for the poet and traveler, a country forever on the far side of where he is. Rimbaud prefers the hell of Aden and barbaric Abyssinia to Egypt and its gods, empire of three hundred fifty pharaohs, sons of the sun god, of Akhnaton inventing monotheism, country crossed by Moses and Jesus. "When the gods lead you back to Egypt,"[16] the

*Genoa, November 17, 1878.
†Mount Troodos, May 23, 1881.

French vice-consul in Suez will later write him; none of these gods will have guided Rimbaud when, dying in his hospital room, the Marseille climate again made him miss Egypt.

In Cairo, it is impossible not to feel the presence of the pyramids of Gizeh, just as one senses the Himalayas even from Katmandu. Chateaubriand was enthusiastic seeing them from a distance of ten miles; Flaubert made his horse gallop toward them; Rimbaud, like millions of noninitiates of the Memphis mysteries, saw the triangles pointing at the setting sun, light like the brown tents at the edge of the Lybian desert, growing powerfully up into the sky as one comes closer. Before Cheops, Chephren, or Mycerinos, all defiance gives way: No other monuments in the world are this overpowering. These millions of blocks of several tons each, like so many walled-up centuries looking out over the bustle of epochs, squelch our obsession with time, frighten and apease. "It seems they keep what escapes the dying," writes Bataille.[17] Neither natural mountains nor quite human monuments, the secret perfection of their proportions attains the purity of abstraction, the absolute. Before the pyramids, there is nothing. The Horizon, the Great, and the Supreme pyramids rise forever at the beginning of everything. Both weighty and immaterial, they assure the presence on earth of the boundless sky, of glory, pride, the will to immortality, and eternal power. They remain, more than tombs, more than names of pharaohs made stone, a place of passage to eternity.

Among the young fellahs and harnessed camels, among the same smell of horse manure that floats at the bottom of the pyramids now, Rimbaud tried to climb the 146 meters of the Cheops pyramid, as Bardey surely told him he had done,[18] pulled by two Arabs and pushed by two more, all singing in unison a verset ending on the old refrain "Eleyson"; Rimbaud climbed, as had Flaubert, who posed for his photo on the top of the pyramid, and Nerval, who shared his lunch with a Prussian officer on the upper platform. Or else he visited the interior, with torches, all the way to the sarcophagus in the king's chamber, on all fours in the corridors, like Flaubert.

He stopped before the sphinx, who at the time was buried in sand up to the ears. The giant keeper of the pyramids, at whose feet Rilke spent a night, is not the sphinx whom the Greek reduced from mystery to riddle,[19] but a god enthroned in the sky, looking death in the face.

Every night, the sun, its energy captured by the pyramid tops, disappears between them in ever changing colors. We move slowly among the ruins, in the providential silence and solitude of an ocher and gold evening with long purple streaks. Nearby, in the dark green and silver valley of the Nile, eternal little donkeys nibble on grain, peasants draw water with a *chadouf,* with age-old gestures. I let my eyes travel along the horizon hillocky with reddish dunes, a runaway horse, the minarets of Cairo, *canges* sailing by in the distance, palm tufts just like on date packages; and circle back to the mastabas, mounds more disturbing for being in the shadow of pyramids. A dragoman lets me enter, head-first, one of the subterranean tombs, a crypt narrow and cool as a washhouse. He lights a match: in the sarcophagus, under my eyes, a dry mummy. Farther on, he crouches down before a dark stela and lights a paper—*Al Arham*—which he throws at the grating: For an instant the daughters of the sun blaze up before me.

Afterward I travel a ways up the Nile. The Nile is as beautiful as *The Book of the Dead.* We land at Karnak among feluccas, lateen sails almost immobile in the reddish fog, the Lybian mountains rising against a cloudless, blazing blue sky that can kill men and plants, long arid mountain range with strange reliefs where I keep seeing faces—on the west bank, on the side of the dead and the hidden Valley of Kings, and here I finally feel the *gift.*

As in Ethiopia, I am allowed to see what Rimbaud saw.

While many writers have spoken of Egypt without ever seeing it, in September 1887, Rimbaud, without ever mentioning it, saw Thebes, the capital of the 100 gates sung in *The Iliad*. He walked through the "forest" of the 134 giant columns of the great pillared hall that counted among the Wonders of the World. He passed between the two colossal, pink granite statues of the pharaoh, one of which shows Ramses walking, one foot forward, arms straight and stiff along the body, the other immobile in the pose of Osiris, arms crossed over his chest and hands on his shoulders—the pharaoh and his double, radiant in life and death.

On horseback he went into the Valley of Kings. Among the burned mountains, in a steep gorge, he went down the sunk entryway into the labyrinthine hypogea deep below ground, a descent into another world according to the twelve hours of the night, to find a starry dark blue sky above stacked sarcophagi, eternity on the ceiling of subterranean tombs.

Here the man who believed that "this life is the only one" saw the bas-reliefs come alive in the temples of the soul: Osiris, the green god, a pharaonic *pschent* on his head, the key of life and the magic whip crossed over his chest; Nut, who enfolds the world in her immense arched body painted with the celestial vault; gods with animal heads, gods with pointed muzzles, cat-goddesses, Horus in golden plumage, Taueret, the hippopotamus midwife. Sekhmet with her lioness's head topped by the moon disk as by a tarnished metal mirror, the insatiable goddess of uncertain embrace; a cruel smile plays over her heavy mouth, she seems to ruminate some voluptuous dream of blood. And in front of each sarcophagus, next to Anubis, the loyal jackal embalming the mummy, our poet of fierce silence, who had amputated his poetry, saw the god of writing, Thoth, an ibis with pointed beak, opening the king's mouth to breathe in life through the word.

On the left bank of the Nile, he wandered through the ruins of the Ramesseum that inspired Shelley,[20] overgrown with mimosas, magnolias, and stinkweed, fragrant ruins full of hidden birds. He wandered through this disintegrated temple of Ramses II, who would have liked to be the beginning of history, a pharaoh now crumbled, whose colossal head has toppled into the shadow of a sycamore, old, sacred tree with bitter bark on which Thoth wrote his eternal scrolls.

Not far off, at Medinet Habu, he may have felt his uneasiness growing with the monuments that each pharaoh wanted larger than his predecessors', with the mania for more colonnades, more funerary chambers where the shadows of kings wearing the Double Crown would come to celebrate their sumptuous anniversaries, with the rows of osiriac pharaohs with feet plunged in the dark, with the uraei rising everywhere, sinuous, their necks swollen with a divine poison.[21]

Then, on his return, he came by the colossi of Memnon sitting placidly by the roadside behind a field of wheat, Amenophis III represented twice, hands on his knees, face worn away, his *pschent* like a shepherd's cap. He was able to read the inscriptions of the Greek and Roman poets who came to hear the colossi sing as the desert wind whistled through cracks in their torsos while the stone began to heat up in the first rays of the sun. Riding through the majestic desert of the Valley of Kings, which surpasses the Valley of Josaphat in lugubrious grandeur, our solitary young man from the African deserts, our searcher for gold, rest, or oblivion, must have thought of the treasures buried under stone and ground by these great conquerors, the "suns" of Africa and Asia, all these Tutmosis, Sesostris, the great nonagenarian Ramses, who, protected by their gods, went down into the entrails of the earth with their prodigious spoils, went down for "thousands and thousands of happy years" of identification with the sun-god, Amon (like Tutankhamon, "Living Image of the Sun God"), still sleeping unsuspected. And the man who had wanted to be a "son of the Sun"* must have thought of the power he had once dreamed of, power of a divine artist who would have been, as in Egypt, "he who gives life."

Finally, coming out of the avenues of mutilated, ram-headed sphinxes that lead from one temple of Amon to another, from Luxor to Karnak,[22] he no doubt carved his name, RIMBAUD, into the stone at the back of the last sanctuary, where it can still be seen,[23] as Byron carved his at Cape Sunium, a trace of passage here and beyond, great solar signature, ultimate hieroglyph.

The signature in capital letters is on the west wall of the birth chamber of Amenophis III, about 2.8 meters from the ground. The noon sun lights on it, leaving all other graffiti in the shadow. Look at the bird feet carved by the Egyptian artist: The signatory probably wanted to extend them in a horizontal accolade to underline his inscription with an airy flourish, pompous or silly, or to give himself wings, identifying with the bird, the Egyptian god.[24]

What does this desire to write our name on monuments respond to? A secret call of the temples? Certainly to the desire for eternity every anonymous passerby feels, our archetypal desire to be named there forever. "A page of history cannot be erased," says a famous inscription on the islet of Philae. After all, with Bonaparte's soldiers and scientific mission leaving inscriptions in Karnak, the innumerable Coptic hammerings, the Latin and Greek poets, the signatures of Emperor Hadrian and his wife Sabina—the great globe-trotters of antiquity—all of mankind has signed Egypt as its golden book. Egypt has always, without interruption, been the great palimpsest: For four thousand years, the pharaohs wrote on top of their predecessors' scrolls, until the last dynasties carved their symbols so that they could not be erased, but instead must be felt with the whole hand, read

*"Vagabonds," *Illuminations.*

by penetration. Now Egypt itself is becoming illegible. The eternal portion of Egypt is not the ruined temples, but the signatures, the desire to inscribe.

So, standing in front of this name that appears in the ruins as new depths of the temple are cleared of sand like a descent into deeper strata of time, I am content to think, even as the dark swallows the inscription at sundown, that it can be read as a trace of Arthur Rimbaud's passage, inspired by the *genius loci,* "this particular power that some places exercise over the mind."[25] By being written there, in Egypt, the name of the man in flight mingles with peace, sun, eternity, and the secret of recovered identity. Because we will never be able to decode it, this signature is *true*— like the mystery of Rimbaud. In the land of the birth of writing, it is written that among so many undecipherable signs there should silently dwell the name of the man who believed in the power of language and then withdrew from it. Here, in front of this inscription is the end of my travels. I could not go farther than this solar boundary.[26] I am satisfied to have found a trace, far from the Ardennes, on a stone from time immemorial, a trace as plain and as inconclusive as a footprint in the snow.

13
GONE

And Van Gogh lost a thousand
summers there.
—Artaud

Rimbaud returns to Arabia; he goes on with all the lights
out, all fire quenched. After this final trace, he signs his
commercial correspondence hastily, in three letters, "RBD,"*
losing his vowels, his breath, a dry, consonant Rimbaud.

I go back to Cairo and try to answer for myself the
questions I was asked in the plane, on this same return trip.
Already Abyssinia, lost to the imagination, settles gently into
my memory. I take away the image of a red and green
country, immense, luminous. At least I know it is necessary
to go to Ethiopia, just as Lawrence held that we cannot understand him unless we have really spent a day in the desert.
Since, in our film, *The Fire Stealer,* I am supposed to be
writing a book, I will have to take up the challenge and
really write one on my return. It is astonishing to see how
ideas also travel, also make their way. I have read Rimbaud
backward, Ethiopia first, then Charleville, as I read Joyce
before Homer. At the start, I thought I had a feeling of
Rimbaud's silence in Africa. I would not have minded if I

*Harar, August 24, 1889.

had found him as he is described in most of the books: cynical, trafficking in anything at all. Later it appeared that, far from "harming the work,"[1] his life explains it, as if he had realized the dreams of the poet at seven "violently longing for sails," of the Seer who wanted a "chalky desert";* as if he had fulfilled the prophecies of *A Season in Hell*[2] in flight and oblivion, in purifying adventures.† So the long red span of the Abyssinian horizon allowed in return an anagogical reading of the work:

> *No hope there,*
> *No* orietur.
> *Science with patience,*
> *Torment is sure.*††

   This still meant distinguishing two periods, two movements. But as I began to find the reality outside time that he had known and to understand that he had lived it with the same relation to the world that his poetry shows, the sense of the oneness of his destiny, of its many constants, gradually became compelling: always on the road, never really with reality, always moving toward the impossible. It is not from 1880 on that Rimbaud thinks of *rest* (not money) as the goal behind the "unimaginable strain," but as early as 1870, at sixteen, in his third letter known to us, which could be a letter from Africa: "I am lost, sick, furious, stupid, upset. I expected sunbaths, endless walks, rest, travel, adventures, bohemian life . . . books. . . . Nothing! Nothing!"§
   Marching through snow in northern Norway, in 1877, or across the "chalky deserts" of Africa, the thirty thousand kilometers Rimbaud covered on foot and the incredible

---

* Sketch of "Delirium" II, *A Season in Hell*.
† "My day is done; I'm leaving Europe . . ." ("Bad Blood," *A Season in Hell*).
†† "Eternity," May 1872.
§ Charleville, August 25, 1870.

multiplicity of his projects took on the sense of a quest for "the one thing,"[3] as with Hölderlin's Hyperion, the quest for a perfection placed beyond this world and at the end of time: Rimbaud was not a writer, but a person who passed through writing among many other experiences, searching in all directions for the one thing or, in his words, "in a rush to find the place and the formula" of the one thing, the unformulable where he would find "freedom in salvation."* I came back convinced that he did not change his object, did not search "in reality" for what he had not found in poetry, nor really for "something else,"[4] but that already his poetry (perhaps more than anything else) was a figure of "the Impossible."

We are flying over Minyeh. I am getting sleepy. A phrase from "The Impossible" comes to me, with the obsessiveness that makes Rimbaud quotations take over my daily life, which tries to absorb them: "But I notice my spirit is asleep. If from this moment on it were always wide awake we should soon reach truth." I experience in the plane what Paul Claudel experienced leaning against a pillar in Notre-Dame: I have my "night" of revelation! Tilt! Yes, this is the essential, this is what I will write my book on, this "from this moment on always"—the fatality of having "always and forever"† been locked inside the body, inside error, carried through time and space; the impossibility of *being before* this moment of thought *always already* too late, of going back to the beginning, of reaching the "primal"†† state of "son of the Sun," the "age of gold,"§ the "ancient feast."‖ This is the regret of "Morning": "Did I not *once* have a lovable, heroic, fabulous youth, fit to be written on sheets of gold— too good to be true!" This longing for the purity of beginnings is in Rimbaud's passion for the sun, his taste for early

* "Night of Hell," *A Season in Hell.*
† April 17, 1871.
†† "Vagabonds," *Illuminations.*
§ 1872.
‖ "Once . . ." *A Season in Hell.*

hours,[5] for "Dawn":* "three o'clock in the morning . . . this unspeakable, first hour of the day."† This is the impetus of all his departures. "If it were always wide awake. . . !" In vain he protests against the fate of beings. Wandering, marching, are his punishment for this essential impossibility, a desperate liberation. At the same time, Rimbaud lived his travels as exploits (crossing the St. Gotthard, the ride to Harar, "six days going, five coming back"††), and most of his poems celebrate exploits ("The Drunken Boat," "Dawn": to marry the summer dawn!). Never satisfied, projects outbidding .one another like the hyperboles in his writing, he always demands more—demands the impossible. So, contemptuous of all idols (to the point of sloughing off *in advance* the one that might be made of him), Rimbaud dashes onward, projects and destroys himself in this momentum. There he goes, Goethe would say, "beyond the graves, and onward!"

Putting away the last cartridge before leaving, the cameraman told me, "You talked ten kilometers."[6] Today, we measure words by length. Ten kilometers of words. A few words in ten thousand kilometers. Perhaps we need as many words as Rimbaud covered miles to join him and fall silent. To arrive at the obvious, the basic truth expressed by Claudel—"a mystic in the raw"—and by Jacques Rivière—"a monster of purity." If we may extend this perfect formula to Rimbaud's whole life and need not take it in the narrow sense of integration into Catholicism, "the grace of being born without original sin" is only one form of understanding this innocence.[7] At the outset of the trip, I carried

* *Illuminations.*
† "Junphe" 1872. Or again, "Good Thoughts in the Morning": "At four in the morning, in summer . . ."
†† November 17, 1878: "The exploit . . . was crossing the Gotthard"; Aden, March 29, 1888: "I made the trek to Harar, six days going, five coming back, eight staying there, and another dozen in dhows and steamers"; Cairo, August 23, 1887: "Exploits like the following."

a small notebook; now, by force of word-kilometers, my suitcase is heavy with a book project; and I in turn have come back with convictions. Yet, stopping at so many places, I have perhaps only reinforced an inner image with space. Have I been wrong? Rimbaud scholars are like Egyptologists: You cannot find two who agree. "You will never get to know Arthur Rimbaud well," proclaimed André Breton—who should have said "I" on this occasion.[8]

By now I have read all of Rimbaud's books, followed most of his tracks, and, I think, see his entire mystery in a more detailed and deeper way. Skimming over the surface of things is a characteristic of traveling. But the encounter with essence that I felt in Ethiopia and Egypt, this kind of truth cannot be reported. Others will come after, more of them, who will not be able to tell it either. . . . The answer, says Blanchot, is "the misfortune of the question."[9] But the question remains, and even grows larger with all the answers. This is the way I think of the ending of Apollinaire's "ocean letter": "You will never get to know the Mayas well."

We are arriving in Cairo. Other planes are taking off for all the corners of the world. All hypotheses are reversible, but the journey continues. This journey has been my truth, a perfect form of happiness. The few ideas I put forward do not matter very much to me. I would even give all the pepper of Ethiopia to be wrong, to learn that Rimbaud had lived exactly as he said in "Vies" ("Lives") III in the *Illuminations:* "In a magnificent place surrounded by the entire Orient, I finished my immense work and spent my famous retirement."

The days have gone by slowly, like barges laden with fruit. It is raining in Athens: This is Europe. Tanned by the Ethiopian sun, I still wear in Rome the djellaba bought in a village behind the pyramids. Greek or Roman, our civilization is under the same cloud. I return as if backward, unable to take my mind off the distant, unreal elsewhere, where at this very moment the sun is shining. It takes skill knowing how to end a dream. The Rimbaldian journey means also return to the point of departure—but in the Nietzschean sense, in a spiral that took Rimbaud to the point of no return. "Always already arrived you'll go everywhere."*

The plane plunges into some kind of felt, with the two cedars of Roissy sticking out. The cold that, it is said, coagulates feelings and causes restraint, is almost pleasant. "Back over our old roads again . . ."† A longing for open space chokes me. In the taxi, with the noise of the windshield wipers, I suddenly see again the Ogadens immobile in the sun, almost invisible among earth and stones. An eagle soars above Harar. . . . Rimbaud's stretcher leaves town, escorted by camels, accompanied by his servant Djami as far as the farewell trees of Kombulcha. A stretcher covered with a leather curtain, faithfully reconstructed, beautiful as Malevich's painted coffin. At what age do we need to start painting our coffin? Rimbaud, who hoped to return soon, designed himself this strange stretcher that carried him off on a journey he was not to come back from. "Yes, for some time already, death would have been preferable!"†† "We contain our death as a fruit its stone," wrote Rilke, who died of the complications of being pricked by a rose. Rimbaud goes alone into his last battle. Curtain drawn on his stretcher, hearing only the breath of his porters and their steps on the dry earth, he keeps a notebook on his last trip. "Arrived in Degadallal . . . the swamps of Egon . . . Left Ballawa . . . A storm . . . in Geldessey. . . . Arrived, stayed, got up, camped, left, left, left, left, passed, arrived . . ." A staggering "notebook of one of the damned,"§ written at the edge of the grave on a journey from life to

---

* "A une raison" ("To a Reason"), *Illuminations*.
† "Bad Blood," *A Season in Hell*.
†† Marseille, June 24, 1891.
§ "Once . . . ," *A Season in Hell*.

death, this *Itinerary from Harar to Warambot* registers the jolts of the stretcher constantly in danger of turning over, registers time going crazy between hours spent in anxiety and endless waiting—"Sixteen hours [without] food or tent . . . under an Abyssinian pelt . . . sixteen hours without cover in the rain . . . thirty hours without any food"—as if adding up hours of departure and arrival, privations and storms, the fine of four talers and the eight men gone in search of camels would give the sum of his misfortunes. Never commented on, these four pages in pale pencil, torn from a soaked, crumpled notebook, might well mark an absolute limit in his work where the highest degree of suffering and reality rejoins the imaginary. Rimbaud was never further from poetry than in these eleven fragments written en route, which record departures and arrivals, unchained elements ("furious wind all night"), real drama ("the stretcher half broken and the people completely exhausted") to the point where this itinerary of death takes on the force and form of an "Illumination," taking us to a land of unknown names like Kimbavoren, Haut-Egon, to unreal people like Mouned-Souyn. . . . The unfortunate fellow tried in vain to "mount a mule by having his sick leg tied to its neck," but had to go back to his stretcher. Evenings, he would write to Isabelle, he was put down and left to dig a hole with his hands beside the stretcher—"I had trouble turning on my side to go to the bathroom on this hole which I then filled with earth."* In the mornings, Rimbaud would shout at his porters to go faster; when they, out of breath, threw him down on the ground at arrival, he would fine them a few talers: Rimbaud is still in a rage, but this time the rage of agony.

Visualizing through the taxi windshield the lava desert crossed by the stretcher and its procession, I thought that Rimbaud's real funeral was not six months later in Charleville, in the rain, a first-class hearse followed only by his mother and sister, the "dear friends" of his letters ("the fate

*Marseille, July 15, 1891.

of the sons of good families, premature coffin covered with limpid tears"*) but this stretcher going toward the Red Sea, carried for two weeks at cargo pace by sixteen natives over three hundred kilometers of Somali desert to the port of Zeila, which had been his gateway to Africa twelve years before. This impetuous convoy, followed by camels that started galloping at the first, faint whiff of the sea, was the true funeral of Arthur Rimbaud, funeral on his own scale in the arid desert, like the "coffins under black canopies with ebony plumes, drawn at a trot by big blue and black mares."†
A last, unbound run on earth, flight from death and hurrying toward it, a cavalcade into the light, new image of topspeed departure toward the inaccessible and desired rest, toward the East, toward Aden where he wanted to be buried, toward "the sea mixed with the sun," toward eternity.†† Obsequies prolonged in wandering and freedom, in the desert he no longer would or could leave, in the large field without beyond where he saw himself "live a long time still, perhaps forever."§ May this rickety stretcher, ark of the covenant at the point of incandescence, tumbledown royal litter with a howling dead man taking his secrets with him for us to dream about, may this caravan take Rimbaud unawares into "affection and the future."‖ Rimbaud! One Rimbaud only, but twice great: great in poetry and great in silence.

* "Bad Blood," *A Season in Hell.*
† "Ornières" ("Ruts"), *Illuminations.*
†† "Alchemy of the Word," *A Season in Hell.*
§ Aden, May 5, 1884.
‖ "Génie," *Illuminations.*

NOTES

Chapter 1: Departure

1. See letter from Paul Verlaine to Emile Blémont, 1873.
2. Jean-Paul Vaillant, *Rimbaud tel qu'il fut (Rimbaud as He Was)* (Paris: Le Rouge et le Noir, 1930).
3. François Mauriac, quoted by Jean-Paul Vaillant, in *Textes africains d'Arthur Rimbaud* (Liège: Editions Dynamo, 1945).
4. Letter from Ernest Delahaye to Ernest Millot, August 9, 1877.
5. Paul Verlaine, "Arthur Rimbaud," *The Senate* (London: October 1895). It is often forgotten that Rimbaud's presence in Harar had been noted in 1886 by *Le Symboliste* of October 22–29 (G. Moréas and G. Kahn, eds.), p. 10. Cf. M. Pakenham, "Trouver le lieu et la formule" ("To Find the Place and Formula"), in *Arthur Rimbaud,* No. 2 (Paris: Minard, 1973), p. 145.
6. Vitalie Rimbaud to her son, Roche, October 10, 1885.
7. Verlaine, preface to *Les Illuminations, La Vogue,* 1886.
8. Ibid.
9. These "Rimbesque informations" were of little use to Verlaine. It was the publisher Léon Vanier who (according to Claude Zissman) added the fantastic details and sold the text to *Entretiens politiques et littéraires (Political and Literary Conversations)*. It appeared (Vol. III, pp. 185–188) over the signature M.D. (Ernest Delahaye) in December 1891, a few days after Rimbaud's death.
10. Frédéric Rimbaud to Rodolphe Darzens, December 10, 1891.
11. "He died laid up in Marseille," the *Écho de Paris* specified. Cf. Henri Matarasso and Pierre Petitfils, *Album Rimbaud,* "Bibliothèque de la Pléiade" (Paris: Gallimard, 1967), p. 315.
12. This is the title of the memoirs of Alfred Bardey, Rimbaud's first employer. *Barr Adjam: Souvenirs d'Afrique-Orientale, 1880–1887* (Paris: Joseph Tubiana/Editions du CNRS, 1981).

13. Concerning the poetry of departures, Julien Gracq said of the Surrealists (although he hardly appreciated them) that they took local trains at random, "full of departures that no arrival could ever disappoint." Or the beginning of Roger Vailland's *Boroboudour:* "At six P.M., I left Sceaux (on the Seine) where I lived at the time, in a truck of my neighbor's who runs a garage. 'Where are you going this time?' he asked. 'To Java!' "

14. "Nuit de l'enfer" ("Night of Hell"), *Une Saison en enfer;* "Democracy," *Illuminations;* letter to his family, November 17, 1878. In the context of the poem "Départ," Pierre Brunel speaks of an *absolute departure:* "With surprising economy, all it takes to evoke this departure is for the poet to write the word *departure.* . . . In fact, this is not a departure *for,* but a departure *within,* as if the mere intention brought a whole world along with it, a *new* world" (*Arthur Rimbaud ou l'éclatant désastre* [*Arthur Rimbaud or the Dazzling Disaster*] [Paris: Champ Vallon, 1983], p. 13).

15. It opens with a sentence by Michel Deguy: "What is left of a trip, where the actual travel took place against all plans, and which was lost on the way back, until it returns, not having been repressed, but lost, without any inconvenience or interest in the loss" (*Donnant-Donnant* [*Giving-Giving*] [Paris: Gallimard, 1980]).

16. "The Correspondence of Vitalie Rimbaud-Cuif, with Thirteen Previously Unpublished Letters," in Suzanne Briet, *Mme. Rimbaud, Essai de biographie* (Paris: Aux Lettres Modernes, Minard, 1968); Isabelle Rimbaud, *Mon frère Arthur* (Paris: Camille Bloch Éditions, 1920).

17. Georges Izambard, *Rimbaud tel que je l'ai connu* (*Rimbaud As I Knew Him*) (Paris: Mercure de France, 1963).

18. Quoted in Jean-Marie Carré, *Les Deux Rimbaud* (*The Two Rimbauds*) (Paris: Éditions des Cahiers Libres, 1928), p. 27.

19. Marc Cholodenko, (Paris: Hachette, 1980).

20. *Galleria,* March 1924; *Revue de France,* September 1, 1928; *Revue hebdomadaire,* August 27, 1932; Paris: Éditions du Sagittaire, 1934; *Comoedia,* June 26, 1943; *Le Mercure de France,* September 1, 1947; *Europe,* special Rimbaud issue, 1954; *Il Mattino del Lunedi,* September 22, 1970.

21. Stéphane Mallarmé, "Rimbaud" (Paris, April 1896), in *The Chap Book,* May 15, 1896.

22. *A page from my notebook:* "Writing on a trip makes us more keenly aware of the uncommunicable. Concentrating on imagining an astronaut's travel, for instance, we can perhaps empathize with some of his probable sensations, but there will always remain, even in the best case, an individual element of the expedition—and the gap between it and our revery shows the value of the methods of Valéry's Monsieur Teste. This gap may be hard to imagine, but even if it were reduced in representation, the body remembers and insists on the difference. When we take the risk of presenting experienced sensations in a story, something keeps out the existential element, but gives in to the desire to travel—not for the sake of saying that we have done it, but to live through it again. So the invitation to travel is based on fear of forgetting, as is love after the death of the beloved. But the telling gradually takes the place of memory, erases it in the process of writing. What is lost in the telling could only be shared in life—the sounds and smells, the tiredness, anxiety, mad laughs, exaltation, surprise or loneliness."

23. In *Rimbaud raconté par Verlaine,* introduction and notes by Jules Mouquet (Paris: Mercure de France, 1934), p. 68.

24. *Rimbaud, le voleur de feu* (*Rimbaud, the Fire Stealer*), directed by Charles Bra-

bant, played on TF1 on the evening of May 30, 1978: two hours, ten minutes. Texts interpreted by Léo Ferré and spoken by Jean-Pierre Pauty; interviews with Jean-Louis Baudry, Alémé Eshete, Émile Foucher, Pierre Gascar, Pierre Petitfils, Stéphane Taute, Vernon Philip Underwood. (And a salute to Dominique Frène, our pilot-fish, to Guy Gourlay who kept an eye on me, to Jean-Louis Soulivet who helped me in difficulty, to Patrick Escudié and Pierre Boucher for their advice.) Annick Hully had obtained authorization to film in Ethiopia—on condition that the film conformed to the idea the new masters of the country had of Rimbaud, and was careful of the national image. They telegraphed to TF1, November 1976: "Rimbaud happy in Harar. Loved an Abyssinian woman and lived happily with her. Supposed to have left a son in Harar. Had excellent, affectionate relations with the natives. Insist Ethiopia did not destroy Rimbaud."

By filming Le Voleur de feu while traveling, on the move, Charles Brabant made the saving gesture—not to have Rimbaud "played" by an actor, as if he were familiar to us, identifiable with what we already know of him. He decided not to represent, but research him. On Le Voleur de feu, see especially Pierre Petitfils, Rimbaud vivant, Nos. 15 and 16. A hot medium for simple messages, TV is the place of formula, not of nuance. But the film, which represents eighteen months of work by thirty people and the filmmaker's vision, lives only one evening, like a dragonfly. So the book compensates for a complex frustration—with a performance always to be done over, with the "whole" remaining out of reach, with even the speed of travel: The eyes cannot take in everything. A film on Rimbaud cannot dispense us from reading Rimbaud; this one tries, on the contrary, to send us back to the book. My notes, born of the film and accompanying it, go a basically different way, but rejoin it on this point.

With regard to Rimbaud on TV: On the occasion of the centenary of Rimbaud's birth, Pierre Dumayet and Pierre Desgraupes had taken an RTF camera to Roche, interviewing the villagers ("Lectures pour tous" ["Reading for all"], 1954). The same Pierre Dumayet recorded a program on Les Deserts de l'amour ("Lire, c'est vivre" ["Reading Means Living"], Antenne 2, 1978). The beautiful black-and-white of the late 1960s was well suited to the Ardennes, where Max-Pol Fouchet filmed a Rimbaud, with Laurent Terzieff (1966). The arcades of the Place Ducale in Charleville appeared in Roman (FR3, 1979) and Portrait d'écrivain, Rimbaud à Charleville (Portrait of a Writer, Rimbaud in Charleville) by J. M. Nokin (TF1, January 1984). The Japanese TBS channel showed two films in 1978, one on Verlaine and the other on Rimbaud, with texts spoken by Jacques Roux, also on Belgian, Dutch, and German TV. Let us also mention Illuminations (ORTF, 1976) and, in order to eliminate it, a film by an Iranian director (FR3, December 1983)—indecent.

A batch of shorts: Bateau ivre (Drunken Boat) by Henri Beauvais, shown as "world premiere" on May 11, 1949, in Charleville (cf. the supplement to Bateau ivre, Nos. 2–3, Bulletin des amis de Rimbaud, May 1949; and Étiemble, Le Mythe de Rimbaud [Paris: Gallimard, 1954], pp. 340–341). Then Bateau ivre by Alfred Chaumel (1950), Les Effarés (Frightened Kids) by J. G. Albicocco (1955), Le Dernier Matin d'Arthur Rimbaud (Arthur Rimbaud's Last Morning) by Jean Barral (1964). After Le Cid, the young lead Gérard Philipe "embodied" Rimbaud in a film by Gilbert Prouteau. Among amateur films, Rimbaud à Harar by Michel Pons (1970, undistributed, as it should remain) and Un Coeur sous une soutane (A Heart Under a Cassock) by Patrick Jeudy (1973).

At the end of his bibliography *L'Oeuvre et le visage d'Arthur Rimbaud* (Paris: Nizet, 1949), Pierre Petitfils observed: "The film remains to be made." There have been some since. *Le Vieux Pays où Rimbaud est mort*, a Quebec film by Jean-Pierre Lefebvre (1977), has nothing Rimbaldian except the title: A "cousin" from Quebec comes to realize that France is no longer the country of Rimbaud. In 1972 appeared the first feature "spectacular," *Une Saison en enfer* by Nelo Risi. Terence Stamp was Rimbaud, Jean-Claude Brialy, Verlaine, and Florinda Bolkan added her legs in the role of Gennet [*sic*], hypothetical Abyssinian wife of the poet. Music by Maurice Jarre. Leaving the empty movie theater, I met the famous linguist Roman Jakobson. He claimed to be enthusiastic about Risi's film—the only one I know. Except for an image set in Stuttgart, the film was a disaster, and was received as such. "The film remains to be made."

"And Rimbaud, a poet, no, a filmmaker who gave up writing before he went to Africa" says the character in the top hat who dances around the filmmaker's car in Fillini's *8½*. It is perhaps in actual films that we can find germs of the quality feature we may still hope for: in *Pierrot le fou*, who gives up everything in order to live his life (Godard inserts two portraits of Rimbaud in this movie, which ends with the poem "Eternity" spoken offscreen over a perfect pan of "the sea gone with the sun"); and even more in *Theorema*. "Rimbaud, my contemporary, my castrator," writes Pier Paolo Pasolini, evoking a "Rimbaud covered with ribbons like Alcibiades." *Theorema* might in part be the first Rimbaldian film (by the way, Rimbaud's *Works* in the Feltrinelli edition appear from the first reel on in close-up, and Terence Stamp—*truer* than in Risi's film—reads Rimbaud several times in the course of the drama). This mysterious young man—hypothetical God *and* conceiver of evil, who sows confusion among a bourgeois family, transforming his hosts into people possessed—joins Verlaine's perception ("Crimen amoris") of a diabolical Rimbaud.

Let us wish for a first festival of Rimbaldian films.

25. Henry Miller, *Rimbaud*, trans. F. Roger-Cornaz (Mermod, 1952); *The Time of the Assassins*, new trans. F. J. Temple (Paris: Pierre-Jean Oswald Éditeur, 1970).

26. Paul Claudel's preface to *Oeuvres d'Arthur Rimbaud*, ed. Paterne Berrichon (Paris: Mercure de France, 1912). Following a pointer by Henri Guillemin, Claudel's most beautiful text on Rimbaud is in *La Messe là-bas* (Paris: Editions de la Nouvelle Revue française, 1919). Let us recall what Claudel said to Mallarmé: "I plan—*for my own benefit*—to write you one of these days at leisure about certain subjects close to my heart, like *Catholicism* and *Arthur Rimbaud* (toward whom you seem unjust). Ever since the initial love at first sight of the issue of *La Vogue* where I first read *Les Illuminations*, I can say that I owe to Rimbaud all I am intellectually and morally. And I think there are few examples of such an intimate marriage of two minds." Later, Claudel will write: "Rimbaud had an effect on me that I would call seminal and paternal, and which makes me believe that there are bloodlines in the realm of the mind like in that of the body" (quoted in Henri Mondor, *Rimbaud ou le génie impatient* (Paris: Gallimard, 1955), and Jean-Claude Morisot, *Claudel et Rimbaud, étude de transformations* (Paris: Minard, 1976).

27. We know that Gide was reminded of the Cévennes mountains on his arrival in Chad. Alfred Bardey compared the "fat fields" of Harar to his native Franche-Comté. And back in 1856, Henri Lebrun wrote in his *Voyages en Abyssinie et*

en Nubie (Tours: Imprimerie Mame): "The greenery often reminds us of Europe. Like at home, the eye often comes to rest on vines, honeysuckles or roses."
Addis Ababa was built in 1891 on a site near Entotto.
See Henry de Monfreid, *Du Harar au Kénia* (Paris: Grasset, 1970): "They lack the concept of charity . . . they would not have understood my giving them care for nothing."

Chapter 2: Living

Concerning the Franco-Ethiopian Railroad (CFE). Do not lean out of the window. Reading lengthy notes is not advisable while traveling. Cf. Willi Loepfe, *Alfred Ilg und die Äthiopische Eisenbahn*, (*Alfred Ilg and the Ethiopian Railroad*) (Zürich: Atlantis Verlag, 1974); and on this book, Jean Voellmy, *Arthur Rimbaud*, No. 4 (Paris: Minard, 1980), p. 115. Willi Loepfe neglects to remember Rimbaud's intuition (it is true, his subject is mostly the years after the poet's stay). But Rimbaud asked as early as 1883 for a *Complete Treatise on Railroads* from France, justly observed in 1887 that "in spite of the invasions, Harar is certainly destined to become the exclusive commercial entryway into Shoa itself and all the Gallas." He was no doubt one of the first who had the good sense to write about the idea of such a railroad:

Menelik himself was so struck by the advantageous location of Harar that on his return he remembered the idea of a railroad that several Europeans had suggested to him and looked for someone to whom he could give the commission or concession of a railroad between Harar and the sea. He later changed his mind, remembering the English presence on the coast! It goes without saying that if it should happen the Shoa government would not contribute to the costs of construction. [Letter to the editor of the *Bosphore egyptien*, August 25 and 27, 1887; on this letter, see Chapter 11.]

The Europeans dangled the advantages of progress in front of Menelik: "In 1883, the engineer Aubry, who accompanied the Brémond mission, demonstrated to Menelik a miniature locomotive and steamboat. The king of Shoa, in love with progress, was delighted" (Ministry of Foreign Affairs [MAE], Africa, 62.606; quoted in Suzanne Briet, *Rimbaud notre prochain* (*Rimbaud Our Neighbor*), [Paris: Nouvelles Editions Latines, 1956], p. 174). Rimbaud was to speak of railroad construction with his temporary partner, Paul Soleillet (cf. Chapter 3), whom Menelik granted a concession for a railroad from Ankober to Obock. However, his company went bankrupt before starting construction. The English were happy about this (Enid Starkie, *Rimbaud en Abyssinie* [Paris: Payot, 1939], p. 58). But Chefneux, Soleillet's younger partner, took over before becoming consul general of Abyssinia. "We have forgotten the brave men who paid with their lives: Chefneux, the instigator of this project, died in misery" (Henry de Monfreid, *Les Secrets de la Mer rouge* [*The Secrets of the Red Sea*] [Paris: Grasset, 1968], p. 9). Makonnen, the governor of Harar, intervened. "He had the courage to combat the nefarious influence of Taïtu, who was hostile against foreigners, and give the concession to France" (Henry de Monfreid, *Les Lionnes d'or d'Éthiopie* [*The Golden Lionesses of Ethiopia*] [Paris: Laffont, 1967], p. 88). Menelik had found his master builder. He thought in even longer terms, allowing France to run the Addis–Djibouti line till December 31, 2016, rather a concession in perpetuity. . . . The rivalry of the European powers had hindered the 1906 Franco-Ethiopian project of a railroad as far as the White Nile (cf. Jean Doresse, *Histoire de l'Éthiopie* [Paris: PUF, 1970], p. 105). *La Dépêche coloniale illustré* (*The Illustrated Colonial Dispatch*) (1910), p. 283, published by *L'Illustration,* reports details of the construction, where we encounter old acquaintances: "By the decrees of March 9, 1894, the emperor Menelik conceded to MM. Ilg and Chefneux . . . the rights to construct and develop a railroad between Ethiopia and the sea, via Djibouti." Starting out from Djibouti, the rails ("English," one meter wide) reached the thirty-seventh kilometer only in August 1899. The first leg from Djibouti to the White Nile was opened for travel on January 1, 1903. Jean-Marie Carré (*La Vie aventureuse de Jean-Arthur Rimbaud* [*The Adventurous Life of Jean-Arthur Rimbaud*] [Paris: Plon, 1926]), who thinks the CFE goes to Harar, could have read:

The initial project had been to connect the town of Harar with the coast, but the nature of the terrain, mountainous from El-Bah (kilometer 288) on, caused the project to be abandoned. The terminal was built at Diredawa, located in a vast basin near an abundant river, the Laga-Harré, which could supply drinking water to a future great city. The construction of a drivable road between Diredawa and Harar was undertaken jointly by the company and the Abyssinian government. By the end of 1903, this road allowed rapid transportation between these two points.

With the benefits of the completed first section, a new company, following an agreement concluded on June 30, 1908, in Addis Ababa between a representative of France and Menelik, the "Franco-Ethiopian Railroad Company Djibouti-Addis Ababa" took over the line, which it extended slowly, from July 1, 1909, on, from Diredawa to Addis Ababa.

The engineer André Provost rode in this train, which, in 1928, took three days from Addis to Diredawa: "The Franco-Ethiopian Railroad, admirable work, but a costly propaganda tool for the name of France, painfully channels part of the rich Abyssinian products toward the port, as many as can reach the railroad in a country without communications in the interior and, besides, drawn toward the English road via Gambela, Sobat, Khartoum and Port-Sudan" ("Sur les traces africaines de Rimbaud," *Revue de France* [September 1, 1928]).

2. Letter to the editor of the *Bosphore égyptien,* op. cit. Danakil is plural of the Arabic *Dankali,* the name the English used for a people who call themselves Afars, and whom the Amharas call Adals. The Danakil, whom even the most open-minded explorers described as most cruel "savages," had wounded Labatut, among others, before his association with Rimbaud. (On the dangers of caravans, see Chapter 9.)

3. In 1974, an AFP telegram among a thousand announces that the CFE has been interrupted by sabotage. Fifty meters of dismantled rails had derailed a maintenance car. In 1928, André Provost wrote: "One travels only in the daytime because the desert blacksmiths like to use the crossbars of the rails to forge spears" (op. cit.). In 1883, Rimbaud's *Report on Ogaden* pointed out "these blacksmiths who wander from tribe to tribe."

4. Rimbaud's letter to the *Bosphore* also says:

Coming to the Haouach, one is stunned remembering the canalization projects of certain travelers. Poor old Soleillet had a special embarcation under way in Nantes for this purpose! . . . Menelik had the Itous construct two bridges over the Haouach, one on the road from Entotto to Guraghe, the other, between Ankober and Harar. These are simple foot bridges built from tree trunks, meant for the crossing of troops during rain and floods, but they are nevertheless remarkable works for Shoa.

It was another colleague of Rimbaud's who was to construct the first bridge that was not makeshift . . . shortly after Rimbaud's departure. In 1897, in the first book on Abyssinia since Rimbaud's departure, Sylvain Vignéras noted "the iron bridge built over the Haouache nearly three years ago by a Frenchman, M. Savouré" (*Une Mission française en Abyssinie* [Paris: Armand Colin, 1897], p. 177).

The final sentence of Carré, *Les Deux Rimbaud* (op. cit.). Rimbaud's name appears for the first time in a periodical in December 1881, as an explorer. If we make exception for Lepelletier's allusion to "Mlle. Rimbaut [*sic*]" (*Le Peuple souverain* [Paris, November 16, 1871]), the Milano magazine *L'Esploratore* (December 1881) appeared before Félicien Champsaur's *roman à clef, Dinah Samuel* (1882) or Verlaine's notice in Lutèce (1883). (Franco Pétralia, *Bibliographie de Rimbaud en Italie* [Institut français de Florence, Ed. Sansoni Antiquariato, 1960], p. 16; the reference is lacking in Etiemble's *Genèse du mythe de Rimbaud*.)

In 1881, Antonio Cecchi was already exploring the southeast of Ethiopia (Kaffa), and Franzoj went from Gallabat to Assab via Gondar and Entotto. Can Rimbaud be considered one of the explorers of his time equal to Count Cecchi, Jules Borelli, Philipp Paulitschke, Count Téléki, Ugo Ferrandi or Robecchi-Bricchetti?

A. (Concerning the route.) Entotto–Harar and the letter to the *Bosphore égyptien*. Pierre Bardey, the brother of Rimbaud's employer, took the CFE when he came for a last time to Harar, before leaving Aden for France. We can imagine the state of mind of this old, tired man who is both sad and happy to leave: Things have not changed much, but the railroad makes trips and commerce considerably easier. Bardey thinks of Lucereau, the young French explorer he met in the Hotel Universe in Aden, who wanted to explore this region for the best route: He was murdered on December 1, 1880. Then he thinks of Rimbaud, who was also his employee, who had signaled "the advantages of a railroad to Harar for Abyssinia" in the *Bosphore égyptien* (see note 1, *above*). This road, Mario Matucci specifies (*Le Dernier Visage de Rimbaud en Afrique* [Paris: Librairie Marcel Didier, 1962]), "would start at Entotto, cross the plain of Mindjar and the Haouach River up to Lake Arro, touch Goro, Herréa, Burka, Oborra, Shalenko, Lake Yabatha and end up, forty kilometers farther, in Harar" (p. 57). In 1887, there were five possible routes, details of which Armand Savouré sent to the Ministry of Foreign Affairs (MAF, Afrique, 107.218; in Briet, *Rimbaud notre prochain*, op. cit., p. 189). For his arms expedition in 1886, Rimbaud was obliged to take the most difficult one, the road of Gobat. On his return he was one of the first Europeans to take what is the present CFE route. For all that we cannot write, as Étiemble and Yassu Gauclère do: "Did he not discover the route the Djibouti–Addis Ababa railroad would take?" (*Rimbaud* [Paris: Gallimard, 1950], p. 224). They imprudently follow Jean-Marie Carré: "It is his tracks that the CFE will follow later" (*Les Deux Rimbaud*, op. cit., p. 44, and earlier in *La Vie aventureuse de Jean-Arthur Rimbaud*, op. cit., p. 211). The railroad did not follow Rimbaud's tracks. This is an error still repeated frequently. Following an article by Louis Lalande in the *Revue des deux mondes* (*Review of the Two Worlds*) of December 15, 1878 (nothing allows us to think that Rimbaud, in Cyprus at the time, could have read it), the late Daniel A. de Graaf even went as far as to claim: "Opening a road for Europe into Central Africa via Obock and Shoa, this was the goal of Rimbaud's explorations in the years 1885–1887, when he aspired to equal the exploits of Jules Borelli, Paul Soleillet, Alphonse Aubrey, and especially Von Hardegger and Paulitschke who had taken the first steps toward the heart of the countries of Galas [*sic*] and Ogaden" (*Arthur Rimbaud, sa vie, son oeuvre* (*A.R., His Life, His Work*) [Assen, 1960], p. 303). Rimbaud indeed said he "desired . . . to take the new, hitherto unexplored road opened by the king through Itou territory, which I had vainly tried to take at the time of the Egyptian occupation of Harar" (Letter to the *Bosphore*). But we have to put this "first" in perspective:

(1) The opening of this road is certainly due to Menelik and his troops, a circumstance of war.

(2) The *Bollettino Della Società Africana d'Italia*, Vol. VIII, Nos. 5–6 (May–June 1889), pp. 135–142) remarks that two Italians had preceded Rimbaud on this road: Vincenzo Ragazzi and Raffaele Alfieri, who were attached to Menelik's troops in a medical capacity: "*Dopo di lui* [Ragazzi], *la strada da Antoto ad Harar fu percosa felicimento dal commerciante francese M. Rimbaud*" (*Bollettino . . . op. cit.*, Vol. II, No. 1 [January 1888], pp. 57–90, in Pétralia, *Bibliographie de Rimbaud en Italie, op. cit.*, pp. 23, 63). The *felicimento* is too much!

(3) Rimbaud was not alone: He was accompanied by the French explorer Jules Borelli, who claimed to be the first European to take this famous route. He was ungenerous in this instance, as Enid Starkie observes (*Rimbaud en Abyssinie, op. cit.*, p. 132), because he owed it to Rimbaud that he could go. Borelli writes: "I decided to leave tomorrow at dawn with M. Rimbaud rather than wait for doubtful promises to be kept or a caravan more in line with my tastes and projects" (Borelli's journal, April 30, 1887). Rimbaud in turn will write to Bardey from Cairo, on August 26, 1886: "It was only after I had obtained Menelik's permission that Borelli thought of coming with me." We may note that this point of detail is apparently contradicted by the letter to the *Bosphore*, written six days earlier, on August 20: "M. Jules Borelli asked the King's permission to travel this way, so that I had the honor to travel in the company of our amiable and courageous compatriot." We shall never know who was first on this road that leads nowhere. Actually, Rimbaud is not contradicting himself: Menelik was suspicious of Borelli and explorers in general. He did not see how one could walk about with scientific instruments and have disinterested aims. But he trusted Rimbaud, who was bringing him weapons. So Borelli benefited from Rimbaud's influence for this trek. In any case, Rimbaud was a day's ride ahead of Borelli, impatient to get the money Makonnen was to pay him for a part of the rifles taken to Menelik. So while Rimbaud rode like the dickens, Borelli serenely made his first observations. Rimbaud will, by the way, stress Borelli's work on the other, more difficult route: "This entire route was first surveyed astronomically by M. Jules Borelli" (letter to the *Bosphore*).

(4) The letter to the editor of the *Bosphore égyptien*, published in a relatively thick volume under the title *Arthur Rimbaud, voyage en Abyssinie et au Harar* by La Centaine in 1928—in a limited edition—has been presented as the work of an explorer, no doubt in place of the book on the Gallas that Rimbaud planned, but never wrote. It is, however, simply a letter, dated Cairo,

August 20, 1887. If it contains information that is precious and new for the time, it nevertheless does not constitute a report of an exploration, but the epistolary story of an extremely painful expedition, in which Rimbaud at times abandons the objectivity required in scholarly communications: "horrible routes . . . presumed horror . . . horrible cesspool," etc.).

B. The *Rapport sur l'Ogadine*. This text of a dozen pages, dated Harar, December 10, 1883, is the only piece in Rimbaud's dossier as an "explorer." "Mediocre writing, [these texts] would have done honor to Ferrandi or Robecchi-Bricchetti," observe Étiemble and Yassu Gauclère (*Rimbaud*, op. cit.). And they were received as they deserved: "Commented favorably in 1887 in the *Geographische Mitteilungen*, in 1888 in the *Proceedings of the Royal Geographical Society*, in 1889 in *Das Ausland*. Even the *Bollettino* . . . (which could not be pleased with a French rival of the best Italians) pays homage to the work of the new geographer." The most famous of East African explorers, Paulitschke, had appreciated this *Report*.

But Alfred Bardey's *Souvenirs* (op. cit., significant passages of which have appeared in *Études rimbaldiennes*, No. 1 [Paris: Minard, 1969] let us know that the exploration of Ogaden was done by the Greek Sotiro, that Rimbaud only wrote it up. Long before writing this text, Rimbaud had told Delahaye (January 18, 1882) that he intended to "work for the Geographical Society" and claimed to have already explored Harar and the Gallas. But he had ventured only to the threshold of Ogaden: At the beginning of his stay in Harar, he stayed mostly at the depot. It was Sotiro, another employee of Bardey's, who went off prospecting and brought back the information that Rimbaud wrote up in a precise and detailed report that Bardey found interesting enough to send to the Geographical Society in Paris, of which he was a corresponding member. The *Report on Ogaden* was published in the *Minutes of the Geographical Society* in 1884 and presented to the said society in the meeting of February 1, 1884. Jean-Paul Vaillant published the last four paragraphs of it in July 1931 ("Rimbaud et la caravane," in the *Bulletin des amis de Rimbaud,* then in *Textes africains d'Arthur Rimbaud,* op. cit.). Sotiro wrote to Bardey around 1919: "I have not gone back to Ogaden since my first trip which I made while with your firm, and of which I gave a report to M. Rimbaud." Sotiro was also sent to the Somali coast under English occupation. In December 1881, he was in Bubassa. Bardey joined him in Bulhar: He was "comfortably set up: his trips to Ogaden and among the Somalis had made him an important person." Then Bardey realized quickly that Rimbaud had a different range of mind from his Greek colleague and took him as second-in-command to Aden.

C. Bubassa. In May 1881 in Harar, Rimbaud had recovered from an illness that kept him in bed for two weeks. He now asked to leave for Bubassa where no white man had set foot, to the south-southeast of Harar, thirty kilometers as the crow flies. The German traveler Hagenmacher had tried to go there in 1875, one year after the arrival of the Egyptians in Harar. "I agreed to the proposition," writes Bardey, "hoping that Rimbaud would at least bring back interesting and useful information for expanding our trade" (letter from Alfred Bardey to Paterne Berrichon, July 16, 1897, in *Le Mercure de France,* April 1, 1930). Rimbaud brought back a pestilential fever that took him two months to get over. His official purpose was not exploration, but clearly defined by Bardey: "Under the protection of the Boko (the Galla chief in Bubassa) he set up . . . two markets in the bush." He will go back to Bubassa with Sotiro. In Galdoa—where nobody will follow him before 1901—Sotiro was taken prisoner by a tribal chief. Rimbaud, who had pushed on alone to the Uebi River, was able to set him free through one of his friends, one of the most powerful chiefs of Ogaden (Louis Jalabert, "Rimbaud en Abyssinie," *Études* [January 20, 1939], p. 176). Some years after Sotiro (and, partly, Rimbaud), other explorers arrived: two Austrians, Dominik Kamel von Hardegger and Philipp Paulitschke in 1885; a German, the Baron Karl von Erlanger in 1900; and a French traveler, the Viscount du Bourg du Bozas in 1901. If the merit of this expedition is mainly Sotiro's, it does not, however, lessen the value of the *Rapport sur l'Ogadine*, which remains of interest even today, as the province has not changed much in the meantime.

D. Rimbaud certainly tried other expeditions without mentioning them in his correspondence (see Chapter 9). If Savouré's memory is exact in 1930, Rimbaud "made only one actual trip to Abyssinia after Menelik's conquest of this ex-Egyptian town [Harar] in 1888–1889. He was the first European to cross the Arussi and Chercher regions following the Abyssinian troops" (letter to Georges Maurevert, *Les Nouvelles littéraires*, January 16, 1947). These final expeditions must have had a commercial purpose—or pretext.

In 1896, *Le Figaro* printed the article in which Rodenbach mentions Rimbaud, the discoverer, the "quite unforeseen and extraordinary precursor." This mythic theme (uncovered by Étiemble) was going to grow. Max Jacob, for example, declared that "in leaving to become an explorer in Abyssinia, Rimbaud proved himself a man" (*Le Mythe de Rimbaud, structure du mythe* [Paris: Gallimard, 1961], pp. 218–219). "It is vain to try and wind him an explorer's crown," writes Jean-Paul Vaillant. We must look elsewhere for the greatness of Rimbaud.

6. The word *Abyssins* means "mixed people" (from the Arabic *Habeschyn*), to which the interested parties preferred the name of Greek origin, *Ethiopians*.

The Abyssins do themselves the honor of the name Ethiopians, *YTIOPIAYAN*, and are glad to call themselves *AMHARA*. The name Abyssins comes from the Arabic word *HABECHI*, which means mixed people, of unknown lineage, a "mixed lot." *HABECHI* was mangled by the Portuguese into *ABEXIOS*, and finally *ABESSIN*, from which modern authors have without effort drawn the term Abyssin. This surname, given to the Amharan nation by the Arabic races, is very insulting, because the most humiliating insult among Orientals is to tell a man, or a people, that he does not know his lineage. [P. Martial de Salviac, *Au pays de Ménélik, les Gallas* (*In the Land of Menelik and the Gallas*) (Paris, Houdin, n.d. [1901], p. 7].

7. Menelik, who claimed to be a descendant of the queen of Sheba and King Solomon, was still king of Shoa in 1886: Vassal and rival of Emperor John who reigned over Tigre, he avoided direct conflict with him. "Menelik cannot afford to disobey Joannès," Rimbaud writes shrewdly in the *Bosphore égyptien,*

and the latter, well informed of the diplomatic intrigues Menelik is involved in, will be able to guard against it in any case. . . . Shoa [around Ankober/Addis Ababa], the only Amharan province in Menelik's power, is not worth a fifteenth of Tigre [in the north of Ethiopia, Aksum being the best-known town]. His other domains are all Galla country [roughly: around Harar] and only precariously subjected. . . . Menelik dreams of extending his kingdom to the south, across the Haouach, and perhaps thinks of emigrating himself

from the Amharan provinces to the new Gallaland . . . to establish . . . a
meridional empire like the ancient kingdom of Ali Alaba.

From 1885 on, England bet on Emperor John IV (or Jean, or Joannès, or
Yohannès IV), whereas Menelik obtained his arms from Italian and especially
French traders. In February 1887, he fought a battle against the Emir of Harar
(Shalenko) and occupied the region. "At his entry into Harar, he declared
himself the sovereign of all tribes up to the coast." Then, at the beginning of
1889, Emperor John ("that horrible Jean," said Rimbaud on May 8, 1889) was
defeated and killed by the Mahdists, and Menelik became emperor: Abyssinia
was reunified.

"That horrible Jean" was a religious fanatic: He had the lips of Christians
mutilated if they dared smoke.

8. See Alain Sancerni, "Le Haleur ou l'épreuve terminée" ("The Hauler or the
End of the Ordeal"), *Europe*, Rimbaud issue, May–June 1973.

9. René Char, *Revue Cahiers d'art*, 1947. In his *Anthologie de l'humour noir* (1950),
André Breton denigrates Rimbaud in Abyssinia as "a rather lamentable clown."
And we know that Jacques Vaché condemned Rimbaud without appeal.
Nevertheless, since the authors gathered in the Surrealist pantheon have in
common the power of reconciling opposites, we may ask if Breton's black
humor at its extreme could not be reduced to the Dada and Surrealist challenge of literature—which we find in Rimbaud's Harar as well as in Germain
Nouveau's pilgrimages. Besides, Breton, who always claimed to admire the
"genius" of the poet Arthur Rimbaud, later considerably modified his opinion
on the African period. In his *Entretiens* (1913–1952), he evokes the "prestige"
of "the man who one fine day turned his back on his work, as if, once certain
peaks had been reached, it in some way 'repelled' its creator. Such behavior
on the part of the latter makes those peaks unsurpassable, somewhat dizzying,
and fascinating to us. *The Harar adventure (the questioning it posits) has been and
largely continues to be the reason for our passionate interest in Rimbaud*" (my italics)
(Paris: Gallimard, 1969). This new position takes back his previous slur of
cowardice. It remains to ask why Breton did not think of explaining what the
courage to stay would have meant.

In February 1886, Rimbaud writes to his family, alone and desperate "on
these cursed shores," in Tadjoura, where his worst troubles are piling up.
Mallarmé is canoeing at Valvins and congratulates Leconte de Lisle on his
election to the French Academy (February 12). These simultaneous facts are
not meant to begin a comparison between the poet of "Brise marine" and the
author of "Le Bateau ivre." It would be unjust and simply wrong. But the
real difference of their lives underlines the importance of the stakes. Perhaps
Mallarmé preserved his life by refusing to leave, one evening. . . . I am reminded of the vizier in Baghdad who refused to travel because it would have
taken four hundred camels to take his bedside books! But it is a matter of
interiority, not only of physical courage or the social life that Rimbaud had
radically rejected. However, does "Brise marine," which, like Baudelaire's
"Pipe," evokes a sea voyage, really allow us to "measure" "*the heroism of the
poet who refuses to flee*" (my italics), as we read in *Mallarmé et le Symbolisme*
(Paris: Nouveaux Classiques Larousse), p. 34. (See note 15.)

10. Concerning Rimbaud's illnesses: "All the Europeans got sick, except me," he
can flatter himself on Cyprus, on February 15, 1879. Likewise from Aden, on
September 10, 1884: "I am more or less inured to all these climates, cold or
hot, humid or dry, and am not scared a bit of catching fevers or other accli-

matization illnesses." Nevertheless, Rimbaud "is ill" in May 1880 and "bothered" by palpitations. He was "sick arriving in Aden" (August 17, 1880) and writes on August 25: "I need at least three months of rest before I'm on my feet again." In February 1881 in Harar, he "caught some illness"; fevers in July, of which he is cured in August. September 1881: "Six months ago I needed medicine; I ordered it from Aden and still have not received it!" In April 1885 in Aden, Rimbaud suffers from gastric fever: "I cannot digest anything; my stomach has become very weak here and makes me miserable all summer long . . . my health is very shaken" (April 14). In Cairo, on August 23, back from his expedition to Shoa: "These days I am tormented by rhumatism in the hips . . . and in my left thigh, which occasionally paralyzes me, a pain in the left knee joint, an (already old) rhumatism in the right shoulder." Back in Aden: "The last trip to Abyssinia took my health down very much" (October 8, 1887). Then in 1891: "I am not well at present" (Harar, February 20). "It's synovitis . . ." (Marseille, May 21). And when last in Aden, Rimbaud says he is "suffering atrocious pains."

11. In 1936, Étiemble describes Rimbaud as "a respectable citizen who sells guns so that he can get married (Étiemble and Yassu Gauclère, *Rimbaud,* op. cit.). In 1984, in *Rimbaud, Système solaire ou trou noir? (Rimbaud, Solar System or Black Hole?)* (Paris: PUF, 1984), Professor Étiemble reprints a few "warmed-over" articles in order to be part of the exhibit at the "*agrégation,*" Rimbaud being part of the exams that year. One can imagine the topic: "Using Rimbaud's correspondence, analyze the ideological and moral assumptions underlying Étiemble's condemnation of Rimbaud. Time: 5 hours." I would not write this essay. As Daumal said about Guénon in the first issue of *Le Grand Jeu,* there are cases where there is nothing to explain. We must affirm.

12. Among authors of books on Rimbaud, only Jean Chauvel and Pierre Gascar spent time in Ethiopia. But not because of their interest in Rimbaud. Ambassador in Addis Ababa, successor of Léonce Lagarde, memorialist and poet, all it took for Jean Chauvel to absorb a Claudel complex was to write on Rimbaud (*L'Aventure terrestre de Jean-Arthur Rimbaud* [Paris: Seghers, 1971]). Pierre Gascar (*Rimbaud et la Commune* [Paris: Gallimard, collection "Idées," 1971]) worked for the World Health Organization in Ethiopia: "This mission led me to remote places where curiosity alone would not have taken me, and if I sometimes followed in Rimbaud's footsteps it was by accident and sometimes without being aware of it" (p. 132).

13. Cf. Marc Eigeldinger, "La Voyance avant Rimbaud," in *Arthur Rimbaud, lettres du voyant (13 et 15 mai 1871),* ed. and commented by Gerard Schaeffer (Geneva: Droz; Paris: Minard, 1975).

14. The turn from metaphor to metonymy, which, according to Jakobson, characterizes modern poetry, would mark the end of this conception of analogy. Rimbaud contributed decisively to this change. After Banville had asked him, Why not write "I am *like* a *drunken boat*"? we know, Rimbaud said to Verlaine, "He's an old dolt."

However, "Le Bateau ivre" remains largely metaphorical, in its general concept and its adverbs (we find four times each: *ainsi que* and *pareil à*). Greimas (*Sémantique structurale* [Paris: Larousse, 1966], p. 100) proposes to speak of *isotopie:* The description of the "Drunken Boat" is truer in regard to Rimbaud (*theme* or *tenor*) than in regard to a boat (*phore* or *vehicle*); Greimas calls this a case of "complex positive isotopism." It is in this sense that there is, if I dare say so, a kind of analogy that includes the passage from metaphor to metonymy. The relative disappearance of the *like* replaces simple metaphor with what Rimbaud called hallucination, where both terms have the same degree of reality.

15. Marcelin Pleynet, in *Aujourd'hui Rimbaud*, a poll by Roger Munier (Paris, Minard, 1976), p. 98 and in *Art et littérature* (Paris, Éditions du Seuil, 1977), p. 193. Verlaine, "Arthur Rimbaud," *The Senate,* London, October 1895.

16. Verlaine, "Nouvelles Notes sur Rimbaud," *La Plume,* November 15, 1895. Also, I have often read, *we are not even trying to find out:* prejudices, contempt (Breton, Étiemble, Gide); preponed death: "I do not have the heart to speak of the rest of Rimbaud's life, which went on for another eighteen years," wrote Claude-Edmond Magny. "We cannot help regarding it as a *posthumous life,* to take up the term Keats used for his eighteen months of biological, apoetical existence" (my italics) (*Rimbaud* [Paris: Seghers, collection "Poètes d'aujourd'hui," 1949], p. 47).

17. *Rimbaud par lui-même* (Paris, Éditions du Seuil, 1961), p. 173. Jacqueline Risset put her finger on the essential problem in her introduction to the *Lettere dall'Abyssinia* (La Rosa, 1979): "*L'enigma Rimbaud . . . turba e mette in questionnne l'immagine della poesia stessa"* ("The riddle of Rimbaud . . . upsets and calls into question the image of poetry itself") (p. vii).

18. *Aujourd'hui Rimbaud,* a poll by Roger Munier, op. cit. Yves Bonnefoy's reply, "Rimbaud encore," is reprinted in *Le Nuage rouge (The Red Cloud),* (Paris: Mercure de France, 1977), p. 218.

19. Stéphane Mallarmé, *Variations sur un sujet,* 1895.

   "I is another": This famous formula that Rimbaud repeats in the two *voyant* letters is clearly defined in context as the universal soul speaking through a singular sensibility. Illustrated by two metaphors (May 13, to Izambard: "Too bad for the wood that finds it is a violin," and May 15 to Demeny: "If brass wakes up as a trumpet"), this singular sensibility distinguishes and designates the poet as an elect (*elein,* to choose: "I recognized I was a poet") within the community ("wood," "brass") in his charge ("he is in charge of humanity"). The notion of being chosen is connected with passivity ("it is not his fault"), which necessitates a paradoxical form of action, working toward availability: "the immense and reasoned disordering of all the senses," "it is a matter of making your soul monstrous"—only this allows us "to arrive at the unknown." This formula has too often been twisted, in the spirit of our time, to fit Freud's definitions of split subject, transference, or narcissistic double (e.g., *Essais de psychanalyse appliquée* [Paris: Gallimard], p. 186), which Lacan takes up in his fashion: " 'I resemble the man I invent by recognizing him as a man, so that I can recognize myself as such.' These various formulas are finally only understood in reference to the truth of 'I is another,' which is less illuminating for poetic intuition than evident to the psychoanalyst's eye" (*Écrits* [*Writings*] [Paris: Éditions du Seuil, 1966], p. 118). Likewise Julia Kristeva: " 'I' is not 'another,' the problematic is not that of psychosis" (*Recherches pour une sémanalyse* [*Research Toward a Semanalysis*] [Paris: Éditions du Seuil, 1966], p. 353). Again, the Rimbaldian formula is unavoidable in the theme of alterity; cf. Michel de M'Uzan: "If I is not exactly another, it has nevertheless the remarkable ability to shuttle between outside and inside without getting lost" (*De l'Art à la mort, Itinéraire psychanalytique* [*From Art to Death, Psychoanalytical Journey*] [Paris: Gallimard, 1977]). Or Edgar Morin: "The *alter ego* is certainly the 'I is another' of Rimbaud" (*L'Homme et la mort dans l'histoire* [*Man and Death in History*] [Paris: Corrêa, 1951], p. 128). Or François Bott: "I is another: This is the feeling of every proletarian with some consciousness" (*Traité de la désillusion* [Paris: PUF, 1977], p. 73). Or again, Blanchot, in "Gog et

Magog" (*Nouvelle Revue Française*, No. 78, p. 1072). The formula has also received a strictly literary treatment in Jacqueline Risset's untranslatable pun: *l'autre est un jeu*, "the other is a game" (jacket copy of her book, *Jeu* [Paris: Éditions du Seuil, 1971) or in Françoise Collin's: "I is no-one, but at the same time I is everything" (*Colloque de Tanger* [Paris: Christian Bourgois, 1976], p. 69).

A good statement of the problem can be found in Roger Munier's philosophical essay, *Le Contour, l'éclat:* "Here is what is at stake, it seems to me. It is a matter of giving up the within as a retreat, as a reserved place, a defended interiority, structured-and-structuring, as a closed *I.* . . . Not a matter of dissolving it. . . . Not of saying that *I* becomes the other, but of establishing ourselves on this side of the antinomy inside-outside, as an *I*-other, in what I call anteriority" (Paris: Éditions de la Différence, 1977], p. 23). Roger Munier's anteriority could historically characterize the evolution of a concept of identity from Villon's *ce-suis-je* to Pétrus Borel's *jo soy que soy.*

The essential commentary on "I is another" is Louis Forestier's "Rimbaud et l'ambivalence," in *Études sur les poésies* (Neuchâtel: La Baconnière, 1979).

20. Kenneth White, *La Figure du dehors* (Paris: Grasset, 1982), p. 65. See also Attle Kittang, *Discours et jeu, essai d'analyse des textes d'Arthur Rimbaud* (Bergen: Universitetsforlaget; Presses universitaires de Grenoble, 1975). According to Yves Bonnefoy:

> Among other acts of revolt or, rather, at the precise point where revolt awakens in the consciousness, Rimbaud states his refusal of the attentive cultivation of writing, of which Mallarmé's disciples claim that it is the restrained, but specific and finally decisive act of the writer. Therefore we must see in him a lost, no: masked, dimension of contemporary criticism: [Rimbaud] remembered very well and even too well that in poetry a *word*—a presence, a call to another—is possible and perhaps the essential. [*Le Nuage rouge, op. cit.* p. 215.]

Elsewhere ("Devant la critique," in *Rimbaud* [Paris: Hachette, 1968], Yves Bonnefoy rightly distinguishes "those who underline the significant and those who cross it out" (p. 169). Here is the great split with Mallarmé (see note 9). Valéry, in "Propos me concernant," writes: "I can vaguely compare Mallarmé and Rimbaud to different species of scholars: One believes in I do not know what symbolic calculation, the other has discovered I do not know what unknown radiation" (see Mondor, *Rimbaud ou le génie impatient, op. cit.* p. 89; and Judith Robinson, *Rimbaud, Valéry et "l'incoherérence harmonique"* [Paris: Minard, 1979]). Obviously Rimbaud got burned in that radiation.

21. Cf. Chapter 1, note 24.

22. Carré, *Les Deux Rimbauds, op. cit.*; Victor Segalen, "Le Double Rimbaud," in *Le Mercure de France,* April 15, 1906, and in book form, Paris, Éditions Fata Morgana (with a preface by Gérard Macé), 1979; Lucien Lagriffe, "Un Problème psychologique, les deux aspects d'Arthur Rimbaud," in *Journal de psychologie normale et pathologique,* 1910; Jules de Gaultier: "Le lyrisme physiologique et la double personnalité d'Arthur Rimbaud," *Le Mercure de France,* March 1, 1924; Hugo Ball, *Die Flucht aus der Zeit (Flight out of Time)* (Luzern: Stocker, 1946), quoted by Jean Voellmy, "Dada, Zürich et Rimbaud," Colloquium *Rimbaud multiple* in Cerisy, 1982; Henry Miller, *Rimbaud, op. cit.*; A. Rolland de Renéville, *Rimbaud le voyant* (Paris: Denoël et Steele, 1929, and La Col-

ombe, 1947); Benjamin Fondane, *Rimbaud le voyou* (Paris, Denoël et Steele, 1933, and Plasma, 1979).

23. "From the point of view of agricultural production, what fertility! what generous soil! . . . Wheat, barley, tef, durra ripen with incredible speed . . . all the vegetables of the temperate regions grow here without trouble, all the fruit trees of our countries prosper" (Denis de Rivoyre, *Mer rouge et Abyssinie* [Paris: Plon, n.d., 1878?]).

24. "Africa's Switzerland," writes Dislère in 1883. Vignéras (*Une Mission française en Abyssinie,* op. cit.): "It's Switzerland, says M. Flemeing who has often been in that country." Louis Jalabert ("Rimbaud en Abyssinie," op. cit.) says more precisely: "It is the climate of Tuscany at two thousand meters altitude, in the tropics." But he borrowed this comparison from Burton. On Rimbaud's contradictory statements on the climate, see Livius Ciocarlie, "Le 'Texte' de la correspondance africaine de Rimbaud," in *Arthur Rimbaud,* No. 3 (Paris: Minard, 1976).

25. Monsignor Taurin Cahagne, coming in 1881 from Zeila to found a Catholic mission in Gallaland, noted on arrival: "We have in front of our eyes the mysterious city of the Adaré Province, where no European has set foot in centuries."

Indeed the Hararis, who claim to be descended from exiled Arabs and Persians that settled in the region in the thirteenth century, distinguish themselves fiercely from the Abyssins and, *a forteriori,* fiercely opposed any Christians coming into their city, from the sixteenth century on. "They barricaded themselves in their city for centuries, so the legend grew about Harar, the mysterious city, impenetrable, hidden behind walls no foreigner ever left alive. The eighteenth-century Scotsman Bruce did not succeed in entering it when he traveled to Abyssinia in search of the source of the Nile. Neither did the Englishmen Harris and Johnston in 1840, nor Rochet d'Héricourt in 1839 and 1842" (Vignéras).

So Richard Burton "invented" Harar. The author of *First Steps in East Africa,* enfant terrible, sent down from Oxford, was no doubt the greatest explorer of his time, notably the first European to enter Mecca, disguised as a pilgrim, and the first in Harar, disguised as an Arab merchant. Rimbaud is not the first to come—but about the tenth European, the first French being Alfred Bardey and his employee Pinchard, on August 22, 1880.

Chapter 3: The Place

1. Edoardo Scarfoglio, *Abyssinia (1888–1896),* Vol. I. (Rome: Éditions Roma, 1936), p. 283.

2. Rimbaud tells us that the emir of Harar, Raouf Pasha, had called on Menelik to convert to Islam (letter to the *Bosphore égyptien*). "After an exchange of civilities on the order of, 'You are the son of a bitch!' and 'You are the son of twelve fathers!' Menelik II, having taken Harar, climbed a minaret and pissed on the mosque in the presence of an aghast crowd. He kept the promise he had made himself, but knowing the importance of such a gesture, he had the mosque replaced by a Coptic church, Medhane Alem, which preserved the form of the old mosque" (Paulette and Maurice Deribéré, *Éthiopie, berceau de l'humanité* (*Ethiopia, Cradle of Humanity*) [SCEMI, 1872], p. 318).

3. Ras (Prince) Makonnen was a cousin of Menelik and father of Emperor Haile Selassie ("Tafari," born in Harar in 1892, who overthrew Lidj Yassou, Me-

nelik's grandson, governor of Harar and short-lived Negus). Makonnen (Rimbaud spells also *Mekonèn, Mokonène, Mékounène;* Zimmermann spells *Meconen*) was the king's representative in Harar (Rimbaud calls him "agent" or "commissar general" or "agent general" in the letter to the *Bosphore*), i.e. governor (occupying the third rank in the Ethiopian hierarchy), *Dedjazmatche* or *Dedjatch.* In his hurried letters, Rimbaud calls him familiarly the *dedj* (and sometimes the "D"). Accompanied by Count Antonelli, Makonnen led a mission to Naples and Florence (which Rimbaud made fun of in 1889) to sign a convention in terms of which the king of Italy recognized Menelik as emperor of Ethiopia, who in turn recognized Italy's sovereignty in Eritrea (Mario Matucci, *Le Dernier Visage de Rimbaud en Afrique,* op. cit., p. 55). Menelik was to denounce this Treaty of Ucciali (1893) and defeat the Italians at Aduwa (1896). Today the Ras Makonnen's monument is a tourist attraction in Harar.

4. Lidj Yassou had Bardey's old trading post demolished to build a hotel, but the project was abandoned. The only Harar hotel *intra muros* was pompously called "Universal" until 1924 (a Rimbaldian name: Rimbaud stayed in the "Hotel Universe" in Aden and was a regular in Charleville's "Café de l'Univers" on the Place de la Gare).

5. Ottorino Rosa, "Souvenirs d'Abyssinie," introduced by Lidia Herling Croce, *Études rimbaldiennes,* No. 3 (Paris: Minard, 1970).

    "The Hararis abuse the aphrodisiac hashish which procures a beatific intoxication and, in the long run, a kind of paranoia very common in Harar" (Bardey, *Barr Adjam,* op. cit., p. 176).

6. Bardey, *Barr Adjam,* op. cit., p. 220. "*Karani* is the name give to any second-in-command." "I expect to become a very mean madman" ("Vies" ["Lives"] II, *Illuminations*). Verlaine to Rimbaud, London, December 12, 1875; Rimbaud to Franzoj, September 1885. (On "Rimbaud's wife," see Chapter 6).

7. The *matads* that Rimbaud sells (letter to Ilg, Harar, August 24, 1889) are not "stoves" (cf. the Pléiade edition, p. 1162), but hotplates to cook the *injira.* We found both traditional and electric *matads,* simple round hotplates, in Harar.

8. Information drawn from an unpublished letter by Alfred Ilg, translated and introduced by Jean Voellmy, "Rimbaud employé d'Alfred Bardey et correspondant d'Ilg," *Parade sauvage,* No. 1, 1984. Rimbaud also made fun of Brémond (see Chapter 12).

9. Vitalie Cuif, "widow Rimbaud," carried her money on her body from March 5, 1905, to August 2, 1907, the day of her death. "If I die, don't let them take inventory of this pocket," she wrote to Isabelle. "Hide it . . . above all, pay for my funeral from it" (see Briet, *Mme. Rimbaud,* op. cit., pp. 79–80).

10. Isabelle Rimbaud to her brother, August 18, 1891.

11. Letter from Rimbaud to "*Chère Maman*" ("Dear Mama"), Aden, December 8, 1882. Having earned up to 416 francs in gold per month, to which add 2 percent on the exchange, Rimbaud had saved and sent to Charleville 2,500 francs, asking to have them invested in securities. "Not in real estate," he insisted, "in stocks." Mme. Rimbaud, good descendant of the peasant Cuifs, instead bought him 37.8 acres of land.

    Cuif-talk: "Don't worry. If my business is not brilliant right now, at least I'm not losing" (Aden, October 8, 1887). Or from Harar, on May 4, 1881: "I'm going to buy a horse and leave. In case this turns out badly and I don't come back, I want you to know that I have the sum of seven times 150 rupies belonging to me deposited with the Aden office, which you must claim."

12. Letter from Alfred Ilg to Rimbaud, October 8, 1889. See Rimbaud's reply on page 54, note 11.

13. She tells him she received the second sum of 1,000 francs he sent (beginning of 1881). She says she sent him a package and talks of money (February 6, 1881). She wonders about the delay of his letters (May or June 1881). She tells him she sent him things—cases, effects—which he has "not acknowledged" (July 12, 1881). On September 8, 24, and 25, she talks of military service, of still not having received the announced money; on October 24, of some check. On October 27, she has received the money from Lyon. To her letter of December 27, 1881, she adds a postcard from Delahaye, and tells him she has written twice about the money. She announces a parcel on December 8, 1881. On January 21, 1882, she has received the money. She has been suffering, but is now well again and speaks of "his interest" (March 20, 1882). On April 23, 1882, she is worried "about you." July 10, 1882, they are both well. In August 1882, she encloses a map with her letter. She tells him he is being robbed in this camera story and since this is the case they will have nothing more to do with his affairs (November 24, 1882). They wish him a good new year (December 1882). On March 26, 1883, she tells him she has mailed two boxes of books and that Isabelle does not want to get married; she also gives him some political news. She has received his photographs from Harar (August 1883). June 1884: She suggests he come back and work in the country. September 23, 1884: They both sent him a "frightened letter" (because he has not written), then tell him that his brother Frédéric is slandering him, and that he should not send him any money. In November 1884, she wishes him prosperity and health, says that his vocation will never be farming and therefore asks him to let her rent out his land; she tells him not to ask for things without sending money, and that he had better come back to Roche and have a rest. In December 1884, she asks if he has received the Korans; Isabelle has thought of visiting him in Abyssinia; she still wishes he would settle on the farm; she asks for a photo, complains of the cold. March 17, 1885: Business is good. Rimbaud kept his mother's letter of October 10, 1885: by accident? (see Chapter 5). September 1885: She is worried about his finances and suggests he come back to France. On December 19, 1885, she tells him his requests are troublesome and asks if a certain title he has asked for is a good book. May 28, 1886(?). December 2, 1886: She tells him she has written him in Tadjoura. September 1887: He had better come back, she is worried about his business. October 8, 1887: "observations." November 20, 1887; They both think of him. December 1887: She confirms having transmitted his letters (Rimbaud says his "sandwiches") to the ministry. June 27, 1888; October 1, 1888: He should come back to France to see them. December 10, 1888: She talks again of illness, deaths; sends him advice and good wishes. April 2, 1889: Everything is fine. November 19, 1889: She complains of not having heard from him since last May 18, whereas they are writing him every other week. (On December 25, 1889, she writes a worried letter to César Tian in Aden to get news of her son). On January 21, 1890, she writes that Tian has reassured her, but is astonished that her son "hardly ever" writes. She speaks of marriage, but that he would have to settle down in that case (September 29, 1890). Everything is fine, except it is very cold (January 5, 1891). We know the letter of March 27, where she tells him that she has sent him an orthopedic stocking: "Good-bye, Arthur." She will see him, for the last time, that summer. But we must remember her letter of 1899, where Vitalie Rimbaud tells her daughter Isabelle of her "emotion" at seeing somebody on crutches near the pew where she kneels at mass. Charleville, June 9, 1899:

I turn my head and am dumbfounded. It was Arthur himself: same size, same age, same face, grayish-white skin, no beard, but a little mustache. And, lacking a leg. This young man looked at me with extraordinary sympathy. In spite of my efforts, I could not hold back my tears, tears of grief, yes, but there was something that I could not explain. I really believed it was my beloved son next to me. And more yet: a very elegant lady passes close to us. She stops to smile at him and says: "Why don't you come to me, you'll feel much better than here."

14. On the places in Harar where Rimbaud lived, see Rosa, "Souvenirs d'Abyssinie," op. cit.; Augusto Orsi in *Il Mattino del Lunedi* (Asmara, 1969): and Michel Barthe's reply in *Arthur Rimbaud*, No. 3, op. cit., p. 189.

15. Gérard Macé, "Rimbaud recently deserted," *NRF*, April–May 1978; reprinted in *Ex-Libris* (Paris: Gallimard, 1980), p. 74.

16. See Isabelle's drawing in *Rimbaud, documents iconographiques* (Geneva: Cailler, 1946), pl. XXIII. Paul Verlaine, "A Arthur Rimbaud," *Dédicaces* (Paris: Vanier, 1894).

17. Gérard de Nerval, *Petits Châteaux de Bohème*.

18. Reassured by de Gaspary, Merciniez recommends Rimbaud a week later as "a very honorable Frenchman" to the marquis of Grimaldi-Régusse, a resident diplomat in Cairo.

19. Armand Savouré to Georges Maurevert, April 3, 1930.

20. Rimbaud knew Armand Savouré, one of the people in charge of the "Franco-Ethiopian Company," very well. They had together prepared a secret unloading of arms in Ambadou in 1888. In the fall of the same year, he had him as his guest in Harar for a month. Savouré, a tradesman, had married an Abyssinian woman and lived in Ankober until he built a large stone house in Djibouti: "I told you I was building a palace," he writes to Rimbaud. According to Enid Starkie, "the most important importer of arms" (*Rimbaud en Abyssinie*, op. cit., p. 151); according to Suzanne Briet, "Menelik's mouthpiece" (*Rimbaud notre prochain*, op. cit., p. 176), Savouré was neither one nor the other, but a mediocre businessman with few scruples, who also spied for the Foreign Affairs Ministry.

21. Rimbaud meets Alfred Ilg in 1887 in Entotto. Ilg has by then been in King Menelik's service for eight years. An engineer with a degree from the Polytechnic in Zurich and experience in the construction of houses, roads, and bridges, he had great prestige with the Negus. Later, the king's trust in him will be affected by Princess Taïtu's intrigues, which made Ilg very bitter. Ilg's company was, according to Jean Voellmy (*Parade sauvage*, No. 1, op. cit.), a kind of "promotion" for Rimbaud. He was, in any case, his only comfort in that country for three years. Rimbaud speaks of him with respect and confidence: "M. Ilg, whom the King uses because of his languages and honesty to handle the court's dealings with Europeans in general, gave me to understand that Menelik . . ." (letter to de Gaspary, Aden, November 9, 1887). "A man of action with broad ideas," gifted with "real common sense and great joviality" (Voellmy, op. cit.), Ilg nevertheless avoids intimate relations. "In spite of the friendly tone of his letters, he has a less complex idea of Rimbaud than Bardey." Ilg acted in a faultless complicity with his fellow Swiss, Zimmermann, which sometimes takes the form of cold duplicity, as one can see in the affair of the "slave boys" (Chapter 11) or in this phrase from an unpublished letter to Zimmermann, translated by Jean Voellmy: "Rimbaud is an

excellent customer for us; we do well to serve him as quickly and as well as possible" (May 22, 1889). No sentiments for Alfred Ilg: learning in Zurich of Rimbaud's death, he tells Zimmermann and Appenzeller in this laconic form: "As I learned from M. Chefneux, M. Rimbaud and M. Deschamps have died" (unpublished letter of March 9, 1892, translated by Jean Voellmy).

22. Paul Soleillet, *Obock, le Choa, le Kaffa, une exploration commune en Éthiopie, Récit anecdotique* (Paris: M. Dreyfous, "Bibliothêque d'aventures et de voyages," n.d. [1886]); *Voyages en Éthiopie, janvier 1880–octobre 1884, notes, lettres et documents divers,* extract of the *Bulletin de la Société normande de géographie* (Rouen: 1886).

Quotation from Mario Matucci, *Le Dernier Visage de Rimbaud en Afrique,* op. cit., p. 45. Cf. Enid Starkie, *Rimbaud en Abyssinie,* op. cit., p. 64. See also "Paul Soleillet" (unpublished documents), in *Bateau ivre,* No. 14 (September 1965), p. 5

23. Auguste Franzoj, correspondent of the Turino *Gazette,* author of *Continento Nero* (republished in 1965), of disinterested and generous reputation.

24. "His pleasure was talking with the workers" (Frédéric Eigeldinger and André Gendre, *Delahaye, témoin de Rimbaud* [Neuchâtel: La Baconnière, 1974], p. 277).

25. Quoted in Paterne Berrichon, *La Vie de Jean-Arthur Rimbaud* (Paris: Mercure de France, 1898), p. 182.

26. Sotiro to Rimbaud, Zeila, July 10, 1891. Armand Savouré to Rimbaud, Harar, August 15, 1891. Bienenfeld (not Felter—Pléiade edition, p. 685), Agenzia di Harar, li [*sic*] July 13, 1891. Dimitri Righas, Harar, juilliet [*sic*] 28, 1891. Michel Barthe (*Arthur Rimbaud,* No. 3, op. cit.) remembers "the list of sarcasms that Rimbaud heaped on Makonnen" to question his friendship for the governor. This (reciprocal) friendship was no doubt formal, and exaggerated by Isabelle, but Barthe seems to forget Rimbaud's constant contradictoriness (see Ilg's letters of May 9 and July 17, 1890), his perpetual irony—and this letter from Savouré.

Chapter 4: Time

1. Achille Raffray, *Abyssinie* (Paris: Plon, 1876), p. 194.
2. The controversial syphilis hypothesis is not difficult to admit. Most of the Europeans in Abyssinia were infected with this chronic illness for which Rimbaud was to consult Traversi (interviewed by Zaghi ("L'Avventura africana di Arthur Rimbaud," in *La Nazione Italiana,* Florence, September 20, 1957). During his first stay in Harar, the Egyptian administration had "insufficient doctors and medicaments" (letter to his family, February 15, 1881). He consulted no doubt Dr. Nerazzini during the years 1889–1891, and finally, in April 1891, was taken on board a steamship to the English hospital in Aden. Dr. Nouks "cried that it was a synovitis advanced to a very dangerous point" (letter to his family, Aden, April 30, 1891), immediately considered amputation and, after waiting for two weeks, sent him to Marseille (see Pétralia, *Bibliographie de Rimbaud en Italie,* op. cit., and Alfred Bardey's letter to Paterne Berrichon, November 30, 1897).

When we consider the ten years of marches and the vastness of the country, the correlation between the swelling of the knee and the causes Rimbaud brings up remains after all primary. . . . In January 1890, Rimbaud hurt his knee in a fall at Dimitri Righas's in Harar; then, wanting to forget his pain in mad horseback riding, he hit his knee against a tree trunk. Let us recall that his sister Vitalie died at seventeen of a knee problem and that Rimbaud complains of rheumatic pains from 1876 on, which Verlaine makes fun of in a dizain: "And which I feel as foretaste of a rhumatisse." The pain resurfaces in 1887, spreads to the legs and arms, then in 1891 is evident and incurable.

3. Pierre Bardey found an occupation for his spare time in Harar: Good Franc-Comtois that he was, he built a small churn. "With the cream of unsmoked milk we manage to get a butter that tastes quite good," writes Alfred Bardey. Pierre Mazeran cultivates the garden, sows (there will be pink radishes) and even harvests for the fathers of the Catholic mission, because the seeds sent by their Angers parish in hermetically sealed boxes do not come up. Rimbaud? "He waits for business to pick up," Charles Cotton writes to Alfred Bardey (*Études rimbaldiennes*, No. 1, op. cit., p. 50). "He seems miserable not having anything to do." He takes care of the depot when Bardey goes away and, "when we stay home, he leaves on 'excursions,'" says Bardey.

4. The *Dictionnaire de la langue française classique* (eds. J. Dubois and R. Lagane [Paris: Belin, 1960]) defines *ennuyer*: "to cause torment, pain; to cause deep disgust; to make impatient, to annoy."

5. "This constant illusion that he will make a fortune," writes for example Monique Garrigue-Guyonnaud, *Rimbaud au Harar*, No. 4 (Charleville-Mézières: Centre culturel Arthur-Rimbaud, 1975).

6. January 15, 1885 (note "arrive"). May 5, 1884 (note "after"). Aden, July 10, 1882. Letter to Isabelle, July 19, 1891.

   "Work leads to riches/Poor poets, to work!" writes Apollinaire (*Le Bestiaire, ou le cortège d'Orphée*) (*Bestiary, or Orpheus's Train*). To work so we won't have to work, we must add in the Rimbaldian perspective: This is what his letters reiterate for ten years. On May 5, 1884, for example: "This money could buy me a little income sufficient to live without working." Or on May 29, 1884: "If only the day would finally come when I can live on my income and be done with this slavery!" Or on January 15, 1885: "I would like to have several thousand francs in regular income and be able to spend the year in two or three different places." Or again on December 30, 1884: "I could not go there except to rest; and in order to rest you need an income."

7. An intertextual echo of "Mauvais Sang" in *Tombeau pour cinq cent mille soldats* (*Tomb for Five Hundred Thousand Soldiers*) by Pierre Guyotat: "Enough. I'm a nigger. I have no money. Enough of this white skin. I'm a nigger. I was with you. I give up."

8. "Europe, Asia, America, disappear!" The poem "Qu'est-ce pour nous, mon coeur . . ." ("What Is It to Us, My Heart . . .") of the end of 1871 is taken to express the Communards' important desire for vengeance. Notice that Africa is excepted: "My heart, it's sure they are our brothers:/O unknown Blacks, let's go, let's go, let's go!"—in the manner of Mirabeau's and Lafayette's 1789 founding of a Society of the Friends of Black Peoples. It is tempting to put on the facing page this letter to Ilg, seventeen years later: "The moral: Be an ally of the Negroes, or do not touch them at all unless you have the power to crush them completely the very first moment" (February 1, 1888)! It would be easy and really unjust: a moment of anger, a single individual exasperated with living under difficult conditions, a defensive reaction ("Europeans are very much despised along the Red Sea"). These are Rimbaud's constant contradictions, which must make us cautious when we consider this violent, but isolated declaration. In the same letter, Rimbaud criticizes "these raids, perquisitions, requisitions, prohibitions, persecutions [which] very much anger

and annoy the natives." Rimbaud's generosity is not to be doubted any more than the quality of his relations with the populace and various tribal chiefs. But, along with political disillusionment, the lyricism of the "unknown Blacks" has vanished on contact with reality, and black is no longer the color of revolution. (Cf. on this point Michel Courtois, "Le mythe du nègre chez Rimbaud," *Littérature*, Rimbaud issue, No. 11, October 1973).

9. *Autour de Verlaine et de Rimbaud, dessins inédits de Paul Verlaine, de Germain Nouveau et d'Ernest Delahaye*, ed. and introduced by Jean-Marie Carré (Paris, Gallimard, 1949).

10. As the Spanish wondered if the Indians had a soul. Or the famous council that met to discuss the problem *Habet mulier animam?* does woman have a soul? Let us recall Bernardin de Saint-Pierre: "The black color of their skin is a godsend for the Southern people because it counteracts the burning sun under which they live" (*Études de la nature* [Paris: Didot, 1868], p. 553).

11. See Gabriel Simon, *L'Ethiopie, ses moeurs, ses traditions* (Paris, Librairie Challamel, 1884).

12. Achille Raffray, in northern Ethiopia, in 1876, wrote: "Even though the Abyssins have black skin they belong to a race quite distinct from what we call the Negro race" (*Abyssinie*, op. cit., p. 329). A.-S. de Doncourt: "What distinguishes the Abyssins is a particular shade which Bruce compares to an olive-brown complexion. . . . There are rather sharp color differences in Abyssinia: The inhabitants of Tigre are almost white, those of the high plateaus, halfway between them, and the inhabitants of the low, swampy plains whose skin is almost black" (*L'Abyssinie* [Lille and Paris: Librairie J. Lefort, 1886]). Sylvain Vignéras: "The name Abyssin, which comes from Arabic *habech* (mixed) was given to them by the Muslims. In Ethiopia, skin color is in fact very varied, and goes from high yellow to darkest black" (*Une Mission française en Abyssinie*, op. cit., p. 63). Concerning *Blaland*, see Jorge Luis Borgès, *Rose et bleu*, trans. Gérard de Cortanze (Paris: Éditions de la Différence, 1978), p. 41.

13. Enid Starkie, *Rimbaud* (Paris: Flammarion, 1982), p. 27.

14. Eigeldinger and Gendre, *Delahaye, témoin de Rimbaud*, op. cit., p. 245.

15. Ibid., p. 249. Henri Matarasso and Pierre Petitfils, *Vie de Rimbaud* (Paris: Hachette, 1962), p. 173.

16. "Les leçons de piano," *La Grive*, No. 83 (October 1954), p. 31.

17. See Dr. Lacambre, assistant medical army officer, *L'Instabilité mentale de Jean-Arthur Rimbaud, essais de psychologie pathologique* (Lyon: La Source, 1923). Or Dr. Delattre, *Le Déséquilibre mental d'Arthur Rimbaud* (Paris: 1928), who speaks of "ambulatory paranoia"; Dr. Jean Fretet, *L'Aliénation poétique* (Paris: J.-B. Janin, 1946); or Dr. Emile Laurent, *La Poésie décadente devant la science psychiatrique* (Paris: Maloine 1897). More interesting, but less funny, is Dr. E. Verbeek, *Arthur Rimbaud, Een Pathographie* (Amsterdam: 1957).

18. On these points, cf. Starkie, *Rimbaud*, op. cit.

19. Alain de Mijolla, "L'ombre du capitaine Rimbaud," in *Les Visiteurs du moi* (Paris: Les Belles Lettres, 1981, p. 41), a chapter that reprints and develops an earlier essay, "La Désertion du capitaine Rimbaud, enquête sur un fantasme d'identification inconscient d'A. Rimbaud," (*Revue française de psychanalyse*, Vol. 39, No. 3 (May–June 1975), pp. 427–458).

20. Alfred Bardey to Paterne Berrichon, November 30, 1897.

21. Letter to his family, Aden, January 30, 1881. Cf. Ciocarlie, *Arthur Rimbaud*, No. 3, op. cit.

22. Statements reported by Isabelle Rimbaud in a letter to her mother, Marseille, October 28, 1891.
23. "Smoothed down with sugar water," according to Paul Claudel's formulation. The Parnassian mane: one thinks of Fantin-Latour's painting, "The Table Corner" and of Ernest Delahaye's drawing, "La Tronche à machin" ("Pate with thingamagig").
24. Cf. Ciocarlie, *Arthur Rimbaud*, No. 3, op. cit.
25. Quoted in Marc Eigeldinger, *Rimbaud et le mythe solaire* (Neuchâtel: La Baconnière, 1964).
26. Verlaine to Ernest Delahaye, April 29, 1875.
27. The average life expectancy in 1891 was precisely thirty-seven, but this was of course because of the high rate of infant mortality. The generation born with Rimbaud in the 1850s was "normally" to live till about 1930: Jean Richepin (1849–1926) or Freud (1856–1939). An example of longevity: Philippe Pétain, born two years after Rimbaud (1856), died in 1951. Gérard Miller, in his essay *Les Pousse-au-jouir du maréchal Pétain* (Paris: Éditions du Seuil, 1975) where he quotes Rimbaud's "A une raison" (as curiously as Lacan in his *Séminaire*, Book XX), reminds us that the *Maréchal* lived forty-four years in the nineteenth century.

The poet Philoxène Boyer also wrote to Banville as a young man and also died at thirty-seven. Banville will say of him: "He died of old age." One is rather reminded of Mozart, who died at thirty-seven with the words, "I have a taste of death in my mouth," and of Isidore Ducasse, dead mysteriously at twenty-two, or of these other artists who died at thirty-seven: Van Gogh, Raphael, Watteau, Caravaggio, Chénier, Pushkin. And Fassbinder dead at thirty-six (or rather after forty films); Crevel at thirty-five; Yves Klein, another figure of the absolute, at thirty-four.

Rimbaud died in a plane crash in Texas, February 1959, with Buddy Holly who was twenty-two. . . .
28. Verlaine, preface to *Poésies de Rimbaud* (Paris: Vanier, 1895), p. xxii.
29. Frédéric Rimbaud sent twenty-five francs as a contribution to the poet's monument—a bust that Mme. Rimbaud never wanted to see, making detours within Charleville to avoid it.
30. We know nothing about this other Rimbaud of the East: "There was perhaps also another poet named Ducasse" (J. Lefrère, *Le Visage de Lautréamont*, p. 120).
31. Macé, *Ex-Libris*, op. cit., p. 76.
32. *In memoriam* Paul Kervan, the late Belgian poet who said: "Rimbaud, an ingot of gold melted in the furnace of the desert."

Chapter 5: Wandering

1. Paul Verlaine to Edmond-Adolphe Lepelletier, September 1872.
2. Ernest Delahaye, "Bombomm bidibidibomm," in *Souvenirs familiers*, Messein, Chapter 14.
3. Louis Pierquin, "Souvenirs . . ." *Le Mercure de France*, May 1, 1924.
4. Paterne Berrichon, *Jean-Arthur Rimbaud le poète* (Paris: Mercure de France, 1912), p. 58.
5. Paul Verlaine, *Les Poètes maudits* (Paris: Vannier, 1884).
6. Quoted in J. Plessen, *Expérience de la marche et du mouvement* (La Haye: Mou-

ton, 1969) on Plessen; and see Eigeldinger, op. cit., on Plessen.

7. "Perfect first drafts," Jean-Luc Steinmetz said to me on a walk (Cerisy, summer 1982).

8. Paul Verlaine, *Les Hommes d'aujourd'hui* (Paris: Vannier, 1888).

9. I had met Émilie Teissier in Rethel a few years earlier. She maliciously pointed at my black copy of Rimbaud's *Works* and asked: "A Bible?" (The "Proses johanniques" is as close as it came.) Pierre Dumayet interviewed her in 1954, Rimbaud's centenary.

10. D. Guerdon, *Rimbaud, la clé alchimique* (Paris: Laffont, 1980), p. 18.

11. Ibid.

12. Quoted in Robert Goffin, *Rimbaud et Verlaine vivants* (Brussels and Paris: Les Editeurs du Monde), p. 53.

13. Victor Segalen, *Le Double Rimbaud*, op. cit., p. 56.

14. Quoted in Goffin, *Sur les traces d'Arthur Rimbaud*, op. cit., p. 65.

15. Pierre Petitfils, *Rimbaud* (Paris: Julliard, 1982).

16. Gascar, *Rimbaud et la Commune*, op. cit.

17. Izambard, *Rimbaud tel que je l'ai connu*, op. cit., p. 47.

18. Verlaine, *Mes Prisons*, 1893.

19. Verlaine, "Laeti et Errabundi," *Parallèlement*.

20. Mallarmé, "Remémoration d'amis belges," ("Remembering Belgian Friends").

21. Quoted in *Rimbaud raconté par Verlaine*, op. cit., p. 87.

22. Louis-Ferdinand Céline, *Guignol's Band* (Paris: Denoël, 1944), p. 42.

23. Quoted in Eigeldinger and Gendre, *Delahaye, témoin de Rimbaud*, op. cit., p. 206.

24. *Études rimbaldiennes*, No. 3, op. cit., p. 19.

25. Henry de Bouillane de Lacoste and Henri Matarasso, *Nouveaux Documents sur Rimbaud, le journals de sa soeur Vitalie* (Paris: Mercure de France, 1938). In front of East Park, Vitalie wrote: "I feel I am in Charleville, on the Square de la Gare." The square station?

26. Rimbaud making fun of Verlaine's pitiful return. He escaped to the docks and embarked, pursued by Rimbaud. They met again for the "Brussels drama."

27. Verlaine to Rimbaud, "At sea, July 3, 1873."

28. All—and more!—in V. P. Underwood's *Rimbaud et l'Angleterre* (Paris: Nizet, 1976).

29. *Rimbaud raconté par Verlaine*, op. cit., p. 87.

30. In the way in which one would like to have known Baudelaire at the time he dyed his hair green and belonged to the club of the "Hashishins," or Gérard de Nervel at the time of the Châteaux de Bohème, when he went for walks with a lobster on a leash.

31. Verlaine, preface to the *Illuminations*, op. cit.

32. Paterne Berrichon, quoted in *Arthur Rimbaud, ébauches*, ed. Marguerite Yerta-Méléra (Paris: Mercure de France, 1937), p. 81.

33. Jean Desgives and Frans Suasso, "Arthur Rimbaud, soldat et déserteur de l'armée des Indes néerlandaises" (Nederlandse Omroepstichting, 1983).

34. Isabelle Rimbaud, *Mon frère Arthur*, op. cit.; Pierre Petitfils, *L'Oeuvre et le visage d'Arthur Rimbaud*, op. cit., p. 269.

35. Rethel, January 28, 1877, quoted in *Delahaye, témoin de Rimbaud*, op. cit., p. 254.

36. Ernest Delahaye, *Rimbaud, l'artiste et l'être moral* (Messein, 1923), p. 51.

37. Verlaine, *Les Hommes d'aujourd'hui*, op. cit.

38. Verlaine's phrase.

39. Isabelle Rimbaud, "Le Dernier Voyage de Rimbaud," *La Revue blanche*, October 15, 1897; and in *Reliques* (Paris: Mercure de France, 1922).
40. Paul Nizan, *Aden-Arabie* (Paris: Rieder, 1932).
41. *Rimbaud par lui-même*, op. cit., p. 178.
42. Letter from Isabelle Rimbaud to her mother, Marseille, 1891.
43. Spinoza.
44. "*Voyages epastrouillants*" is Delahaye's phrase.
45. Segalen, *Le Double Rimbaud*, op. cit.
46. Gilles Henry, "L'Ascendance d'Arthur Rimbaud en ligne directe," *Études rimbaldiennes*, No. 3, op. cit.
47. *La Grive*, No. 83.
48. De Mijolla, "L'Ombre du capitaine Rimbaud," op. cit. (see above, Chapter 4, note 19).
49. Ibid., p. 41.
50. I am referring to a brand of Japanese whiskey that uses Rimbaud on its labels. It is true that Rimbaud is better known in Japan than, say, Basho is in France.
51. An allusion to Colonel Godchot, a sprightly Rimbaldian bent on defending Captain Rimbaud: *Arthur Rimbaud ne varietur*, 2 vols. (Nice: self-published, 1936–1937). *La Voyance de Rimbaud* (St.-Cloud: self-published, n.d. [1934]). *L'Agonie du poète Arthur Rimbaud* (St.-Cloud: self-published, n.d. [1937]).
52. Quoted in Robert Goffin, *Rimbaud vivant* (Paris: Éditions Correa, 1937).
53. Jean-Pierre Richard, *Poésie et Profondeur* (Paris: Éditions du Seuil, 1955), p. 11.
54. Adam Biro, *Loin d'où* (Paris: Éditions Recherches, 1983): "Two Jews meet at the airport. 'I'm going to New Zealand,' says one. 'To New Zealand?' replies the other, astonished. 'But that's far!' 'Far from where?' "
55. Gérard de Nerval, "Les Femmes du Caire."
56. This is a montage inspired by Rimbaud's letters of April 11, 1885; April 14, 1885; November 9, 1887; April 4, 1888; May 15, 1890. We know that Buffalo Bill (1846–1917) prided himself on having killed three thousand bisons—and ended up in a circus.
57. Gérard Tougas, *Puissance littéraire des États-Unis* (Paris: L'Age d'homme, 1979).
58. *Delahaye, témoin de Rimbaud*, op. cit., p. 261.
59. Jean Todrani, *Ici et ailleurs* (Paris: GLM, 1954).

Chapter 6: Solitude

1. Starkie, *Rimbaud en Abyssinie*, op. cit., p. 122. Menelik's grandson, Lidj Yassou, undertook "out of love" to bring the Negus's empire back to Islam, which led to the conspiracy of Tafari (Makonnen's son, Haile Selassie, "Power of the Trinity, Elect of God, Defender of the Faith"). See Monfreid, *Les Lionnes d'or d'Ethiopie*, op. cit.
2. *Les Apocryphes éthiopiens*, trans. by René Basset (Paris: Librairie de l'Art indépendant, 1909), p. 6. The belief in the coming of this Messiah was also widespread among the Falashas, the pre-Mosaic Jewish community of Abyssinia.
3. P. Émile Foucher, "L'Arrivée d'Arthur Rimbaud à Harar," *Missions-Messages*, November–December 1980. Also "L'Arrivée de Mgr. Taurin à Harar," ibid., September–October 1975.
4. Gaëtan Bernoville, *Mgr. Jarosseau et la mission des Gallas* (Paris: Albin Michel, 1950). See also François Mauriac, "L'ami de Rimbaud," *Le Figaro*, October 4, 1937.
5. Quoted in Max Guineheuf, "Rimbaud et Mgr. Jarosseau," *Le Mercure de France* (April 1948), p. 760.

6. In Isabelle Rimbaud, "Le Dernier Voyage de Rimbaud," op. cit.
7. Alfred Bardey, *Le Mercure de France*, January 1930.
8. *Delahaye, témoin de Rimbaud*, op. cit., p. 252.
9. Isabelle to her mother, Marseille, October 28, 1891.
10. Isabelle's notes, October 4, 1891.
11. Pierre Petitfils, "Les manuscrits de Rimbaud," *Études rimbaldiennes*, No. 2, 1970.
12. Isabelle to Louis Pierquin, October 23, 1892.
13. Mathilde Verlaine, *Mémoires de ma vie* (Paris: Flammarion, 1935), p. 269.
14. Yves Reboul, "Les Problèmes rimbaldiens traditionnels et le témoignage d'Isabelle Rimbaud," in *Arthur Rimbaud*, No. 1, 1972. But Henri Guillemin (*À vrai dire* [Paris: Gallimard, 1956], pp. 201–208) vouches, against Etiemble, for the authenticity of Isabelle's letter. Readers who are not doubtful, see also the beautiful book by André Thisse: *Rimbaud devant Dieu* (Paris, José Corti, 1975).
    Isabelle could also have discovered her brother's past by reading the letters (Bourde, Gavoty) he brought back.
15. Isabelle to her mother, October 28, 1891.
16. Quoted in Goffin, *Sur les traces d'Arthur Rimbaud*, op. cit., p. 67.
17. Quoted in Briet, *Rimbaud notre prochain*, op. cit., p. 193.
18. Most mosques are invisible from the outside. In any case, there are not "three hundred mosques" in Harar, as Miss Starkie rashly claims (*Rimbaud en Abyssinie*, op. cit., p. 31).
19. Petitfils and Matarasso, *Album Rimbaud*, op. cit., p. 254. Sheik Si Hamza Borbakeur, *Le Coran*, Vol. II (Paris: Fayard, 1979), p. 1651.
20. Petitfils, *Rimbaud*, op. cit., p. 357.
21. Ugo Ferrandi, letter to Ottone Schanzer, published by Benjamin Crémieux in *Les Nouvelles littéraires*, October 20, 1923. Petitfils, *Rimbaud*, op. cit., p. 414.
22. Ugo Ferrandi, in Pierre Petitfils, "Des Souvenirs inconnus sur Rimbaud," *Le Mercure de France*, January 1955.
23. Rochet d'Héricourt, *Voyage sur la côte orientale de la mer Rouge, dans le pays d'Adel et le royaume de Choa*, op. cit., p. 331.
24. H. d'Acremont, "En Abyssinie sur les traces de Rimbaud," op. cit.
25. Isabelle Rimbaud, *Reliques* (Paris: Mercure de France, 1921), p. 81.
26. Letter from Léon Valade to Émile Blémont, October 5, 1871.
27. In Pétralia, *Bibliographie de Rimbaud en Italie*, op. cit., p. 73. Ferrandi, 1923: "*Dettaglio intimo: quando aveva il piccolo bisogno di mingere, si chinava come gli indigeni: onde questi li consideravano un poco come musulmano; e lo consigliava anche a me, vedendo la conoscenza che già avevo degli usi islamici, che io avevo appreso nelle mie peregrinazioni, qualche anno prima nell'estremo Fayum.*"
28. Isabelle Rimbaud to Louis Pierquin, October 28, 1892.
29. Gabriel Bounoure, *Le Silence de Rimbaud*, ed. Edmond Jabès (Cairo: Librairie LDF, collection "Le Chemin des sources," 1955).
30. Verlaine: "Malheureux! Tous les dons, la gloire du baptême" (Wretch! All your gifts, the glory of baptism), *Sagesse* (*Wisdom*).
31. In Briet, *Mme. Rimbaud*, op. cit., p. 29. Carré, *Autour de Verlaine et de Rimbaud*, op. cit., p. 51.
32. Verlaine, "Paysages belges, Walcourt" ("Belgian Landscapes: Walcourt").
33. Germain Nouveau, in *La Bataille*, July 14, 1891.
34. Emmanuel Lévinas, *L'Au-delà du verset, lectures et discours talmudiques* (Paris: Éditions de Minuit, collection "Critique," 1982).
35. Edmond Jabès, *Le Livre des questions: El ou le Dernier Livre* (*The Book of Questions: El or the Last Book*) (Paris: Gallimard, 1973).

36. Yves Bonnefoy: "A philosophy of the absolute can very well establish itself in the ruins of language: but having withdrawn from any hope of exchange, it cannot test the act of being-there where it is a mystery, in life" (*Le Nuage rouge*, op. cit., p. 218).
37. Daniel Paul Schreber, *Mémoires d'un névropathe* (Paris: Éditions du Seuil, collection "Le Champ freudien," 1975).
38. Jean-Louis Backès, in "Rimbaud musicien" (*Romantisme*, No. 36, 1982), proposes a comparison with Wagner.
39. Mathilde Verlaine, *Mémoires de ma vie*, op. cit., p. 181.
40. He disdained the banal "thank you": The other one, the sincere "thank you . . . swells his chest, but does not come out, does not dare to come" (Izambard, *Rimbaud tel que je l'ai connu*, op. cit., p. 171).
41. He addressed this letter to "Alfred" rather than "Ernest": a confusion with Bardey? Mme. Rimbaud neglected to give her son's letter to Delahaye: Perhaps we must attribute this mistaken identity to her?
42. Isabelle claims that Djami stayed in Rimbaud's service for eight years, which seems improbable. Rimbaud left him 3,000 francs in notes and 750 talers (about 50,000 francs Fabius). Cf. the receipt of Monsignor Taurin-Cahagne for Rimbaud's legacy (Harar, June 7, 1893), *Album Rimbaud*, op. cit., p. 316.

    Djami was in Aden in 1891. He saw Sotiro there, with whom he spoke of Rimbaud and César Tian. Then he was in Harar in the service of Bienenfeld (July 1891). Then we lose track of him. The only way of conjuring up Djami: the fiction, poetry, liberties and fantasms of Jean Senac's "finds" (*Dérisions et vertige* [Marseille: Actes Sud, 1983], pp. 61, 103).

Djami's Sleep
(sanguine)

1

You are asleep. Even Endymion
Couldn't put more grace
Into the beauty and offering of this pose.
Seeing you has set my eyes ablaze.
O curly time of youth, bull-calf of space!

2

You arch your back. My loins call names.
ABDAALLAH RIMBAUD
(Ebdoh Rinbo)
From Harar I receive in Tipasa
The seal,
Djami's inheritance . . .

It is perhaps Djami one sees next to Rimbaud on a mule in Harar (unpublished photograph, private collection, New York).

43. In the logic of his literary enterprise, Rimbaud would have renounced homosexuality. Bardey's and Borelli's testimony on this point confirm Rimbaud's determination to forget, to condemn his past, his effort to "find a morality."

    One word only, *ménahins*, leaves this hypothesis open. Alfred Ilg wrote to Léon Chefneux from Zurich (May 31, 1888): "Rimbaud tells me he's going to Harar for . . . business; but he doesn't say of what kind, probably for coffee, gum and skins. (Ménahins!?)." According to Jean Voellmy, who published and translated this letter (in *Rimbaud vivant*, No. 15 [1978], p. 22), "*Ménahins* designates in Arabic 'those who predict the weather,' which makes no sense in this context. Possibly the word is misspelled and really meant to be *mélahins*, which designates vagabonds and perverse children. This last explanation seems the most acceptable, considering not only Rimbaud's past, but also the punctuation following the word in the letter." Alfred Bardey replied to Jean-Paul Vaillant: "Sexual inversion may be frequent elsewhere, in Turkey for example, but it is not at all current in Abyssinia. Rimbaud was neither debauched nor a pervert" (Vaillant, *Rimbaud tel qu'il fut*, op. cit., p. 34). This comment tells us more about Bardey than about Rimbaud's morals in Abyssinia.

Let us remember, on the other hand, that the Swiss engineer cultivated *Witz*, broad humor (Freud's *Zoten*, or dirty jokes). Ilg for instance wrote to Rimbaud on June 16, 1889: "We are always very-very-very happy if we can touch something in some parts (no pun intended)." To round out the hypothesis, the word *ménahins* could just as well concern Ilg.

On this aspect of Rimbaud's life we must suspend judgment.

44. This woman was supposed to be from Tigre or an Argobas, one of the Galla tribes. Testimony of Françoise Grisard, Alfred Bardey's servant who taught her to sew, states; "I think I was the only person he invited into his house. He seemed to be very good to this woman. She was very gentle . . . Catholic. . . . He wanted to teach her and marry" (letter of Françoise Grisard to Paterne Berrichon, Marseille, July 22, 1897, in *La Vie d'Arthur Rimbaud*, op. cit., pp. 158–159). Bardey specified to Berrichon that there were no children (letter of July 16, 1897, in *Le Mercure de France*, April 1, 1930).

In *L'Impero del Leone di Guida, Note sull'Abyssinia* (*The Empire of the Lion of Judah, Notes on Abyssinia*) (1913, p. 154), Ottorino Rosa published the photograph of a woman in the characteristic Shoa headdress and claimed: "This woman lived with the great poet Arthur Rimbaud in Aden, 1882."

Cf. Starkie, *Rimbaud en Abyssinie*, op. cit., p. 75. Pierre Mille, taking a "poll" in Djibouti in 1896, heard a rumor he spread under the formula of "dictionaries bound in skin"—a harem of women speaking different languages that Rimbaud was supposed to have kept. Of no interest. See Étiemble.

Savouré writes to Rimbaud from Harar on August 15, 1891: "Everybody is bringing women. It leaves only you and me to get married."

45. "The customs of the whole country are terrifyingly licentious"; "The women exercise a very noticeable influence on their husbands"; "The Abyssins consider marriage as a social contract whose formalization does not require a priest . . . the least whim of the man, or the woman, is sufficient for a divorce" (*Le magasin pittoresque*).

A certain Laminne, who had in his time been a hunter in Ethiopia, wrote to Paterne Berrichon on January 24, 1912: "Here is what Righas [Ottoman] told me: one day, when Rimbaud was at home in Harar, a fibulated girl came into the house. Rimbaud was going at her a bit fast and came up against the obstacle, then wanted to operate with his penknife on the unfortunate girl who screamed her head off. A mob gathered and things almost turned out badly" (unpublished letter, Library of Charleville-Mézières). Berrichon replied to Laminne that Righas's testimony was not at all trustworthy.

Chapter 7: Innocence

1. Alfred Ilg, January 18, 1889, translated by Jean Voellmy: "The miserable inhabitants of this part of the world have the gift to alarm and annoy" (Bruce, *Voyage* . . . , op. cit., p. 196).
2. "Thirst limbers up the camel drivers and loaders; they abandon their animals to run to the wells dug in the Ansa River and throw themselves on them" (Alfred Bardey, *Journal de route de Zeilah à Harar*).
3. Maurice Blanchot, *La Part du feu* (*The Share of the Fire*) (Paris: Gallimard, 1972), p. 158.
4. Alexandre Merciniez, Massawa, August 5, 1887. Righas, in Segalen, *Le Double Rimbaud*, op. cit., p. 56.
5. Raffray, *Abyssinie*, op. cit., p. 122. As Bachelard composed "Lautréamont's bestiary," Sartre had long thought of establishing "Rimbaud's lapidary."
6. The stretcher is preserved in the Harar museum—where it becomes more authentic by the year.
7. *Delahaye, témoin de Rimbaud*, op. cit., p. 259.
8. These infantry marches were used to moving effect all through the unforgettable performance of *A Season in Hell* by Bruno Sermonne (Brussels, 1981).
9. Exempted at his request from military service in 1874, Rimbaud kept being obsessed with his "service record" in Abyssinia and even on his deathbed. His *livret militaire* was put in order *in extremis*. Frédéric had enlisted for five years in 1873, which took care of his obligations. Referring to his brother with irony, Rimbaud wrote his mother in 1875: "I salute the army" (Stuttgart, March 17, 1875).
10. Isabelle Rimbaud, "Le Dernier Voyage de Rimbaud," op. cit., p. 121.
11. Ernest Delahaye, *Verlaine* (Paris: Messein, 1919), p. 227.
12. Verlaine to Rimbaud, December 12, 1875.
13. Izambard, *Rimbaud tel que je l'ai connu*, op. cit., p. 72.
14. Bardey, *Études rimbaldiennes*, No. 1, op. cit., p. 52.
    Bardey wrote to Paterne Berrichon (December 9, 1897): "Why treat the Egyptians as dogs and bandits when all the governors of Harar have been very paternal and useful to us and him, and the Egyptian Officers' Corps (of much higher quality than thought in Europe) was always very affable and obliging. . . . And why this quirk of always being insulting when he did not mean a word of what he said."
15. Paterne Berrichon, in *Arthur Rimbaud, ébauches*, op. cit., p. 161. Verlaine spoke of the "diamond prose" of the *Illuminations*, but with Berrichon there are only pearls. Cf. Chapter 10.
16. Borelli, touchy and generous like Rimbaud, wrote him a moving letter of reconciliation from Entotto, on July 26, 1888.
17. Pierre Arnoult, *Rimbaud* (Paris: Albin Michel, 1943), p. 490. Cf. also Daniel A. de Graaf, *Arthur Rimbaud, sa vie, son oeuvre*, op. cit., p.314; M. Guigniony, *Bulletin des amis de Rimbaud*, July 1957; Jean Voellmy, *Rimbaud vivant*, No. 15, p. 12. The following letters to Rimbaud are from Savouré (April 11, 1889) and Brémond (February 10, 1889).
18. This is based on the account of a descendant of this surgeon.
19. Germain Nouveau to Verlaine, October 20, 1875. Verlaine to Rimbaud, London, December 12, 1875.
20. Jacques Lacan, *Écrits*, op. cit., p. 140.
21. Statements reported by Verlaine (in Matarasso and Petitfils, *Vie de Rimbaud*,

op. cit., p. 101) and by Ernest Millot (in Carré, *Les Deux Rimbaud*, op. cit., p. 25).

22. *Études rimbaldiennes*, No. 3, op. cit.
    Ottoman Righas also said to Laminne (see above) that "Rimbaud arrived in Djibouti (or Obock) in a native dhow, fleeing from I don't know which Greek island where he must have committed some misdeed"—which would corroborate Rosa's testimony.

23. Jules Borelli to Enid Starkie, *Rimbaud en Abyssinie*, op. cit., p. 210.

24. When Alfred Bardey learned of these statements he was bitter and refused to write a preface for the *Lettres d'Afrique et d'Arabie*.

25. Cf. Steve Murphy, "L'Oeil du policier," *Cahiers du Centre culturel Arthur-Rimbaud*, No. 9, 1984.

26. Rimbaud declared his good faith, which was obvious, to M. de Gaspary, consul in Aden (who seems his good conscience, France in a gray suit). Rimbaud won his case. Before the opening of the Harar road (1887), Menelik and the *azzaze* "invariably judged in favor of any Bedouin against a *Frangui*."

27. Verlaine, end of the preface to the *Poésies de Rimbaud*, op. cit.

28. Tristan Corbière, *Gens de mer* (*People of the Sea*).

29. Ernest Delahaye, in a letter to Ernest Millot, January 28, 1897. Paul Verlaine, *Sagesse*.

30. Brunel, *Rimbaud ou l'eclatant désastre*, op. cit., p. 48.

31. *Delahaye, témoin de Rimbaud*, op. cit., p. 262.

32. Isabelle Rimbaud, *Mon frère Arthur*, op. cit.

33. Quoted in ibid.

34. Lost. "It was a socialism opposed to state control, though it amounted to more or less the same" (*Delahaye, témoin de Rimbaud*, op. cit., p. 184).

35. Verlaine, "Arthur Rimbaud," op. cit. On Verlaine's conduct during the Commune, see Petitfils, *Rimbaud*, op. cit. Let us only recall the story of Verlaine arrested by the Arras police: "I was just getting over being a bit of a Communard and not averse to raising my voice. I added that I was from Metz and had to choose between France and Germany and, by God, now, with this arbi-tra-ry arrest I would really hesitate" (*Mes prisons*).

36. This verdict is given by prosecutor Étiemble ("Rimbaud et les barricades de Mai 68," reprinted in *Rimbaud, système solaire ou trou noir?*, op. cit.): "Arthur Rimbaud, you ('a youth of seventeen,' p. 134) who perhaps participated in the Paris Commune (only to be 'picked up by soldiers' and 'more or less willingly raped,' p. 140), the Court, in Truth, judges you unworthy of being invoked on the barricades by these Sorbonne and Nanterre students (also 'hoodlums and *Katangais*' [a quasi-military group that invaded the Sorbonne in May 1968], p. 140—as Mauriac has rightly said—and who on top of it all are challenging me).
    "Second, worse, count of the accusation: Seeing that you were 'a harsh racist and colonialist merchant' (p. 134), seeing that you dared say France was wasting its money in Tonkin, as it did, and that it should have colonized Madagascar, as it then did, seeing that as an 'imaginary criminal and occasional sodomite' (p. 144) (here it is a question of the poet), you cannot have participated in the Commune. I, Vice-Curator of the Myth that also bears My Name, declare that you have betrayed the ideals of the Commune. In consequence I judge you unworthy of being quoted in the context of Vietnam by Mlle. Enid H. Rhodes, in the *MLA Newsletter* of March 1969. . . . The Court is adjourned."
    Étiemble's thought is as profound as a cup of tea! How could one sum-

marize it except by burlesquing it. I myself published this article in the *Rimbaud* issue of the magazine *Bérénice* (Rome, 1980). I should have read it beforehand.

37. Verlaine, preface to *Poésies de Rimbaud*, op. cit.

38. ". . . the sad colony of Obock where we are at present trying to set up a post; but I don't think anything will come of it. It is a deserted, burned beach without food, without trade, good only for a coal depot" (Aden, October 7, 1884). Rimbaud anticipated without knowing it the pessimistic prognosis of Lemay (Foreign Affairs) and Dieulafoy (an archaeologist who in an 1889 report proposes to limit Obock "to being a coal and provisions depot").

39. In 1883, Count Antonelli gave Menelik a credit of 75,000 francs for opening the road from Massawa to Shoa. He offered him first 5,000, then 38,000 rifles, 38 cannons, millions of shells, and signed with the new emperor the Treaty of Ucciali that Menelik was to repudiate with such cunning. "Italy then announced to the world that Abyssinia was as it were an Italian protectorate. Menelik feigned being a stupid and ignorant black, but simply reserved the right to shake off the Italian yoke as soon as he could walk on his own" (Starkie, *Rimbaud en Abyssinie*, op. cit., p. 167). We also know the Negus's hostility toward England, which had supported Emperor John. "If France's policy had been shrewder at that moment," notes Starkie (p. 66), "it could have captured the whole eastern coast of the Red Sea as far as Zeila, probably even as far as Berbera. France was in a better position for this than England or Italy." Let us also note that Rimbaud did not think Menelik capable of keeping Harar, which he had just conquered (letter to the *Bosphore égyptien*).

40. See note 36.

41. La Bruyère: "Speaking and offending are one and the same thing with certain people" (*Les Charactères* [Paris: Les Grands Maîtres, 1949], p. 79).

42. ". . . un uomo assolutamente pacifico, alieno affatto dalla politica, tutto occupato dai suoi commerci e da una grave malattia a una gamba, è in continue e cordiali relazioni con tutti gli italiani che lavorano nel mar Rosso" (Edoardo Scarfoglio, *Corriere di Napoli*, June 16, 1891, in Pétralia, *Bibliographie de Rimbaud en Italie*, op. cit., p. 78).

43. Rémy de Gourmont, "Le Joujou patriotique," *Le Mercure de France*, March 25, 1891: "Personally, I would not give a little finger for these forgotten territories, neither that of my right hand: it helps support my hand while writing, nor that of my left: it is good for shaking my cigarette ash." See the introduction of J.-P. Rioux to the J.-J. Pauvert edition of this text (1967), where we found some of the quoted documents. One dignified reaction in this troubled time: that of Alphonse Allais (born like Rimbaud on October 20, 1854), who withdrew into bitter irony.

44. Paul Verlaine to Rimbaud, London, September 12, 1875. Again, later, Verlaine will celebrate (after four absinths?) Rimbaud's "supreme gifts, magnificent testimony to Intelligence, a proud, French, very French (let us insist on it in these days of cowardly internationalism) proof of the natural superiority of race and caste, incontestable affirmation of the immortal kingdom of the human Mind, soul and heart," etc. Without mentioning the speech Izambard made before Verlaine's statue in the Luxembourg Gardens in 1916, a prototype of reactionary clichés.

45. Bardey, April 15, 1881, *Études rimbaldiennes*, No. 1, op. cit., p. 39. At night, the hyenas "howl with shrill laughter." The odor of blood attracted them because the Hararis butchered every day great numbers of goats, sheep, and cows, held on wooden forks and stakes (ibid., p. 34). The cowardly, stinking,

and scavenging hyenas are the night crew of the Harar garbage dump, as vultures are in Aden: "In this town without canalization they know they are invulnerable. They are the sanitation department. They are city employees" (Francis de Croisset, *La Féerie cinghalaise* [Paris: Grasset, 1928], p. 27). Or as goats are in Saudi Arabia: "the gluttonous goats that love cigarettes and are more or less officially in charge of garbage removal" (Philippe Soupault, *Revue de Paris*, May 1951). "The hyena is transformed into a useful animal: it clears the towns of decaying matter which would cause epidemics and thus takes the place of a sanitation department, whose existence is not even suspected in Abyssinia" (Doncourt, *L'Abyssinie,* op. cit., p. 44).

Chapter 8: Literature

1. President of the Organization for African Unity with headquarters in Addis Ababa (1976).
2. Sylvain Vignéras had been able to meet César Tian himself (*Une Mission française en Abyssinie,* op. cit., p. 57).
3. Besse told Soupault of "his very sincere admiration for Rimbaud's flair: it was his example that allowed him to build up [his] immense fortune by monopolizing the trade on incense, sheepskins, coffee, *cat,* dhows, arms. . . . Rimbaud," he said, "was a precursor. He did not know Rimbaud had been a poet" ("Sur les traces de Rimbaud," op. cit., p. 34). One could imagine this Ethiopian millionaire as another form of anti-Rimbaud—one who waited to be rich in order to write.
4. *Lettres de Jean-Arthur Rimbaud, Égypte, Arabie, Éthiopie,* ed. Paterne Berrichon (Paris: Mercure de France, 1899). Marcel Coulon, *La Vie de Rimbaud et de son oeuvre* (Paris, Mercure de France, 1929), p. 332 ff. Paterne Berrichon, whose name should really be Patachon (as messy kids are called), also changed passages of Rimbaud's letters that would have embarrassed the hagiography. Rimbaud writes: "Everybody here wants to have his picture taken; I can get as much as a guinea per photograph." Berrichon adds: "But this is not what I bought my camera for, I need it for other things." See also Izambard, *Rimbaud tel que je l'ai connu,* op. cit.
5. "César Tian . . . told me that he handed him a small fortune when he returned to France" (Armand Savouré to Georges Maurevert, April 3, 1930). The franc-or, which was currency from April 1803 (*germinal an XI*) to August 1914, contained 0.2900322 gram refined gold (law of March 28, 1803). César Tian's draft represented a weight of 10.86171 kilos refined gold, which at the current rate of 96,500 francs per kilo (July 25, 1984) could be converted into 1,048,155 francs Fabius.

   We must add (letter to César Tian of May 6, 1891) half the assets of the Harar depot, the eight kilos of gold deposited in Cairo, the money invested in land by Mme. Rimbaud. "I would have had more," writes Rimbaud, for he had "money outstanding all over the place . . . but because of [his] unfortunate departure [he] lost several thousand francs" (letter to his family, Aden, April 30, 1891).

   Curiously, Rimbaud's financial position in 1891, at the time of his precipitate departure, is on the scale Berrichon wrongly claimed for 1884. Since Étiemble goes no further than Berrichon's falsification of Rimbaud's finances in 1884 in order to deflate the "fable" of the rich merchant (*Le Mythe de Rimbaud,* op. cit., Vol. II, p. 217), the operation is once again at his expense.

6. In Martial de Salviac, *Au pays de Ménélik, les Gallas*, op. cit.
7. Contrary to Lévinas's absolute equivalence of word and money, the word given and the word due.
8. Yves Bonnefoy evokes the gold-belt Rimbaud wore in Egypt in the context of the poem "Le Pauvre Songe" ("The Paltry Dream") (*Rimbaud par lui-même*, op. cit., p. 173). Then, in the context of "Ce qu'on dit au poète à propos des fleurs" ("What is Said to the Poet in Regard to Flowers"): "Foreclosure forever repeated as proved by the merchant and colonist of the African years who carries his fortune in his belt in bullions of the yellow metal" (in *Denis de Rougemont* [Neuchâtel, La Baconnière, 1976], p. 240, and in *Rimbaud, Opere* [Mondadori, 1975]).
9. Georges Bataille, *Haine de la poésie* (*Hatred of Poetry*) (Paris: Éditions de Minuit, 1947).
10. Berrichon, *La Vie de Jean-Arthur Rimbaud*, op. cit., p. 132,
11. Letter to Georges Maurevert: "He gave me hospitality for the month [fall 1888]. Rather good house without furniture. I had to sleep on the field bed I carry and during the entire month could never make out where he slept—seeing him spend day and night writing at a rickety table."

Pierre Mille, private secretary of Paul Bourde (then secretary general of Madagascar):

"Used a stopover in Djibouti to investigate the businessman Rimbaud. It was easy to find traders in the cafés who remembered the poet [the Righas?]. But when he told them about the young genius they were astounded! They had never considered him as anything but a good merchant, somewhat adventurous in business, even having "ideas," which in their mind was not altogether a compliment. But they added that they could never have known about the poetical career of their former colleague. Rimbaud never spoke to them either about his previous existence or about literature, not even in the most general way." [*L'Action française*, November 20, 1938; quoting *L'Age nouveau*, No. 1.]

12. "*Rimbaud . . . già letterato in Francia, e che abbandonate le muse, messa da un canto la critica e gittata la penna, era venuto in Africa a spennare i suoi ideali, tuffando le strofe alate, le odi epiche . . . nel prosaico ma lucroso bagno di un commercio . . .*" (Luigi Robecchi-Bricchetti, *Nell'Harar* (Milano: Galli, 1896), p. 152).
13. Jules Borelli to Enid Starkie, September 1936.
14. From "The Snail" (in the collection *Le Reliquaire*, ed. Rodolphe Darzens, 1891) to *La Chasse spirituelle* (Paris: Mercure de France, 1949). André Tian stopped the rumors spread by the press in 1947 about the forty thousand unpublished verses Rimbaud wrote in Abyssinia ("40,000 Unpublished Lines of Verse," *Les Nouvelles littéraires*, February 13, 1947): After having published a note under this title, we received a letter of the keenest interest from M. André Tian. M. Tian tells us that he is working on a book on Rimbaud's long stay in Abyssinia. He adds:

Rimbaud wrote nothing in verse after 1873. Among his papers, which in 1891 were left in Aden, in my father's hands, there were no poems. His correspondence with my father was exclusively commercial and also concerned, I now feel free to say, with France's stakes in Ethiopia. But neither my father nor his manager Maurice Riès nor their friend Jules Borelli, whom I knew well, nor Msgr. Jarosseau suspected before 1893 that Rimbaud was a

308 / Notes

poet. Nothing in his life in Harar, nothing in his papers of that time drew their attention to what he had been before 1880.

In 1942, my letter to *Confluences* took care of the revelations Maurice Riès was supposed to have made to André Pourquier, which the latter published in Saint-Étienne's *Les Amitiés*. Riès knew nothing about Rimbaud the poet before the latter's death. The firm César Tian, later César Tian and Maurice Riès (September 1, 1891–April 1, 1909) remained deaf and dumb to the objurgations of "poor Arthur's" admirers asking for details about him.

My late father had been adviser to M. de Gaspary, the French consul in Aden, then himself a specially appointed consul. Maurice Riès, also dead now, had been French vice-consul in the same city. They were sworn to professional silence. Rimbaud was an intelligent and devoted agent providing information about Menelik and acting as liaison between him and my father. These activities, which did not officially involve the French government, brought both of them the lasting hatred of the Foreign Office. The reports quoted by Miss Starkie are proof of this. During the three years that Rimbaud was my father's buyer and retailer in Harar, poetry was dead for him. I am convinced that the repeated news of the discovery (first in a little Ethiopian village, then in Addis Ababa) of manuscripts and finally of forty thousand lines of verse is the prelude to a cleverly orchestrated fantasy, a literary hoax to make Mérimée dream and turn over in his grave.

André Tian.

15. Maurice Blanchot, "Le Sommeil de Rimbaud," in *La Part du feu,* op. cit., p. 153.
16. "Rimbaud is above all this unforgettable silence which is there, hauntingly, when we get involved in writing. He forbids us even to fall silent, because he has done it already, better than anybody" (Gérard Macé, in "Des Poètes d'aujourd'hui lecteurs de Rimbaud," special issue of *Cahiers de recherches,* Nos. 34–44, ed. Pierre Pachet [University Paris-VII, series "Sciences des textes et des documents," 1984]).
17. André Breton, *Flagrant Délit* (Paris: Thésée, 1949), p. 13.
18. "Alfred Poussin, the poet of the *Versiculets,* told us he ran into him on November 1 near the Odeon. . . . Rimbaud was pale and silent as usual. His attitude as well as his face betrayed something virile, bitter and formidable. . . . Poussin was to remember this encounter all his life with a sense of terror" (Berrichon, *Jean-Arthur Rimbaud le poète,* op. cit., pp. 294–296).
19. The Belgian lawyer Léon Losseau found the rest of the edition, unpaid, in the cellar of the publisher Poot in Brussels. Rimbaud did not burn the "almost untouched stack of copies" (Berrichon, ibid.), but no doubt the manuscript and the copies in his possession. See Léon Losseau, *La Légende de la destruction par Rimbaud de l'édition princeps de Une Saison en enfer* (Mons: Dequesne, n.d. [1914]).
20. "Corbière and Mallarmé have printed—this small immense thing. M. Rimbaud, too disdainful, more disdainful than Corbière who at least threw his volume in the face of the century, did not want to publish any poems" (Verlaine, *Les Poètes maudits,* op. cit., 1884). Rimbaud had at first tried everything to get published, but it is no doubt against his wishes that we read *A Season in Hell* or the *Illuminations.*
21. Chamfort, *La Fontaine,* Vol. III (Paris: Éditions des Grands Écrivains, 1920), p. 249, n. 7. [Chamfort's examples are *hommes* and *où nous sommes, tous tant que nous sommes,* the point being the predictability of the rhyme.]

22. We might also note this condensation to a sign—the number of books that take their title from Rimbaud's work. Books contain words—but Rimbaud's words contain books: *Ce que l'homme a cru voir* by Albert Chambon (Paris: Éditions du Cerf, 1969); *Après le déluge* (novel) by Paul-André Lesort (Paris: Éditions du Seuil, 1977); *Les Remembrances du vieillard idiot* (novel) by Michel Arrivé (Paris: Flammarion, 1977); *Du même désert à la même nuit* (poems) by Vahé Godel (Jacques Antoine, 1978), etc. Without mentioning allusions: *Une Saison au Congo* by Aimé Césaire (Paris: Éditions du Seuil, 1967); *Une Saison au purgatoire* (novel) by Thomas Keneally (Paris: Denoël, 1978); *Une Jeunesse en enfer* by Maureen Peters (Paris: Jean-Claude Lattès, 1975); *Le Coeur violé* (novel) by Henry Bonnier (Paris: Albin Michel, 1977); *La Vie est ailleurs* by Milan Kundera (Paris: Gallimard, 1973); *Le Zoizeau ivre* (novel) by José-André Lacour (Paris: Laffont, 1977), etc.

23. Martin Heidegger, *L'Etre et le temps* (Paris: Gallimard), p. 203.

24. Pierre Debray, *Rimbaud, le magicien désabusé*, preface by Daniel-Rops (Paris: Julliard, 1949), p. 241. Cf. Petitfils, in *Le Bateau ivre*, Nos. 2–3, op. cit., p. 9.

25. In Berrichon, *La Vie de Jean-Arthur Rimbaud*, op. cit., p. 237.

26. *Delahaye, témoin de Rimbaud*, op. cit., p. 305.

27. Verlaine recognized himself in the "pitiful brother" (letter to Charles de Sivry, August 1878).

28. Verlaine, "Malheureux, tous les dons . . ." ("Wretch, All Your Gifts . . .").

29. Edmond-Adolphe Lepelletier, *L'Écho de Paris*, November 17, 1871.

30. C. A. Cingria spoke of the "sex appeal" of Rimbaud's poetry, of which he also said: "It is young, democratic and young, a Sunday, your hands in your pockets" (*Poésie 42*, No. 1, January 1942; quoted by Jacques Réda, "Des Poètes d'aujourd'hui lecteurs de Rimbaud," op. cit., p. 57).

31. Verlaine to Delahaye, November 27, 1875.

32. "I tell you," Rimbaud supposedly said to Delahaye on his return from Paris in 1872, "I went to Cabaner's room while he was not there and discovered a cup of milk waiting for him, so I jerked off into it" (*Delahaye, témoin de Rimbaud*, op. cit., p. 197).

33. On Rimbaud's nicknames, see ibid., p. 243.

34. Verlaine to Rimbaud, Paris, May 1872.

35. Germain Nouveau to Verlaine, January 27, 1876.

36. Félix Fénéon, *Le Symboliste*, October 1886.

37. Verlaine, "Arthur Rimbaud," *Les Hommes d'aujourd'hui*, op. cit.

38. Maurice Riès to Émile Deschamps, March 15, 1929. See also, apropos Rolland de Renéville, *Action française*, June 6, 1929: "Rimbaud had a horror of his past."

39. Borelli to Enid Starkie: "He never spoke of his previous life" (September 1936).

40. Italian version of this document, reported by Lidia Herling Croce (in *Études rimbaldiennes*, No. 3, op. cit., p. 11): "Entirely devoted to commerce, he never spoke of his past, and there was no reason to suspect under this extravagant and somewhat cantankerous shell his genius as a poet and man of letters. He never said one word about Verlaine. Once only he had to tell me that, disgusted with the Bohemian life he had been led to by his restless, adventurous temperament and the company he had kept as a very young man, he had suddenly and definitely decided to leave France."

41. "Voyelles" ("Vowels") and "The Drunken Boat" had appeared in *Lutèce* in October 1883. Paul Bourde was best known for an article in *Le Magasin pittoresque* extolling the explorer Stanley. . . . He later wrote a condescending letter to Rimbaud: "As you live so far from us, you are no doubt unaware

that for a very small Parisian coterie you have become a kind of legendary figure. . . . several young men (whom I find rather naive) have tried to base a literary system on your sonnet on the colors of letters." He was appropriately named, Bourde (meaning "fib," "howler"). This letter (Argelès, February 29, 1888) had in part been published in Berrichon, *La Vie de Jean-Arthur Rimbaud*, op. cit., p. 203 (reprinted in Starkie, *Rimbaud*, op. cit., p. 445). It appears as No. 264 in the catalog of the auction "Precious Autographs and Literary Manuscripts" (Paris, Nouveau Drouot, Room No. 3, December 1983) and is quoted *in extenso* in *Un Sieur Rimbaud, se disant négociant* (Paris: Lachenal et Ritter, 1984).

42. Sigmund Freud, *Totem et tabou* (Paris: Gallimard), p. 42.
43. *La Révolution surréaliste*, No. 2, 1925.
44. Verlaine, *Les Hommes d'aujourd'hui*, op. cit.
45. Roger Munier, "Du silence," in *Le Parcourse oblique* (Paris: Éditions de la Différence, 1979), pp. 127–131.
46. The merit of having been the first to suggest the needed study of the connection of Rimbaud and Nietzsche belongs to Paterne Berrichon, in his presentation of *Lettres d'Égypte, d'Arabie et d'Afrique*, op. cit., p. 14.
47. Colonel Godchot, *L'Agonie du poète*, op. cit., p. 32.

Chapter 9: Reality

1. Hiroo Yuasa, communication at the colloquium *Rimbaud multiple*, Cerisy-la-Salle, 1982.
2. According to Giuseppe Raimondi: "Africa represents for Rimbaud the will to pursue, on the level of life and in exceptional conditions, the same aim that the 'exploits' of his *voyance* had tried to reach . . . after the poetry of the word, the poetry of action" ("Rimbaud mercante in Africa," *Civiltà della macchine*, September 1954). Pierre Debray (*Rimbaud, le magicien désabusé*, op. cit.) also claims that since language has no strictly magical value, Rimbaud, the man of action, would be in the lineage of Rimbaud the poet. Moreover, F. Castelli claims that Rimbaud realizes through action in Abyssinia the poetry he had previously realized in words (*Arthur Rimbaud, demoniaco genio delirante*, 1954).
3. Gérard Macé, "Rimbaud Recently Deserted," in *Ex-Libris*, op. cit., p. 59.
4. Duncan Forbes, *Rimbaud in Ethiopia* (Taiwan and Edinburgh: Volturna Press, 1979), p. 24.
5. Mickaël Taylor, "Rimbaud, le réel même," in *Vent des royaumes ou les voyages de Victor Segalen* (Paris: Seghers, 1983), p. 110.
6. Tristan Tzara, *Le Surréalisme et l'après-guerre* (Paris: Nagel, 1947), p. 16.
7. See Voellmy, "Dada, Zürich et Rimbaud," op. cit.
8. Antonin Artaud, March 18, 1936, *Oeuvres complètes*, Vol. VIII, 1971, (Paris: Gallimard), p. 212. "I . . . am more and more bored by written poetry . . . and find that all of French poetry of the last hundred years is contained exclusively in a dozen sonnets by Nerval, a few poems by Baudelaire and *A Season in Hell* by Arthur Rimbaud" (to Henri Poupet, August 26, 1934, ibid., p. 327). "Finally Rimbaud's legacy, a dynamic notion of poetry, is freeing poetry from text and writing and gives us again a magical idea of life" (to Jean Paulhan, August 6, 1935, ibid., p. 339). "Rimbaud's gesticulating with long crazy arms seems to sweep away the planets, and an ecstatic Breton throws diamonds at Soupault. It is Rimbaud with his sand-burned hands who dares the

infinite descent into the I, with images where a trembling Life takes shape at the border of Nothingness, he, Rimbaud, and before him Novalis who said: A style is the more perfect the closer it comes to Nothing" ("Propos d'un pré-dadaïste," *Complete Works*, Vol. II, p. 224).

9. Isabelle Rimbaud, in *Ébauches*, op. cit., p. 182.
10. *Delahaye, témoin de Rimbaud*, op. cit., p. 201: a series of prose texts in 1872.
11. Bardey to Rimbaud, Vichy, July 24, 1883.
12. Ciocarlie, "Le 'Texte' de la correspondance africaine de Rimbaud," op. cit., p. 26. "We want to show that in Rimbaud's correspondence the overthrow of Romantic poetry is accompanied by a real transgression . . .; to find an example of what Derrida has called a *renversement-transgression*, an 'overthrow-transgression,' etc." Since the referent indeed cannot be defined, formalism can continue its analyses at leisure, and consider the correspondence as a "text" having, like "The Drunken Boat" or *A Season*, a double, semantic and semiological, structure. To us who start out from the Referent and do not find it again in the correspondence, the misunderstanding seems quadruple.
13. Verlaine, *Les Hommes d'aujourd'hui*, op. cit.
14. Raffray, *Abyssinie*, op. cit., p. 246.
15. Title page of the work just quoted, and Martial de Salviac, *Au pays de Ménélik, les Gallas*, op. cit. (Chapter 8).
16. Quoted in Jean-Paul Vaillant, *Le Mercure de France* (November 1930), p. 17.
17. See *Avant-Guerre sur l'art*, No. 2, 1982.
18. Op. cit., Chapter 1.
19. Provost, "Sur les traces africaines de Rimbaud," op. cit., p. 148.
20. See the beautiful work of Jacques Mercier, *Rouleaux magiques éthiopiens* (*Magic Scrolls of Ethiopia*) (Paris: Éditions du Seuil, 1979).
21. Michel Leiris, "L'Abyssinie intime," in *L'Ire des vents*, Nos. 9–10, p 38.
22. H. Lebrun, *Voyages en Abyssinie et en Nubie*, op. cit., p. 8.
23. Capitaine Rimbaud, "Les sauterelles," military report, Sebdou, June 10, 1849, in *Rimbaud vivant*, No. 5 (1974), p. 12.
24. Doncourt, *L'Abyssinie*, op. cit., p. 48.
25. Eleven times according to Isabelle, nine according to Jean Voellmy.
26. Raffray, *Abyssinie*, op. cit., p. 81.
27. Vignéras, *Une Mission française en Abyssinie*, op. cit., p. 12.
28. Dr. Venette, *Traité de l'amour conjugal* (Paris: Imprimerie Dersi, 1920), p. 307.
29. Bardey, *Barr Adjam*, op. cit., p. 274.
30. Monfreid, *Les Lionnes d'or d'Éthiopie*, op. cit., p. 149.
31. Berrichon, *La Vie de Jean-Arthur Rimbaud*, op. cit., p. 219.
32. The insult comes from Étiemble, see Chapter 2, note 11.
33. Starkie, *Rimbaud*, op. cit., p. 513.
34. So remarkable that Delahaye did not allow Marcel Coulon to reprint it in 1924. Armand Lods waited for Delahaye's death to publish it, self-censored, in *Le Figaro* of April 2, 1932. Verlaine, irritated by some money problem was annoyed, "calmer" and all the more lucid.
35. Gabriele-Aldo Bertozzi, *Rimbaud attraverso i movimenti d'avanguardia* (*Rimbaud Across the Avant-garde Movement*) (Roma: Lucarini, 1976).
36. Rimbaud left Marseille for Alexandria; "he got sick at the start of the crossing. Gastric fever . . . consequences of excessive walking, this was textually the doctor's diagnosis." Rimbaud was put ashore at Civita-Vecchia. "Recovered, he used the occasion to visit Rome" (*Delahaye, témoin de Rimbaud*, op. cit., p. 258).
37. Jacques Gengoux, author of two "Rimbaldian classics" (*La Symbolique de Rim-*

baud [Paris: Édition La Colombe, 1947], and *La Pensée poétique de Rimbaud* [Paris: Nizet, 1950]), told me that Rimbaud could have lived this reality without speaking about it, keeping it inside him (Cerisy, summer 1982). We must however observe the constant tendency toward abstraction in Rimbaud, and the gap between his letters and Abyssinian reality does not essentially hide his interiority ("I never find anything interesting to say . . .").

38. André Dhotel, "Roche, vue par Rimbaud," in *Le Pays de Rimbaud*, a photographic exposition (Charleville, n.d.). At my return, André Dhotel seemed amused by my telling him of this striking difference between Ethiopia and what Rimbaud writes about it. Then he cried, in a tone of complicitous familiarity with Rimbaud: "It was already like that in Roche!"

Chapter 10: The Middle Term

1. Quoted in *Delahaye, témoin de Rimbaud*, op. cit., p. 262.
2. Maurice Riès to Émile Deschamps, March 15, 1929.
3. Isabelle Rimbaud, *Reliques*, op. cit., p. 124.
4. *Philomath*, defined as "one who loves knowledge" in Littré. The noun was applied to Rimbaud by Verlaine in a letter of August 1875 and taken up by Delahaye in February 1876. Verlaine scoffs at "the wild beast who advised the École Polytechnique" for Rimbaud (letter to Delahaye, November 27, 1875) and makes fun of "Rimbaud, engineer abroad" (*Complete Works*, Vol. II, pp. 1420–1421). Delahaye suggested that Rimbaud prepare for the École Centrale or the Polytechnique: "He told me to get lost." "A *pipo* [Polytechnique student] is just what I need," Verlaine writes, thinking of Rimbaud.
5. Quoted in Berrichon, *La Vie de Jean-Arthur Rimbaud*, op. cit., p. 183.
6. Françoise Grisard, letter, July 2, 1897; quoted in Berrichon, ibid.: "I have learned that all his books and papers were left with Father François," a Franciscan of Spanish nationality, who replied on August 10, 1897, to Berrichon that Rimbaud never entrusted any papers to him (unpublished document in the Jacques Doucet Library, quoted in Petitfils, *Rimbaud*, op. cit., p. 359).
7. Izambard reports their rivalry in this area, in *Rimbaud tel que je l'ai connu*, op. cit. About the lost articles, see Chapter 12.
8. "I cannot find even a stamp in this horrible country" (Tadjoura, January 6, 1886). There was not even a rudimentary postal system in Abyssinia before 1892. The caravans served also as couriers. "It takes approximately three months for an exchange of correspondence," wrote Monsignor Taurin from Harar on July 27, 1881. The envelopes of Rimbaud's letters were not kept by his mother and became the object of a "blatant and clumsy fraud": See Henri Tristan, "Les enveloppes du prétendu courrier d'Arthur Rimbaud à l'époque de son séjour en Éthiopie," *Documents philatéliques, Revue de l'Académie de philatélie*, Vol. VIII, 3rd trimester, No. 141, 1969.
9. Carré, *Les Deux Rimbaud*, op. cit., p. 40. Jean Fretet likewise speaks of the "slack" (*avachi*) style of the correspondence (*L'Aliénation poétique*, op. cit.).
10. In Henry de Bouillane de Lacoste and Henri Matarasso, "Nouveaux Documents sur Rimbaud," *Le Mercure de France* (May 15, 1939), p. 27.
11. Sentences beginning with "I," rare subordinate clauses, few relative pronouns, adverbs "here" and "at present," inchoate verbs, most often in the present indicative, imperatives, etc. Principal themes: solitude ("I" repeated seven times), unique relation ("I-you"), projects ("an enterprise"), demands ("send me"), pressing needs ("I absolutely need"), climate ("good"), money ("earn some-

thing"), hyperbole ("extreme goodness"), departures ("I'm leaving in a few days"), precipitation ("have not yet found a way to send you a letter"). Brief notes, written in haste.

12. Catherine Valogne (*Dialogue à travers les siècles* [La Louvière: Daily-Bulletin, collection "Les Poquettes volantes," 1966]) "interviews" Rimbaud by taking the information for his answers from his correspondence.

> I ask him about Aden. "What is it like?"—"The crater of an extinct volcano filled up with sand from the sea. So you see and touch nothing but lava and sand that cannot produce the slightest vegetation."—"And the country around?"—"Aden's surroundings are absolutely arid sand desert. But in Aden, the sides of the crater keep the air from coming in . . ."—"Were you in Aden while the English were at war with the Sudan?"—"The war against the Sudan ended shamefully for our English. Now they are giving up everything to concentrate their efforts on Egypt . . ." [etc.].

> (This procedure for an interview had already been practiced by André Rousseaux in *Le Figaro,* September 28, 1935: "What Rimbaud would have said," Rousseaux imagines meeting with a Rimbaud in his nineties.)

13. Colloquium in Cerisy, summer 1982.
14. Blanchot, *La Part du feu,* op. cit., p. 159.
15. Paris: Gallimard, 1931. Paris: Mercure de France, 1899. Paris: Gallimard, 1965. One may prefer to Jean-Marie Carré's edition the preceding incomplete *Correspondance inédite (1870–1873) d'Arthur Rimbaud,* introduction by Roger Gilbert-Lecomte (Paris: Éditions des Cahiers libres, 1929).
16. For example, if we choose this excerpt following the much quoted sentence from the important letter of May 6, 1883—". . . and find a family and at least have a son whom I would spend the rest of my life bringing up according to my ideas, preparing and arming him with the most complete education possible at this time. I see him becoming a famous engineer, a man powerful and rich through knowledge"—we would have to sort out the details of well-worn themes strung together in a very dense concatenation (the Other, riches, the impossible, the absolute, arms, wandering, knowledge, modernity, desire of normalcy, salvation, etc.). Observing their surfacings and scattering in any Rimbaldian text makes for inexhaustible reading.
17. Mme. Delamain, "Étude graphologique," *Rimbaud vivant,* No. 17, p. 20: "Two letters from Africa, one of 1885, the other of 1888. In the dynamic, large and curly writing, we find all the characteristics of the adolescent: his tough courage, impulsive whimsy, imagination, even his pride."
18. Albert Camus, *L'Homme révolté* (Paris: Gallimard, 1951), p. 117.
19. Agnès Rosenstiehl (author of an—illumined and luminous—anthology, *Ce qu'on dit au poète à propos de fleurs* [*What One Says to the Poet on the Subject of Flowers*][Paris: Gallimard, 1981]), "Tâchez de raconter ma chute et mon sommeil," *Circeto,* No. 2 (February 1984), p. 37 ff.: "The dressing up (of the *Report on Ogaden*) consisted in carefully cleansing it of all stylistic strangeness. And the execution was perfect except for the 'superb dollars of golden abbayas,' dross that escaped the furious erasure of any literary effect." But listening for the "musicality of Rimbaud writing," Agnès Rosenstiehl finds in the African correspondence the devices and dynamics of the earlier texts, uncovers "nuggets," watches "the unfolding overseas alliterations, the rolling paronomasia: *Je suis aRRivé ici apRès avoiR ROULé La meR ROuge* ("I aRRived heRe afteR Rolling on the Red Sea").
20. Georges Schéhadé, *Anthologie du vers unique* (Paris: Ramsay, 1977). Rimbaud:

"Un bateau frêle comme un papillon de mai" ("A boat frail like a butterfly in May").

21. "That Mozart was a genius of incredible creativity we all know, but even he—even Mozart—could be menaced by silence. That a very great artist's inspiration might give out, is this not what stuns, nay frightens us about the year 1790? Absolute silence is by definition without witness: the letters from Abyssinia tell us very little about Rimbaud, about the reasons of what was perhaps a spiritual suicide, but Mozart's works, not all, but those of 1790, can paradoxically tell us about the reverse of creation" (Roger Laporte, *Mozart 1790* [Paris: Portail, 1983], p. 17).

22. Alfred Ilg to Rimbaud, Entotto, October 26, 1889.

23. Letter from Monsignor Jarosseau, September 22, 1936.

24. Verlaine, *Mes prisons*, 1893, op. cit.

25. *Études rimbaldiennes*, No. 3, op. cit., p. 19.

26. See Suzanne Briet, "L'humour de Rimbaud," *Études rimbaldiennes*, No. 2, op. cit.

27. Verlaine, *Mes prisons*.

28. Alfred Ilg to Rimbaud, Ankober, June 16, 1889.

29. Alfred Ilg to Rimbaud, Zurich, February 19, 1888. Alfred Bardey to Paterne Berrichon, quoted in *Le Mercure de France* (May 15, 1939), p. 14.

30. On the question of Rimbaldian drama, cf. Petre Solomon, *Actes* of the Colloquium in Cerisy, 1982.

31. On the photo showing Rimbaud in a garden café, one notices left of his feet a strange anamorphosis: a rock? the mask he dropped?

32. But Mallarmé's information came no doubt from Paterne Berrichon, whose information came from Isabelle. What are we to make of this sentence about Rimbaud (April 1896): "It made for a delightful harmony to hear him sing in Arabic or Greek"? This passage appeared in *Chap Book*, a Franco-American magazine in Chicago ("an exquisite and daring periodical" according to Mallarmé himself) and was not included in *Divagations*. Perhaps Mallarmé did not recognize it as his own. In any case, Rimbaud had not yet learned Arabic when he met Mallarmé—and a true encounter of the two did not take place.

33. Charles Bruneau, "Le Patois de Rimbaud," *La Grive*, No. 53, April 1947. Verlaine to Cazals. Verlaine in 1877, quoted by Delahaye (1905 and 1919).

34. Paul Errard, 1934, quoted in "Du nouveau sur Rimbaud," *Le Mercure de France*, January 15, 1955. Alfred Bardey, *Études rimbaldiennes*, No. 1, op. cit., p. 36.

35. Ibid., p. 52.

36. Armand Savouré, letter to Georges Maurevert, April 3, 1930.

37. "*Poliglotto*": Robecchi-Bricchetti, *Nell'Harar*, op. cit., p. 152. Ugo Ferrandi: "*Rimbaud conosce inoltre a fondo la lingua araba e i costumi dell'Africa Orientale*" ["Rimbaud moreover thoroughly knows Arabic and the customs of Eastern Africa"] ("Lettera dell'Harar," February 1889). Borelli: "He knows Arabic and speaks Amharic and Oromo. He is indefatigable. His aptitude for languages . . . puts him among the most accomplished travelers" (*Éthiopie méridionale*, February 9, 1887). Arthur and Constantin Righas to Victor Segalen: "He spoke English, German, Spanish, Arabic and Galla" (*Le Double Rimbaud*, op. cit., p. 31). Bardey: "Rimbaud spent his spare time deciphering Arabic books and perfecting his languages." But it was slander to speak with Pierre Mille of "dictionaries bound in skin." And V. P. Underwood (*Rimbaud en Angleterre*, op. cit.) shows that Rimbaud's English was rudimentary.

38. Letter from Jules Borelli to Enid Starkie.

39. Alfred Ilg to Rimbaud, Ankober, June 16, 1889.

40. Alfred Ilg to Rimbaud, Entotto, May 9, 1890. The same formula appears twice, and again in his letter from Entotto, January 30, 1891. And again on October 26, 1889: "Come on, my dear Monsieur Rimbaud, you live only once. . . . If nothing else works any more, we'll team up and annoy the others."

41. So Bruno Sermonne in Cerisy, summer 1984.

42. Antonin Artaud, *Les Nouvelles Révélations de l'être*, 1937, *Oeuvres Complètes*, Vol. VII.

43. Claude Minière, "La grammaire somali," *Bérénice*, No. 3. (Rimbaud, Harar, September 23, 1883: "some ammunition that we have twice asked for and the aforesaid Somali grammar").

44. Juels Borelli to Enid Starkie. "Intelligence . . . personified," Bardey wrote to Berrichon (December 9, 1897).

45. *Delahaye, témoin de Rimbaud*, op. cit.

Chapter 11: The Slave

1. Paterne Berrichon, "Rimbaud et Ménélik," *Le Mercure de France* (November 16, 1914), p. 720.

2. The books or essays that constitute this dossier on "Rimbaud and the Slave Trade" are indicated in the notes of this chapter by the following capital letters, in chronological order:

 A. Enid Starkie, *Rimbaud en Abyssinie* (Paris: Payot, 1938).

 B. Mario Matucci, *Le Dernier Visage de Rimbaud en Afrique*, using unpublished documents, ed. Sansoni Antiquariato (Paris: Librairie Marcel Didier, 1962).

 C. Jean Voellmy, "Connaissance de Rimbaud," in *Arthur Rimbaud, Correspondance 1888–1891* (Paris: Gallimard, 1965).

 D. Mario Matucci, "La malchance de Rimbaud," *Critique*, No. 231–232, August–September 1966.

 E. Jean Voellmy, "Rimbaud à l'ouest d'Aden," *Rimbaud vivant*, No. 15, fourth trimester, 1978.

 F. Mario Matucci, "Sur Rimbaud en Abyssinie," *Bérénice*, No. 2, special Rimbaud issue, Rome, March 1981.

3. Jules Borelli, *Éthiopie méridionale*, August 28, 1889.

4. Bardey, *Barr Adjam*, op. cit., pp. 125, 127.

5. Borelli, op. cit., p. 356. After Monfreid, Paulette and Maurice Deribéré (*L'Éthiopie, berceau de l'humanité*, op. cit., p. 334 f.) described in 1972 the vestiges of this "customary right."

6. Or a paradoxical desire for alienation that joins the "love of the censor" analyzed by Pierre Legendre (Paris: Éditions du Seuil, collection "Le Champ freudien," 1974). Pierre Gascar observed: "Slavery, except in the case where a master owns very many slaves, is a personalized advertisement. The man loses his dignity, but keeps his name. It is the other way round for the proletarian . . . I have seen legally freed slaves in Ethiopia who stayed on with their master and shared his poverty" (*Rimbaud et la Commune*, op. cit., p. 158).

7. Provost, "Sur les traces africaines de Rimbaud," op. cit., p. 155.

8. Quoted in B, p. 114.

9. Oxford, Clarendon Press, 1937.

10. Miss Starkie's historical information is not exempt from British nationalism. Neither are, on the French side, the "Foreign Affairs" archives presented by Suzanne Briet in *Rimbaud notre prochain*, op. cit.

316 / Notes

11. A, p. 153.
    Enid Starkie claims to have quoted *in extenso* Rimbaud's letter stating that there is no correlation between the two kinds of traffic, and that this letter was unpublished. She certainly was unaware that the letter was already published in *La Centaine*, in 1928, which she later learned from André Tian, the son of Rimbaud's employer, eager to defend his father's name. She nevertheless "forgot" to quote the crucial passage (p. 265). Cf. André Tian: "La Vérité sur Arthur Rimbaud en Abyssinie," *Le Feu*, June 1941; and a critical commentary on the latter in *Poésie 41*, No. 6, "Mystères abyssins," p. 19.
12. F, p. 108.
13. Antinori, letter to Professor Della Vedova; quoted in B, p. 140.
14. *Abissinia, 1888–1896;* quoted in B, p. 36.
15. Doncourt, *L'Abyssinie*, op. cit., pp. 66–67. Ali, a member of the Abou-Beker family, was himself kept as a slave by his nephew, Rimbaud tells us in the letter to the *Bosphore égyptien*. After his conquest of Harar, Menelik freed the unfortunate man and entrusted the provisional administration of the city to him.
16. Antinori, letter to Professor Della Vedova; quoted in B, p. 140.
17. Bardey, *Barr Adjam*, op. cit., p. 306.
18. Vignéras, *Une Mission française en Abyssinie*, op. cit., p. 140.
19. Letter of the English minister in Aden to his colleague in Cairo, May 1889; quoted in A, p. 156.
20. Pétralia, *Bibliographie de Rimbaud en Italie*, op. cit.
21. Bardey, op. cit., p. 170.
22. Paul Morand, *Papiers d'identité* (Paris: Grasset, 1931), p. 178.
23. In 1793, 1815, 1848, and two "reintroductions" in 1802 and 1816. The First Consul is often given the excuse of having been influenced by Josephine, who was Creole—which says everything. We are not happy to remember that, by ignoring the decree of March 29, 1815, Napoleon tried to please England more than Louis XVIII would ever be able to. France hesitated for over six months, from March 29, 1815, to the end of January 1816, between an abolition more radical than the English and reintroduction. In 1870, when Cardinal Lavigerie organized the Order of the White Fathers, the British consul in Zanzibar suspected him of wanting to reestablish the treaty and took steps in Paris. The consul had reason to worry: French slave traders, tracked down on the Atlantic, had taken refuge in the Indian Ocean. In fact, until the conquest of Dahomey (1892), and through acts of faith like that of Savorgnan de Brazza, who exalted colonization as liberation, the nineteenth century forgot the true French abolitionists of the eighteenth century.
24. Briet, *Rimbaud notre prochain*, op. cit., p. 181.
25. Ibid.
26. Three Franco-English treaties: 1884, 1886, 1888.
27. A, pp. 159–160.
28. Italics Enid Starkie's. It is astonishing that in the second edition of her *Rimbaud*, Miss Starkie neglected to modify the hypotheses she had retracted. Cf. *Rimbaud*, op. cit., Part III, Chapter 3.
29. A, pp. 152, 155; B, pp. 69–77; C, p. 27; D, p. 741; E, pp. 12, 14; F, p. 108, III. After Chadwick, only Duncan Forbes in a little photocopied work for anglophone readers, *Rimbaud in Ethiopia*, op. cit., (Chapter 7), still thinks Rimbaud could have joined his caravan to that of Abou-Beker, neglecting Matucci's irrefutable evidence (B, p. 78).
30. D, p. 742: "This operation would have had to be airborne at the very least." Savouré to Rimbaud, Paris, January 27, 1888: "Ask for 225 camels . . ."

31. B, pp. 52–53.
32. D, Mario Matucci.
33. A, p. 154; B, pp. 78–88; C, p. 26; D, pp. 738–739; E, p. 14; F, p. 109.
34. Discovered by Zaghi in 1940 and published integrally for the first time by Matucci (B, p. 81 f.).
35. "It follows that news is known within a few hours although it comes from regions one could not reach in less than several days" (Bardey, *Barr Adjam,* op. cit., p. 120).
36. B, p. 38.
37. *Non obstant* his personal political opinions, which will lead him to designate England as an enemy in 1940.
38. A, p. 155.
39. Alfred Ilg to Rimbaud, Entotto, August 23, 1890.
40. F, p. 746.
41. A, p. 155.
42. Alfred Ilg to Zimmermann, January 22, 1890, translated by Jean Voellmy, E, p. 14; C, p. 189.
43. Alfred Ilg to Rimbaud, January 30, 1891.
44. Edoardo Scarfoglio, *Corriere della Sera,* December 1891.
45. Armand Savouré to Rimbaud, January 27, 1888.
46. Alfred Bardey to Paterne Berrichon, December 9, 1897, quoted in *Le Mercure de France,* May 15, 1939.
47. Juels Borelli, Marseille, March 28, 1939.
48. Forbes, *Rimbaud in Ethiopia,* op. cit., p. 103.
49. Soupault, "Sur les traces de Rimbaud," op. cit., p. 35.
50. "A monument of infamy," Pierre Gascar writes (*Rimbaud et la Commune,* op. cit., p. 159).
  "An infamous myth," writes Augusto Orsi, repeating Mario Matucci's argumentation (*Arthur Rimbaud, poète et aventurier* [Addis Ababa: Instituto Italiano di Cultura, 1972], p. 26).
51. Étiemble, *Le Mythe de Rimbaud,* Vol. I (Paris: Gallimard, 1954), p. 44; Vol. II, pp. 261–262. Although he should have made amends and blamed Miss Starkie (*Le Figaro littéraire,* April 21 and May 5, 1965), the polemicist relapsed in his "updated" "Classiques Larousse" edition (*Pages choisie d'Arthur Rimbaud* [Paris: Larousse, 1972], p. 11), and continued to spread this fable of the trader in human flesh. . . . This same man talks about ethics, elsewhere.
  Revealing Miss Starkie's errors, Mario Matucci has proved "how partial and demanding some critics are in regard to Rimbaud" (B, p. 748). One of the most renowned biographers of his time, Jean-Marie Carré (but also Jalabert, Pétralia, Provost, Zaghi, etc.) subscribed without qualification to Miss Starkie's inconsistent hypotheses. Even at that, this eminent Rimbaldian was putting forth an innovative hypothesis; the others just jumped on the bandwagon to spread the dirt. Ever since Berrichon, Rimbaud has had spies on his tail.
  "The case is closed" (Étiemble, *Le Mythe de Rimbaud, structure du mythe,* op. cit., p. 24). It is what one wants to hear: it persists (numerous audiovisual echoes), and F. Mitterand in his film *Lettre d'amour en Somalie* (1982) again evokes a Rimbaud, "protector of slaves."
  In a letter to Mario Matucci, Enid Starkie admitted that she had been hasty in consulting the documents, and led into errors. She concluded: "I bow to your severe criticism, which I accept in all humility" (quoted in F, p. 114).
  The first Pléiade editions of Rimbaud's works (by Renéville and Mouquet) did not reproduce, or only in part, Ilg's letter to Rimbaud of August

23, 1890. But in the chronology (p. li) of his 1972 edition, Antoine Adam was explicit about the finally available letter: "Imprudent historians have interpreted this to mean he was a slave trader."

Suzanne Bernard, for her part, showed intuition in the "biographical summary" (p. xiii) of her edition of Rimbaud's *Oeuvres* (Paris: Garnier, 1960): "It seems doubtful that he [Rimbaud] should also have tried slave trade, as it has been thought." When Mario Matucci's work (B) appeared, Suzanne Bernard sent a note to her publisher that this crucial point should be clearly rectified in subsequent editions. It is a pity that after Suzanne Bernard's death, the new Garnier edition (1981: "revised and corrected") was modified in a fashion both anachronistic and incongruous: "It seems that he [Rimbaud] then tried to get into trading slaves or wanted to procure some for his own use." An error (or fault) sweetened in the 1983 reprint to: "It seems he tried to procure slaves for himself."

52. Berrichon, *La Vie de Jean-Arthur Rimbaud*, op. cit.

"Slave in Uganda": *L'Écho de Paris*, November 12, 1891. In the same aptly named newspaper, Lepelletier writes in September 1897: "[Rimbaud] did not have such a horror of work since he chose to exercise in Harar, in Arabia Petraea and Ethiopia, the rough trade of camel driver and slavetrader." Izambard, *Rimbaud tel que je l'ai connu*, op. cit., p. 37 ("How One Becomes a Phenomenon," *La Liberté*, July 16, 1898). In *Le Moniteur des Côtes-du-Nord* of July 27, 1901, Edouard Beaufis wrote: "It was long believed that [Rimbaud] was a slave trader." Then, in 1938: see the welcome Enid Starkie's book gets in "Les Avatars d'un poète maudit," *L'Action française*, September 12, 1938. Or again in 1946: "Already in 1942, American information" found "important Rimbaldian manuscripts" in Diredawa, "a kind of reportage . . . on black slavetrade." (Aline Treich, *Ordre*, October 14, 1946).

53. Étiemble, *Le Figaro littéraire*, op. cit. (see above, note 51).

54. Gascar, *Rimbaud et la Commune*, op. cit., p. 158.

55. D, p. 747.

56. Montaigne, *Essais*, Vol. III, p. 12.

57. B, p. 41.

58. Jorge Ricardo Gomez, *Massimissa* (Paris: R. Deforges, 1976).

59. In a superficial and skimpy argument, Ahmed Al-Hubeishi (in *14 Arbatacher* [the weekly *14 October*] of November 19, 1982, unfortunately reprinted in *Nota Bene*, No. 12, spring 1984) supposes that Rimbaud lived on this island "reserved . . . for the slave trade" and that therefore "Rimbaud worked at the heart of a slave society."

60. Unpublished letter.

61. Combes and Tamisier, *Le Magasin pittoresque*, 1837, p. 54.

62. Charles Gosselin, *L'Empire d'Anam* (Paris: Perrin, 1904). The ancients distinguished three Cushes or Ethiopias, each peopled by descendants of Cush, son of Ham: Arabian, African, and Red Sea Ethiopia.

63. Combes and Tamisier, op. cit.

64. Galla women constantly smeared their bodies with rancid butter. Bruce had observed a Galla vagabond "rubbing his arms and body with melted lard" (Lebrun, *Voyages en Abyssinie et en Nubie*, op. cit., p. 60). Achille Raffray encountered "a dignified matron, still beautiful and attractive, except that the butter she had poured on her head dripped all over her shirt and chemma" (*Abyssinie*, op. cit., p. 69). Henry de Monfreid evokes an Aicha whose "clothes are always dipped in goat butter which melts in the heat" (*Les Lionnes d'or d'Éthiopie*, op. cit., p. 160).

65. Martial de Salviac, *Au pays de Ménélik, les Gallas*, op. cit.: "The prodigious expansionist urge that took the Gauls as far as Africa" (p. 326) was, according to this highly poetic but unlikely hypothesis, at the origin of the Galla tribe descended from a wandering tribe of Gauls. According to Romanet de Caillaud, a popular Galla prophecy announced that the "Francs" would come one day and "restore the Ethiopian empire in all its splendor." Cf. also Duncan Forbes, *Rimbaud in Ethiopia*, op. cit., p. 8.
66. Lebrun, *Voyages en Abyssinie et en Nubie*, op. cit., p. 14.
67. Friedrich Nietzsche, *Genealogy of Morals*.
68. Michel Deguy, "Esthétique de Baudelaire" (in *Figurations* [Paris: Gallimard, 1969], p. 219): "Our life is like a repetition, at the expense of freedom, of a primary scenario of 'de-paradisation.' "
69. Verlaine to Matuszewicz, Brussels, July 5, 1873. On Rimbaud's lost works, cf. Petitfils, *L'Oeuvre et le visage d'Arthur Rimbaud*, op. cit., pp. 120–136. One thinks notably of *La Chasse spirituelle*, which Verlaine considered even superior to *A Season in Hell* (by default: Bruce Morissette, *La Bataille Rimbaud, l'affaire de la Chasse spirituelle* [Paris: Nizet, 1959]).

Chapter 12: Egypt

1. "I am sorry to leave Addis. I liked the lively crowds, the *guebi* and papier-mâché houses, the steep, rocky alleys, the shops with always at least one lion on their signs" (Michel Leiris, *L'Afrique fantôme* [Paris: Gallimard, 1934], p. 515).
2. Gérard de Nerval, *Voyage en Orient*, Vol. II (Paris: Gallimard, "Bibliothèque de la Pléiade"), pp. 90, 92.
3. Alexandre Merciniez to M. de Gaspary, Massawa, August 5, 1887.
4. Mentioned by MM. Bourguignon and Houin (*Revue d'Ardenne et d'Argonne*, 1901, p. 142), the "Letter to the Editor of the *Bosphore égyptien*" was published by Jean-Marie Carré in *Le Mercure de France* of December 15, 1927.
5. Armand Savouré was in Paris January and February 1888. On February 13, he wrote to Ilg, who had stayed in Entotto, getting ready to return to Zurich: "The newspaper gossip . . . is getting more and more unlikely and each morning contradicts the news of the day before. Now Rimbaud is having fun in Aden sending hoaxes to the press." Could it be that some of the articles written in Cairo in August or those Rimbaud wanted to write in December were actually published?
   Scrolling through *Le Figaro* on microfilm at the Beaubourg library, scanning *Le Temps* by pushing a button, in the company of Agnès Rosenstiehl, this is the hypothesis we come up with: "If you would like, I am sure I can place in *Le Temps* correspondence about these regions you know so well and which the Massawa business has brought to general attention," Paul Bourde wrote to Rimbaud on February 29, 1888. "They would pay fifty centimes per line," he specified. But Rimbaud demanded much more—exorbitant sums, Paul Bourde will tell Berrichon—and his articles were not published. This hypothesis seems confirmed on consulting *Le Figaro* or "*Le Temps*, a serious, gray, pedantic and balanced newspaper" (says Maupassant in *Boule de suif*). These newspapers of four pages (one of which is for advertisements) were hardly interested in anything but operettas and the health of the Kronprinz. A sleepy Europe considered itself the center of the world, unconcerned by America, Russia, or distant Asia. By way of foreign policy, there was an occasional

"letter from Bulgaria" from Madrid or Abyssinia, like a letter carried on stage in a play. *Reporters* did not yet exist, and the press, far from any modern concern for information, indifferent to truth or fact, only reports official releases. The *Figaro*'s "letters from Abyssinia" are signed Jacques Saint-Cère, [a pun on "sincere" that makes it] a transparent pseudonym for articles written along the cramped political lines of an opposition paper. It is hard to imagine that an unknown and in fact sincere correspondent could take his place. In 1884, Germain Nouveau also sent the *Figaro* an article from Alexandria on "The Jews in Jerusalem," also in vain.

Savouré, the old sharper, who was preparing a new arms-expedition to Abyssinia for early March (in which he tried to interest Rimbaud) had to keep up with the news. He told Rimbaud of his "puzzlement" in a letter from Paris of January 14. Worried about the turn of events, he bought the papers every day—"the papers say . . . every day that Menelik is staying neutral" (ibid.)— at least the major papers and particularly Le *Figaro*. On February 9, he came across a short article (not so short actually, a double page in current layout): disastrous news that the *Figaro* felt obliged to print in spite of its admitted desire to lie in order to please the Italians. Announcing the imminent Italian defeat, the *Figaro* spoke of an inofficial "cable from Aden." Savouré, who did not want to believe in the Italian setback, attributed this cable to Rimbaud. The only interest of his letter is actually that it attests Rimbaud's relatively intellectual reputation and the fact that he had not hidden his project to write articles from his colleagues. The suspicion of a *fumisterie*, or "hoax," which reminds us of François Coppé mocking the "accomplished hoaxer" apropos the poem "Les Voyelles" ("Vowels") and of the *fumisteries* of Rimbaud's *Album zutique*, confirms the sarcastic Rimbaud of Abyssinia. But it was in Egypt that Rimbaud took up the pen again and again put it down. By December he had only "intentions" left, and soon after not even any memories "in this direction."

6. Ch. Maunoir to Rimbaud, Paris, October 4, 1887.
7. Gabriel Bounoure, Le *Silence de Rimbaud*, op. cit.
8. Pierre Petitfils, *Rimbaud*, op. cit., p. 335.
9. Antoine Adam, chronology in Rimbaud, *Oeuvres complètes* (Paris: Gallimard, "Bibliothèque de la Pléiade"), 1972, p. l. This page contains several errors. We cannot consider as fact that Rimbaud "spends approximately five weeks in Cairo." He probably left the city right after August 26. The articles Savouré mentions on February 13, 1888, are not by Rimbaud (cf. above, note 5). On March 28, 1888, Rimbaud is still in Aden (cf. Mario Matucci, *Bérénice*, No. 2, special Rimbaud issue, op. cit., p. iii).

After his article, "Rimbaud au Caire" (*Image*, December 22, 1929), Jean-Marie Carré received a letter from Mlle. E. B. Paul, telling him that Jules Borelli was in Cairo at the same time as Rimbaud, "very depressed by the trip": We also know that Rimbaud was introduced to the explorer's brother, Octave Borelli, a "rich lawyer, renowned, rich, influential," thanks to whom the letter to the *Bosphore* was published. But it is difficult to "suppose" with Mlle. Paul that he spent much time in Cairo for all that.

10. Gérard de Nerval, *Voyage en Orient*.
11. Vicomte de Petiteville to Rimbaud, Beirut, December 3, 1887. Cf. Rimbaud, *Lettre du Baron de Petdechèvre* . . . (Geneva: Pierre Cailler, 1949). [A work attributed to Rimbaud.]
12. A character in the *Alexandria Quartet* says to the narrator: "You should leave . . . go back to Europe. This city [Alexandria] is sapping you. And what will

you find in Upper Egypt? Blinding heat, dust, flies, a servile job. . . . After all, you are not Rimbaud" (Lawrence Durrell, *Justine*).

13. A theme that persists in 1894 in Léon Dierx's deplorable verses, "Soura Hé" (*Oeuvres complètes* [Paris, A. Lemerre]). See also "Le Rêve égyptien," *Silex*, No. 13, 1979.

14. Henri Mondor, *Eugène Lefébure, sa vie, ses lettres à Mallarmé* (Paris: Gallimard, 1951).

15. Germain Nouveau to Rimbaud, Algiers, December 12, 1893.

16. Lucien Labosse to Rimbaud, Suez, April 22, 1888.

17. Georges Bataille, *Oeuvres complètes*, Vol. I (Paris: Gallimard), p. 505.

18. Bardey visited Cairo on his way back to Lyon from Aden via Port Said in 1880.

19. Nor the image of the cruel, unnatural woman one finds in Germain Nouveau's poem "Sphinx" (*Valentines*).

20. Shelley, "Ozymandias."

21. Paul Valéry (*Cahiers* II [Paris: Gallimard, "Bibliothèque de la Pléiade," 1960], p. 962): "All of a sudden an extraordinary idea about Egyptian art comes to me. . . . They have the art of knowing what we do not and of building a complete, ideal world—and solid." "For ever since [the waters] abated—O buried jewels and open flowers!— what a bore! and the Queen . . . will never tell us what she knows and we do not" ("Après le déluge" ["After the Flood"], *Illuminations*).

22. Germain Nouveau, "The people of sphinxes with marble hearts," "La Charité," *La Doctrine de l'amour*, op. cit.

23. And not on the "pyramid of Louqsor" [*sic*] as the *Bateau ivre* wrote (No. 5, spring 1950, p. 7), correcting an error it had not committed in the preceding issue (No. 4 [October 1949], p. 8) by adding two more.

24. "Rimbaud's signature" was the object of simultaneous discovery in 1949, as if it had suddenly become legible. Jean Cocteau claimed to have "suddenly" come across it (*Maalesh, journal d'une tournée de théâtre* [Paris: Gallimard, 1949], p. 115), but also, more certainly, Henri Stierlin (*Formes et Couleurs*, March 1949) and (or) Théophile Briant ("Le sourire du sphinx, du Caire à Assouan à la recherche d'Arthur Rimbaud," in *Les Nouvelles littéraires*, March 31, 1949). Since 1949 was the year of the "Chasse spirituelle" affair that created such a big stir, the hypothesis of a fraud comes to mind immediately. "The work of cutting this deeply into flint takes much time and leisure, which is astonishing in a man of Rimbaud's stamp" (Stierlin)—unless he had decided, as he said, to take a rest. Let us play Maspéro . . . : The inscription is at a level that was accessible only in the period 1830–1899 as the neighboring signatures indicate (not 1891–1899 as Stierlin claimed), then was buried in sand. We can therefore state with Enid Starkie (who researched this in April 1950) that "Rimbaud being quite unknown before the temple was completely dug out . . . the hypothesis of an apocryphal signature is absurd" (*Rimbaud*, op. cit., pp. 402, 676). "Impossible," Stierlin agrees. "Would a joker have thought of placing his work at the level of the other, dated signatures?" And, adds Starkie, "nobody could nowadays perpetrate a hoax of this kind, not even with the help of a long ladder, without being noticed."

The surprising form of the graffito would support the hypothesis of a homonym—perhaps a soldier in the Egyptian Army (although the spelling "Raimbaud" was more current before the nineteenth century), or the Rimbaud signaled on the coasts of the Red Sea, employee of the Messageries Maritimes, the Other again. In this case, the forgotten, nameless Arthur Rimbaud, could have encountered his name on an Egyptian pyramid!

"A very close examination of the stone allows us to notice before the name the presence of a lightly scratched (A) of the same size as the letters it precedes," affirms Stierlin. The detail is complicated by the fact (unnoticed by the "inventors" of the signature) that *two more* RIMBAUD graffiti in small capital letters figure at the same time on the nearest column. Scratched much lower and nearly opposite the large name (they could be made later, or perhaps the temple was a meeting place of all the Rimbauds . . .), one only sketches RIMB, as Rimbaud sometimes signed his correspondence in 1889, and seems like its neighbor a sketch for the large signature. Nothing speaks against "our conclusion that the poet was indeed in the vicinity of ancient Thebes" (Stierlin).

As the graffiti are not dated (except by their neighbors), Starkie proposes: "Perhaps he visited Luxor when he was in Alexandria, in 1880" (op. cit., p. 306). An altogether unlikely date: Rimbaud did certainly not take this route in 1880, and only the Cairo period in summer 1887, when he is without projects, allowed for the time and intention of such a trip. The neighboring dates confirm our supposition. If Rimbaud carved his name in Luxor, it was no doubt in the first week of September 1887.

Before this inscription, Théophile Briant (*Le Goéland illustré, album souvenir 1936–1949*, No. 90, spring 1949) asks himself "if the Harar adventure was not simply an alibi for the man with Soles of Wind, if he did not behind the screen of a too willfully commercial life pursue his quest of the Orient" (p. 26). Stierlin tries to measure "how deep the conversion was that made him forsake all poetic sensibility" and is astonished that Rimbaud "was not also moved by the sight of this beauty"—a silence that, on the contrary, seems logical and necessary to me.

"If it was by Rimbaud, which I do not believe," Étiemble again airs prejudice, "this 'document' would only prove the silliness of its author" (*Le Mythe de Rimbaud, genèse*, op. cit., p. 316). At the top of the Cheops pyramid, Nerval "finds an antidote to excessive enthusiasm. All the English who have risked this climb have of course carved their name into the stone. . . . A shoe-polish dealer in Piccadilly had even had the merits of his invention (protected by 'improved patent of London') cut into an entire block" (op. cit., p. 216). Today everybody is like Gustave Flaubert "irritated by the number of names of idiots written everywhere" (*Voyage en Orient* [Paris: Librairie de France, 1925], p. 35). However, the second half of the nineteenth century with its birth of "tourism" is the period when inscriptions only just began to be viewed as a mutilation, mostly because of their proliferation. They had barely stopped being a rare and noble gesture, like Byron's or like Chateaubriand's request on his return from Jerusalem that a French tradesman write his name, as customary, on the pyramids, which he was unable to approach: "One must fulfill all the little duties of the pious traveler." Champollion, who had a certain prerogative here, carved his own name in hieroglyphs on the Ptolemaic temple of Deir el-Medineh. Nerval was moved to encounter in Gizeh the "visiting card of our Egyptian Army carved on a marble block sixteen feet wide." . . . But of the campaign of "Abounaparte" (as the Egyptians called him) we should only keep the eighteenth of August 1788, when the military band joined the Arabic orchestras to celebrate the Nile . . . and Egyptology.

25. Michel Butor, *Le Génie du lieu* (Paris: Grasset, 1958).
26. See Julien Gracq (*Préférences* [Paris: José Carti, 1961]): "I must admit that all

that counts for me, all that really is worth the trouble, always comes to my imagination at the end of a trip."

Chapter 13: Gone

1. We can guess the author.
2. "I'll return with limbs of steel, dark skin and furious eyes. With this mask, people will think I am of a strong race. I shall have gold: I shall be idle and brutal. Women nurse these fierce invalids back from hot countries. I shall be involved in politics. Saved" ("Bad Blood," *A Season in Hell*). Starkie makes the point that his return was quite different (*Rimbaud*, op. cit., p. 184). Guillemin, Underwood, Strentz, consider it, on the contrary, as a prophetic passage.

    Because "quille" is a slang word for "leg," Jean Genet is persuaded that in writing: "O que ma quille éclate" [O that my keel would burst] ("The Drunken Boat"), Rimbaud anticipated his amputation (Jean Genet, *Vidéo-livre Témoins*, 1982).
3. Hölderlin, *Hyperion*, Book II.
4. Carré, *Les Deux Rimbaud*, op. cit., p. 63: "The adventurer of the real has supplanted the adventurer of the ideal. It is basically the same person, the same insatiable, mobile, perpetually unstable character with his need for change and fresh starts, his devouring, passionate greed for possession: only the object of his conquest has changed." I would have liked to be able to ask this biographer what he meant by "adventurer of the real," what was the "object of his conquest," and whether he had thought about the way in which Rimbaud was "perpetually unstable." But the essential point of his study of the "two Rimbauds" is no doubt that he ends up concluding that they were only one.
5. Jean-Pierre Richard, "Rimbaud ou la poésie du devenir," *Poésie et profondeur* (Paris: Éditions du Seuil, collection "Points," 1976), p. 189: "Rimbaud gets up with the sun. Three o'clock in the morning." Pierre Pachet has complemented this study by analyzing the term of "veille" (night before): cf. "Rimbaud de la veille à l'aube," *Poésie*, No. 26 (1983), p. 87 ff.
6. On 2.8 meters of film per second.
7. Jacques Rivière, *Rimbaud* (Paris: Kra, 1930; Émile-Paul Frères, 1914). Cf. *Dossier 1905–1925*, ed. and annotated by Roger Lefèvre (Paris: Gallimard, 1977).
8. In the case of Rimbaud, there are always people who *know*. Rimbaud was a saint, and Paterne Berrichon his prophet. Claudel held in 1912 that all has been said and that too much time is between us and "Jean-Arthur Rimbaud, the poet." Stronger yet, Marcel Coulon, after denouncing the hagiography of Rimbaud's family, gave his study the victorious title: "Le problème de Rimbaud, sa solution." Just like Mallement des Messanges, who published in 1682 "The Great and Famous Problem of the Squaring of the Circle, Solved Geometrically by Circle and Straight Line" (Paris: Coignard).
9. Maurice Blanchot, *L'Entretien infini*, I. We shall understand "mystical" in the sense of "eternal dissatisfaction, the longing for something other, the need to be elsewhere, to go beyond his limits" (J. Ancelet-Hustache, *Maître Eckhart et la mystique rhénane* [Paris, Éditions du Seuil, 1978], p. 184)—the pursuit of the unreachable (rest, salvation) where the figure of the impossible unfolds, to the point of making life impossible.